D1485759

THE AMAZING WORLD OF NATURE

THE AMAZING WORLD OF NATURE

THE READER'S DIGEST ASSOCIATION LIMITED
LONDON AND CAPE TOWN

The Reader's Digest
The Amazing World of Nature
First Edition © 1969 The Reader's Digest Association Ltd

The Reader's Digest Association Ltd
25 Berkeley Square, London W1 and Parkade, Strand Street, Cape Town

CONTENTS

———————•———————

PART ONE

This Planet Earth

PART TWO

The Miracle of Living Things

PART THREE
Man and Nature

PART FOUR
Worlds Without End

PART ONE
THIS PLANET EARTH

Nature's Mightiest Forces

We live precariously on the thin, shifting crust of a turbulent, changing
planet, the liveliest in the solar system. Our destiny has been
shaped by such incomparably powerful forces as
volcanic explosions, shattering earthquakes,
upheaving mountain ranges and mile-deep
ice-sheets that grind inexorably across entire continents

An Island is Born

In 1963 the North Atlantic sea-bed spewed up
an island of sterile lava. It had
scarcely cooled before the first rudiments
of life became established there

Early on the morning of November 14, 1963, a fishing vessel was cruising some 4 miles west of Geirfuglasker, Iceland's southernmost offshore island. At about 7.30 a.m. the skipper, engineer and cook felt the boat sway irregularly as if it were caught in a whirlpool. A strange odour of sulphur permeated the atmosphere.

Towards the south, the skipper spotted dark smoke coming from the ocean surface; he trained his binoculars on what he thought might be a burning ship. Instead he saw the black columns of a volcanic eruption rising grotesquely above the sea.

Although he could have no inkling at the time, Captain Gudmar Tomassón was witnessing the very beginning of an awesome miracle of creation. Spewed out of a submarine volcanic eruption, a new island was being born before his eyes.

For the first time, scientists with 20th-century instruments would be able to observe, record and analyse each stage of a volcanic island's emergence from the sea and its struggle against the might of the waves to retain a place in the sun.

The birth pangs of the new island, which was subsequently named Surtsey after a legendary Norse giant, were violent. Days before, a volcanic fissure had rent the basalt ocean bottom 425 ft below the surface. Embryonic cones and vents breathed forth from the bowels of the earth the fearsome gases and solids that started building a solitary islet. Now, at the surface, the eruption column was belching gas and steam thousands of feet towards the skies, while black columns of ejected solid particles called tephra rose hundreds of feet into the air.

That night the island of Surtsey was born. The incredible new land had reached a height of some 33 ft above the waves by the morning of the second day of the eruption. Four days later, the isle was 200 ft high and some 2000 ft long. Explosions were catapulting incandescent lava bombs 4000 ft away in the North Atlantic. During the long Arctic nights, residents of Iceland's capital, Reykjavik, 75 miles away to the north-west, were able to see the awesome eruption.

One of the first of the international group of scientists to arrive on the scene itself was Icelandic geologist Sigurdur Thorarinsson, who wrote:

'Few hours of my life do I treasure as much as one late afternoon near the volcano. Waves washed our small coastguard vessel from stem to stern. The eruption column was rushing continuously upwards, and when darkness fell it was a pillar of fire, and the entire cone was aglow with bombs which rolled down the slopes into the white surf around the

A soaring 5-mile high tower of steam and volcanic ash heralded the violent birth of the island of Surtsey off Iceland's southern coast in 1963. This spectacular event has given scientists a rare opportunity to observe plants and animals colonising a barren habitat entirely cut off from other land by the sea.

in the air, trying not to dodge the bombs until the very moment they seem to be about to land on your head. When the biggest bombs, almost a yard in diameter, crashed on the wet sand, they cupped out holes that soon filled with water which boiled against the red-hot lava.

'After we had stayed on the island for an hour and a half, these bomb showers relented enough so that we could row our dinghies to our ship. It was an experience none of us will forget, but no further attempts were made to go ashore while an explosive vent was still active.'

An aerial view reveals the open vent of the infant island of Surtsey as molten lava was explosively turning seawater into steam. Static charges in the rapidly rising eruption sometimes produced brilliant lightning.

island. Lightning flashes lit up the eruption cloud and peals of thunder cracked above our heads. The din from the thunderbolts, the rumble from the eruption cloud and the crashes of bombs into the sea produced a most impressive symphony. High in the sky the crescent moon rushed headlong between racing clouds. How hopelessly beyond my powers it is to do justice to such a grandiose performance of the elements. To do so one would need the romantic genius of a Byron or a Delacroix.'

In the weeks and months that followed the eruption, Surtsey continued to grow until the tephra cliffs towered hundreds of feet above the Atlantic. Then came the day when Sigurdur Thorarinsson actually set foot on Surtsey:

'Seven of us, including two women, stood on the sandy beach. We had not stayed there many minutes when Surtsey began to fire warning shots, and we saw water spouts in the sea off the beach. They came from lava bombs crashing down, which soon began to fall all round us. Under such circumstances there is only one thing to do—suppress the urge to take to your heels and endeavour to stand still and stare up

Fiery rivulets of lava solidified to form the island of Surtsey. Only a year and a half after it was formed, Surtsey harboured its first leafy green plant. Within five years, scientists visiting the island had identified 23 bird species and 22 insect species.

Tephra is too unstable a substance to withstand the pounding of waves, and Thorarinsson was elated when, at the end of the explosive phase, lava began to flow in April 1964. Since lava cools into hard rock, the permanence of the island was assured. In June 1967, Surtsey boasted noble dimensions: height, 567 ft; length, just over 1¼ miles; area, more than 1 square mile—almost twice that of the Principality of Monaco.

The last and most portentous stage in Surtsey's evolution occurred like a quiet finale to a thunderous symphony. After months of breathtaking pyrotechnics, a miracle wrought silently by wings and fins and seed-bearing currents brought life itself to Surtsey. A creature from the depths of the sea began wriggling on a sandy beach, and a first plant grew in a rocky cranny on this new Atlantis. The creation of Surtsey, son of the sea, was now complete.

But its evolution continued. By the summer of 1967, other plants had rooted, and the newborn cliffs were alive with birds. In June the first flower bloomed—a white sea rocket. Even human beings had found a place for themselves—a hut for international scientists, who come and go in tiny aircraft, watching how the world is eternally created anew.

When Krakatoa Blew Up

Ernst Behrendt

Dust from the biggest explosion
ever heard by man coloured the world's
sunsets for almost a year

The world is awed by the might of the blasts that devastated Hiroshima and Nagasaki, but there was an explosion once that was incomparably greater. Those atomic bombs flattened two cities, yet people a few dozen miles away were oblivious of the fact.

When the East Indies island of Krakatoa blew up, on August 27, 1883, the whole world knew about it. The noise was heard 3000 miles away. The great waves which the explosion caused in the sea reached the shores of four continents and were recorded 8000 miles away. An air-wave generated by the blast travelled right round the world, not once but several times; and where there had been a mountain half a mile high was now a hole a thousand feet deep and miles across.

Red-hot debris covered an area larger than France, to a depth of sometimes 100 ft on land. For nearly a year afterwards the dust of the explosion, blown upwards for 30 miles, filled the high atmosphere over almost the whole globe. Even though there were no large towns within 100 miles of the volcano, 36,000 people lost their lives.

The biggest blast in history was caused by nothing more mysterious than the old-fashioned force that rattles the lid on a kettle. But the fire under the kettle was a mile-long pocket of seething lava and it changed a cubic mile of ocean into super-heated steam. The lid blew off, and the kettle exploded.

Krakatoa was a volcanic island of about 18 square miles in the Sunda Strait, in what was then the Dutch East Indies, between Java and Sumatra.

Early in the spring of 1883, there were warning signs. Smoke and steam poured from recent fissures in the rock. A river of lava cut a wide swath through the tangled jungle. But the Dutch in Java and Sumatra were not alarmed. Old Krakatoa had puffed and rumbled before. Even when the Dutch Captain Ferzenaar arrived in Batavia in August with a report that two new volcanoes had appeared on Krakatoa, the Dutch were not impressed. There were scores of volcanoes in the East Indies; besides, Krakatoa was a hundred miles away.

'The ground was so hot it burnt right through the soles of my boots,' Captain Ferzenaar said. Well, if it was as warm as that on Krakatoa the few natives who lived there would have to take to their boats and wait until the island cooled off.

Captain Ferzenaar was the last white man to set foot on Krakatoa before the eruption. By this time navigation through Sunda Strait was becoming difficult. Several captains turned back when they saw the narrows covered with a foot-thick layer of cinders. But the skipper of one American freighter battened down the hatches and calmly sailed through the hissing sea. His cargo—paraffin!

No one after him attempted the passage. By now Krakatoa's rumblings had grown into a continuous, angry roar heard along the entire east coast of Java. In Buitenzorg, 61 miles from Krakatoa, people were seeking shelter from what they thought was a gathering thunderstorm.

'In the afternoon of August 26,' R. D. M. Verbeek wrote in his description of the catastrophe, 'the low rumbling was interrupted by sharp, reverberating detonations. They grew louder and more frequent. People were terrified. Night came, but no one thought of sleeping. Towards morning the incessant noise was drowning every other sound. Suddenly, shortly before seven, there was a tremendous explosion. Buildings shook, walls cracked, and doors flew open as if pushed by invisible hands. Everybody rushed into the streets. Another deafening explosion, and then everything was quiet as if the volcano had ceased to exist.'

The volcano *had* ceased to exist. Seething with the expansion of its gases, the white-hot lava found temporary outlets in the two craters seen by Ferzenaar, which normally acted as safety valves. But the pressure became too great. Unimaginable energies were straining against hundreds of feet of solid rock overhead. The rock heaved, buckled; on the evening of August 26 it cracked wide open like the wall of a faulty boiler.

A stream of lava burst forth in a deafening roar. Seconds later the sea rushed into the opening. On contact with the hot lava, the water changed into super-heated steam. Colossal blocks of granite and obsidian rocketed upwards amid a cloud of dust and smoke. Again the sea rushed in, battling with the pent-up lava, changing into expanding, exploding super-heated steam, breaking down barrier after barrier of rock.

No one knows how many times the white-hot magma pushed back the sea and how often the sea returned to the assault. In the end the water won. Early in the morning of August 27 the sea reached the volcanic centre of the island. Even the fury of the previous explosions was but a faint prelude to the final cataclysm as the heart was ripped out of Krakatoa and 14 cubic miles of rock streaked into the sky.

The sun was blotted out behind a curtain of ebony torn by jagged lightning. Miles away, Krakatoa's pyrotechnics awed the sailors of the British ship *Charles Bal*, who saw the island shoot up over the horizon, 'shaped like a pine tree brilliantly illuminated by electric flashes'. The sea was covered with fish, floating belly up on the churning water.

Long afterwards came the noise—the loudest ever heard by human ears. 'The concussions were deafening,' wrote Lloyd's agent in Batavia. They hammered every eardrum in Java and Sumatra and put fear into the hearts of Borneo's headhunters. People in Victoria Plains, Australia, 1700 miles to the east, were startled by what seemed to be artillery fire. The sound-waves travelled 2968 miles westward to Rodrigues Island near Madagascar.

With the noise, concentric waves of air started on their way round the globe. A day and a half after the explosion, the first of them hit London from the west. Then a second wave rushed over the city from the east. Four times the eastbound wave swept over London—and over Berlin, Leningrad and Valencia as well—and three times it swept back. The stratospheric see-saw continued for more than ten days before the blast had spent its force.

Far more violent was the effect of the eruption on the sea. In Anjer, on the west coast of Java, a retired sea captain suddenly noticed a new island that had bobbed up in the strait. The next moment he was running for his life. The island was a wall of water, 50 ft high, advancing across the narrows at incredible speed, battering down the wharves, engulfing Anjer, racing uphill, smashing everything in its path. The wave flung a log at him, and he went down. When he regained consciousness he was sitting on the top of a tree half a mile inland, stripped of every shred of clothing but otherwise unharmed.

He was one of the few who saw the wave and lived to describe its fury. Anjer had vanished. The wave, rising to a height of 100 ft, wiped out scores of villages and killed thousands of people. On the coast of Sumatra, the wave tore the warship *Beroun* from her moorings and drove her, anchor dragging, 2 miles inland, where it left her, stranded in the jungle, 30 ft above sea level.

The wave raced across the entire width of the Indian Ocean; when it reached Cape Town, 5100 miles away, it was still over a foot high. It rounded the Cape of Good Hope, turned northwards into the Atlantic, along the coast of Africa, and at last spent itself in the English Channel.

Whole districts of what is now Indonesia were buried under ashes; the jungles were choked, the rice paddies changed into deserts. The sky was so filled with ashes that for a time lamps were needed all day in Batavia.

But what covered the land and the sea was only a small part of the volcano. Most of Krakatoa's solid rock had been pulverised and blasted to a height of 150,000 ft. Clouds of volcanic dust hung suspended in the stratosphere for months. Air currents carried them across oceans and continents. All over the world, the rays of the sun were filtered through a veil spun in the depths of Sunda Strait. In Paris, New York, Cairo and London, the setting sun appeared blue, leaden, green and copper-coloured, and at night the earth was steeped in the light of a green moon and green stars.

The phenomenon lasted into the spring of 1884;

then the colours faded, and Krakatoa's magnificent shroud disappeared. The final chapter in its history seemed to be over. Krakatoa was utterly dead. Nothing was left of it but a few square miles of rock buried under a mountain of ashes. All plants, insects, birds and mammals had been dissolved in a fiery cloud.

Then a miracle happened—the miracle of the rebirth of life. Four months after the eruption, a botanist found an almost microscopic spider, gallantly spinning its web where nothing was to be caught. It had apparently drifted in on the wind.

Then, in a few years, came the grasses and shrubs, the worms, ants, snakes and birds. They arrived by air—seeds dropped by birds on their flight over the barren land; small caterpillars carried by the wind; beetles and butterflies winging their way over from Java and Sumatra. They arrived by water—eggs of worms and reptiles flung ashore with flotsam; snails and scorpions riding the waves on decayed tree trunks; pythons and crocodiles swimming across the narrows. Parasites clung to their bodies.

Plants and animals came by accident, but there was nothing accidental about the sequence in which they established themselves. It was a rigid chronological pattern telescoping millennia into months. It was necessary for some forms of life to be there first before others could live.

For a while some forms prospered through the absence of enemies and competitors. In about 1910, Krakatoa was overrun by swarms of ants; ten years later, when there were plenty of birds and reptiles, the ants had all but disappeared. By 1919 the first small clusters of trees had taken root, and by 1924 they had grown into a continuous forest. A few years later, climbing plants were choking the trees to death and transforming the forest into a tropical jungle with orchids, butterflies, snakes, numberless birds and bats.

Krakatoa became a naturalist's paradise, and the Dutch made it a nature reserve and allowed no one but accredited scientists to set foot on the island. They worked out a complete inventory of life on Krakatoa. They counted the steadily growing number of new arrivals and observed how they lived with each other and fought each other. They even discovered several sub-species—birds and butterflies with peculiar characteristics not to be found anywhere else. Krakatoa was not only drawing on the forms of life around it; it was creating a life of its own. Then, one day, the scientists discovered that another sort of life was stirring on Krakatoa. The old volcano was by no means dead.

Deep down under its rocky foundation a pocket of lava was seeking an outlet for its energies. The bottom of the inland sea was heaving and buckling again. A submarine cone was building up; on January 26, 1928, it broke the surface and showed its top, a flat, ugly island a few hundred feet across, which the waves washed away a few days later.

A year passed. Then suddenly a geyser began to spout steam and ashes. Sulphurous fumes drifted over the ocean. Again the sea was covered with dead fish floating belly up.

The new geyser is still there. It is a part of the old crater rim with mud deposited on its top and a flue in its centre—a safety valve for the stupendous pressure generated by the lava pocket underneath. The natives call the new volcano 'Anak Krakatoa', 'Child of Krakatoa'. No name could be more ominous.

Earthquakes — the Underground Menace

Ira Wolfert

Earthquakes can make solid rock heave
like the sea. By comparison,
H-bomb explosions are child's play

A geophysicist I know, who has been living with earthquakes on charts for years, finally experienced one in person. He says it felt as if the whole world had become a rug that had been given a good strong double shake and then dropped. 'The people, the buildings, the mountains—we were no more than dust in the rug,' he said.

It was all over in about 30 seconds. But it is amazing how much a man can live through in the amount of time he might devote to a yawn.

My friend was about to leave his house when, without warning, a force equivalent to 100 atomic bombs of the Hiroshima model broke loose in the earth's subterranean rock and began racing towards him under the landscape. There had been a crunching shock, the kind you get when wood gripped in a vice splits. The pressure had been accumulating in the rocks for years. Then it had become more than they could contain and now it was loose, a powerful, terrible bursting smothered by stupendous weight.

Along the split, or fault as it is called by scientists, there was slipping of the rock. As a result, riding out in all directions from the fracture were vibrations, or elastic waves, such as a bomb blast would send out if it occurred in solid rock, not air.

The rock shuddered, its particles jarring back and forth like the trucks of a goods train jolted from behind. The jolt travelled miles before dwindling down to a gentle shoving. That was the first effect, the 'P' (for primary) wave. Then came the 'S' (for secondary) wave, which travels about half as fast. It doesn't jolt; it twists. A subterranean mass of rock had been wrung out like a wet sock. When the S wave passed, the rock untwisted itself and lay twanging and quivering, retching back into place.

Sometimes, if it is quiet, you can hear earthquake waves coming—like a train roaring over a bridge, or with the snappings and cracklings of a brush fire. There is no outrunning it—just dive and duck. For the P wave travels at 5 miles a second, more than eight times faster than a high-velocity bullet. The S wave travels at $2\frac{3}{4}$ miles a second.

My friend was in midstride, nearing his front door, when the jolt hit. His front foot landed on the floor somewhere behind him. He toppled and clutched at the wall and was flung away, as if hit by a moving train. That was how he knew it was an earthquake, not something he had stumbled over.

He remembered what various authorities on earthquakes have said: 'Get under something that will protect you from falling debris, and count to 40.' He tried to get under the door lintel, but the floor had become one of those undulating floors found in fun fairs. Then there was a lull. The P wave had passed. He lunged across the floor, threw himself down under the lintel and gripped the door jamb.

Above the thudding of his heart he could hear church bells ringing, set in motion by the quake. He began to count. Suddenly an incredibly long washboard was being pulled out from under him at terrific speed. The S wave had arrived. Just as suddenly it was gone, leaving a spattering of plaster on the floor and the big hall chandelier swinging like a pendulum.

It was a relatively minor quake, though 52 people were killed. My friend's chief reaction, as a scientist, was: 'How much we have to learn!'

An earthquake is perhaps the most deeply buried page in the book of Nature's secrets. Only one thing known to man can explore it for him—earthquake

16

An earthquake registering 8·5 on the Richter/Gutenberg scale demolished the Alaskan town of Anchorage in March 1964. The most severe quake ever recorded struck Colombia and Ecuador in 1906 with a force of 8·9 on the Richter scale.

Yawning fissures in Anchorage's snow-clad earth show the terrible energies unleashed by the Alaskan quake (below). The rubble pile at upper right is all that remains of a newly built, but fortunately still unoccupied, apartment house.

waves; and now he is learning to translate what the waves say into a language he can understand. The most valuable maps of hidden treasure now known are drawn by seismologists for oil companies by setting off explosives and getting the seismic waves to tell what they have seen on their travels.

An earthquake was once believed to be a reminder to the wicked of God's wrath. If it is a reminder of anything, it is of the cunning of creation. We live out our lives on a space ship—a weirder one, more superbly engineered, than any in science fiction.

Father Joseph Lynch, seismologist of New York's Fordham University, says that earthquakes are one of the earth's safety measures. The earth is in perpetual motion, not only through space but within itself. It suffers wear and tear, yields and breaks under strain. This happens an average of 2700 times every day—little breaks releasing a force equalling about 50 lb. of dynamite, big ones mounting up awesomely. We feel a big break as an earthquake, the repair job that follows—when the rock settles back into shape—as after-shocks.

Only so much energy can accumulate in rock before the rock will break. However, that amount is at present unknown. When there is a fault that has suffered a previous fracture, the break is likely to come before prodigious energy has piled up. For a really big quake to occur, one scientist says, there must be an area of rock at least 50 miles in diameter, each part strained to breaking point simultaneously.

The largest recorded earthquake registered 8·9 on the magnitude scale devised by Charles Richter and Beno Gutenberg of the California Institute of Technology. There has been only one such quake since 1904, when scientists first began to measure accurately the energy in an earthquake. It struck Colombia and Ecuador in January 1906, the most terrible of all earthquake years scientifically recorded. In April of that year, the famous San Francisco earthquake struck: 8·3 on the scale. In August, the rock burst in Chile with a magnitude of 8·6, and the following month in New Guinea with a magnitude of 8·4. During the last ten years disastrous earthquakes have occurred in Colombia, Turkey, Yugoslavia, Iran and other areas of the world. In May 1960 an earthquake with a magnitude of 8·5 rocked Chile, and on March 27, 1964, an equally violent earthquake struck Alaska.

How is the energy generated that powers these shocks called 'earthquakes'? One theory may give a partial answer. There are tides in the solid earth, which physicist Dr Albert Michelson measured. Every 12 hours, all the water, mountains, cities and people on half the globe rise 1 ft into the air, then sink 1 ft down in the next 12 hours when the moon is pulling on the opposite side of the world. This action creates enormous subterranean pressures.

As the earth rotates, its motion also creates a tremendous internal force. In addition, the earth's surface is continually cooling; and as it contracts it clamps more tightly round the interior. All these forces are among the causes of earthquakes.

Japan is by far the greatest sufferer from earthquakes (the ghastly Yokohama/Tokyo disaster of 1923 killed some 142,000 people). But no place is immune. The interior of a continent is generally regarded by geologists as stable, yet in 1811 one of America's greatest earthquakes hit New Madrid, Missouri, 600 miles from the Atlantic coast. Felt as far north as Massachusetts, it destroyed a forest and created the 20-mile long Reelfoot Lake in Tennessee. 'The ground rose and fell in successive furls like the ruffled waters of a lake,' reported the naturalist John James Audubon. Then came the after-shocks, which lasted the better part of a year, and were strong enough to make people seasick.

Earthquakes in the ocean bed occur almost daily. But you cannot twist something out of shape when, like water, it has no shape to begin with. That is why liners passing over earthquakes have encountered only a single upward jolt like that caused by a bump in the road. But when a submarine earthquake is of some magnitude, the convulsive movements in the depths can create a tidal wave, which scientists prefer to call by its Japanese name, *tsunami*, since it has nothing to do with the tides. Springing from the ocean bed above the focus of an earthquake, it can stretch scores of miles and race along at speeds up to 500 mph, pushing the ocean water before it.

As the *tsunami* approaches land, the first sign is likely to be a sharp swell, hardly different from an ordinary wave. Then there is an enormous draining withdrawal. The ocean floor gapes open, exposing a litter of stranded fish far beyond the furthest ebb of low tide. Finally the gigantic wave, which may reach a height of 200 ft, comes crashing in. In 1946 one of these waves drowned 173 people in Hilo, Hawaii.

This *tsunami* made history when a throng of oceanographers observing the Bikini atomic bomb test were caught in its path. Never before had a tidal wave been the object of such intense, on-the-spot observation. Out of it came a life-saving warning system. Earthquake reports are sent from seismographic stations to Honolulu. There the position of each earthquake is plotted, and the arrival time of *tsunamis* is estimated.

Today about 1000 seismograph observatories are scattered around the world, watching the shock waves and translating what they say into a universal language of numbers and mathematical symbols. Big shocks are reported by urgent cable to Washington, where the information is collated and analysed for the reporting observatories. In Britain the International Seismological Summary in Edinburgh, and in Strasbourg the Bureau Central Séismologique International, follow up with a more detailed report of the world view of the same earthquake.

It will be some time before scientists can tell us as much about the sombre storms in the subterranean rocks as they can about the more visible storms which occur in the atmosphere. But every day they are learning more and more what an awe-inspiring, humbling miracle this earth of ours is.

Are the Earth's Continents Adrift?

Rutherford Platt

There is mounting evidence that the lands
we live on may be wandering slowly
but inexorably over the face of the globe

Facts have been found to bolster a startling scientific theory: that our continents were once part of greater land masses, and that, broken apart, they are drifting across the face of the earth. Africa, for example, was at the South Pole. North America may even now be ploughing westwards through the Pacific Ocean, to collide eventually with Asia!

The theory of drifting continents was first seriously proposed in 1915 by Alfred Wegener, a German geologist. Until recently the arguments against it were at least as impressive as the arguments for it; but data accumulated during the International Geophysical Year of 1957–8 provided new evidence in favour of the theory.

Wegener likened the continents and big islands to icebergs floating in a sea of hot, soft volcanic rock.

As proof that they were once joined together, he pointed out that the continents fit together like pieces of a jigsaw puzzle. The east coastline of South America matches the west coast of Africa, with the rounded corner of Brazil fitting neatly into the Gulf of Guinea. The facing coasts of Europe and the United States could be fitted together if some moving around were done.

Mountain ranges of the same geological age and with the same rock structure can be matched on coasts that face each other across wide oceans. They stand as though broken and pulled apart. This is true of the coastal ranges of Brazil and West Africa. It is also true of North America's Appalachians, whose ancient rock ends abruptly with a great headland in Nova Scotia, but reappears in Newfoundland, Greenland, eastern Ireland and in the Grampian Mountains of Scotland.

There is also zoological evidence of drifting continents. For example, guinea pigs, chinchillas, peculiar land snails that must live in woods, and giant lizards that lay their eggs in termite nests, are found wild only in South America and Africa. All fish and freshwater creatures in South America have close relatives in Africa, including the electric eel and lungfish, which stick their noses out through the scum of stagnant swamps to breathe lungfuls of air. Unless the two continents were once linked, what explanation is there for this amazing resemblance of unique creatures on opposite sides of the ocean?

Assailants of the drifting-continents theory talk of land bridges like that which once existed between Asia and North America at the Bering Strait. But no evidence for such a land bridge across the Atlantic has ever been discovered. On the other hand, a great ridge runs north and south down the middle of the Atlantic floor, paralleling the coastlines of the facing continents with mysterious accuracy. No one has ever explained it—but it looks as it might look if it were a residue left where a land mass broke apart.

Botanists also support Wegener's theory. In his book *The Geography of the Flowering Plants,* a classic in its field, Professor Ronald Good, formerly of the British Museum, writes: 'The opinion of plant geographers is almost unanimous that the present distribution of plants cannot be explained without assuming that the continents have been joined to one another at some time in the past.'

I myself have seen some of the botanical evidence. In a Greenland ravine 300 miles north of the Arctic Circle, I found thin layers of shale, separated like the pages of an old book. Almost all the fragments had imprints of plants—sassafras, sycamore and fig leaves, elm seeds with their hat-brim wings. These are not the plants of a raw polar place, but of more temperate woodlands.

In Greenland, too, I found a colony of peculiar saxifrage plants, which also grow on the other side of the world in the high Himalayas. This peculiar flower uses no seeds, but spreads by reaching out with a short stem and planting a tiny bulb. Through many millennia it could have crossed thousands of miles of land by taking 3 in. footsteps, but could it have leapt across the ocean?

Such clues would seem to indicate, as Wegener believed, that North America and Greenland were once joined to Eurasia, drifted away, and that Greenland 'ran aground' while North America continued on its western course.

Some 200 million years ago, the greatest ice age of all spread up from the South Pole. From the evidence of boulders, sediments and rock scratches, the ancient glaciers buried South America under ice as far north as the Equator, and covered both western Australia and India.

But glaciers could *not* have reached up into tropical South America, nor crossed the Equator into India. The Equator always receives a constant supply of heat from the sun—too much for glaciers. The only answer to the mystery, said Wegener, is that those lands were not always located where they are today. They have drifted. Moreover, he reasoned, at the time of this ice age those lands—Antarctica, South America, India and Australia—must all have been joined together in one super-continent, which he called Gondwanaland.

What evidence is there for this idea? When the ancient glaciers melted back, a strange shrub grew on the raw tundra left behind—one never seen since or elsewhere on earth. Its name is Glossopteris, or tongue fern, a tough, cold-weather plant with coarse, tongue-shaped leaves. Tongue-fern fossils have been found in the Argentine and Brazil, in Central Africa, in India, Australia and Antarctica. Since tongue fern could not have leapt thousands of miles of sea, the only explanation seems to be the existence of the super-continent Gondwanaland.

As the enormous glaciers slowly melted back, and tongue fern spread, the huge land-mass was revolving and drifting northwards. The strain of revolving caused Africa to break off, and South America, and two more huge pieces. India drifted into the Tropics, hit Asia and formed a tight bond; the impact is thought by some scientists to have pushed up the Himalaya Mountains. Australia moved to its present location. The nucleus of Gondwanaland continued to drift towards the present South Pole, where eternal cold buried its rocky bulk under an immense white ice-cap. Today, with sonar soundings, explorers are finding great cracks and chasms of continental proportions under the Antarctic ice—scars such as might have been left by the stresses and strains of the past adventures of the land.

But the most conclusive evidence of continental drift has been the discovery of 'fossil magnetism'. When rock materials are first laid down they are either fluid lava or watery sediments, in which microscopic particles of magnetised iron oxide are free to rotate. Before the rocks harden, these particles align themselves like compass needles, all pointing north.

Geologists can date rocks quite accurately on the geological calendar; and from the direction of the fossil compass needles, it is possible to calculate the latitude and longitude of the rock at the time it was deposited. These findings indicate different directions at different times for north. Magnetic north appears to have been out in the middle of the Pacific near Hawaii. It has visited Japan, and more recently found itself in Kamchatka in northern Siberia.

But the earth is a good gyroscope, spinning at an eternally fixed angle, and long-distance pole-wander is an impossibility. The explanation, therefore, is not that the North Pole has shifted, but that the very continents on which the rocks were laid down are sliding about over the face of the globe.

P. M. S. Blackett, Professor of Physics at Imperial College, London, has said: 'Measurements of Indian stones prove without doubt that India was situated south of the Equator 70 million years ago. Measurements in South Africa point to the fact that the African continent has drifted directly over the South Pole in the last 300 million years.'

What causes the continents to shift? For years no force on earth was known great enough to move a continent. Now one has been discovered. It is called a convection current, a heat-flow which causes actual motion of the material through which it moves. Convection currents are set in motion by radio-activity in the centre of the earth. They flow up through the 2000-mile thick mantle of rock which underlies the rocky crust, horizontally along the upper mantle, then plunge again towards the earth's core, completing a circuit.

It is as though great wheels were turning, underneath the surface, causing areas of the earth's crust to move where they are in contact with them.

Where are the continents going, and how fast? There is no telling, for this utterly amazing motion is subject to the caprice of convection currents and to unpredictable stresses and strains, such as sudden volcanic cracks that torture the earth's mobile crust. From his measurement of fossil compass needles, Professor Blackett estimates that in the last 150 million years Britain has drifted north from a place much closer to the Equator, and that it has also turned clockwise by more than 30 degrees.

Presumably the drift is continuing. It need not worry us unless it goes much faster.

Beyond Control

George Gamow

If man survives long enough, he will
see new mountains rise
and a new ice age cover his cities

We are now living in the midst of a revolutionary epoch of the earth's history, when its crust trembles and crumples under the action of accumulated internal stresses resulting from the cooling of the earth's body. There have been two gigantic outbursts of volcanic and mountain-making activity in this epoch so far: one about 40 million years ago, responsible for the formation of the Himalayas, the Rockies and the Andes, and the second 20 million years ago, which elevated the Alps. Although the formation of these mountains represents quite an achievement, it still falls short of the accomplishments of any previous revolution. It seems more probable that the present period's mountain-building activity is far from complete, and that at some future date humanity will witness catastrophes for which there is no precedent in its past history.

Unfortunately, it is impossible to predict the date of the next outburst or to specify a 'safety period' during which such a catastrophe can be guaranteed not to occur. To calculate the future behaviour of the earth's crust, we must know the distribution of materials in it, its compressibility and ultimate strength, the distribution of existing stresses and the position of cracks and other weak spots. But, even if field geologists were able to give us all this information with the desired accuracy, the calculations would probably take thousands of years.

We cannot say much about the symptoms that will announce the catastrophe's approach—earthquakes, volcanic eruptions and general motion of the ground—since we do not know how violent these phenomena must become to be considered no longer routine adjustments of the crust, or how long before the main outburst they will become prominent. But we can be fairly certain that when the crumpling begins, the earth will not be a very comfortable place to live on. In the localities immediately affected by mountain-forming activity the ground will be shaken by a wild *danse macabre*, and tremendous amounts of red-hot lava, erupted through the cracks opened in the crust, will spread over hundreds of thousands of square miles. Even in places far removed from the site of the new mountain birth, violent earthquakes and giant waves of the disturbed oceans will make life perilous.

It is some consolation that this catastrophe is unlikely to happen during our lifetime. Since the revolutionary period extends over tens of millions of years, the probability that the outbreak will occur in the next ten or hundred years is negligibly small.

We can do much better in predicting the climate of the future and the date for the next advance of polar ice on the continents which are the present-day sites of human culture. The periodicity of extensive glaciation seems to be connected with recurrent changes in the earth's orbit and in the direction of its axis of rotation. Since an astronomer can calculate the expected changes in these elements, even for hundreds of thousands of years ahead, predicting ice ages becomes a comparatively easy task.

The conditions for the glaciation of the northern hemisphere will again be fulfilled between AD 50,000 and AD 90,000, when much of Europe and North America will be covered by thick sheets of ice. The eccentricity of the earth's orbit during these epochs is expected to be greater than during the last glacial period but smaller than during the previous four. Thus the ice descending from the Scandinavian highlands and brushing away Oslo, Copenhagen, Stockholm and Leningrad will probably stop before reaching London, Paris and Berlin. However, as the interval separating us from the next advance of ice is ten times longer than that which has elapsed since ancient Egyptian civilisation, it may be that by the time the glaciers begin to descend from the polar regions these cities will be of interest only to contemporary archaeologists.

21

Rocks sometimes bear eloquent testimony to the enormous forces that have repeatedly racked the earth's crust. The photograph on the left shows layers of Bude sandstone, formed about 200 million years ago, in the 70-ft high cliffs at Efford Ditch in Cornwall. When these layers of sedimentary rock were first formed—by the pressure of the sea on thick deposits of sediment lying on the sea-bed—they were horizontal. Later, movement of the earth's crust forced them into their present almost vertical position. Igneous rocks—which form when molten material breaks through the earth's crust and cools in the air, or forces its way into surface layers of the earth and cools there—can also be folded and contorted by movements of the crust. But since they are not often formed in layers, as sedimentary rocks are, contortions in them are not usually as obvious as they are in the strata of sedimentary rocks.

In the photograph on the right, layers of black slate, siltstone and laminated sandstone on the neck of land between Penally Hill and Penally Point in Cornwall show how movements of the earth's crust can not only thrust a layer of rock into a vertical position, but also fold it into bizarre, violent contortions. These rocks were also formed about 200 million years ago. The geologist's hammer in the middle of the picture is 1 ft long.

Before the next advance of ice the earth's climate will become much warmer than at present, reaching the maximum about AD 20,000.

During the present interglacial warm spell, tropical forests extended up as far as northern Germany, and there is every reason to believe that the situation will be repeated 20,000 years from now. This future extension of tropical vegetation, accompanied by the northward migration of animals that are now found only in equatorial Africa or South America, will probably be even greater than during former interglacial stages, since it is believed that the eccentricity of the earth's orbit will then reach an unprecedentedly low value.

Looking still further ahead into the future of our planet, we can expect the same monotonously regular cycles that characterised its past. For the

first tens of millions of years, while today's mountains still stand on the surface of the continents, with new mountains rising in the catastrophes of crust-crumpling, the earth's surface will look much as it does now; and periodic glacial advances of smaller or larger intensity will alternate with interglacial warm spells. Later on, the present revolutionary activity will slowly die out, and the laborious work of rain will obliterate the last hill on the earth's surface. Continental surfaces will become flat and uninteresting, and large areas will be inundated by ocean water, forming extensive shallow seas. The climate will become mild and uniform, and one will be able to travel from Cape Town to Moscow without changing into warmer clothes.

These flat, inter-revolutionary continents will still be dominated by the representatives of the

mammalian kingdom, which will probably increase considerably in size. All the animal races which have dominated the world during one era or another grew in size up to the point where they became extinct, and there appears to be no reason to believe that the present size of living mammals represents the upper possible limit. It may be that elephants, which are too large even today, will be unable to continue their development and will vanish from the face of the earth (they are already vanishing), but all the other animals, including man, seem to be quite capable of further growth. Thus one can easily imagine a picture of the 'Palaeontological Museum of the year AD 80,000,000', where visitors 10 or 15 ft tall inspect the fossil skeleton of a pony, which seems to them no larger than a dog.

But one should not go too far along the path of fantasy, even if it is based on scientific fact; the extinction of our human race may take place, for example, simply because of the degeneration of mankind's cells, and the corresponding drastic reduction of the human birth rate.

It is impossible to know which breed of animals will take precedence as 'Dictator of the Earth', and we may now look with suspicion and a feeling of rivalry at any small creature crawling at our feet.

The earth itself is expected to grow a thicker and thicker solid crust, which will become sufficiently strong to withstand any further stresses. At this stage of development the periodic revolutionary crumpling of the earth's surface layers will be checked, and after the last mountains have been washed away by rain, the continents will remain forever flat and smooth.

THE CHANGING FACE OF THE EARTH

Our planet moves like a living thing. As regular as breathing, the tides of its seas move against continents and islands and alter shores and coastlines. In a steady cycle of evaporation and condensation, water circulates between the sky and sea. It falls as rain, and forms rivers which can eat their way even through solid rock. Deep inside the earth, the molten rock moves, and at weak places forces its way volcanically through the earth's crust to the surface.

But not all the earth's changes are as violent as volcanic eruptions; even the invisible wind changes the earth. As the globe spins, winds are generated that drive sand grains like chisels, and carve the seemingly unchanging rocks into a fantasy of strange shapes. By a similarly imperceptible process, the minute labour of coral polyps builds whole islands.

The face of the earth can change suddenly and violently. Or it can change so slowly that we are unaware of it, except when the strange shape of a wind-carved rock reminds us that the processes of change continue, silently, all around us.

A volcanic eruption is one of the most violent and spectacular manifestations of Nature's power to change the face of the earth. The volcanic 'belts' around the earth follow the more recently formed 'belts' of mountain-building activity—the Alps, Andes and Rockies. The eruption in November 1959 of Kilauea Volcano, 4000 ft above sea level on Hawaii (above), sent a fountain of molten lava gushing 1000 ft into the air. Eruptions are accompanied by heavy falls of volcanic cinders, sand, ashes and dust, which have been known to crush the roofs of buildings by their weight, and suffocate human beings.

Kapoho Volcano (above), on the most eastern point of the island of Hawaii, erupted during 1960. The lava fountain shown is over 600 ft high. In the foreground, a river of molten lava—they have been known to travel at speeds of 40 mph—pours down the slope.

The Haleakala Crater (above), in Haleakala National Park on the island of Maui, Hawaii, is 7 miles long; 1000-ft high cinder cones, painted in variegated shades, rise from the lava-strewn floor. The actual rim of the crater marks the horizon in this photograph.

The Jupiter Terrace at Mammoth Hot Springs in Yellowstone National Park, Wyoming (above), is an example of quieter geographical change. Sunlight catches the hot waters as they drip over the slowly evolving ledges, coloured by chemicals and living organisms.

Stalactites such as these in Treak Cliff Cavern, Derbyshire (above), are pendent masses formed where water containing mineral solutions drops very slowly from an elevation. Beneath each stalactite a pillar of deposit, called a stalagmite, rises vertically.

Heron Island, Wistari Reef (above), is part of the Great Barrier Reef which stretches for over 1000 miles along the coast of north-eastern Australia, the largest reef of its kind in the world. Coral reefs are formed of the calcareous bodies of various marine organisms, particularly corals and millipores, which in calm, warm conditions attach themselves to firm rock or a shallow bank, die, and in time form a new reef there. The process is a slow one, taking many thousands of years, but eventually islands such as Heron Island are formed which are soon able to support life.

25

The Atlantic beats savagely on the Orkneys, to the north of Scotland, and the wind there blows so fiercely that only a few stunted shrubs grow on the islands. Under these forces of wind and sea, the coastline has been weathered into stark, dramatic shapes. This photograph shows a typical example, the rock of Yesnaby Castle which was once part of the main coastline.

The aeroplane in this photograph of Knik Glacier, in South Alaska, indicates the size of the glacial ice mass. Glaciers move at speeds ranging from a few inches to 60–70 ft each day, and over the years gouge out valleys (the Norwegian fjords were carved by glaciers). When glaciers melt, lakes are often formed; the Great Lakes of North America were formed in this way.

Where there is a prevailing wind, rock is often eroded in lines following the direction of the wind. This has happened to these rocks in central Turkey, which, in the course of years of weathering by wind and sand, have come to resemble desert sand dunes.

The Fish River Canyon (above), in the south of South West Africa, is the world's second largest canyon—after the Grand Canyon in the U.S.A. Here the Fish River has torn a ravine 2500 ft deep and 40 miles long out of the barren earth. It is one of Africa's greatest sights, but as unexpected as it is huge—from more than a few feet away, the edge of the ravine is almost invisible.

The fluid sand forms of the Rub' al Khali (The Empty Quarter), in Saudi Arabia, reflect the constantly shifting nature of the whole surface of the world. Some of the sand dunes here may reach heights of 800–1000 ft; but even this ocean of sand is not permanent. As one part of the changing face of the earth, mountains, a forest or the sea will in time take its place.

The Ocean of Air

As the earth spins on its axis and circles the sun, heat pours in
and drives the prevailing winds of the world. These great
globe-girdling currents in the 20-mile deep ocean
of air create the weather in all its variety—
from spring's soft rains to the
screaming fury of a hurricane or a tornado's deadly suction

The Atmosphere – Our Invisible Guardian

George Gamow

If the earth is the mother of all life,
its father must surely be
the air, a spectacular sea of gases that
feeds all living things

We live at the bottom of a vast ocean of air which surrounds our globe as a thin, transparent veil. A quarter of the atmosphere is below the level of Santa Fé, New Mexico, which has an elevation of 7000 ft; a half below the altitude of 16,500 ft, which is just the height of Mount Ararat; and three-quarters of it is below 30,000 ft, which is the height of Mount Everest. But highly rarefied fringes of terrestrial atmosphere extend hundreds of miles above the earth's surface, and it is difficult to say where our atmosphere becomes merely the very thin gas which fills all interplanetary space. The total weight of terrestrial atmosphere is 5000 million million tons which, although a large number in itself, is nevertheless only a third of 1 per cent of the total weight of water in the oceans. Atmospheric air is composed of 75.5 per cent nitrogen, 23.1 per cent oxygen, 0.9 per cent of the inert gas argon, 0.03 per cent carbon dioxide, and negligible amounts of some other gases.

Up to the height of about 6 miles, air contains varying amounts of water vapour which originates from evaporation of moisture from the ocean and land surfaces and is carried upwards by ascending convective currents. When the warm air rises, it expands and becomes cooler, which accounts for the steady decrease in temperature with increasing height. At an altitude of $1\frac{1}{2}$ miles above the ground, air temperature drops to the freezing point of water; it continues to decrease steadily, dropping to about $-100°F$ at an altitude of 6 miles. The vertical convective currents do not penetrate beyond that height, as a result of which the air at greater altitudes remains free of humidity and always stays at a constant temperature.

The part of the terrestrial atmosphere extending up to the height of 6 miles is known as the troposphere, and the physical phenomena occurring in it are of paramount importance for life on the earth's surface. Storms, hurricanes, tornadoes and typhoons originate here; all kinds of clouds are formed, to shower rain, snow and hail on our heads. Beyond the upper limits of the troposphere, conditions are much quieter and the sky is always blue. This is the stratosphere, through which airliners usually fly on long journeys.

With the exception of the chemically inert gas argon, all components of air play an important role in supporting life on the earth. Proteins, which form

A photograph taken from the Gemini 4 space capsule during its earth-orbiting flight of June 4, 1965. It shows the edge of the earth at twilight, and the bands of blue, yellow and white light in the atmosphere over the earth's rim. The sky above that is black because it contains no atmospheric particles to reflect the light and make it visible.

the major part of all living organisms, are composed essentially of carbon, hydrogen, oxygen and nitrogen. Growing plants get their carbon by absorbing and decomposing atmospheric carbon dioxide under the action of sunlight.

Carbon is used to build sugars and other organic material, while oxygen is liberated back into the atmosphere. Hydrogen and oxygen in the form of water are brought in through the roots from the soil, where water gathers from rainfall. Atmospheric nitrogen is assimilated by certain bacteria in the soil and turned into a variety of fertilising materials necessary for the growth of plants. Thus it is only fair that, when we speak about 'Mother Earth', we do not forget 'Father Air'.

Plants and animals living on the surface of the earth exert, for their part, a considerable influence on the composition of the atmosphere. It has been estimated that plants consume yearly 500,000 million tons of carbon dioxide, transforming it into organic materials. This figure is about a third of the total carbon-dioxide content of the atmosphere; if the

A photograph of the Florida peninsula, taken during the flight of the Gemini 5 space capsule on August 23, 1965. The whole peninsula is covered with light cloud, which closely follows the coastline; the sky above the sea is cloudless. This happens because during the day the land heats up more quickly than the sea. Cool, damp air flows over the land from the sea, is warmed, and rises; as it rises it cools again, condensation occurs, and clouds are formed.

supply were not constantly replenished it would run out in only three years. It may be mentioned here that only a tenth of the total carbon-dioxide consumption is due to grass, bushes and trees, the other nine-tenths being accounted for by algae in the oceans. The consumption of atmospheric carbon dioxide is com-

pensated for by its formation in the processes of animal and plant respiration (plants consume oxygen at night); by the rotting of dead plants and fallen leaves; and by forest fires. In this way a steady balance is maintained throughout the millennia between the consumption and formation of the gas.

If there were no organic life on the earth, atmospheric oxygen would gradually disappear as the result of various inorganic oxidation processes, being transformed mostly into carbon dioxide. Such a situation seems to exist on Venus, whose atmosphere, according to spectroscopic studies, contains very large amounts of carbon dioxide and no detectable trace of free oxygen. This fact represents a strong indication that there is no life on the surface of that planet.

Another important function of the terrestrial atmosphere is that it turns the earth into a giant greenhouse, keeping it at a mean temperature of about 60°F, higher than it would be otherwise. The functioning of greenhouses is based on the fact that glass, being almost completely transparent to visible light, which brings most of the sun's energy, is opaque to the heat rays which are emitted by the object warmed up by the sun's radiation. Thus, solar energy entering through the glass roof of a greenhouse is trapped inside and maintains a temperature well above that of the outside air.

In the case of our atmosphere, the role of glass is played by carbon dioxide and water vapour which, even though present in minor amounts, absorb very strongly heat rays emitted from the earth's warm surface and radiate them back to the earth. Thus the excess heat which is removed from the earth's surface during the daytime by the convective air currents is resupplied during the cold nights.

The moderating effect of the atmosphere can best be demonstrated by comparing the earth with the moon, which gets exactly the same amount of heat but has no atmosphere. Measurements of the moon's surface temperature, carried out by special heat-sensitive instruments known as bolometers, show that on the illuminated side of the moon the temperature of the rocks rises to 214°F, while it drops to −243°F on the moon's dark side. If our earth had no atmosphere, water would boil during the daytime and alcohol would freeze during the night.

While controlling the visible sunlight to keep the earth's surface warm and comfortable, our atmosphere protects us from various much less pleasant kinds of radiation from the sun. Apart from visible light, our sun is known to emit large quantities of ultra-violet radiation, X-rays and high-energy particles, which would have a deadly effect on plant and animal life if permitted to penetrate all the way to the surface. But all these dangerous rays are absorbed in the upper layers of the atmosphere and only a negligible fraction of ultra-violet comes through—in just the proper amount to tan the bodies of holidaymakers on beaches.

Last but not least is the mechanical protection our atmosphere gives us against constant bombardment by meteorites (with the exception of the biggest ones, which come rarely) and against artificial satellites and the rockets used to put them into orbit, which burn and disintegrate completely after their re-entry into the air.

The Wonder of Winds

J. D. Ratcliff

Winds can destroy or make fertile,
confound or help us; they are among the most
powerful forces in the earth's affairs

The wild wind can be a demon out of control, a bearer of death and destruction. But day in, day out, the wind is the earth's breath of life—an awesome wonder that shapes and blesses our lives in a hundred ways.

As bearers of rain, the winds determine which portions of the globe are habitable and what crops can be grown. They keep northern Europe from being a polar waste and moderate the heat of South America's west coast. Winds virtually created one country, the Netherlands. They spun windmills that ground grain, sawed wood, pumped out the sea; and they helped to make Holland one of the great trading nations, driving her ships to every corner of the globe.

The names men have given to winds have an allure —the poison wind, the doctor wind, the barber wind, the wind-of-120-days; the roaring 40's and the howling 50's; Alaska's *knik*, Japan's *narai*, and the Argentine's *pampero*. Hurricanes, typhoons and tornadoes make the headlines. But the real stars are the great wind systems: the monsoons that water southern Asia; the westerlies that drive the Gulf Stream and warm northern Europe; the Antarctic winds that push the cold Humboldt Current, with its enormous cargo of sea nutrients, up the west coast of South America—giving rise to some of the world's greatest fisheries.

Early sailors hugged the shore. The Romans were among the first to note wind patterns and take advantage of them. Rome had to have 20 million bushels of Egyptian wheat a year to survive. Roman sailors observed a prevailing wind blowing up from Egypt across the Mediterranean in the spring; in summer the wind reversed. They therefore did most of their transporting in spring.

We say we live *on* earth. We also live *in* a vast sea of air. At times this sea around and above us is as calm as a mill-pond; at others it moves faster than a bullet. The cause of this unrest? The wind has two great propellant forces. First, there is a constant interchange of air between the warm Tropics and the polar ice-caps. Second, the earth exerts a rotational force—at the Equator it moves at about 1000 mph, dragging a sea of air behind. These two forces generate the great primary winds that flow in regular paths over thousands of miles.

In the North Atlantic and North Pacific these winds flow in a clockwise pattern around low-pressure areas, pushing before them the great sea currents—the Japan Current, or Kuroshio, and the Gulf Stream. In the South Atlantic and South Pacific they flow anti-clockwise, pushing along the Humboldt, the Brazil and the other great currents that have such an enormous impact on world weather.

The North Atlantic trade winds are part of the pattern, blowing with amazing constancy from North Africa to the west. These winds frightened Columbus's sailors. How would they ever get home? They did not know that, further to the north, the westerlies blew in the opposite direction.

Ferdinand Magellan, on his round-the-world exploration of 1519–21, rode the trade winds across the Atlantic and down the east coast of South America. Then, below the 40th parallel, approaching Cape Horn, Magellan encountered the roaring 40's that howl around the earth in an easterly direction at speeds up to 50 knots. After bucking these terrors he found another set of gentle trade winds, in a new ocean that he named 'Pacific'.

Ships followed the great routes of the primary winds to open the world for trade and colonisation. One route was from England down to Africa on the wind-driven Canary Current, with a cargo of trade goods; thence to the West Indies on the trade winds with a cargo of slaves; then home on the westerlies with rum and molasses.

It was Matthew Fontaine Maury, a U.S. Navy hydrographer, in the mid-19th century, who began putting the global wind picture together. He collected thousands of ships' logs, noting the set of the wind at specific spots on specific dates. Maury showed that a roundabout course often provided the quickest passage. If an English ship bound for Australia, for instance, rode trade winds to the coast of Brazil, then dropped down, passing round the Cape, it often took only half the time—although the route was thousands of miles longer than the voyage down the African coast.

Nothing demonstrates man's utter dependence on the winds so well as the monsoons. In summer the great central land-mass of Asia heats up; air becomes light, and a vast low-pressure area forms, which sucks in air from as far away as Australia. Passing over seas, it picks up moisture and drops it as rain on Malaysia, India, Japan and other areas. With

astonishing regularity June marks the arrival of the rainy season, and planting can begin. Indians by the thousand pour out into parched fields and streets to let the water splash on their upturned faces, and to give thanks for this recurring miracle.

In winter, as the Asian land-mass cools, the air over it cools; a great high-pressure area forms, and the outward flow of air begins. When it strikes the towering fence of the Himalayas, it drops moisture as snow. By the time it arrives in India the air is dry, cloudless. For six months the sun will shine. Rainfall figures tell the story: in March, Bombay has virtually no rain; in July, it has 25 in.

Among the most interesting of local winds are the Föhns. Passing over the Alps, damp winds rise, cool, drop their moisture; then, as they tumble down the other side, they become compressed and heat up, in the same way that a bicycle pump gets hot as it compresses air. Thus a cool wet wind on one side of a mountain becomes a hot dry one on the other.

The Föhn effect is noted at dozens of places around the globe, but the chinook, which sweeps over Montana and Alberta, is the most spectacular example. On western slopes of the Rockies this great sea wind drops snow or rain, to feed rivers and irrigation ditches. Then it tumbles down eastern slopes as a hot dry wind whose performance is almost past belief. In Havre, Montana, it shot the temperature up by 31°F in three minutes. Calgary, Alberta, reported an incredible rise one February: from −14° to 76°F.

Great deserts are powerful wind-breeders. Iran's maddening, desiccating wind-of-120-days often carries enough sand to bury whole villages. Southern California's Santa Ana wind, which sweeps in from the desert, heats up as it drops down the Pacific slopes of the Rockies. It withers vegetation and opens the way for raging brush fires. The sirocco, born over the Sahara, sweeps northwards, picks up water crossing the Mediterranean and strikes Spain, Italy and France as a hot, sodden, enervating wind cursed by all.

The northers are winds that occur when low-pressure systems suck in polar air. Most great land-masses in the Northern Hemisphere have east/west chains of mountains that block the flow of polar air, but North America does not. Hence the devastating northers that sweep down from Siberia and Alaska, chilling the air as far south as Central America.

France's mistral, sucked southwards by low-pressure areas over the Mediterranean, is a norther. It has overturned lorries and blown chains of

With tons of dust swirling up its funnel, a tornado twists across the plains of Kansas against a lowering sky. Destructive 'twisters' like this one are formed when a vortex drops out of a thundercloud and sucks into its vacuum air or anything else in its path. Tornadoes passing over ponds and streams sometimes drain them dry. Those passing over larger bodies of water become waterspouts and suck up great columns of water, just as land tornadoes suck up dust, trees and buildings. The winds in a tornado's funnel, which is quite narrow—about 200 yds across—may reach velocities of from 300 to 600 mph, and are the most powerful winds on earth.

parked railway trucks for miles. In southern France houses present a solid stone wall or only small windows to the anger of the wind, and most village main streets run east-west.

Although a vast store of wind knowledge has been accumulated, great areas of mystery remain.

For instance, no one is sure what causes a tornado. That is why, more and more, Tiros, Nimbus and other satellites are sending to earth television pictures of the wind-driven cloud patterns.

The World Weather Watch of the World Meteorological Organisation is now being set up, and observations from land stations and ships at sea are being planned. The data collected will be analysed with the aid of high-speed computers located at meteorological centres in Washington, Moscow and Melbourne. In addition, there are also plans developing which include provision for more effective international communication systems for transmitting information about the weather.

The winds have always been great shapers of human destiny, and man does well to continue to try to discover what the wild winds are saying.

SPLENDOUR OF
THE SKIES

Men have worshipped the sun as a supreme God, lightning has been thought of as the weapon of Zeus, and the rainbow was the sign of Jehova's covenant with Noah. Today, we think of the sun as a nuclear furnace, describe lightning as an electrical discharge, and know that rainbows are caused by the diffraction of sunlight among water-drops. But the sun is still the source of all life,

rainbows can still enchant us, and inexplicable things are still seen in the skies.

Nearly all the phenomena that we see above us are caused by the sun's radiation entering and acting upon the earth's atmosphere. In this way auroras—shimmering displays of colour, licking the sky like flames or fading into ghostly streaks—are created, and the sun's radiant heat and the earth's rotation combine to whip tornadoes into spiralling fury. Sometimes the moon also takes a part in the heavenly spectacle and, passing between the earth and the sun, blots out the sun's disc entirely. When this happens, only the sun's corona is visible, a pearly halo too pale to be seen except during a solar eclipse.

Spectacular mirages, like this one photographed in the Niger–Temesna region of Africa, are usually only found in desert and polar regions. But mirages are also familiar in temperate climates—as when on a hot day a dry road appears in the distance to be covered with water. This is a mirage of the sky, caused in the same way as the mirage shown above: by light being reflected and refracted between a layer of hot air at ground level, and the successively cooler layers above.

When the sun shines through a thin cloud of ice crystals—usually at a very high altitude or in polar regions—it often shows a halo. The moon can also be haloed when its light is refracted by ice crystals.

A solar eclipse, occurring when the moon passes between the earth and the sun and partially or totally obscures the sun's disc. In the British Isles an eclipse can last for a maximum of 5½ minutes.

Many atmospheric phenomena occur in the cold, clear air of the polar regions. Above are sun-dogs—mock suns on the arc of an incomplete halo around the sun.

Left: a double rainbow at sunset near Milford Haven in Pembrokeshire, showing the orange light of the sun on the rain. Rainbows are caused by raindrops acting as prisms and splitting sunlight into its basic colours. In a double rainbow, the order of colours in the second bow is reversed because they are reflected twice.

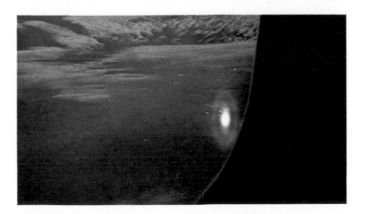

The sun with an elliptical ring round it, reflected from the top of a cloud. This phenomenon, known as a sub-sun, was photographed above the Mississippi river. Sub-suns are sometimes mistaken for flying saucers.

A photograph taken just before sunrise east of The Long Mynd in Shropshire. Above the line of darkness, over the horizon, not yet lit by the sun, is a line of shadows cast by mountains on to the sky.

Side view of a funnel-shaped tornado photographed in Texas (above). The swirling funnel appears to grow at a slant from the base of a dark, heavy thundercloud; it reaches the ground, twisting and bending slowly, the base dragging because of friction. North American tornadoes average 300–400 yds in width, although they can be as wide as a mile or even more. Tornadoes do not travel far—sometimes for as short a distance as 3 miles.

Aurora borealis, or northern lights, photographed in Alaska. Auroras are seen in the northern and southern hemispheres, and are the result of streams of electrically charged particles from the sun encountering the earth's magnetic field above the North and South Poles.

A dreaded 'haboob', the violent squall preceding a dust-storm, approaches Khartoum in the Sudan. These winds, often over 100 mph, pick up sand from the desert and carry it overland in an almost vertical wall. In a 'haboob', day turns to night in the space of seconds.

36

As the sun's radiation passes through the lower atmosphere, it is scattered by particles roughly the same size as the wavelength of radiation. Scattering is most intense at sunset and sunrise, when only the long yellow and red waves reach our eyes directly. These rays reflecting from the red rock of the Olga Mountains in central Australia (above), produce one of the most beautiful and striking sunsets in the world.

A cloudburst, such as this one photographed in Monument Valley, southern Utah, is a sudden, violent rainfall. The downpour is usually localised and, though brief, is capable of causing heavy 'flash' floods, which pour over the desert but soon dry up.

Snow reflects sunlight at the base of Mount Discovery in Antarctica. There is so much of the sun's invisible ultra-violet radiation in the Antarctic that sunburn is a severe hazard; however, the same radiation also destroys bacteria, making the air here the purest on earth.

The Howl of the Hurricane

Benedict Thielen

We call them by friendly names like Carol, Edna, Connie and Hazel—but these havoc-wreaking furies are as much beyond our control as the tilt of the earth

Between the great trade winds of the North and South Atlantic lie the doldrums—a broad belt reaching across the tropical sea from the Guianas in the west to the bulge of Africa in the east. It is a place where breezes falter, a place of calms but not of peace. Behind the calms there is a restlessness. The slowly heaving sea, shivering from time to time with flurries of wind or brief showers, glistens pale as lead. Grey curtains of distant cloud and rain form, drift and disappear below the horizon. Sometimes, in the hot summer months, they form and grow.

The heated air, weighted with water, rises slowly from the sea. As it rises, other air moves in to take its place. This motion in the calmness is imperceptible at first, but growing as the misty air is drawn off the sea like smoke up a chimney. The earth, too, is moving, spinning; and as the air moves, it takes on the movement of the earth as well. Around the hollow centre the air begins to spin and spiral. Rising, the warm air expands, cools; and the water it is charged with condenses as rain.

So the air-column grows, spinning in one place like a top, with occasional erratic darts forward or to the side. Presently, touched by the edges of the trade winds, the column begins to move westwards. It moves slowly at first, sometimes stopping altogether as it sucks up the hot dampness that is its fuel. But a direction has been set. Out of motion a shape has been born. It is a hurricane.

On a distant shore, a thousand miles away, the sound of the sea changes. The light, quick rhythm of the breakers becomes heavier and slower. When the long swells, visible far out on the horizon, reach the shore, they fall with a deep, reverberating boom, grave as a tolling bell. Hearing the sound, a man who remembers other storms will look to the sky. It is clear, with a still and luminous clarity that seems to stem from an immense innocence. Far above, wisps of high cirrus cloud gleam with a pearly lustre; and as evening falls the sunset will blaze with an even greater splendour than usual.

Many men and instruments have been watching the sea and sky. From weather satellites in orbit above the earth, and from men on freighters, liners and tankers at sea, comes information about the changing weather conditions. High in an office building in Miami, at America's National Hurricane Centre, men analyse this data.

Next morning the waves are breaking high over a lighthouse on an offshore reef. A breeze is blowing now, but instead of blowing off the sea, it blows from the land. Yet it is not a land breeze, dry and smelling of dust and late summer flowers. It is heavy and damp, and there is salt in it, bitter on your lips.

The sky is no longer clear but veiled in a milky haze. As the day wears on, the veil thickens, grows yellowish. As the sun sinks, the sky is streaked with unusually brilliant orange and red light.

At sea, the air has begun to hum and throb. The dark mass has moved forward, as the confused waters are lashed by the rain and wrung and twisted by the wind. The clouds spin faster, advance faster, rumbling like distant guns. Coming in low above the churning water, a plane flies straight into the eye of the storm. A long time after, it reappears, wings quivering. Then it wheels, rises and sends its message to shore.

In Miami the man at the plotting board can now mark the exact centre of the storm. The radar grilles swing to face it, and men bend over the screens waiting for its picture to appear—the hollow centre with its spiralling cloud arms, the octopus shape. Now the storm is given a name. It has become a personality, malevolent and dangerous, a criminal at large. At the Hurricane Centre the teleprinters click faster.

As the storm approaches, the air ahead of it becomes charged with an unaccustomed tension. Not knowing why, people become more aware of the beating of their hearts. They feel a restless need to be doing something and at the same time a difficulty in concentrating on the thing to be done. Fear twitches. It was fear that gave the hurricane its name: *hurrican*, the Carib Indians' word for evil spirit.

The storm now spins at 100 mph—an immense, shallow disc, its top curved with the curve of the earth, its centre filled with sunlight and plunging air. It still advances slowly, at 10–12 knots. As it moves west and north, its outer edge strikes a well of air, the great oval of high pressure that covers the Atlantic from Bermuda to the Azores. Unable to go further north, it heads due west. The westward-flowing winds urge it faster on its course.

Watchers on the shore can see it approach now. Through the milky veil a greyish blur appears on the

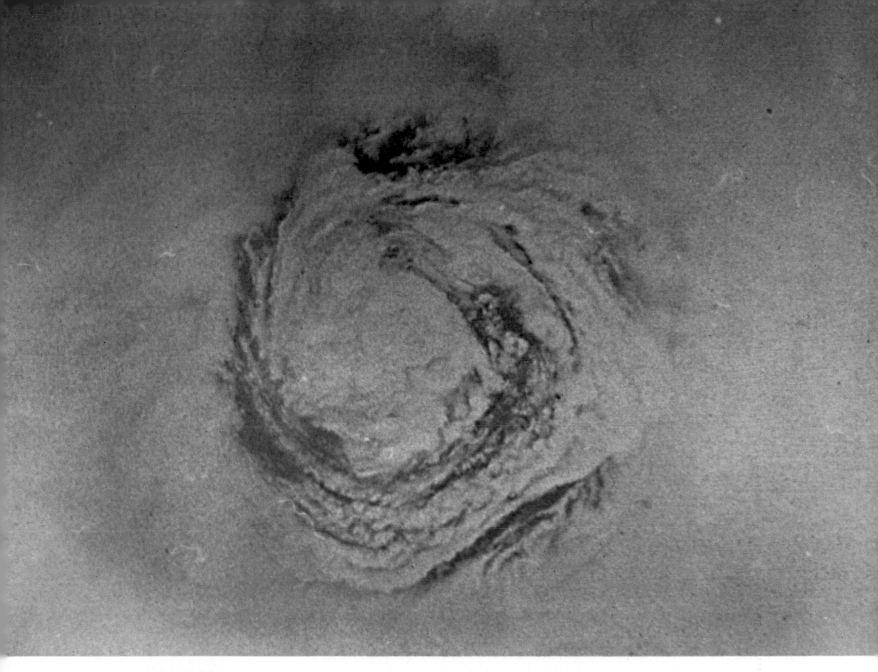

The eye of hurricane Beulah, photographed from a reconnaissance plane. Beulah began in the tropical Atlantic 35 miles west of Martinique, on September 5, 1967. From there it travelled north-west across the Caribbean, made landfall on the Mexican island of Cozumel on September 16, and went on to cause unprecedented damage to the lower Rio Grande Valley on the Texas–Mexico border. By September 22, when the hurricane finally blew itself out in the mountainous region near Monterrey in Mexico, it had caused damage costing over 200 million dollars and had killed 59 people.

horizon, shot through with a coppery light. Other clouds, broken, fast-moving, come like outriders at its side, scudding low across the sea. As it nears, the body of the storm becomes black, swelling and rising, blotting out what light still lingers in the sky. The driven rain rakes the sea, and for a long time gusts punch and pound at the torrents of rain, now pausing, now striking again.

The pauses grow gradually longer. Finally, only gentle air currents are moving. The sky clears, and the sun comes out. The air is warm and dry and very light. This is the eye of the storm. For perhaps half an hour the quiet persists. Then from far away comes a faint humming. Clouds creep over the rim of the sea and begin to spread across the sky. The wind returns, at speeds of 150 mph and more.

Now, with the passing of the centre around which it spins, it blows from the opposite direction. Trees that had bent before it are jerked back. Like someone kicking and gouging an opponent who already lies gasping, the wind clutches and shakes the helpless land. Then, as the blackness touches the zenith, the whole world seems suddenly to burst apart. From someone's throat comes a cry as the sea, piled up by the wind, breaks from its own weight, and falls— obliterating houses, boats, trees and, here and there, the small running figure of a woman or a man.

The water flows over the defeated land. When a tree falls, its splash is lost in the universal thundering. The flight through the air of a roof, an oar, a bucket, is without sound. There is no sound as a

39

splinter no bigger than a matchstick penetrates the skull of a man. Now the sun comes out again. The air smells fresh and clean with the sweetness of crushed leaves. Boats and houses lie broken and scattered along the shore. Some people are dead.

To the meteorologist the hurricane is a 'cyclonic vortex', a circulation of air revolving around a core of low pressure. It spins clockwise below the Equator, anti-clockwise above. To be classed as a true hurricane, it must have a circular speed of at least 75 mph; speeds of 160 mph are not unusual. Above this point, wind-measuring instruments are generally carried away, but there have been storms with gusts estimated at 250 mph. It was to express this, the inexpressible, that a shipmaster once entered in his log, 'Winds infinite'.

A hurricane's course is influenced by neighbouring areas of pressure, for it takes the path of least resistance. If a body of high pressure lies on both sides of a storm path, the hurricane will move up the channel created between. It was through such a channel that a hurricane tore into New England in 1938 at a mile a minute.

That disaster ushered in an era of northern storms. With each succeeding one—the Great Atlantic Hurricane of 1944; Carol, Edna, Hazel in 1954; Donna, surging from Florida to New England in 1960; Carla, devastating the Texas coast in 1961; Betsy, hitting New Orleans in 1965—people wonder whether a new and permanent pattern has been set.

Once having listened to the rising wind or watched the rising sea, one can never again enjoy quite the same feeling of security one knew before. In Massachusetts I have seen the red, black-centred warning flags fly many times, and in Florida as well, where I have sat in a shuttered house and listened to its tiles being riffled like cards by the wind, while coconuts thudded like cannon-balls against its sides. But when I think of a hurricane, it is still my first one—the New England hurricane of 1938.

At five o'clock on the afternoon of September 21, the house I lived in stood on a strip of beach. Behind it lay a salt-water lake: in front of it dunes faced the sea like ramparts. An hour later no trace of the dunes remained, and the house was floating towards the far shore of the lake. I can still hear the crash of glass as a wave smashed the front window. I feel the water, ankle-deep, then waist-deep, then bottomless in a single huge surge. I see the point of land towards which I am swimming disappear. The wind, blowing at 90 mph, whips the surface of the water into spray and drives it down my throat. It crosses my mind that I may drown. But slow strokes and the wind

carry me to a hillside; I grasp the thorny branches of a wild rosebush and slowly pull myself out and beyond the reaching sea.

In places where hurricanes occur often, they say that people get used to them. In a sense it is true. They know what precautions to take—what supplies to have on hand, which windows to close and which to leave open. But there is always the feeling of ultimate helplessness.

In a small Cuban town I once asked a friend what people there did when a hurricane came. 'Why,' he said, looking at me in surprise, 'we get drunk.'

I can think of no more reasonable course of action.

The Miracle of Lightning

Ira Wolfert

In a few violent seconds lightning can vaporise the sap in a tree trunk, burn holes in concrete and turn the air into plant food

When you see lightning, it has already missed you. When you hear thunder, relax; the show is over. The noise is just the audience rushing for the exits.

One of the great figures in thunderstorm exploration, the late Dr Karl McEachron, used to reassure nervous laymen by telling them this. If a big bolt were to hit you, you'd never know it. In the meantime, enjoy the spectacle.

Lightning is one of the most dramatic examples in Nature of the ill wind that blows good. It is true that it kills a score of people a year in Britain, injures 50 others and starts about 130 fires. Yet it is also true that without lightning plant life could not exist.

Almost 80 per cent of our atmosphere is nitrogen—an essential food for plants. About 22 million tons of this nutriment float over each square mile of earth. But in its aerial form nitrogen is insoluble, unusable. Before plants can take life from it, it must undergo what our food undergoes in our digestive machinery: a series of chemical reactions. Lightning touches off the series.

This is how the extraordinary process occurs. Air particles are made white hot by lightning. They reach temperatures as high as 30,000°C. Under this intense heat, the nitrogen combines with the oxygen in the air to form nitrogen oxides that are soluble in water. The rain dissolves the oxides and carries them down to earth as dilute nitric acid. You can smell this acid—the pungent, tingly odour that hangs in the rainy air of a thunderstorm. Reaching the earth, the nitric acid reacts with minerals there to become nitrates on which plants can feed. This is a wonder, indeed: lightning, which meteorologists estimate to be bombarding the earth at a rate of more than 100 times a second, transforms the upper air into fertiliser for earthbound plants.

The story of lightning is one that sings the greatness of science. Every schoolboy knows that the story began with Benjamin Franklin and the kite, which led to his invention of the lightning conductor. This simple device, which has remained basically unchanged since Franklin's day, must be included in any list of great inventions.

Very little more was learnt about lightning until an August afternoon in 1920, when a bolt struck a gnarled 'snake tree' a foot away from an unoccupied shack owned by scientist Charles Steinmetz. The bolt bounced off the tree and broke a window; it splintered a work-table, then leapt across the room to shatter a mirror. Discovering the debris, Steinmetz had every fragment and splinter of the mirror collected and fitted together between two sheets of glass. It was the first time that the pattern struck off by a lightning charge had been studied.

Then scientists devised instruments to measure and record bolts. They hunted lightning, trapped it on film, learnt how to make it in the laboratory. They even developed a camera that takes a high-speed, slow-motion picture of a lightning bolt.

Scientists were urged to make these studies because of the growing dependence on electric power. Lightning plays havoc when it hits electric power-lines, and it hits them frequently. Lightning can run along the line directly into expensive machinery in the power station or transformer or, if it makes an arc to the ground before it travels that far, it can be followed into the earth by all the electricity in the line, until the line is drained or shut off.

The scientists eventually learnt how to control the power failures by discovering how lightning strokes are formed. To begin with, a thundercloud gets under way when warm, humid air rises from the earth in a steady up-draught, generally over a hill or mountain-top. The humidity condenses as the air cools on rising. We see the tiny water droplets as mist that gradually assumes the familiar shape of a cumulo-nimbus cloud. Sometimes looking like a huge cauliflower, or an enormous white anvil, the cumulo-nimbus is often topped by a 'cirrus umbrella'. It is composed of millions of minute ice crystals.

These formations can be enormous—up to 50,000 ft or more in height. They can contain as much as 300,000 tons of water. In them is a so-called 'chimney current'—a column of air rising at a full gale force of about 100 ft a second. The moisture in this column condenses rapidly, and the droplets are swept upwards to freeze into hailstones. The hailstones do not fall. They dance on the chimney current like table-tennis balls on a gushing fountain, rising steadily higher until, near the top of the cloud, the force of the current is exhausted. There the hailstones shower out in all directions, carrying cold air with them as they descend. Frequently they are sucked back into the chimney current, to be dissolved and reformed again and again.

In this turbulent motion something still unexplained happens. There is a separation of electric charges. The smaller particles near the top of the cloud become charged positively, while the raindrops in the lower portion are charged negatively.

Meanwhile, on the surface of the earth directly below the cloud, there is a corresponding build-up of a positive charge. As the cloud drifts, a positive charge on earth follows it like a shadow, climbing trees, church steeples, towers, poles. It races into houses, and climbs water-pipes, television aerials, lightning conductors—whatever can bring it closer to the cloud.

Enormous differences of electric potential develop between the top and bottom of the thundercloud, and between the bottom of the cloud and its image on the earth.

Suddenly a thin white arm reaches down for perhaps 50 ft from the base of the cloud—a 'leader'. It is a gaseous arc path, reacting to electricity like the gas in a neon tube. The leader hangs, hesitating a moment, thickening and brightening as the electrons in the cloud swarm into it. Then it reaches down again, perhaps as much as 300 ft.

The activity of the positive particles on the earth may have increased now to where 'streamers'—the opposite of leaders—can be noticed leaping up from the high points in the vicinity. Photographs have been made showing them snaking as high as 50 ft upwards. This phenomenon is familiarly called 'St Elmo's fire'. Now, in time, a streamer meets a leader and a path between the earth and the cloud has been opened.

A unique time exposure, taken at Castleford, Yorkshire, records this weird phenomenon— a·'ball' of lightning bouncing off a brick chimney and exploding in front of a house. Ball lightning has never been satisfactorily explained (and a few scientists deny that it exists), but it appears to be formed of electrified gases resembling those on the sun.

The great sky-splitting spear of light that we see is actually hurtling up, not down. It starts at the point of first contact between negative and positive charges and rips up to the cloud along the gas path that has been formed by the descending leader. The fact that the spear of light seems to travel down is an optical illusion that occurs when speeds become too great for the eye to follow.

There is often a great pulsing in the light, made by successive strokes along the same path. There may be as many as 40 pulses in a second, which is about how long the lightning's path stays open. The heat in the path rises so abruptly that the surrounding air breaks the sound barrier in moving away. The result is thunder.

Lightning usually 'strikes' one of the higher points in any area—a tree, a house, a golfer on a fairway. Current flows through the object struck via the best conducting path that object offers. If your clothing is wet, the current will go through *it*. You may even survive such an experience, for moisture is a good conductor of electricity. But when lightning strikes a tree with dry bark, it travels inside the bark, in the sap. The sap is instantly super-heated to steam, and expands so abruptly that the tree explodes.

It is lightning's tendency to seek out the best path offered which makes the lightning conductor work as successfully as it does. When no path is offered, lightning builds one—brutally. From the top of a chimney on a country cottage, a bolt crashed like a bomb through the wooden wall to ground level. But there was no metal, no plumbing or wiring, and the ground itself at that point resisted the passage of electricity. Whereupon the lightning ripped open a trench 155 ft long, two or three feet wide, a foot or two deep, through the soil to the house of a neighbour who had put in modern improvements. There it punched a hole 6 in. wide through the concrete foundation to leap across the cellar and finally land on a well-pipe.

At Ascot in 1955, 47 race-goers received shocks and burns when lightning, hunting for a pathway, struck the metal fence on which they were leaning.

Far older than man are the horrors and terrors wrought by lightning,· and they never change. The work of the devil, it was called, and in the last century the civilised world shot off cannon to frighten it away. Now science has learnt at last that there is good in this most awesome force; and lightning is recognised as one of the great spasms in the continuing miracle of creation and existence.

Lightning occurs when the build-up of static electricity in clouds and the ground overcomes the air's resistance to the passage of an electrical current. Dry air has a high resistance, but in damp air electricity can force a way for itself between the ground and a cloud, between two clouds, or between different parts of the same cloud. When this happens, the air along its path is heated to incandescence, and we see a lightning flash. The heated air expands, produces a shock-wave, and we hear thunder.

The Waters of Life

Whatever form it takes—whether in the world's great oceans,
in mile-wide rivers, quiet meadow streams, lakes or
thundering thousand-foot waterfalls—water
has a fascination and enchantment all
its own, as it makes its endless,
life-bringing journeys between sea, land and sky

The Restless Tides

K. F. Bowden

The tidal pulse of the oceans is a response
to the attraction of the moon and sun;
but in time the world's seas will be tideless

The rise and fall of the sea twice a day is such an obvious thing that it must have been well known to people living along the coasts of tidal seas from very early times. These people also must have noticed that the tides came later and later each day—50 minutes on the average—as did the rising of the moon. Some may have associated this with the rise and fall of the sea.

The tides vary greatly from place to place, often within a surprisingly short distance. Only 40 miles separate the Atlantic and Pacific Oceans along the Panama Canal, yet at the Atlantic end the tidal range is about 2 ft, while at the Pacific end it is about 14 ft. Around the British Isles the tidal range is greatest in the Bristol Channel where, at Avonmouth, the spring range reaches 40 ft. At Portland Bill, near the centre of the English Channel coast, the spring range is only 7 ft. The largest range in the world is at the head of the Bay of Fundy, between New Brunswick and Nova Scotia, where the spring range reaches 50 ft at the head of the Minas Basin.

As tidal ranges vary from place to place, so do tidal rhythms. Along the shores of the Gulf of Mexico, where the range is no more than a foot or two, the rhythm of the tides would seem remarkable to anyone accustomed to two high waters and two low waters a day. Here the tides are diurnal, with only one high water and one low water each lunar day of 24 hours and 50 minutes. On the other hand, the Pacific coasts of North America have mixed tides—two highs and two lows a day, but usually of markedly unequal heights.

Since Greek and Roman times men have known that the rhythm of the tides was somehow related to the apparent motion of the moon and sun, but it was not until Newton's time that we were given a rational explanation of the link. In 1687 Newton showed that the tides are one of the consequences of the laws of gravitation. Every particle of matter on the earth is attracted by the moon, and the force of attraction is directed towards the moon's centre; also, the further away from the moon's centre the particle is, the weaker the attracting force. So the force varies slightly both in direction and in strength, depending on the position of the particle on the earth. It is this variation in the attracting force that causes the ocean waters to move to and fro over the earth's crust and so produce the tides.

We know that the sun also exerts a tide-generating force on the earth's waters. It may seem surprising that the sun, nearly 25 million times larger than the moon, does not have a greater effect; but mass is not

A rock hollowed by the backlash of waves striking at its foot. The shapes that erosion can produce in the course of centuries always reflect the direction of the eroding force—wind, rain, ice or sea—and the strengths and weaknesses of the material being eroded.

the only key to the explanation. Although tidal force is directly proportional to the mass of the heavenly body concerned, it is also inversely proportional to the cube of its distance. The sun's greater distance from us, then, is the dominating fact, with the result that its ability to raise tides on earth is less than half that of the moon.

But there are other influences at work. In 1775 the French mathematician Laplace showed that the tidal picture is made much more complex because of the earth's rotation and the inertia of the ocean waters. The complexity is added to by irregular coastlines and the varying depth of the sea.

While the tides in the deep oceans ebb and flow in accordance with the changing positions of the moon and sun, the tides in coastal seas, such as the English Channel and the Red Sea, are secondary effects and depend on the oceanic tides. If these seas were cut off from the oceans, the tides in them would be almost imperceptible; it is the tidal waves coming in from the ocean that set them oscillating. Wherever we find a large vertical rise and fall of tidal water, we know that enormous quantities of sea are also flowing horizontally from one place to another; in the Bay of Fundy tidal currents twice daily move 100,000 million tons of water. In restricted passages and straits these tidal currents sometimes attain speeds of more than 10 knots, as they do in Discovery Passage and in Seymour Narrows, British Columbia. In coastal seas, tidal currents frequently attain speeds of 2–3 knots, but in the open oceans they are rarely more than a quarter of a knot. One of the most notorious tidal current areas in the world is around the Aleutians, where ships have been cast

45

up on the rocks as they attempted to work their way through the Akutan and Unalga Passes.

When tides flow into an estuary, they become distorted and slowed down by the restricting effect of shallow water. In extreme cases the flood stream rushes up the river in the form of a tidal bore—a turbulent mass of water with an almost vertical wave front, followed by a series of choppy waves. There are some half dozen or more well-known tidal bores in the world. In the British Isles, bores occur in the River Trent, a tributary of the Humber, in the River Severn and in the Solway Firth. One of the most striking bores is in the Chien-Tang Kiang, which flows into the Bay of Hangchow in China. There, at high tide, the bore surges upriver as a wave up to 11 ft high with a speed of up to 12 knots or more. Within 10 minutes the river rises 9 ft, and about $1\frac{3}{4}$ million tons of water flow upstream per minute.

Since the tides depend on the motions of the moon and sun, we can normally predict them rather accurately—the times of high and low water to within a few minutes, and the heights of the water itself to within a few inches. Sometimes, however, meteorological disturbances invalidate predictions.

These disturbances are known as storm surges, and they can be disastrous over a large area. The most destructive surge occurring in north-western Europe in recent years was the one on January 31 and February 1, 1953, when strong northerly winds caused a piling up of water in the southern part of the North Sea. Because the peak of the surge came very near the time of high water of a spring tide, this storm tide inundated the coasts of Holland and eastern England at levels up to 10 ft higher than were predicted; and high waves generated by the gale added to the destructive force of the water. In Holland more than 1800 people were killed, in England more than 300 died, and in both countries there was extensive damage to property. This disaster made it obvious that some sort of flood warning service should be set up in Britain. Such a service is now operated jointly by the Admiralty and the Meteorological Office; by methods based on a study of previous surges, we can forecast the probable height of a surge about 12 hours before it strikes.

The surges born of hurricanes in the Gulf of Mexico and along the Atlantic coast of the United States, and those brought on by typhoons in the China seas, have a special character. The wind piles up the water in the storm region, as it did in the 1953 North Sea surge, but at the same time the low pressure area of the storm causes a temporary rise in sea level. And a third effect—resonance—may build up the surge to even greater heights if the cyclone or hurricane happens to be moving at almost the same speed as that at which a tidal wave, once set up, would travel freely.

Destructive surges of still different character can be produced by submarine earthquakes. These surges are popularly known as 'tidal waves', although they have nothing to do with the tides. Scientists prefer to call them by their Japanese name, *tsunamis*. When an earthquake jars the ocean floor, the resulting disturbance in sea level sets up a wave that fans out for hundreds or thousands of miles in all directions at a speed of about 500 mph. In the deep ocean the height of a *tsunami* is only 1–2 ft, and a ship overtaken by one may not even detect it; but on entering shallow water, although the wave's speed is greatly reduced, its height may build up to 30 or 40 ft before it overwhelms the shore and rushes inland. These waves do not occur singly but in a long train, and in deep water 100 miles or more may separate them from crest to crest. On reaching the shore the third or fourth wave in the train is usually the highest and most destructive, after which waves of decreasing height follow one another at intervals of 10–20 minutes for some hours.

There have been many highly destructive *tsunamis* throughout history. When a series of violent shocks shook the west coast of South America in 1868, the sea withdrew ominously from the coast, but shortly afterwards returned as a great wave that swept boats a quarter of a mile inland. When the volcanic island of Krakatoa exploded in 1883, the resulting *tsunamis* swept a gunboat inland for 2 miles.

Whether we are concerned with surges or simply with normal tides, there are enormous amounts of energy locked up in the movement of the water. Tidal energy enters the western end of the English Channel from the Atlantic Ocean at the rate of about 240 million horsepower, but 87 per cent of this energy is dissipated by friction with the channel floor. On a global scale this tidal friction acts as a kind of brake that is slowly but decisively slowing down the rate of the earth's rotation, with the result that the length of our days is increasing at a rate of about one-thousandth of a second in a hundred years. At the same time, the tidal friction is slowly pushing the moon further away from the earth, which means that the moon is taking longer and longer to circle the earth—which in turn means that the length of our months is also increasing.

In its early life the moon rotated rapidly on its own axis, but tidal friction on its surface gradually slowed it down until it became 'frozen'. Today we see only one side of the moon as it revolves about us. Its far-side face is forever turned away. Astronomers tell us that, if conditions continue as at present, a similar fate awaits the earth 50,000 million years from now. As the earth spins more slowly, our days will continue to lengthen and the moon will continue spiralling away from the earth until the length of a day and a month will eventually be the same—equal to about 47 of our present days. By then, tides as we now know them would have ceased to exist; but astrophysicists say that, long before this state of affairs comes about, the sun will become so much brighter and radiate such intense heat that all our oceans will be boiled dry.

The Unearthly World at the Bottom of the Sea

Rutherford Platt

Oceanographers' discoveries surpass
sailors' yarns in their strangeness—yet we
still know less about the depths
of the ocean than we do about the moon

Today, strange lands more inaccessible than the planets are being discovered at the very bottom of the sea. Down there in an unbelievable world are plains vaster than the Steppes, and mountain ranges more massive than the Alps. The sea-bed is utterly dark. But it is not silent, nor is it motionless: muffled shock-waves from earthquakes travel through the deeps; horizontal wrenchings and vertical shiftings result from stresses and strains in the earth's crust and the elastic mantle that underlies it. Incredible forms of life have been found in this dark region where it was previously thought to be impossible for life to exist.

But explorers will never walk about down there, for no 'space suit' could protect a man from being squashed to death under a weight of water that can reach a pressure of 7 tons per square inch. The Piccard bathyscaphe can descend to the bottom of the ocean, but men in it can make only a spot check of what they encounter in the little circle of their electric lights. They cannot go outside.

This world of incredible grandeur is now being revealed by remote control. Ingenious deep-sea equipment is being invented to explore and map undersea regions. Electronic, mechanical and sonar sensors are helping scientists to find clues to some of the great mysteries of the earth, such as how the oceans and continents were created, and whether the continents are drifting.

This dark realm lies far beyond and below what people on beaches think of as deep ocean, where dolphins play and seaweed jungles teem with life. These are actually just the waters upon the continental shelf. The famous experiments in underwater living conducted by Jacques-Yves Cousteau and by the U.S. Navy's Sealabs take place on this shelf, which is the shoulder of a continent upon which the ocean has trespassed. It slopes outwards very gradually to a maximum depth of 600 ft, and ends suddenly at the true rim of the continent, known as the shelf break. Beyond lies the continental slope, which rapidly descends to the appalling depths that are just now beginning to be explored.

Among the extraordinary devices developed for this exploration are specially designed cameras mounted with lamps and encased in heavy aluminium-alloy cylinders to withstand the extreme pressures. Lowered miles into the depths to within 6–20 ft of the bottom, the cameras provide superb pictures of the ocean floor.

Another device is a 1600 lb. weight at the top of a hollow steel shaft. Triggered to plunge into the sea-bed, it can penetrate as far as 60 ft and bring up a core of sediment for study under microscopes.

Oceanographic ships are being fitted with new deep-ocean exploring instruments capable of extraordinary precision. They are floating laboratories designed for work in the open sea. One result is increasingly detailed maps of our under-ocean lands.

A surprising revelation is the ruggedness of the terrain: the vertical distances (depths of valleys, heights of mountains) are much greater than on the continents; when averaged out, the depths on the bottom are five times greater than the heights reached on continents above the sea.

Seen from the perspective of the ocean floor, the continents are tremendous blocks of granitic rock thrusting abruptly upwards. In some places the walls of the continents are cut by underwater canyons bigger than Arizona's Grand Canyon. Such a one is the Hudson Canyon, which cleaves the continental

*Dwelling in waters so deep that no light penetrates,
this female anglerfish attracts prey with her 'fishing rod',
a jointed spine of her dorsal fin with a luminous,
wriggling lure at its tip. Some anglerfish have no
luminous organs, making it difficult for the sexes to find
each other and mate. When a young male and female
meet, the male attaches himself permanently to the
female's side; the female grows to maturity, while
the male becomes nothing but a small parasitic machine
whose only function is to fertilise the female's eggs.*

shelf off New York. The canyon slopes gradually downwards, starting from under the Verrazano Narrows Bridge in New York harbour. Sixty miles offshore, the Upper Gorge cuts through the shelf break, plunging to a depth of 8000 ft. From there the Lower Gorge cleaves the gently sloping hillside formed by centuries of deposits until it reaches the Sohm Abyssal Plain, 16,500 ft under the waves. There towers Caryn Peak, a weird volcanic pinnacle five times higher than the Empire State Building.

The puzzle of what formed the giant canyons was solved in a surprising way. One day in 1929, 12 telegraph cables between the United States and Europe, running parallel but spaced miles apart,

were mysteriously broken, one after the other, over a period of 13 hours. The breaks took place in deep water beyond the continental rim off Newfoundland and began approximately one hour after a local earth tremor had occurred.

Twenty-three years later oceanographers were able to solve the mystery. A great event had occurred in the mysterious deep. A mass of stones, sand and mud, which had been torn from the coast by waves and deposited on the shelf of the Grand Banks, was shaken up and toppled off the shelf by an earthquake. Travelling as fast as 50 mph, this turbid mixture tumbled down the continental slope to the floor of the ocean, cutting one cable after another. The phenomenon is known as a turbidity current. Until then, no one had realised its magnitude or the power of which it is capable. Composed of water mixed with heavy rock and sediment, it moves like quicksilver—and attains great velocity and gouging power. Geologists say that this process, repeated again and again over millennia, has carved the big canyons in the deeps.

The Sohm Abyssal Plain extends north-east from Caryn Peak. The Hatteras Abyssal Plain stretches south-east of Caryn. These two flat bands, about 3 miles deep and 200 miles wide, curve until they almost encircle a comparatively rough terrain named the Bermuda Rise. This area is about 12,000 ft below sea level, except at its centre, where a steep, sharp mountain stabs up through the ocean—Bermuda.

Abyssal plains are the deep-sea floor of the ocean. Here are no swaying seaweeds, no cycle of day and night, no apparent tides or waves. All is dark. Most abyssal plains are studded with volcanoes, called sea-mounts. Some, especially in the Pacific, are beheaded and are called guyots. In ancient ages these volcanoes repeatedly erupted through the ocean floor, belching fiery lava that built up until it emerged above the sea. Later the volcanoes became extinct and the tops, eroded by wind and waves, flattened to sea level. But the crust of the earth is thin and elastic under the ocean depths; in time it sagged, drowning the volcanoes. Today we discover the guyots with their flat tops as much as a mile under the surface.

Strange chasms called trenches are sometimes found at the edges of the abyssal plains near the continental margins. Their origin is still unknown. Averaging 20 miles wide at the top and hundreds of miles long, a trench has steep sides and a flat floor, and is usually about 25,000 ft deep. The Challenger Deep in the Marianas Trench east of Guam is the deepest spot yet discovered—7 miles under the blue water of the Pacific.

In the Atlantic, beyond the abyssal plains, under mid-ocean, lies a huge highland region called the Mid-Atlantic Ridge, whose mountain peaks break through the water into the sunshine at the Azores, Iceland, Ascension and other islands. The ridge was detected in 1873 by the famous expedition of the British ship *Challenger*, which sounded the depths with a lead weight.

Today, the new ocean-exploring devices have revealed that the Mid-Atlantic Ridge is a segment of the longest mountain range on earth. It runs from the Arctic Ocean basin the full length of both the North and South Atlantic oceans. Continuing in the deep water between Africa and Antarctica, it bends east and then branches northwards under the Indian Ocean, loops south of Australia, through the South Pacific, then north up the eastern side of the Pacific, where it runs ashore in Lower California. These globe-circling mountains are labelled Mid-Ocean Ridge—a colossal geological mystery that stretches over 40,000 miles and emerges from the sea in only a few isolated places.

The most exciting discovery about the Ridge is that it is sliced down the middle. This slicing has been carefully studied in the North Atlantic, where it is called the Rift Valley of the Mid-Atlantic Ridge. There the astonishing crack averages more than 6000 ft in depth; the severed sides stand 8–30 miles apart, suggesting a hellish tearing asunder.

In the Atlantic the line of the Rift follows the turns of the opposite coastlines. If the American continents and Europe/Africa were pushed together, and turned slightly, they would fit at the Rift like a jigsaw puzzle—a dramatic hint that these continents may have been formerly one land-mass that split apart at the Rift.

The key question is: what force is great enough to displace continents? One exciting suggestion comes from the discovery of unusual amounts of heat in the Mid-Atlantic Ridge and Rift, leaking out from the mantle through the crust at the bottom of the ocean. Is this kind of heat merely the result of volcanic eruptions, or is it being brought up slowly from the hot interior of the earth by convection currents? According to the convection-current theory, hot materials deep within the earth's mantle become excessively heated, perhaps by radio-activity, expand and rise towards the ocean floor. Just below the crust the ascending material slowly divides and spreads horizontally, dissipating heat as it does so. As it cools, the material grows denser and sinks back towards the deep interior where it heats up again. Thus a kind of wheel, revolving with infinite slowness, is formed within the mantle, and the moving mantle carries the crust along with it. Many geologists think that the slow spreading apart of the mantle creates a stretching force sufficient to cause the Rift Valley. This force, they say, tore the continents asunder, inched them apart through geological time, and is even now continuing to separate them.

Why, in the course of millennia, is there so astonishingly little sediment on the ocean floor? And what happens to the 8 cubic miles of land sediments that are washed by rivers into the oceans each year? Part of the answer is that some sediments dissolve as they run into the sea, and more disintegrate on the long slow trip to the bottom. Only the nearly insoluble materials in the sediments survive the journey. Nothing is left on the floor of the ocean except fine clay particles that come from the land, and a peculiar ocean deposit called ooze, composed almost entirely of the skeletal remains of countless millions of microscopic marine animals.

The clay particles and ooze are deposited by a perpetual 'phantom snow' with flakes so tiny that they are beyond the range of most microscopes and so nearly weightless that one may take years to sink from the upper layers 5 miles down to the floor. The sediment accumulates at an estimated rate of $\frac{1}{25}$ in. every thousand years. Even at that rate it should have reached a thickness of 10,000 ft after 3000 million years—which is about the time that the deep oceans have existed.

Yet the carpet of ooze is much thinner than this. Moreover, photographs taken by deep-sea cameras show that large areas of the ocean bottom are bare rock. Where have the sediments gone?

Some explain this by a theory about a grand cycle which scientists suspect may be occurring in the deeps, especially under the trenches. According to this theory, developed by Dr Robert Dietz of the U.S. Environmental Science Services Administration, the ocean floor on which the sediments are falling is also slowly moving, being nudged by the convection currents. It could be that the sediments are gradually being carried back towards the continental margins as though they were riding a conveyer belt.

Why don't they pile up against the continental margins? Perhaps they are pulled into the trenches. According to Dr Dietz, the trenches occur where the convection currents in the mantle are starting to descend. They drag a bit of the earth's crust with them and thrust it, with its veneer of ocean sediments, under the continents. At such depths, the earth's interior heat is intense enough to melt the sediments which, because of their granitic origin, slowly crystallise into fresh granitic rock.

Since these sediments are deposited so slowly, it is possible that they are carried under the continents and turned into new granite as fast as they collect. Thus the continents of the earth may be constantly renewing the materials that are steadily washed out of them, by reabsorbing them through the action of convection currents.

The utmost penetration of light into mid-ocean is about 3000 ft. Most sea-life is far above that depth, at no more than 300–600 ft, where there is enough sunlight energy for marine plants to manufacture food through photosynthesis. In the 1870's British and American ships discovered, in the blackness below the light-line, a mid-depth band of life, where sizeable fish swim happily under water pressure of 2 tons. These strange fish have evolved internal adaptations that enable them to survive the tremendous pressure of the water where they live. Many are luminous and have big mouths with long, sharp teeth. Some lure their prey with their eerie glow to within striking distance of their huge jaws. Others are scavengers which feed upon the carcasses of dead fish and other debris as it descends from above the light-line.

But can life exist on the very floor of the abyssal wilderness? The answer is, surprisingly, 'Yes'. Ocean-bottom cameras have shown living things on the firm ooze of abyssal plains and trench floors— mostly small, burrowing creatures: worms, sea cucumbers, molluscs. By a rare stroke of good luck the camera of one such probe caught a vivid picture of an acorn worm, 40 in. long. It was devouring ooze and defecating modernistic coils and spirals as it went on its way.

These inhabitants of the ocean floor, marvellous as they are, have cells similar to those of all other living things on earth. Because of the miracle we call evolution, they are able to survive by adapting their internal pressure to that of the surrounding water. Their existence is one more testimony to the astonishing hardiness of life.

How Rivers Change the Earth

R. de la Croix

The cycle of water between sea, sky and land sustains life on earth; it also produces rivers, which constantly alter the landscapes they flow through

One night in July 1890, when the French three-master *Fédération*, bound from Saigon to the Philippines, was 50 miles off the coast, the watch signalled that an island had been sighted. The commander thought it was a mirage; there were no islands marked on his charts at this latitude. Fifteen minutes later, however, he had to yield to the evidence: the ship was passing alongside an archipelago.

At first the commander thought that the islands had been created by volcanic action, but trees were

At the Bec d'Ambes, 14 miles north of Bordeaux in south-west France, the waters of the Garonne and Dordogne unite to form the Gironde, one of the greatest estuaries in Europe. At their junction a port has been built for petrol tankers, and despite its sandbanks and treacherous tides, the estuary—about 44 miles long and 7 miles wide—is navigable from its opening in the Bay of Biscay as far inland as Bordeaux. Some of France's finest vineyards lie along its west coast.

growing in the moist earth. These latitudes were too well travelled to leave hope of a new discovery. Then, to the astonishment of the crew, an element of danger was added. In the darkness, the helmsman did not see one of the mysterious islands. There was a crash, a cracking sound, and a tree rose level with the foremast. Branches lay strewn all over the superstructure of the French ship.

Luckily, the *Fédération* was able to free itself the next day and continue on its way, but it was not until later that the puzzle was solved. The islands which the three-master had encountered were simply clusters of clay and mud, with plants and bushes clinging to them. Rising waters had torn them away from a river bank.

The face of the earth is always changing, under the combined attack of several forces. The sea eats away our coastlines, but wave action is restricted to a narrow strip. Massive white glaciers also play a role in changing the face of the earth, but their

The tributaries of the Amazon can stretch for hundreds of miles; this photograph, taken at the end of the rainy season, shows one of the largest, the Tapajos, which joins the Amazon at Santarem in the Para region of Brazil. At its widest the Tapajos is 12 miles across, and its largest head-stream, the Arinos, rises some 900 miles south of Santarem in the Matto Grosso highlands.

effect is confined to mountains high enough to retain snow. The chemical decomposition of rocks stops when the layer of decomposed matter becomes thick enough to prevent the circulation of water. Wind action is effective only on loose soil.

But a river is always at work. It carves valleys, fertilises one place, erodes another, moves a forest, changes the face of a city, moulds a shoreline and alters its own course. It is a potent, formidable sculptor of the land.

The essence of a river is water: water which falls from the sky and feeds the sources of the river. This water is set in motion by the slope of the land, and the energy it thus acquires is the source of the river's strength. When the river meets an obstruction, it adjusts the width and depth of its channel. If a rock is too hard for it to wear away, it runs round it. If the river encounters a depression, it forms a lake or pool while the waters work to restore the continuity of its

course. A river is an agent of change because it is perpetually forced to carve out a channel for itself. With its weapons of mud, gravel and pieces of quartz a river is capable of great works: for example, cutting the great transverse valleys of the Himalayas or the Alps.

The strength of a river is less influenced by average rainfall than by the amount of rain which falls in a short space of time. A violent rainstorm gives a river new force, and in some countries powerful disruptions are common after storms. It has been calculated that each year the Ganges, for example, transports enough material to build 42 pyramids the size of the Great Pyramid.

A river is characterised by its flow, the width of its bed, its current and also by the colour of its waters. When the water level begins to rise, when the flood's ravages or benefits are close at hand, the water becomes muddy.

Then, especially in tropical countries, it grows red, a sign that it is full of laterite, iron-rich clay scraped from the basin. On the other hand, green and clear water is a sign that the river is doing little work and carrying very little sediment. If it is fed by melting snow, the green becomes milky, as in the Alpine rivers, the Aar or the Swiss Rhône. A yellow,

A meander in the course of the River Ain, which rises in the Jura mountains in eastern France, and follows a tortuous course for 118 miles before joining the River Rhône west of Lyon. The turbulent waters of the Ain cascade through many spectacular gorges and ravines as they descend from the mountains, and hydro-electric dams have been built to harness their power.

churning, muddy river is carrying a heavy load of sediment.

This shows clearly in the confluence of the two Niles at Khartoum. In July the river is dark from the mud of the Blue Nile, which has drained its waters from the Ethiopian plateau during the rainy season. In October it becomes whitish with microscopic plants carried by the White Nile from the swampy area to the south. Upstream, during the rainy season, the Nile breaks loose. Large chunks of the banks cave in. Trees are uprooted. The debris unites and forms islands cemented together with mud, which grow at random as the river deposits more debris. Birds bring grain picked from the river banks. Plants sprout up. The islands solidify, another witness to the creative power of the river. They impede the current and the banks are submerged. Then the sun dries them out and the Nile destroys what it had created: the islands crumble and float away.

For a long time, the source of the great rivers was a mystery. The Mississippi, the 'great water' venerated by the Algonquin Indians, rises in Lake Itasca, in the mountains of Minnesota—a fact which was only established in 1832; and it was not until 1941 that Bertrand Flornoy determined the source of the Amazon. Today, geologists have deduced the laws that govern the birth of rivers. Because it is fed mainly by precipitation, and only in a smaller measure by subterranean waters or other sources, a river can be born only when the rainfall is above a certain level—in the tropical desert regions it must not be less than 8 in. annually.

Only a third of the water which falls on a river basin reaches the sea. The rest evaporates or is absorbed by the roots of trees or by the earth. The regularity of the flow depends on the stability of the source, the river profile and the amount of sediment carried. When the load of sediment becomes too heavy, it is deposited on the bank. Almost by instinct the river regains its proper equilibrium.

One of the most beautiful sights a river can present are the meanders, those calm arabesques, majestic, complicated, logical or fantastic, whose design seems to have come from an artist's brush. But the river does not limit its artistic endeavours

53

to the meanders. The heroic gorges of the Rhine, the gigantic Iron Gate of the Danube and, on the Yangtze Kiang, those wild gorges, bordered with natural castles fashioned by the rain, erosion and floods—all these bear witness to the power of the river, master of Nature and also of men. For rivers also mould human geography. They give rise to great capitals, to commercial centres and strategic points. They play a political role, serving as the frontiers of the states which border them, and when their course changes, sometimes the state lines change too.

All rivers flow into the sea, but they do not necessarily die once they reach there. Often they undergo one last metamorphosis, which again attests to their power. Sometimes the sea advances to meet the river, but in a delta the river continues its work. It has gathered detritus all along its course and carried it to the coast, and now it will change the outline of the coast. The Po turned Ravenna and the ancient port of Adria, on the east coast of Italy, into inland cities. Its deposits are 6 ft higher than the level of the plain.

The Rhône, that 'furious bull descended from the Alps', has engaged in a victorious struggle with the sea. In prehistoric times, its delta began at Donzère, which is now about 75 miles from the sea. The enormous quantity of mud, stones and debris of all sorts has made the salt water recede. As we have seen happen with the Nile, islands are born, are destroyed again and deposits accumulate all along the banks. The Camargue is a creation of the Rhône, just as, on a much larger scale, Egypt is a creation of the Nile. The Mississippi delta begins 300 miles from the sea. It is a succession of marshes and impenetrable canals, or 'bayous'. From time to time rows of cyprus and poplar break the monotony of the landscape.

Every delta is a secret universe, with its dead ends, its swamps seething with fish, its diseases—malaria or cholera—and its silent people: the fishermen, and sometimes men who are living on the margins of society. Once there were political refugees living in the Danube delta. Convicts who escaped from the prisons of the Guianas tried to reach the islands of the Amazon delta, which they believed would be a paradise of freedom. What they found there instead was an inferno of mosquitoes, heat and suffocating humidity. For the estuary is as monstrous as the river itself, and the hostility of its climate seems to match the battle fought between the Atlantic and the giant river, whose yellow waters flow 200 miles out to sea before the ocean finally swallows them.

The Nile

Lord Kinross

'The bringer of food . . . creator of all good, lord of majesty' is no longer worshipped as a god, but it still controls the lives of the men who live along its banks

The River Nile, stretching across half of Africa, flows northwards from the tropical mountains and forests of the Equator to the temperate Mediterranean Sea. It is the world's longest river, reaching 4150 miles from the lakes that feed it and the streams that feed those lakes. Of Egypt, the land with which it is most closely associated and which the Nile makes fruitful for the last thousand miles of its course, the ancient Greek historian Herodotus wrote that it is an acquired country, 'the gift of the river'. So it is; but the river itself is, in a sense, the gift of man. 'Help yourself,' runs an Egyptian proverb, 'and the Nile will help you.' The Nile as we see it today is the product of peoples who have been helping themselves for the past 5000 years. It is a supreme gift, not only of the equatorial rains, but of man with his inherent adaptability, industry, inventiveness, courage, curiosity and sense of adventure.

During the millennia preceding the dynastic history of Egypt, which began around 3200 BC, the ending of the Ice Age gradually dried up the grasslands which bordered the Nile, transforming the pastures of herdsmen and hunters into waterless desert. Yet the river itself remained, sprawling through this desert, overflowing its banks into jungle swamps and waterlogged marshes where hippopotamuses and crocodiles flourished and vegetation ran rife and unproductive. A new challenge thus confronted the inhabitants of the valley and its neighbouring lands.

Some evaded the challenge, taking the line of least resistance. Their progeny survive among the Nilotic tribesmen of the Southern Sudan, primitive men still living in a natural environment. Here, in a tropical region perennially watered by rain, is a wilderness of swamps known as the Sudd, in which the river loses half its waters. Traversing a labyrinth of streams, inlets and lakes, its main channels have no fixed banks, but pass between floating masses of vegetable matter—'floes' of

*Desert sands drift to the very edge of the Nile near
Abu Simbel in southern Egypt. This photograph was taken
before the completion of the Aswan Dam in 1968 turned
this reach of the river into a reservoir and freed
most of Egypt from its dependence on the Nile floods.*

matted papyrus and reeds, forever shifting this way
and that to block the river's course. Where a foothold exists in these sprawling, steaming marshes,
naked African tribesmen, the Dinka and the Shilluk,
have perched. 'Gentle savages', long-legged like
waterfowl, long-speared to hunt game, they live in
primeval indolence, ruled by kings they believe have
magical powers and worshipping the same totems
and fetishes that the pre-dynastic Egyptians did.
Such still is life over much of the upper Nile valley.

Below the First Cataract near Aswan, where
Egypt properly begins, it is different. Here other
tribesmen made a more positive response to the
challenge. They faced up to the change in their
climate by changing their whole way of living.
Stirring themselves to action, they drained the
swamps and the marshes, canalised the river between
dikes and diverted some of its flow into ditches and
basins with low mud walls. Thus they reclaimed soil
on which they grew their food instead of gathering
it. Unlike their less spirited neighbours, they imposed themselves on their environment and thereby
transformed Egypt into a cultivated land rich in
cereals, vegetables, fodder, oil crops and, in later

times, sugar cane and cotton. Their descendants are the industrious *fellaheen*, toiling in their millions throughout the lower Nile valley today.

The land of Egypt was the gift not only of the Nile but of the sun, which was visible all day in a cloud-free, mist-free sky. The slow, undeviating cycle of the sun was Egypt's life-beat, setting the rhythm of every man's day. Thus the Egyptians worshipped, above all other deities, the sun-god.

The ancient Egyptians knew no other world but their long river valley, a secure 'oasis' walled in between the broad desert wastes which only occasional raiding Bedouin tribes would venture to cross. The world beyond it meant little to them, and the source of the Nile was unknown to them beyond the fact that it was located in an unfamiliar 'Land of Ghosts and Spirits' somewhere to the south. At first the river was believed to gush forth from the underworld through a mythical cavern above the First Cataract. But early in the 3rd millennium a military expedition into Nubia, beyond the First Cataract, showed that the river rose in remoter African lands hundreds of miles to the south.

It was not until the 19th century that the source of the Nile was finally discovered. The Blue Nile pours out of Lake Tana, in the Ethiopian highlands, and passes over a series of cataracts and rapids to join the main stream of the river, the White Nile, at Khartoum. From here these waters run distinct for a while, side by side in the same bed, more grey and green than white and blue; they finally merge and, fed by only one more stream, the Atbara, flow unbroken for 1600 miles to the Mediterranean.

Thus the blank space on the map of Africa was filled; no longer was there a 'Land of Ghosts' beyond the First Cataract. European man had met the ultimate challenge of the Nile, completing the work of Egyptian man in the earliest days of his history.

British administration led to the co-ordinated construction of dams and barrages throughout the length of the Nile, from the great lakes to points close to the river's two mouths at Rosetta and Damietta. This control of the waters was designed to replace the old system of basin irrigation by one of perennial irrigation. The conversion was accomplished in an area that covered five-sixths of the cultivated land of Egypt, permitting the growth of two or more crops each year instead of one, as before, and facilitating the production of cotton, which needs water at a season when the river is naturally low. The old Aswan Dam—completed by the British in 1902 and heightened twice since then —conserves water in the flood season and releases it as the flow abates, thus affording an even supply. Thanks to this, the lower Nile valley is today the most intensively cultivated agricultural area in the world. Thus if Egypt is still, as in the days of Herodotus, essentially an acquired country, 'the gift of the river', it is a country more than ever acquired by man, through his progressive subjugation of its waters. The Nile valley is in truth a gift to civilisation by the people of Egypt themselves.

The Mississippi – an Almost-Living Thing

Wolfgang Langewiesche

Chafing against its banks like a giant animal, the Mississippi winds 600 miles across the southern plains of the U.S.A. to the Gulf of Mexico

In the spring I spent two weeks flying over the Mississippi and watched it flow down its majestically winding course to the sea. From the ground, small parts of it can be seen, but not the river itself—it is simply too gigantic. But studying it from the air, I began to understand it.

I started at Cairo, Illinois. This is where the Mississippi takes in the Ohio, doubles in size, and begins its final march to the sea. Down to this point it has been just another river, though a big one. From this point on it is unique, the classic river of Mark Twain, the Cotton Delta, the showboats— Old Man River.

At Cairo it starts to wind, to meander. Sometimes it almost flows in circles—and for no apparent reason. No hills are in its way. The country is flat, an immense plain that slopes imperceptibly towards the Gulf of Mexico, 600 miles away.

River winding has become less of a mystery since the U.S. Army Corps of Engineers built a laboratory river, fed by city water, running 150 ft on an inclined, sand-covered floor. To begin with, they gave it a straight channel. Yet in due course it developed all the peculiarities of the Mississippi—meander loops, sand-bars, deeps and shallows. Using patches of coloured sand as tracers, the army engineers studied everything.

It seems that the fundamental cause of meandering is the power of flowing water to pick up and carry earth material. As a river flows through loose, fine-particled soil, it eats into the banks; a bank caves in somewhere; a sand-bar forms downstream of it. Then the water has to make a detour round the bar. As the current on the outside of the curve speeds up, it eats into the river bank on that side, undermining it. At the same time the water on the inside slows down, loses earth-carrying power and drops some of its sand load. So the sand-bar grows. In this way the river shifts its channel further and further outward.

Through the years, the original slight detour becomes an exaggerated loop; and where the river comes out of that loop and turns back towards the sea, the same things now happen in reverse: the river pushes its channel out to the opposite side. One loop causes another, which causes a third, and so on down the river. That is how a river starts its amazing dance.

But there is more. Not only does the river swing back and forth in curves; the curves themselves keep moving, squirming, snaking. The whole river country is a maze of former river courses, now abandoned, all curving and swinging and criss-crossing each other. Geologists have sorted them out and dated them quite accurately back to the time of Christ, fairly accurately for 4000 years before that.

Each meander loop, once formed, moves downstream slowly, so many miles per century. Occasionally one loop gets into tougher soil and its motion slows up. The loop next above catches up with it in a sort of rear-end collision: as the two touch, the current short-cuts, and a whole curving loop of river, now abandoned, becomes a lake. They are there by the dozen in the Mississippi Valley, beautiful crescents and loops of water, known as 'oxbow lakes'. They are one of the Deep South's many unsung treasures, especially beautiful from the air.

Another river motion is the formation of 'chutes'. When a meander loop has become too much of a detour, the river gets impatient and, during high water, starts flowing across the bend. A sort of gully forms, called a chute. Over the years, the chute becomes the main channel.

But now the current, no longer coming round the bend, flows into the next bend at the wrong angle. So now that bend must change its shape and, after it, all other bends the whole way down. This makes the river an almost-living thing. It squirms and writhes; it never gets comfortable in its channel.

That is why civilisation stays away from its banks. The river flows in solitude. Few roads go near it. Most towns are well away from it, except for those like Memphis, Vicksburg and Natchez, which are on bluffs. The levees—flood-control dikes—are set back at a respectful distance from the river, sometimes over 5 miles away. The country between is the flood plain: a wild country, mostly woods, old river branches, oxbow lakes—no people.

Floods on the lower Mississippi can be gigantic. The river drains more than one-third of the United States, from Virginia and New York to the Rocky Mountains; also one small section of Canada. The run-off from all that area flows down this one slot below Cairo.

On so big a river, floods are not caused directly by heavy rain—it is the small river that floods in response to rain. Big rivers flood when too many tributaries happen to have high water at the same time.

Normally, the timing of the Mississippi tributaries dovetails. The Ohio's high water passes Cairo between January and April, and high water from the upper Mississippi and Missouri rivers pours in between April and July.

The biggest flood in the lower Mississippi occurred in 1927. The Ohio was late and poured into a river that was already full. The Mississippi rose 20 ft above 'banks-full', and the levees gave way.

These levees form an almost unbroken earth dam, hundreds of miles long. Now the responsibility of army engineers, they average 30 ft high. The more effective they are, the more they have to grow. If a levee really holds, it keeps the water from spreading out sideways. That makes a flood higher. So the levees have to be built higher to contain it.

Naturally, I wanted to see a flood. The Mississippi was not performing, but one of its tributaries was in flood—the Red; and also *its* tributary, the Ouachita.

One thinks of a flood as a raging thing. I found it to be more of a soggy mess. Only along the main channel of the Red River was the current strong, the brown, muddy water angry and rippling. For the most part, I just saw water standing in the woods that covered the flood plain.

Here and there the muddy water of the Red had actually flowed up the side rivers for a mile or so and, backed up, these streams were now beginning to overflow. This backwater flooding puts a great burden on the flood controller. It is not enough to build a levee along the river; he must branch out and build more levees along the tributaries, and along *their* tributaries, until he gets into the hill country. If he leaves any low spot unprotected, the main river flood, backing up, will find it, break out there and come running down on him from behind.

Now I understood for the first time the great problem of flood control. The place where the damage is done is not the place where the damage can be prevented. To protect his house, a man might have to build a levee on someone else's property, perhaps in some other state. He might have to build a flood-control dam that would drown half a county. To do these things the local citizen (or his small flood-control district) lacks the knowledge, the money and the legal power.

When the Mississippi decides to change its course, the levees are no help. Levees, after all, are only earthen dams, designed to hold back slow, standing water, not the main angry current. So the army engineers decided to put the river into a strait-jacket. Here and there along the banks are fields where they have been casting concrete blocks by the millions. With these blocks they are, in effect, paving the river banks and the river floor.

This is called a revetment, and its object is to hold the river where it is and protect the levees. Revetments do not depend solely on brute force. By paving the banks so the current cannot cave them in, they starve the river of sand with which to build bars. In this way they interrupt the whole meandering process.

In recent years, army engineers have also shortened the river by 152 miles by making artificial cut-offs. The new river cuts across the lovely old meandering river, straight, cold and efficient—it makes a landscape something like a dollar sign. This, too, is flood control. On the upper part of a river you hold a flood back with dams. On the lower river, you shorten the route and shove the flood on—get rid of it.

Thus life on the Mississippi, as elsewhere, tends towards management and control. But sometimes the river gets out of control. For several years it poured more and more water into Old River in Louisiana, where it discovered a new route to the sea, 173 miles shorter than the present one. The new route was the Atchafalaya River. This distributary had always been there, but in its original state, choked off by a mass of dead logs, it did not amount to much. Then the steamboat came in the 1850's, and local people, with enormous labour, cleared out the logs. The flow speeded up. Now, more than 100 years later, we saw the result.

Each year at flood time, more Mississippi water poured down the Atchafalaya. Each time the channel was deepened so it drew more water. By 1970, if

nothing had been done about it, the new route would have become the main river. Then the present lower Mississippi would silt up fast; harbours and ship channels would be laid dry; New Orleans and Baton Rouge would wither.

But army engineers started to tackle the Atchafalaya with bulldozers, draglines and lots of concrete. They made canals with floodgates, spillways, locks for shipping. Now there are two passageways for flooding waters: the West Atchafalaya and the Morganza floodways. In time of flood the engineers can open floodgates and let a lot of water out of the Mississippi down the Atchafalaya ways. This is one of the safety valves for the lower river, assuring flood protection for New Orleans and Baton Rouge.

A stern-wheeled paddle-boat plies the Mississippi between Hannibal and St. Louis, Missouri. A mile and a half at its widest point, the river begins as a 12 ft stream that flows from its source, Lake Itasca, in Minnesota.

As I followed the Mississippi down I saw why this safety valve is so important. In the lowest section, below Baton Rouge, the levees are set hard against the river edge. With no flood plain to spread the water sideways, the river cannot handle the floods; and with plantations, towns and cities lining the shores, the situation would be impossible without the Atchafalaya safety valves.

All this comes to a dramatic point at New Orleans. Here the city is on one side of the levee, the river is right on the other side, and sometimes higher than the city. What is more, the river does not merely flow past the city but half-way around it, in a big curve. From above, this curve can be seen as a typical meander loop.

The river would love to make a chute right across the town. To make quite sure it does not, there is another floodway just above the city—the Bonnet Carré, which at flood time can bleed water out of the river sideways into Lake Pontchartrain, which connects with the Gulf of Mexico.

Below New Orleans the river flows another 100 miles, while on both sides the country fades away in a twilight zone between land and sea. In the end the river flows through the sea—incoming ships meet the muddy water 30 miles out. In the old days, it is said, a steward would get a pail of the water and serve it in glasses. The passengers would then drink a patriotic toast with it.

A steamship was coming in now, and I flew a few miles out over the Gulf to circle it. Its churning propeller was bringing clear seawater up from underneath, and you could see how the river still maintained its identity—now as a thin sheet of muddy fresh water, spread over the heavier salt water of the Gulf.

That is what I saw along the Mississippi, air-age style. For 600 miles I was looking the river straight in the face. I came to feel its presence like that of a person, like that of a gigantic, almost-living thing.

Twenty Times Higher than Niagara

Michael Scully

In the 'Lost World' setting of the Venezuela Highlands, Angel Falls plunge over 3000 ft into nearly impenetrable jungle

Jimmie Angel had no urge to carve his name on the map when he nosed his little Flamingo plane up that weirdly wonderful Venezuelan canyon in 1935. He was just a journeyman pilot, a First World War veteran, looking for a river full of gold in the fantastic chaos of stone and jungle called the Guyana Highlands.

In Panama a few years before, a secretive old prospector named Williamson had hired Angel to fly him to Venezuela and inland to Ciudad Bolívar on the Orinoco River. Williamson had pointed out a zigzag course over the Orinoco llanos, a vast grassy basin studded with iron hills that jerked the compass into impotent jitters. Further south they entered a crazy world of mesas, rearing thousands of feet from the jungle and split by plunging streams. They lurched to a stop in a grassy clearing and the old man went off to the river near by. An hour later he returned—bringing with him about 20 lb. of gold nuggets.

Jimmie Angel's skill got them safely home again, and he was paid 5000 dollars for that flight into fantasia. A short time later Williamson died.

Angel returned to Venezuela. First he flew from Ciudad Bolívar, scouting from mesa to mesa. But that took too much time and fuel, so he built a camp and cleared a landing strip near Auyán-Tepuí —Devil's Mountain—150 miles nearer his goal.

Auyán-Tepuí is a giant among mesas. Its flattish top covers 250 square miles and bears a peak nearly 10,000 ft high. Aeons of erosion have cut a crooked, V-shaped canyon into its northern face, and from this surges a stream that stirred Jimmie's curiosity. He had found a few nuggets and diamonds, but nothing like the rucksack-load that Williamson picked up in an hour. Perhaps he could never locate the golden stream again, but there must be others like it, and this canyon looked inviting. So he poked the Flamingo's nose between its blue-brown walls, and flew into an unexpected kind of immortality.

From high in the wall on his right, a stream spurted and plunged to the jungle below. From a higher hole beyond it another one dived. Then another; then four side by side. And more beyond, right and left. The pilot soon lost count, for this gallery of spectacular waterfalls went on for miles.

Then, as he rounded a promontory, Angel came upon an unbelievable sight—a vertical river plummeting from the clouds above him, its roar drowning the sound of his engine. He craned to see the white column vanish in a mass of foam where it crashed into the valley. He went down perilously close to the jungle floor and made a rough calculation of the fall's width. It was perhaps 500 ft. He climbed again, trying to estimate height by his altimeter. Somewhere between half a mile and a mile, he calculated. Even half a mile would make that sheer drop the great-grandfather of all waterfalls.

Angel made a layman's guess that there was nothing else like this in the world. He was right. When a National Geographic Society expedition measured the august marvel named Angel Falls in 1949, it found that the great cataract was 3212 ft high, 20 times the height of Niagara; almost three times as high as the Empire State Building. The first straight drop is 2648 ft; then the column bounds from a ledge and falls another 564 ft.

In a series of spectacular leaps, the world's tallest waterfall, Angel Falls, drops 3212 ft from the rim of a mesa to the floor of Venezuela's Gran Sabana (Great Plain) region. Its longest section, fully visible here, is a 2648 ft plunge down a sheer cliff.

For centuries men had skirted and probed the region—a place where geography is so mad that a river flows in two directions. In 1800, Baron von Humboldt followed the Orinoco, which empties into the Caribbean, to a point where the upper river splits and one branch, the Casiquiare, is shunted southwards via the Amazon into the Atlantic. A few years later, Robert Schomburgk climbed Mount Roraima, far to the east, and found a plateau jungle of plant life unlike, and older than, any other known to science. When Conan Doyle wrote of such discoveries in his novel *The Lost World*, he scarcely exaggerated the realities of this region.

Before the aeroplane came, Auyán-Tepuí, 300 miles from Humboldt's trail and half as far from Mount Roraima, was only a piece of mapmakers' guesswork. Moreover, it was shielded by superstition. Its name, Devil's Mountain, had real meaning for the few jungle Indians of the region. The awesome thunderstorms it brewed were adequate proof that the devil himself lived there, and Indians gave it a wide berth.

In Caracas, Gustavo Heny, a veteran mountaineer, and Felix Cardona, a Spanish explorer, were the first to become actively interested in Angel's story of his discovery. In 1937, in separate expeditions, they explored the canyon and saw that this was no orthodox waterfall: it was the end of an underground river roaring from an enormous tunnel 200 ft below the mesa top. How could that lost plateau, measuring only 15 by 22½ miles, produce the immense daily flow from the great falls and its satellites, of which there were nearly a hundred?

From the nearest point accessible on foot, Heny and Cardona, who had met at Angel's base camp, set out to climb the cliffside. Aided by Angel, who dropped food from his plane, they reached 4000 ft. But horizontal progress from there was impossible. Ages of erosion had cut away the soft surface rock, leaving an insane pattern of fissures, some hundreds of feet deep, between jagged ridges of Cambrian sandstone. These offered an explanation for the streams that burst from the cliffsides.

The mesa is a colossal natural condenser, squarely in the path of the almost ceaseless trade winds from the Caribbean. As these meet the warm air rising from the low forests, they produce a constant mist. Precipitation is estimated to range up to 300 in. a year, and this may be the wettest area on earth. The honeycomb of deep fissures serves as a gigantic reservoir, feeding the underground rivers that form the falls. In the far distance Heny and Cardona spotted a level stretch through their field-glasses. If they could land a plane on it, the major falls might be accessible. Angel scouted the spot and decided that a landing might just be possible.

It was agreed that Heny and Angel would make the attempt, while Cardona would man the camp radio to keep contact and, if necessary, summon help. But when Jimmie's wife, Marie, who was also in camp, discovered their plan she delivered an ultimatum: 'You are not going up there without me!'

The three landed safely, but the grass hid a soggy surface, and the wheels quickly bogged down. Angel found that a take-off was impossible. It was also impossible to reach the falls. They surveyed their chances, then called Cardona by radio, describing the route by which they would try to escape.

In answer to Cardona's radioed appeal, William Phelps, American businessman of Caracas, chartered a plane and started out the next day. The Venezuelan army sent another. But shifting cloud masses and their shadows made spotting three tiny human figures impossible.

Cardona and the rescue flyers had all but lost hope when, after two weeks, the two men and Marie Angel dragged one another into camp. They had rationed the food, and water was no problem, but their boots were shredded by the rocks, their clothes were torn away and their bodies were cut and bruised.

Like so many trail-blazers, Angel was unrewarded except for the satisfaction of giving his name to the world's highest waterfall and the fact that his find focused attention on a region that is now proving fabulous in raw wealth—diamonds, gold, iron ore.

Of the few people who have ever seen Angel Falls from its base, most were with the National Geographic expedition of 1949. A few other determined souls have made the one-week, round-trip journey by dug-out canoes, leaving from Canaima, site of a small tourist camp some 40 miles north-west of the falls. Hundreds of tourists on weekly excursion flights have seen the falls from the air.

Jimmie Angel's plane sits today on the mesa where it landed in 1937. A few years ago my wife and I flew just above it with Captain Charles Baughan, air veteran of both World Wars, who has put his wheels down on as many unlikely spots as Angel, except one. The little Flamingo marks that spot. It is Auyán-Tepuí's captive for ever.

Jimmie Angel died in 1956 as the result of an air crash in Panama. As he had requested, his ashes were scattered over the falls. Four years after his death, the Venezuelan government commemorated Jimmie and his magnificent discovery by proclaiming the still-mired Flamingo a national monument.

The Oldest Lake in the World

Pierre Pfeffer

Lake Baykal in Central Asia is the oldest lake
in the world, and the deepest.
In its amazingly pure waters flourish many
animals that are found nowhere else

The Siberian Taiga is the
biggest forest in the world. It covers over $4\frac{1}{2}$ million
square miles—an area about one-third bigger than
the United States. It stretches from the Ural mountains in the west to the coast of the Sea of Okhotsk,
north of Japan, and is studded with lakes.

Of all its lakes, the most famous is Baykal. Situated at the edge of the highlands of Central Asia, it
is surrounded by strikingly sculptured mountains
with bare summits, but with slopes covered with
green pastures painted in the spring with poppies,
irises and wild anemones. Lower down are vast
forests of cedar, larch and fir, strewn with stands
of birch, ash and aspen. Steep valleys, natural
amphitheatres covered with eternal snows, and
the slashed sides of numerous fjords are relics of
great glacial activity.

The entire region is a huge collecting basin from
which nearly 300 streams and rivers flow towards
Lake Baykal. Although not the largest lake in the
world, Baykal is the deepest, at 5314 ft. It is also the
largest freshwater reservoir in the world: 5520 cubic
miles, or a fifth of the earth's total reserves. Astonishingly clear and rich in oxygen, the water makes it
possible for plants to grow as far down as 220 ft, and
for animal life to flourish near the bottom of the lake.

The purity of the waters of Baykal was dramatically pointed out recently by Dr Grigory Galazy,
head of the Soviet Institute of Limnology. According to Dr Galazy, victims of drowning in the lake
vanish without trace. Their flesh is quickly consumed by crustacea, and their bones dissolve in
the almost mineral-free water.

But the most extraordinary fact about Lake Baykal is its antiquity. Even though geologists do not
agree on its age, the most conservative estimates
date its appearance back to the Miocene Period,
25 million years ago, making it by far the oldest lake
in the world. This antiquity makes Baykal zoologic-
ally interesting, for residual animals from Asiatic

and North American fresh waters—which were
still connected at the time of the lake's birth—
have been able to survive and evolve in almost
unaltered conditions.

The result of this long evolutionary process is that
out of nearly 600 species of algae and more than
1200 species of animals, three-quarters are endemic,
truly peculiar to Lake Baykal. Among these are
an entire family of sponges, and a unique mammal,
the Baykal seal *(Phoca sibirica)*.

The greedy Baykal crustacea are eager to gobble
up any fish eggs that appear, and the fish have had to
develop curious spawning habits. Some travel up the
rivers to breed; others lay eggs that are poisonous
or foul-smelling to predators.

The most extraordinary fish in the lake are the
Comephoridae. The size of a pencil, they have transparent bodies without scales and an extremely pure
fat that accounts for 26 per cent of their weight.
If one takes this little fish out of the water and leaves
it in the sun, it literally melts away.

The other endemic family of fish is that of the
Cottocomephoridae. These live on the stony bottom
and, with their short bodies and large triangular
heads, resemble bullheads. In May, when they
spawn near the shores and in the mouths of the
streams of the forest, all the bears in the neighbourhood gather on the lake shore to turn over the
stones and spear the fish with their long claws. The
noise the bears make is like that of a gang of ditch-
diggers. Not until they are satiated, late at night, do
they rest for a few hours.

The *Cottocomephoridae* are also the basic food of
the Baykal seal, which zoologists agree is closely
related to the species dwelling on the Arctic coast.
Many theories have been put forward as to how
these seals could have been isolated in the heart of
Asia. The most persuasive is that they reached Lake
Baykal at the time of the melting of the big glaciers
by swimming up the Lena River.

The Baykal seal came very close to being wiped
out by fur hunters, but conservation measures
have fortunately been taken by the Soviet Union,
and the seal population has been brought up to
30,000 individuals. Concern is now focused on
preserving the lake itself and all the unique and
remarkable species it harbours. A typical threat is a
huge new pulp mill which is reportedly discharging
its wastes into the lake and will alter or destroy
the life that has evolved in it over the ages. The
volume of Baykal is so great that a bucketful of
water—or pollutants—flowing into it will remain
there for about 400 years before flowing out again.

Sun and Ice

Over 260°F separate the highest temperature ever recorded on earth
(136·4°, in Mexico) from the lowest (−126·9°, in the Antarctic).
Between these extremes, living things are ingeniously
adapted for survival, and conditions
at extreme temperatures—in deserts, at the Poles and
in the Tropics—continue to fascinate both laymen and scientists

The Top of the World

Edwin Muller

As scientists probe the mysteries of the polar
north, the Arctic Circle is having the
world's most unexpected population explosion

The North Pole and the
Arctic used to be a remote end of the earth. Before
the Second World War only a handful of explorers
had been to the Pole. A few Eskimoes and other
natives lived in the Arctic, and there were a few
towns inhabited by pioneers; apart from these the
area was deserted.

Today, things are very different. The Arctic is
much busier and more heavily populated. The extraordinary city of Thule is only 950 miles from the
Pole, and there are permanent settlements further
north in both Canada and the Soviet Union.
Hundreds of people have flown over the North
Pole. Regular passenger flights follow the polar
route, and there are routine flights for observing
the weather and sea-ice conditions.

Many of us have misconceptions about the
Arctic. We call it an ocean, but it is actually about
one-sixth the size of the Atlantic. Over 50 years ago,
explorer Vilhjalmur Stefansson rightly called it a
'mediterranean sea'—a sea surrounded by land.

We think of the North Pole as the coldest place on
earth, but the lowest temperature registered there is
some 50 degrees warmer than the South Pole's low
of −126·9°F. In summer the temperature can rise
above freezing at the North Pole, but this never
happens at the South Pole.

To find real cold in the Northern Hemisphere you
have to go some 1500 miles south of the North Pole.
The coldest inhabited place, the northern 'cold
pole', is the Siberian town of Verkhoyansk, just
inside the Arctic Circle. It has recorded 93·7° below.
(Incidentally, it gets warm in the summer—temperatures at Verkhoyansk average 60°F.) The
lowest temperature recorded in North America was
−81·4° at Snag in the Yukon.

The Arctic is variously defined. To some it is the
region north of the Arctic Circle; to others, the
region north of the tree-line, or the 50° isotherm for
the warmest month. Most of us generally think of
the Arctic as a land of constant snow and ice. It is
true there is plenty of ice, but Eureka, in central
Ellesmere Island, has an annual precipitation of
only 1·74 in., comparable to the deserts of the world.

On the west coast of Greenland, near the Circle,
are many lovely meadows. There are no trees—
almost none anywhere in the Arctic—but in July and
August there is a wealth of shrubs and flowers.
These meadows are better to look at than to walk
on. Just under the surface is the permafrost, or permanently frozen ground. In summer, when the top
few inches thaw, the ground is like a saturated

A glacier flowing into Baffin Bay from Tanquary Fjord on Ellesmere Island, Canada. The speed at which glaciers in this area flow into the bay has been measured and found to be between 1¾ and 2½ miles per year— although one, the Great Qarajaq Glacier, travels at just over 4 miles per year. The lumps of ice floating on the sea are icebergs 'calved' by the glacier.

sponge—just the right conditions for mosquitoes to breed. However, while mosquitoes appear to be the most abundant insects in the Arctic because of their persistent annoyance to man, they are actually out-numbered by both midges and root maggots. Bumble-bees and butterflies are common, too, and the ice worm is not a myth but actually does live on the surface of glaciers.

The Arctic has been described as silent; on the contrary, however, it is apt to be noisy. The millions of ice-floes, from a few inches up to several hundred square miles in size, are in constant motion. Floe grinds against floe with a roar that can be heard for miles. When one floe is forced over the surface of another, there is an ear-splitting screech.

Nor is the Arctic lifeless. In fact, life in northern waters is abundant and, as elsewhere, is like a pyramid. At the base are phytoplankton. Feeding on them are millions of shrimps, and similar organisms, the animal plankton. Eating the shrimps, too, are large numbers of seals; and at the top of the pyramid is the polar bear, which lives chiefly on seals, and which spends most of its life on the floating ice.

This abundant life was little known up to 60 years ago. When Stefansson proposed an expedition far out on the sea ice, 'living off the country', no less a polar authority than Roald Amundsen said it was suicidal. Arctic whalers agreed. So did the Eskimos, not one of whom would accompany Stefansson.

With two companions, Stefansson started north from Alaska, carrying enough food for one month. In a 700-mile journey they spent three months on the ice, far from land. They lived chiefly on seals. The meat provided ample food and the blubber provided fuel. Drinking-water was no problem. Sea ice is salty when it first forms, but it loses its salt and in six months is fit to drink. In a year it cannot be distinguished from freshwater ice. Year-old ice was always available.

Thule, the United States Air Force's northern-most base at the north-west corner of Greenland, has a 14,000 ft ice runway and a complement of more than 6000 men. Established in 1951 on a site leased from Denmark, Thule is also an outpost for the powerful Ballistic Missile Early Warning System, built over two years at a cost of 500 million dollars. The original town of Thule was established by the Danish explorer Knud Rasmussen as a base for his expeditions. A few years ago the Greenlanders still living there elected to move to another site further north, so that they would be free to continue their own way of life, uninterrupted.

The climate is not as harsh as you might think. In summer there are many days when you can take off your shirt and sunbathe. In winter the average temperature is $-24°F$.

It is difficult at first to get used to more than four months of constant day and nearly four months of almost constant night when you are above the Arctic Circle. But even on a moonless night in winter it never gets pitch dark. There is always enough starlight reflected from the snow to distinguish objects up to a hundred yards away.

Other permanent settlements nearer the Pole than Thule are three of the five weather stations maintained jointly by the United States and Canada on the Canadian Arctic Islands. The furthest north is 'Alert' on Ellesmere Island, about 450 miles from the Pole. There are also several scientific research stations throughout the Arctic, such as the Arctic Research Laboratory of the United States Office of Naval Research, at Point Barrow in Alaska, which is open all the year round, and North America's Arctic Institute at Cape Sparbo on Devon Island, open for summer work.

About $1\frac{3}{4}$ million people live in the North American Arctic and sub-Arctic regions from Alaska to Greenland. On the Russian side there are about $29\frac{1}{2}$ million. In Canada some 38,000 inhabitants, including about 18,000 natives, live above 60° north. In the Soviet Union about 300,000 people live in the Arctic, but then the total area of the Russian Arctic is larger than that of the North American. Russian assets in the Arctic and sub-Arctic are coal, oil, meat, fur and minerals. In summer, steamers go up and down the three great rivers—the Ob, Lena and Yenisey—and regularly traverse the Northern Sea Route, re-supplying the northern settlements. In winter these rivers are highways for tractor-drawn trains. Railways also run beyond the Arctic Circle to Murmansk and Vorkuta.

People in the travel business are now quite accustomed to planning trips to the Arctic. Of all Arctic scenery, the coasts of Greenland are probably the most spectacular. Few people have seen the east coast, where constant ice makes shipping almost impossible; but in the summer, supply ships and Danish passenger ships ply up and down the west coast. Tourists in Greenland generally travel by aeroplane and helicopter.

The air is usually clear. From 100 miles away the great snow peaks of the west coast begin to rise from the sea. Close in, your ship is dwarfed by dark headlands towering a sheer 3000 ft. Now and then, through a gap in a cliff, you get a breathtaking glimpse of a vast, swelling hump of glittering white. The Greenland ice-cap is one of the wonders of the world. Except for a coastal fringe 10–100 miles wide, it covers the whole of Greenland (665,000 square miles) with an average thickness of 4800 ft. If the climate were to change enough to melt the ice-cap, all the oceans of the world would rise by about 24 ft, and many of the world's greatest seaports would be inundated.

The ice-cap is in a state of equilibrium now—the annual accumulation of snow is virtually balanced by melting, evaporation and iceberg production. Tongues of ice flow down the mountains to the sea. One of them, Jakobshavns Isbrae (a glacier), moves at more than 3 ft an hour and discharges millions of tons of ice into Disko Bay in the form of icebergs. Great chunks topple like falling skyscrapers; they make a deafening thunder and throw out mighty waves.

From a ship's deck in Disko Bay you can see hundreds of icebergs 'calved' by the glacier. They tower above you, the visible eighth as big as a cathedral, carved into fantastic shapes—spires and pinnacles and rounded domes. At their water-line the pounding waves have undercut them: you can peer into lovely blue-green caverns.

Full use of the Arctic as an airway will not come until there is unrestricted travel between North America and the Soviet Union. But Arctic commercial flying has not waited for that. Jet aircraft regularly fly over the North Pole, the shortest route between the Scandinavian countries and the Pacific coast of the United States. Emergency landing fields have been established along the route at Thule, Coral Harbour and Frobisher Bay.

Polar flying has shown that Arctic air travel is even safer than present commercial passenger flights across the Atlantic. Theoretically, flying is safest at the Poles (and at the Equator), where there are clear skies and an absence of fog, sleet and icing conditions; and if a trans-ocean plane has to come down, it is better off on floe ice than it would be in the open water of the Atlantic.

The under-ice voyages made to the North Pole a few years ago by the nuclear submarines *Nautilus* and *Skate* pioneered a possible route for future commercial shipping. This route, for example, cut the distance from London to Tokyo from 11,200 to 6500 miles.

So have a look at the top of the world in your atlas —you may be there before long.

The Wonder of Snow

John Stewart Collis

Fallen snow gives little hint of the fragile beauty of snowflakes, or the prodigal inventiveness that Nature bestows on them

It has snowed all night, and the evergreens are holding up thick fists of snow like white boxing gloves. On other trees long twigs, thin as wire, serve as the base for high walls of snow. The laying of the pure white bricks on the clear black boughs has been so gentle, and each brick in itself is so light, that a perfect balance is achieved.

We shall not encounter a more delicate miracle than the birth of snow. Snow, like rain, is born from water dust—molecules of vapour that flow freely and invisibly in their swarming millions through the air. When the temperature of the air cools, the motion of these vapour molecules is slowed down and, drawn together by the mutually attractive power that all molecules possess, they unite and become visible as fog or clouds.

They come together, and with the temperature below freezing, they form solids that we call crystals; and here is another marvel—snow crystals build themselves into definite and lovely forms. We are in at the very beginning of symmetry and geometry.

There is a further point to notice about the architecture of these crystals. They need a supporting substance as a foundation upon which to grow. They get this from the particles in the air—of which there are a vast amount. Not only is there earth dust and smoke, volcanic ash, salt spray and so on, but there is meteoric dust from outer space. We do not

By the time a snowflake reaches the ground, it has already begun to lose its crystalline perfection. Evaporation destroys its sharp edges and corners, and makes the crystal shrink until it becomes dense and granular. The most elaborate and perfect snowflakes are formed only in low, very moist clouds, in windless conditions.

normally notice all these particles, but we are able to see some of them distinctly when they are caught in a sunbeam. Upon this foundation tiny discs or needles of ice are built, and upon them the finished article, the snow crystal, is displayed. The variety of appearance is inexhaustible, but very often (though not always) a hexagonal shape is adhered to, so that each is a little star with six rays crossing at an angle of 60°.

If the crystal looks like a composition of ferns, it will have six out-pointing leaves; if like a windmill, it will have six sails; if like a starfish, it will have six ribs; if like a fir tree, it will have six plumed stems in perfect symmetry.

Only through the science and art of photo-micrography has the snow crystal been revealed in all its glory. We think of Wilson Bentley, who devoted his lifetime to the study of snow. Constructing a photomicrographic camera in 1885, when he was 20, he photographed snow in his lonely New England mountain retreat for 46 years; some 3000 of his pictures were published in the great work, *Snow Crystals*. He introduced mankind to the beauty of snow.

Bentley was unable to discover, out of his 5300 pictures of snow crystals, two identical shapes. In the boundless prodigality of her beauty, Nature rains down vast numbers of these fleeting flowers of aerial ice—each one different. Yet this is not surprising. It is a wonder of wonders that the dance of the molecules produces these geometrical designs in the first place; it would be too much to ask that exactly the same shape be duplicated.

When these billions of crystals alight, falling layer upon layer, they become banks of one white substance. Yet snow is not white in itself; it is frozen water, colourless ice. The whiteness is produced by the reflection and refraction of light from myriad minute surfaces of the crystals. However, whiteness is what we see, and that is the image of snow that we remember.

The crystals fall upon the earth so weightlessly, so delicately (though ultimately house roofs can be caved in under their massive multiplicity), that a great amount of air is present. For this reason men who have been buried deep in snow for as long as two days have not been suffocated. For the same reason snow is an aid to agriculture; it serves as an excellent insulator, conserving heat in the lower ground levels and saving seeds from freezing to death.

It is comforting to think of one particular office that Nature can perform with snow. Here is our city; here are our roads. Our civilisation is in full swing; the great principle of moving from one place to another at all costs, and as quickly as possible, is working well. The absolute necessity of combustion is law in the modern world.

Now see those falling flakes. The feeble filigrees, the fairy ferns descend. They stick and stay where they have fallen. Now an inch, now a foot, many feet at last. A hush, a pause, as the soundless feathers fall. The roads become empty and traffic comes to a halt. Civilisation has been stilled. Silence has fallen. These, the frailest of all earthly envelopes, and perhaps the most beautiful, have yet the power to bestow peace upon the world.

Land of Fantasy and Phantom

Thomas R. Henry

Mirages blossom in the pure air
of the Antarctic, and on 'white days' a man
there may have to protect the
underside of his chin from sunburn

Explorers of the Antarctic encounter phenomena far beyond ordinary experience. They are eerie and beautiful and terrible, and science still gropes to understand many of them.

Antarctica is a land of white darkness, where two men, dressed in white, can walk across the snow side by side and find themselves in a world of complete whiteness. The air is white; earth and sky are white; the wind in the face is white with clouds of snow. Suddenly one man becomes conscious that the other is no longer walking beside him. He has disappeared, as though the thin, white air has dissolved him. Yet he continues to talk as if nothing has happened, unaware that he has become a substanceless phantom. His voice is unchanged; it seems to come from the same direction and the same distance. A moment later he reappears—perhaps floating in the air a few feet ahead and at about eye-level. Still he talks as if he were walking beside the other man.

Intense cold, dry air and seemingly limitless expanses of snow and ice combine to make the Antarctic landscape almost as alien as the face of another planet. Mirages and other illusions are common as the low-slanting rays of the southern sun are bounced and twisted in apparent defiance of the normal laws of optics.

These disappearances occur only on 'white days', when the sky is overcast with white clouds—which causes, scientists believe, the physical phenomenon of 'multiple reflection'. At such a time the accumulation of imprisoned light between earth and sky—like the accumulation of heat in a greenhouse—causes vision to become drowned in light. This results in the complete antithesis of darkness: absolute whiteness, to which the human eye is little better adjusted than to darkness.

In 'white darkness' there are no shadows. The illumination is so diffuse that there is no perspective by which one can estimate the contours, size or distance of white objects. The feet cannot find the snow underfoot. One staggers and stumbles like a drunken man.

Accompanying the white light is an enormous amount of invisible ultra-violet light that makes sunburn a serious problem. It radiates from all directions, and on a white day the most likely part of the body to become sunburnt is the exposed bottom of the chin, or the palms of the hands if the weather is mild enough for gloves to be discarded.

Another apparent contradiction to the laws of physics was first experienced by Dr Paul Siple, chief scientist of one expedition. While engaged in surveying an ice-shelf 2 miles from his camp, he became aware that the tents had enormously enlarged. The camp loomed before his eyes like a city of pyramidal skyscrapers. Then a cloud drifted across the sun and there was a slight change in the wind direction.

In the twinkling of an eye the tents disappeared completely, and before him stretched an empty field of snow. Mystified, he dropped to his knees. The camp of brown skyscrapers immediately came back into view. When he rose to his feet it disappeared once again.

Much of the Antarctic's topsy-turviness can be explained by comparing it to a great hall of mirrors in the sky. The illusions are caused by the refraction of light as it passes through warm and cold layers of air. There are double and triple sunrises and sunsets.

Above the mountains in this view across McMurdo Sound in the Antarctic is the mirage of another mountain range, caused by layers of air at different temperatures acting as a huge lens and bending the light to produce the image of a distant scene. Mirages are common in desert and polar regions, where temperature ranges are extreme.

Ships sail upside-down in the clouds. In the middle of the ice-shelf one may see floating vessels, smoke pouring from their funnels, although no open water lies within a hundred miles. Wild mountain landscapes, grossly distorted, loom on the skyline. They look as though they could be reached easily in a few hours, but in reality they are beyond the horizon, weeks away.

A diary kept by Sir Ernest Shackleton describes the false sunrises and sunsets observed by his party just before the long Antarctic night:

'I had taken the sun for the last time and said we would not see it again for 90 days. Then after eight days it got up again. It had gone away and risen by refraction. On other days we watched the sun set, come up again, and set, over and over, until we got tired of it.'

The crew of a U.S. Coastguard ice-breaker pushing southwards through the ice-pack on New Year's Eve, 1946, saw on the southern horizon what appeared to be a green shore; close-mown lawns, bordered by hedges, sloped gently upwards into eider-down clouds. The effect was like a Chinese landscape painting, 50 miles long and 10 miles high, suspended over the horizon.

Another Antarctic phenomenon is the uncanny pull to the left. When a blizzard arose suddenly over the Antarctic one winter evening, the drivers of two tractored jeeps became lost while attempting to make their way from the petrol dump to the base camp—a distance of only 200 yds. The drivers floundered helplessly in the dense whiteness for some time, then suddenly found themselves back at the petrol dump from which they had started. Later examination of the tracks showed that they had made a complete circle, nearly a mile in radius; the tracks always turned to the left, although both men insisted they had meant to bear to the right, in the direction of the camp.

This instinctive turning left is common. The sun in summer moves 24 hours a day around the high horizon, always from right to left. Members of Admiral Byrd's expeditions reported instances of men deliberately trying to move with the wind, which was blowing from left to right. After a short while they found themselves turned left and facing the wind, unable to understand how they had got themselves into this position.

The exact opposite is true in north polar regions, where everything naturally turns right. The instinct appears to become more pronounced the further north or south one goes. In some complex way the consciousness of man, bird and seal is integrated with the whirling of the planet in space.

After crossing the Antarctic Circle, each man gains almost a pound without putting on any extra flesh. This is due to the greater pull of gravity in the south polar region.

Here men exhale rainbows in extremely cold weather. The moisture in the breath freezes instantly, forming clouds of millions of floating ice crystals. Sunlight shining through these crystals creates a succession of rainbow-coloured circles that appear to come from one's lungs.

Antarctica knows no rot, rust or mould. There are no bacteria to spoil meat, no spores to turn bread mouldy. In 1947 Admiral Cruzen visited the camp at Cape Evans that had been abandoned by Captain Scott more than 35 years before. From the camp's appearance, the occupants might have just left. Boards and rafters of the cabin looked as if they were fresh from the sawmill; there was no rot in the timbers, not a speck of rust on the nailheads. A hitching rope used for Manchurian ponies looked new and proved as strong as ever when it was used to hitch the helicopter. Biscuits and canned meat were still edible.

At the Little America camp that he had abandoned 14 years before, Admiral Byrd came upon a strange phenomenon. Among the stores was a crate of apples; they were frozen hard, but when thawed had about the same taste, texture and juiciness as apples baked in an oven. There is reason to believe that cold baking would be successful with most fruit and vegetables.

This land on the edge of time could have considerable potentialities as a health resort. It has the earth's driest, purest air. Ultra-violet radiations tend to destroy germs.

The experience of one expedition to Antarctica was a typical example of this phenomenon. Colds and influenza disappeared among the men until the aircrews arrived, bringing a supply of germs; a mild epidemic broke out that lasted for about a week. Following this there were no more colds until the expedition's ships had docked in New Zealand.

Perhaps the most terrifying of Antarctic phenomena was reported by British explorers on a nearly motionless glacier inland from the Ross Sea. Over this glacier towers a lofty mountain. At almost the moment that a shadow of the mountain falls on the ice on a sunny day there starts a succession of loud explosions, like mortar fire in battle. Sometimes the detonations last for half an hour, while networks of crevasses, some of them as much as 100 ft long, appear in the glacier.

The earth's richest pasture is the 2 million square miles of ocean, 2 miles deep, which rings the Antarctic continent. The plant growth in these icy seas is so abundant that millions of the largest extant animals, the biggest of which require more than a ton of food a day, find pasturage. There are countless billions of tons of microscopic plants and animals for the herds of whales and porpoises and the little crustacea that colour thousands of acres pinkish-red. A spoonful of Antarctic water under the microscope shows thousands of little plants, together with the minute animals that eat them—to be eaten in turn by shrimps and fishes, which themselves become the sustenance of seals, birds, whales and dolphins.

The broad base consists of diatoms, almost invisible plants which can move, like animals, of their own volition. Each has a shell of silica. Some of these diatoms live and multiply in cakes of ice. Their colonies sometimes cover acres, colouring the surface of the ice-pack yellowish-brown. They appear to be the hardiest form of life yet discovered on the earth.

It is unlikely that primitive man ever existed in the Antarctic. Remains of abundant life in its rocks indicate that at one time in the past—perhaps at several times—large parts of the continent enjoyed a temperate or even semi-tropical climate. But the storms and cold of a hundred million year-long winters have swathed in a shroud of ice what was once a country of green swamps and forests. Now there is only an endless glittering white desert with mountains that rise like tombstones in a cosmic graveyard.

This is the Antarctic continent. About the size of the United States and Australia combined, it is the world's coldest land. Although the temperature may rise above freezing on the sea's edge in the middle of the summer, it has been known to drop as low as −126·9°F in the interior during the long winter months. Antarctica is a land of wonder and adventure—a threshold to an infinity of mystery, beauty and danger.

Waterpocket Fold (left), a 150-mile long ridge of rock in south-east Utah, is named after the numerous stone basins, like the one shown here, which catch the rain.

A flash flood pours over the desert after a sudden hailstorm. Steam rises from the racing water, and after only a few hours the earth will be dry again.

Portrait of a Desert

Edward Abbey

The Utah desert in western America is beautiful but deceptive, a place of sudden changes and startling contrasts

The air is so dry here that I can hardly shave in the mornings. The water and lather dry upon my face as I reach for the razor: aridity. The inch of snow that falls during a stormy night in May has all disappeared an hour after sunrise, except in shaded places, and an hour after the snow melts the surface of the desert is again bone dry.

Stream beds flow only after rain in the canyon lands, and then only for a few minutes or at best a few hours. It seldom rains. The geography books credit this part of Utah with 9–10 in. of precipitation per year; but this is merely an average, with actual rainfall and snowfall varying widely from year to year. There are a few perennial springs hidden here and there in secret places deep in the canyons, waterholes known only to the deer, the coyotes and the mourning doves, to myself and a few friends. Water rises slowly from these springs, flowing in rills over bare rock, over and under sand, into miniature fens of wire grass, bulrushes, willow and tamarisk. It does not flow far before vanishing into the air and under the ground.

Along canyon walls are horizontal crevices between rock formations, cracks thinner than paper, where water seeps forth by almost imperceptible degrees to support hanging gardens of monkey flower, maidenhair fern and species of orchids. This water never reaches the canyon floor but is taken up by the thirsty plant life and transformed into living tissue. Even the rain in these parts, when it comes, does not always fall to the ground but can often be seen evaporating halfway down between cloud and earth—curtains of blue rain dangling out of reach, hope without fulfilment. The clouds disperse and melt into nothingness.

After long enough in the desert, man like other animals can learn to smell water. He learns, at least, the smell of things associated with water—the unique and heartening odour of the cottonwood tree, for example, which out here might well be called 'the tree of life'. In this wilderness of naked rock, burnt auburn or buff or red by ancient

The still waters of Harris Canyon (left), in south-east Utah reflect the desert's golden cottonwood trees and the sandstone cliffs towering above them.

Green plants clinging to the sides of Davis Gulch, in the Glen Canyon area of Arizona and Utah, are kept alive by water seeping through the gulch walls.

fires, there is no vision more pleasing to the eye and gratifying to the heart than the acid-green leaves (bright gold in autumn) of this venerable tree, signifying not only water but also shade, in a country where shade from the sun is almost as precious as water.

In some places you will find clear, flowing streams, as in the Salt Wash of the Arches, where the water looks beautifully drinkable but is too saline to swallow, or if swallowed too brackish to keep down. You might think, beginning to die of thirst, that any water, however salty, would be better than none at all; but this is not true. Small doses will not keep you going or keep you alive, and a deep drink will force your body to expend water in getting rid of the excess salt; the result is a net loss of bodily moisture and a hastening of dehydration. Dehydration first enervates, then prostrates, then kills.

North-east of Moab, Utah, in a region of gargoyles and hobgoblins, a landscape left over from the late Jurassic Period, is a peculiar little waterhole named Onion Spring. A few wild onions grow in the vicinity; but more striking, in season, is the golden princess plume, an indicator of selenium, a mild poison often found in association with uranium—a poison not so mild. Approaching the spring you notice a sulphureous stink in the air, though the water itself, neither warm nor cold, looks clear and potable enough. Unlike all other desert waterholes, however, this one shows no trace of animal life. Nothing comes to drink. In addition to the sulphur, and possibly selenium, the water of Onion Spring contains arsenic. The water is too clear. There is no life in it. When in doubt about drinking from an unknown spring, look for life. If the water is scummy with algae, crawling with worms, grubs, larvae and spiders, full of tadpoles and toads, be reassured, drink heartily; you will get nothing worse than dysentery. But if it appears innocent and pure, beware. Onion Spring, except for the smell, wears such a deceitful guise—out of a tangle of poison-tolerant grass and weeds, dripping into a basin of sand and mud, flowing from there over red sandstone in a rill so slight, so steady that only the glisten of sunlight reveals the motion, these potent solutions go to mix with the harmless water of Onion Creek.

The prospector Vernon Pick found a poison spring at the source of the Dirty Devil River, when searching for uranium in the San Rafael Swell. At the time he needed water—he *had* to have water—and in order to get a decent drink he made a colander out of his canteen, punching it full of nail holes, filling it with charcoal from his camp-fire, and straining the water into a basin. How well this purified the water he had no means of knowing, but he drank it anyway; and though it made him sick, he survived, and lives today to tell about it. He found uranium, too.

In July and August, here on the high desert, come the thunderstorms. The mornings begin clear and dazzlingly bright, the sky as blue as the Virgin's cloak, unflawed by a trace of cloud from the Book Cliffs in the north to the Blue Mountains 80 miles to the south, from the Sierra La Sal on the east to the notched reef of the San Rafael 100 miles to the west. By noon, though, the clouds are beginning to form over the mountains—coming, it seems, out of nowhere, out of nothing, a special creation. They merge and multiply, cumulo-nimbus piling up like whipped cream, like mashed potatoes, like seafoam, building upon one another into a second mountain range greater in magnitude than the terrestrial range below. The massive forms jostle and grate, ions collide, and the sound of thunder is heard on the sun-drenched land. More clouds emerge from empty sky, anvil-headed giants with glints of lightning in their depths. An armada forms, advances, floating on a plane of air that makes it appear, from below, as a fleet of ships must appear to the fish in the sea.

At my observation point on a sandstone monolith, the sun is blazing down as intensely as ever, the air crackling with dry heat. But the storm clouds are taking over the sky, and as they approach the battle breaks out. Lightning streaks among the clouds like gunfire; volleys of thunder shake the air. As long as the clouds exchange their bolts with one another no rain falls, but now they begin bombarding the ridges and buttes below. Forks of lightning, like illuminated nerves, link heaven and earth. The wind is rising and for anyone with sense enough to get out of the rain, now is the time to seek shelter. A lash of lightning flickers over Wilson Mesa, scorching the brush, splitting a pinyon pine. North-east, over the Yellow Cat area, rain is already sweeping down, falling not vertically but in a graceful curve, like a beaded curtain drawn lightly across the desert. Between the rain and the mountains, among the tumbled masses of vapour, floats a segment of a rainbow; but where I stand the storm is only beginning.

Above me the clouds roll in, unfurling smoking billows in malignant violet, dense as wool. Most of the sky is lidded over but the sun remains clear, halfway down the western sky, shining beneath the storm. Overhead the clouds thicken, then crack and split with a roar like that of cannon-balls tumbling down a marble staircase; their bellies open—too late to run now—and suddenly the rain comes down.

Comes down—not softly, not gently, with no quality of mercy, but like heavy water in buckets: raindrops like lead pellets smashing and splattering on the flat rock, knocking the berries off the juniper, plastering my shirt to my back, drumming on my hat like hailstones, running like a waterfall off the brim. The pinnacles and arches and balanced rocks and elephant-backed fins of sandstone, glazed with water, but still exposed to the sun, gleam like old grey silver in the holy—no, unholy—light that slants in under, not through, the black ceiling of the storm.

For five minutes the deluge continues under a barrage of lightning and thunder and then trails off quickly, diminishes to a shower, to nothing, while the clouds, moving off, rumble in the distance. A fresh golden light breaks through and now in the east, over the turrets and domes, appears the rainbow sign, a double rainbow with one foot in the canyon of the Colorado and the other far north in Salt Wash Valley. Behind the rainbow, framed within it, jags of lightning play across the stormy skies.

The afternoon sun falls lower; above the mountains and the ragged black clouds floats the new moon, a pale fragment of what is to come; in another hour, at sundown, Venus will appear, planet of love, to glow bright as chromium low in the western sky. The desert storm is over and through the pure, sweet, pellucid air the cliff swallows and nighthawks plunge and swerve, with cries of hunger and warning and—who knows—perhaps of exultation as well.

Stranger than the storm, though not so grand and symphonic, are the flash floods that burst with little warning out of the hills and canyons immediately after the storm has passed. I have stood, not a trickle of moisture to be seen, sunlight pouring down on me and the buzzing flies and busy ants, and watched a wall of thick, rich rust-red foam and water come tumbling round a bend upstream and surge towards me like—like what? What can the front of a flood be likened to? There is nothing else in Nature like it.

Think of the water as being as thick as gravy, dense with mud and sand, and lathered with reddish froth, bearing on its crest the trunks of dead junipers, tangled masses of shrubs and tumbleweeds, and roaring as it comes like a train, like a waterfall, like a horde of rioters bent on revolution. The flood comes with a forelip perhaps a foot high, making hissing, sucking noises like some kind of giant amoeba running amuck, nosing this way and that as if on the spoor of something good to eat. I got out of there, quickly.

An hour later the flood is past and gone, the flow dwindles to a trickle over bars of quicksand, and soon new swarms of insect life come in to take over the provinces of those that were swept away. Nothing has changed except the contours of the watercourse—and that not much—and the personnel of its inhabitants.

After the storm has passed and the flash floods have dumped their loads of silt into the Colorado River, leaving the stream beds as dry as they were a few hours before, water still remains in certain places—on rimrock, canyon bench and mesa top. These are the pools which fill, for a time, the natural tanks and cisterns and potholes carved by wind and weather out of the sandstone. Some of these holes in the rock may contain water for days or weeks after rain, depending upon their depth, exposure to the sun and consequent rate of evaporation. Often far from any spring or stream, these temporary pools attract doves, ravens and other birds for as long as they last, and provide the deer and the wandering coyotes with a short-lived water supply.

Such pools may be found in what seem like improbable places: at Toroweap in the Grand Canyon I found a deep tank of clear, cool water almost over my head, countersunk in the top of a sandstone bluff which overhung my camp site by 100 ft. A week after rain there was still enough water there to fill my needs; hard to reach, it was worth the effort. In the canyon lands of south-east Utah there are hundreds of the same; the doves and the eagles know where they are.

The rain pools, set in naked and monolithic rock, are usually devoid of plant life but not always of animal life. In addition to creatures of microscopic size, these pools may contain certain amphibians such as the spadefoot toad, which lives in a state of torpor under the dried-up sediment in the bottom of a pothole until rain comes, when he emerges from the mud, singing madly in his fashion, mates with the nearest female and fills the pool with a swarm of tadpoles, most of them doomed to an ephemeral existence. With luck a few may survive to become mature toads, and as the pool dries up they, like their parents, utilising their long-toed feet, dig themselves into the mud in the bottom of the hole, make themselves a burrow which they seal with mucus to preserve that moisture necessary to life, and wait down there, week after week, patiently, hopefully, indefinitely, for the next rain. If the next rain comes soon enough the cycle can be repeated; if not, this particular colony of spadefoot toads is reduced to dust, a burden on the wind.

There is no shortage of water in the desert, only exactly the right amount, a perfect ratio of water to rock, ensuring a decent, habitable spacing among plants and animals and its human inhabitants also. I have mentioned but not described the perennial springs, where the rushes and willows and tamarisk grow, where green, blue, scarlet and golden dragonflies hover and dart on transparent, fine-veined wings, where schools of minnows move through the clear shadows, where the deer and the bobcat, the kit fox and the ringtail cat, and the coyote, the jackrabbit and the wild bighorn sheep come at night.

Most of these precious springs are inaccessible to cattle, so for them we have the government wells drilled in the 1930's, the water pumped out of the ground by windmills of wood and steel. The windmill, with its skeletal tower and rattling vanes, is a classic symbol of the American desert, as typical as the pinto horse, the giant cactus, the lone juniper growing out of solid rock, the silver-blue sage, the purple distances that lead men on and on into wonder and heartbreak. No lack of water out here, except when you try to build a city where no city should be.

The engineers and developers complain of a water shortage in the South-west and propose schemes of inspiring proportions for diverting water by the damful from the Columbia River, the Snake River and others of the North-west, down into Utah, Colorado, Arizona. Why? 'In anticipation of future needs, in order to provide for the continued industrial and population growth of the South-west.'

The pattern is fixed and protest alone will not halt the iron glacier moving upon us. No matter. Time and the winds will sooner or later bury the Seven Cities of Cibola, the ruins of Phoenix and Albuquerque, under dunes of glowing sand over which blue-eyed Navaho Bedouin will herd their sheep and horses, following the river in winter, the mountains in summer, and sometimes striking off across the desert towards the red canyons of Utah, where great waterfalls on the Colorado plunge over silt-filled, ancient, mysterious dams.

Only the boldest among them, seeking visions, will stay for long in the strange country of the standing rock, far out where the spadefoot toads bellow madly in the moonlight on the edge of a rainpool, where the arsenic-selenium spring waits for the thirst-crazed traveller, where the thunderstorms blast the pinnacles and cliffs, where thick rust-red floods roll, where the community of quiet deer walk at evening up glens of sandstone through tamarisk and sage towards hidden springs of sweet, cool, still, clear, unfailing water.

Africa's Garden of Eden

Katharine Drake

Africa's Ngorongoro crater
is the nearest thing to Paradise
remaining in the world

The place: a primeval rain forest. The time: a March morning in 1892, when maps still had 'Unexplored' printed across great chunks of equatorial Africa. The action: a pioneering party is crashing through jungle undergrowth towards a mountain shoulder. In the lead is a white man in a sun helmet. Behind him toil porters, mostly naked except for bead aprons and ear-rings.

Suddenly, rounding a bush barricade, the white man halts dumbfounded. Yawning at his feet, its sheer sides nearly half a mile in depth, is a gigantic emerald-green amphitheatre. He raises his field-glasses and stares incredulously, for the scene is straight from Genesis. At the bottom, roaming over a grassy carpet, are unending herds of elephants, zebras, wildebeeste and antelopes, all pursuing a way of life belonging to the Garden of Eden.

What Dr Oskar Baumann, German scientist and explorer, stumbled upon that day is now acknowledged as one of the great marvels of the world—the Ngorongoro crater, a volcanic caldera in the Great Rift valley of northern Tanzania. The upper rim is 12 miles across; its flat floor (5800 ft above sea level) covers 102 square miles.

Ngorongoro has belonged for aeons to the beasts, although today it is also inhabited by the Masai, a tall warrior-herdsman tribe. Game-killing is forbidden, however, and animals still abound in such profusion that 10,000 visitors a year cheerfully submit to six hours' bumping along the rough dirt road from Arusha (Ngorongoro's nearest town) for the incomparable thrill of discovering zoo favourites in natural surroundings, living as they have always lived. Nowhere else can such a concentration of animals still be seen.

As we step from the overnight cabins on Ngorongoro's south rim, a bonfire dawn is spreading up behind Kilimanjaro, Africa's highest mountain. Its 19,340 ft summit is nearly 100 miles away, but the strange light seems to bring the blazing snowcap almost overhead. Our Land Rover is being checked like an airliner—brakes, winch, tow-rope, crankshaft, spare tyre, petrol, oil. The route into the

crater is a precipitous one-way track hacked from the 2000 ft walls. We carry no guns, but the game warden assures us that visitors, if they remain inside their vehicles, are safe from animals; petrol fumes camouflage the human presence.

Our half-hour descent begins. We slide round hairpin bends, squeeze beneath dangling tree roots, shudder over ruts of red glue. Halfway down, sunshine swamps the amphitheatre, and we see black ants turn into herds of wildebeeste and zebras, silvery hairlines into rivers. One look backwards up those towering walls, and we feel like a microbe at the bottom of a salad bowl.

Now begins a day of joy and wonder. We are unprepared for the flowers. The crater floor is one vast garden: acres of pink, blue and white lupins, of candle-white lilies; sheets of butter-coloured marguerites, flame-coloured gladioli, gold and purple thistles, white petunias; millions of blossoms scattered across a layer of knee-deep clover, a hyacinth-blue variety that grows nowhere else.

These zebras, seeking new grazing land, have wandered from the floor of Ngorongoro crater to the rim. In the daytime, because of their black and white stripes, zebras are unmistakable. But at dusk, when lions are on the prowl, the zebras are camouflaged by their stripes.

Crunching our metal monster over this lovely carpet seems a desecration.

Wherever we look now we see graceful, satin-flanked antelopes in all shapes and sizes, from huge dewlapped eland nearly 6 ft at the shoulder to pint-sized dik-diks no bigger than a hare. Soon personalities begin to show. The tail-wagging Tommy (Thomson's gazelle) is the out-giving type, endlessly exuberant. The massive waterbuck, shaggy grey-brown coat and classic head capped by elliptical horns, is a ladies' man, basking in the admiration of his devoted harem.

Suddenly, from behind, comes a snorting and woofing as up from the nearby swamp, fly-swatter tails bolt upright, trots a family of wart-hogs—father, mother, three young—all enamelled in mud.

The boar has tusks like twin scimitars (they can rip a hyena in two), warts as big as horns, and gargoyle features. One look at the messy apparitions and some nearby gazelles react as though to an electric shock: their ears quiver, their necks arch, and then away they bound, in 15 and 20 ft leaps, incomparably graceful.

Further along we come upon a herd of frolicsome zebras several hundred strong, their stripes dissolving, disappearing, intermingling, reappearing, providing magnificent camouflage. High overhead a flock of Egyptian geese flies by in a neat formation against the cobalt-blue sky. And now, as we circle some boulders, we slam on the brakes. Lions—right alongside.

Three fully grown males arise majestically—the nearest close enough to shake hands. We get a pit-of-the-stomach sensation as, nostrils twitching, the lions regard us thoughtfully with amber eyes. We can count flies on the muzzle of the closest one, spot a tick in a nostril, get a whiff of his breath, which is

77

*Every year 10,000 people come to visit Ngorongoro crater
in Tanzania, south-east of Lake Victoria. The crater
is a natural amphitheatre with 2000 ft walls, a paradise
where zebras, gazelles, lions, elephants and other
creatures roam free in a perfect environment.*

formidable. Behind are three lionesses and two plump cubs, wrestling in a whirl of paws, tails and round, mischievous faces. Romping excitedly, they almost collide with our front wheels. The largest lioness lets out a gravelly roar, and in a split second the cubs are back to safety. The males relax, stop staring at us and slide back into their familiar Trafalgar Square pose.

Soon we come on the cause of their lethargy—a zebra carcass, no head, no legs. A gingery jackal and two spotted hyenas are snatching flesh from the rump of the lion's kill. In this animal kingdom death strikes like a sledge-hammer, and now we watch Nature's disposal system in action. Marabou storks are pacing about, impatiently waiting for the hyenas to finish. Circling in the sky are the vultures, buzzards and kites, which feed next. What the birds leave, the small rodents will handle. Then armies of ants will get busy, leaving only the skeleton which, in turn, will be wafted away by huge bearded vultures, with a 10 ft wing span. By sunset, nothing but

a patch of trampled flowers will mark the spot where fate overtook a little striped horse in order to nourish a multitude.

Yet, as we joggle along, romance is more evident than tragedy, for it is spring. We watch a paradise widow bird embark on his fascinating courtship ritual, tangerine breast aglow, black tail hanging down like a fan. He is tamping a ring into a grass patch, doing it the hard way, bouncing up and down in 50 and 60 ft leaps. In the centre, ensconced on a tuffet, sits his beloved, ogling two other widow birds, goading her swain to stratospheric effort. Such a courtship is not something that can be cut short with a blunt yes or no.

We select a grove of trees as a place to eat lunch and, as we approach it, a herd of elephants slowly emerges, one at a time, extending across our bows like a frieze in a Hindu temple. At the front is a gigantic cow with ears like capes, tusks so powerful that they could scoop up our Land Rover and pitch-fork it wherever she wished. At the rear is another behemoth. Boxed in the middle are three baby elephants, small trunks latched to the tail of the animal ahead. The herd, 13 strong, must have known we were coming (an elephant's hearing is sharp), but the withdrawal is unhurried, almost ceremonious. As we watch these weird, proud, tragically persecuted titans making for the acacia forest, their departure seems somehow symbolic, for elephants are high up on the 'heading for extinction' list, mercilessly butchered for their tusks by poachers.

Over by the swamp, parading among reeds and water lilies, we see almost every known water-bird. Our glasses pick up sooty-black faces of sacred ibises, the gold topknots of slender crowned cranes. All around us are fish eagles, guinea fowl, duck, teal, quail, egrets, storks of all kinds, while thousands of shell-pink flamingoes rocket up from the water like an explosion of rose petals.

And now, across the indigo tree-shade, advances an apparition bizarre enough to be in a dream—a young Masai whose home, a dung-plastered hut, is here in the crater. His hair is coral-red; his earlobes, weighed down with hoop ear-rings, sag halfway to his shoulders. His only garment is a rusty knee-length cloth, knotted at the right shoulder.

We take him in bit by bit as he approaches, the bronze, arrow-slim body with its arrogant assurance, the fine-featured face, neither friendly nor unfriendly, the long, razor-sharp spear. To our Swahili greeting, 'Jambo', the Masai answers with a slow smile. But he declines offers of fruit and sandwiches (his diet is meat, fresh cattle-blood and milk), and after a moment makes a courteous departure. His receding figure is an unforgettable picture—bare feet, spear carried lightly as if lions held no terror.

We drive along haphazardly until suddenly above the clover appears a great spotted cat's head—a female cheetah, streamlined, her yellow-green eyes glued to the rump of an unsuspecting Thomson's gazelle. Right behind toddle three roly-poly youngsters, ludicrously mimicking mother's stealth and concentration. Blind luck enables us to watch a rare sight, a kindergarten class in the three S's—spotting, stalking and springing. For cheetahs, born without the killing instinct, must be carefully taught to survive. A moment later the big cat springs, a leap of quicksilver beauty. The gazelle drops as though clubbed. The youngsters scamper up, overjoyed at the prospect of eating.

A hundred yards ahead another thrill awaits us. We come across a rhino snoozing on a flower carpet; three armour-plated tons arise on short, stocky legs, every pound registering petulance at the interruption of his siesta. Fortunately his eyes, set midway down his cheeks, are too short-sighted to bring us into focus, and his entourage of tickbirds, gorging on his gaping sores, is too absorbed to sound the customary warning. Our hearts skip a beat, listening to that thunderous snorting, for the rhino is the rarest of the great beasts—only a few thousand remain.

The sun is nearing the crater's west rim when we come across a herd of wildebeeste, or gnu, several thousand strong. It is calving time, and more than a square mile of floor is churning with the blue-grey, short-maned, buffalo-sized creatures. Then, before our eyes, the unbelievable happens—the miracle of birth, Garden of Eden style, no suffering, no bleeding, no distress.

We have been watching a number of females group themselves, heads out, around a bulky matron who is holding her tail out as rigid as a rod. Now, to our astonishment, we see two tiny hoofs protruding just below it. Mother-to-be seems unaware of her predicament; presently she lies down for a roll in the flowers. Soon we are watching a small head being born and now, as the matron stands up, out slides a brown-black body almost vertically, two little forelegs groping for the ground. In no time a perfect little calf is lying on the flowers, and we watch the mother expertly remove the membrane, snip the cord, dispose of the afterbirth and turn her attention to jacking the baby up on to his wobbly legs. The calf flops down once or twice, but a few minutes later he is happily taking his first meal. The whole performance has taken little more than half an hour.

Suddenly the group breaks into a frantic dance of alarm. In a moment we see the trouble—a hyena. It is slinking past us, jaws slavering, eyes on the suckling calf. Unthinking, we bang loudly on the metal sides of our vehicle, stamp our feet, yell 'Shoo! Scat! Beat it!' To our dismay the din scares off not only the hyena but every other creature within earshot. We watch helplessly as the herd canters away, leaving the mother and calf trailing woefully behind. Will this late-afternoon drama end in another killing? No. Through binoculars we see mother and child safely reunited with the rest.

Our day ends with a Technicolor sunset. Back at the crater's rim, we look down at the toy trees where weird, sad elephants are hiding; at the swampy lake where flamingoes settle in a shell-pink mist; at the vast velvety carpet where little cheetahs attend nursery school and terrifying rhinos snooze like Ferdinand the Bull among the flowers.

The hush is as holy as a benediction. It is as if an all-compassionate, all-loving Presence were looking down, blessing the living creatures—the great, the small, the strong, the weak—and bidding them 'Be still, and know that I am God!'

PART TWO
THE MIRACLE OF LIVING THINGS

Microscopic Multitudes

The microscope has given us a window on the vast world that
stretches just beyond our unaided vision—a world inhabited
by countless millions of tiny creatures, plants and
strange beings that are half animal,
half vegetable. Sparking this teeming microcosm
is the greatest unknown of all: the secret of the living cell

When Life on Earth Began

Rutherford Platt

Under the sun's glare and the action of
wind and rain, the oceans of the
newly formed earth gradually became
reservoirs of life's vital chemicals

After centuries of bitter argument about how life on earth began, an awe-inspiring answer is emerging out of shrewd and patient detective work in laboratories all over the world—an answer that is even more startling than Darwin's theory that all human beings evolved from a common, ape-like ancestor. Scientists, probing to the very dawn of life, have traced mankind's beginnings to an astonishing and peculiar scum of the primordial seas.

Deep in a void of time, perhaps 3000 million years ago, the earth's infancy came to an end. The temperatures on the surface of our planet were now determined by sunlight. The raw crust, a metallic desert of lava, scoria and granite, was a battlefield of the elements, illuminated by the lurid glare of lava fountains, rumbling and shaken by earthquakes. Steam gushed out of vents all over the globe, great geysers spouted boiling water until the atmosphere was saturated and black clouds blotted out the sun.

Then came the rains. As the clouds condensed, they released downpours that continued for centuries, until wide, low areas of the crust were filled with fresh water. When at last the clouds parted, the sun shone on blue, new oceans. Yet the earth was a dead ball of rock and water. The elements vital for life were there—hydrogen, carbon, nitrogen and oxygen—but none was accessible.

There was no free oxygen in the air, for example: the atmosphere was a mixture of water vapour, ammonia and methane. The earth's fund of oxygen was tied up with hydrogen, or in iron ore, or in granite (which is half oxygen) and other rocks deep in the crust. The supply of nitrogen was in a similar state. Carbon was gripped in the clenched fist of heavy metals (as in iron carbide), and buried under massive layers of granite and lava. All the odds were against such a fantastic occurrence as the creation of life.

The lifeless earth was now bursting with dramatic events—volcanoes thrusting up their cones, ultra-violet radiations bombarding land and sea, great winds churning the waters. Melted and torn loose by these upheavals, the vital elements began colliding in the volcanic fluids and gases, dissolving and mixing in the seas. Rain washed chemicals out of the air; rivers carved valleys and canyons, dissolving the salts from the rocks. This chemical treasure flowed into the seas, which became the cradle of life.

The reservoirs of the earth's oceans were a unique *milieu* for chemical adventures. The sun's glare made land surfaces scorching hot by day, but the water at the surface of the sea was held at moderate temperatures by the circulation of cool water underneath. Here, in the mixing currents, chemicals that washed out of the atmosphere reacted with salts washed from the rocks.

If we had been there to witness the coming of life, we would have seen an ocean looking much as it does today—restless, blue under a clear sky, grey under an overcast sky, white-plumed in the wind. But the surf would have been crashing against rocks bare of barnacles and seaweed, the waves sliding on dark, empty beaches uncoloured by shells, crabs and dead fish.

We would be looking for hydrocarbons, for they are the first step in the chemical evolution of life. Molecules of hydrogen and carbon have weird powers. For one thing, they reflect a trait of living stuff in the way they can grow. Instead of being a finished speck of matter, a hydrocarbon can repeat and elaborate its patterns and thus grow bigger and bigger.

For a long time chemists thought that the hydrocarbons, like other 'organic' substances, could be made only by living cells. This posed a puzzling question. How could there be hydrocarbons without life, and how could life start without hydrocarbons? Today, laboratory experiments have demonstrated how the early hydrocarbons could have been formed when methane molecules in the air were bombarded by cosmic rays and electrical charges—lightning.

Even with the release of elements and the formation of certain chemical compounds basic to life, something else was needed—the stability of shape. Everything that lives must have a body.

We do not have to look far to find the beginnings of form among the hydrocarbons in the pre-life sea. When a clump of organic matter is suspended in water, its molecules tend to stick together, forming a jelly. Chemists call this a colloid, a form of matter half way between a fluid and a solid (colloids are familiar as gelatin, egg white and drops of oil). If the colloid is shaken up in watery fluid, instead of dissolving it breaks into tiny drops. Thus, hydrocarbons in the pre-life sea, agitated by currents and tossed in windy seas, formed sticky droplets.

Ultra-sensitive instruments have detected a curious fact about these gel droplets. They have a whisper of magnetism on their surfaces that induces molecules of water in which they float to cling to the droplet in tight parallel ranks. This gives the gel droplet a peculiar skin of water, through which dissolved materials can pass in and out. Thus the gel droplets can maintain themselves by refreshment from their surroundings and enjoy individual existence.

The myriad gel droplets in the sea were only mimics of protoplasm in living cells. No more alive than sea foam, they gathered in quiet clusters in the midst of massive turmoil. But each droplet body fenced off a tiny, isolated portion of the sea, where chemical reactions were able to gain some control and direction.

The curved, transparent skins of the gel droplets acted like microscopic burning glasses, focusing light rays heavily charged with ultra-violet. Today, ozone in the upper air shields delicate protoplasm in living cells from ultra-violet rays. In the Era of Creation there was no ozone and the ultra-violet light cooked the chemicals of life in the flotsam of the primeval ocean. When this energy flashed through the gel droplets, it fomented creativeness.

We cannot know how long it took for the first signs of life to appear. There was no demarcation of time. Through dim epochs, the gel droplets simmered in the tepid seas. Infinite combinations of atoms must have occurred in the organic jelly, only to vanish into oblivion. The best-made droplets survived, the weaker ones collapsed, in a kind of pre-living natural selection. Thus, on a silent, invisible and majestic scale the elements struggled towards life.

Now we reach a late period in the Era of Creation; the oceans of the earth have grown old. The scum that will bring life lies upon the water, giving it the tang of many mineral salts. In the last few million years, evolution in the gel droplets has been speeding up, under the influence of catalysts—substances that quicken chemical reactions. The first catalysts were probably particles of clay washed into the sea. These attracted molecules of other kinds of matter in large numbers, bringing them into tight contact so that more reactions took place and new compounds were formed.

Gradually some giant molecules or clusters of molecules, complex descendants of the simple gel droplets, emerged until eventually, after almost infinite time and infinite chemical combination, the incredible molecule we call protein was formed. We speak of this event as though it happened suddenly, when certain atoms collided and stuck together in a particular arrangement. The fact is that we simply discover protein in the void of time, and cannot know how it got there.

The chance of carbon, oxygen, nitrogen and hydrogen atoms, as well as phosphorus and a constellation of metallic elements, coming together in the right proportions, under the right conditions, can be likened to the chance that a pack of cards, thrown in the air, will fall to the table with all the suits in sequence—virtually impossible, even though the cards were tossed in the air every second without pause through history. But we have been observing molecules evolving towards greater complexity and colliding at electronic speed through endless time. On these terms, the remotest chance might one day turn up—even a protein molecule.

The new substance was something utterly different from rock, gas and liquids. Quite possibly, nothing like it had ever existed in our solar system before. A giant compared to ordinary molecules, composed of hundreds of atoms, it had a peculiar structure that gave it weird powers.

Electric charges of different magnitudes play within the towering scaffolding of a protein molecule. Acids and alkalis react on each other. Bonds are made and broken. The thing has tremendous chemical energy, and it can grow in every direction. It expands and contracts; elongates, shortens and flexes. It may become as straight as a stick, wind into a ball, or coil at one end like a figure 6. Protein and certain other molecules called nucleic acids, also evolving in the sea, are together the wand of life. In the course of time they will summon up protoplasm, enzymes, genes, insulin, haemoglobin; they will create muscles and organs and co-ordinate their work; they will command the beating of hearts, the breathing of lungs, the vibrations of nerves and, ultimately, the flow of thought. But first, out of the flotsam of the ancient sea, they had to make a living cell. For these molecules, in all their glory, are not yet life. The first need is to speed up activities in the flotsam with super-catalysts. The special catalysts of life are a kind of protein molecule called enzymes. When by the chance of evolution they occurred, they electrified the flotsam. Chemical unions that had taken millions of years were accelerated to enormously greater speeds. In a vast epoch, bridging millions of years, chemical trial-and-error fabricated the green pigment we call chlorophyll. The gels of the flotsam, equipped with chlorophyll and thus endowed with photosynthesis, could now make food within their own bodies out of light, air and water.

With this achievement, we have reached the mysterious threshold. Only one more step remains to be taken for lumps of jelly, floating in the primeval sea, to become the first life on earth.

To be called life, the gel droplets and the complex molecules in them must be able to carry their banners across the horizons of future time by passing along their natures to descendants. Otherwise, this near-life stuff is doomed to be forever making a fresh start. The vital step was when protein and nucleic acid (with accessory substances) mysteriously joined to form the first protoplasm. The long-chain nucleic-acid molecules, rich in nitrogen and phosphorus, appear to carry within them 'blueprints'; thus the protein–nucleic-acid systems were duplicators that could strike other molecules at the right time and angle to break them up and reassemble them into their own likeness. So the magic of heredity became possible; and, though the complex cells we know today were still far in the future, the threshold had been passed. Life had begun.

The Invisible Hordes in your Life

Rutherford Platt

In worlds too small to be seen by the naked eye, one-celled organisms lead lives as hazardous, cunning and ferocious as any we know

Recently, Professor David Pramer of Rutgers University in America, using a powerful microscope, witnessed a thrilling drama. He saw a tiny, one-celled fungus plant lasso and strangle a ferocious nema worm. Out of its single cell this speck of a plant had grown a gossamer thread 1/200th of a millimetre in diameter but as strong as steel. When the nema came charging in, the plant formed a loop at the end of its thread and gripped the monster round its middle. The loop inflated like a rubber tyre until it strangled the victim and the fungus then devoured the carcass at leisure.

Weird battles like this are constantly being fought under lawns and in fields. In this strange, invisible world, fantastic beings are duelling, minute throngs are warring for survival. These invisible hordes, the original forms of life, are giving up many of their secrets as modern microscopes penetrate deeper into their realms. The distinction between the plant and animal kingdoms disappears, and

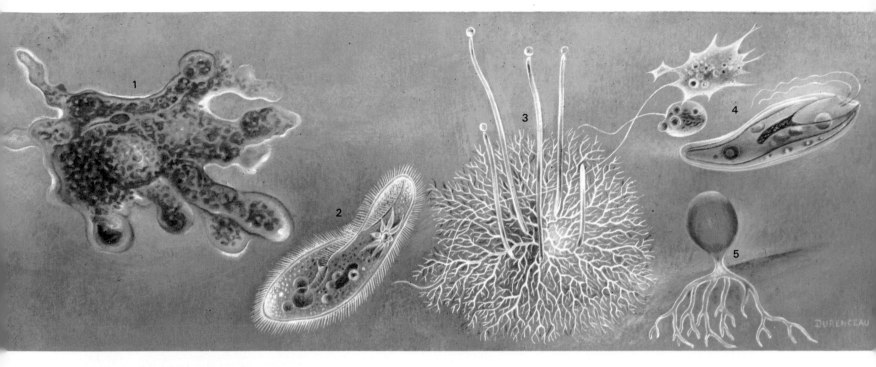

*In a drop of pond water or a grain of garden soil,
creatures like these live, reproduce and die. Their
world lacks clear distinctions between plant and
animal, and they form the basis of all higher life. The
amoeba (1) lives in ponds and damp places; to reproduce,
it splits in two. Paramecium (2) live in still water,
and move by means of their hair-like cilia. A fungus (3)
cannot make its own food, and lives on other organisms.
Flagellates (4) live in still water and move by
whipping their tails. Blue-green algae (5) may be
one-celled or many-celled, but lack a distinct nucleus.
Without such organisms as these, we could not exist.*

astonishing lines of evolution point all the way back
to the time when non-living elements combined
to create the first living cell.

Nature used one-celled organisms as pilot models,
so to speak, for big plants and animals. For several
millions of years these basic organisms tried out
different forms of living, moving and growing. They
responded to light in ways leading to eyes. They
'invented' eating, drinking and digestion. They perfected photosynthesis and a system of inheritance
with genes. They initiated sexual reproduction. All
the cells of the body reflect life processes developed by the invisible hordes. Their profound importance is not often honoured because, since Pasteur,
research has concentrated on germs—'gangster'
microbes that throw human life off-balance.
But the truth is that the invisible hordes are the
mainstream of life.

How do these hordes travel? To them the air is a
magnificent transportation system which has enabled
all their races to colonise the globe.

The fungi are the supreme aerialists. These
microscopic specks live in damp, dark places on the
ground, but break out by erecting mushrooms and
puffballs to launch their spores into the winds. Astronomical numbers of spores are always whirling in
the sky; they have been detected at a height of
35,000 ft. Algae torn from their clinging places ride
the winds, and clouds of bacteria are launched by
coughs and sneezes.

But the chief homeland of the invisible hordes is
the soil. An acre of typical farm soil (to a depth of
6 in.) has a ton of fungi, several tons of bacteria,
200 lb. of protozoa (one-celled animals), 100 lb. of
algae and 100 lb. of yeasts. Soil thus contains the
highest concentration of life-power on earth.

The frontier between this invisible world and the
visible one is a millimetre, or 1/25th of an inch. This
is about the smallest dimension that can be clearly
seen by the naked eye. The living beings beyond this
milestone are grouped in three categories according
to size. The largest are the big protists, which average only one-fifth of a millimetre. These protists are
mostly the 'giant' one-celled animals called protozoa—amoebas, parameciums, etc.

The second group, the little protists (average size
1/200th of a millimetre), includes primitive one-
celled algae and fungi. Algae are egg-shaped and
have green chlorophyll. Fungi are slender threads
with no green pigment.

Far smaller are the monerans of the third group,
only 1/1000th of a millimetre in size. These most

primitive of living forms include the bacteria and a mysterious form of life, the blue-green algae.

Single-celled evolution reached its limit with the big protists. Of these, the most developed and most arresting are the protozoa—such as the amoeba, an irregular blob with an elastic skin. From any part of its body it pokes out a bulge known as a false foot, that elongates and withdraws, giving this formless animal an uncanny method of creeping about.

Certain protozoa, the flagellates, or 'flag-wavers', use very long hairs, made of many fibres twisted together, which they whip about to propel themselves in pursuit of food or a mate.

Most spectacular of the protozoa is the giant paramecium, which revolves among the smaller forms by means of spiralling rows of hairs that the creature uses like oars. Batteries of poison arrows are embedded in its skin, enabling this masterpiece of one-celled evolution, with no sense organ, no muscles and no brain, to rout its enemies.

Another protozoan, didinium, is shaped like a fat jar with a snout puckered as though it were whistling. The snout is surrounded by two circles of vibrating hairs that create whirlpools to suck its victim within range. The didinium's mouth stretches enormously —and the prey is gradually devoured.

However, it was not the big protist animals that led the way in evolution towards beings of many cells. The individuals with the fanciest equipment in this top level of one-celled life represent a dead end of evolution, for such self-sufficient bodies could not fuse easily to form many-celled life, and did not have the urge to do so. It was the little protists—the algae—that unlocked the secret of sun power and with this energy carried life to higher spheres.

The secret was the green pigment, chlorophyll, the magic ingredient of photosynthesis that catches the energy of sunlight. In a split second this energy is imparted to a molecule in which carbon from air and hydrogen from water are combined. The resulting product is carbohydrate, or sugar. It is a nugget of energy that can be released later when digested, and is the chief food of all living things.

The green algae had inherited this power to make food chemically with the help of sunlight from the ancient pigmented organisms, which first did it differently, with sulphur and iron and without free oxygen. Oddly, it seems that the green algae almost gave us our red blood. The chemical formula of chlorophyll is the same as the red pigment of blood, except for a slight detail. If one atom of magnesium in a molecule of chlorophyll is replaced by one atom of iron, the substance turns into red blood.

By using chlorophyll the green algae multiplied enormously and created a great surplus of food energy, available to fungi and to the monerans below and the big protists above. The nations of the invisible were energised in a tidal wave of carbohydrates—and tremendous mergers of cells began that created big seaweeds, and then complex new species with skeletons, limbs and organs.

The oldest, tiniest and most primitive one-celled organisms are the monerans, which include the all-important bacteria. Their shadowy silhouettes have three shapes—sticks or rods (bacilli), corkscrew spirals (spirilla), and plain ovals and spheres (cocci).

Another type of moneran is the mysterious blue-green algae—many times tinier than the green algae, and ages older. They are even considered to be the ancestors of bacteria.

Some of these remarkable infinitesimal blobs do not obey the familiar laws of life. Quite independent of heat and cold, they can live on polar glaciers or in hot springs close to boiling point. With no apparent way of moving, they have a mysterious way of travelling: they cling together in chains, whose tips bend from side to side as the colony glides forward and back with a revolving motion. They are able to live without breathing oxygen—yet use oxygen when it is available.

The blue-green algae represent one of Nature's ancient 'experiments' at one of the turning points of evolution. For some of these cells are red, yellow, orange and purple. Here is a veritable laboratory test of the effects of different pigments for photosynthesis, as it was made by the first living cells, around 2500 million years ago. (Multicellular life began much later—about 600 million years ago.) Thus, biologist Dr Lawrence Dillon believes that at the base of the tree of life stand the blue-green algae, the oldest form of cell life known still to exist on earth.

In the light of these revelations about the domain of life beyond the millimetre marker, the line between the two classical kingdoms—the animal kingdom and the plant kingdom—has vanished. Some biologists today propose that the tree of life has a tall trunk that is all plant. This trunk rises from the blue-green algae at its base through the various green algae forms, culminating in the seaweeds at the top of the trunk.

Then two sub-kingdoms branch off. One is the sub-kingdom of many-celled plants, from which evolved the flowering plants. The other branch is the sub-kingdom of many-celled animals, with man at the top. This means that we share the same point of origin with the trees and flowers. The brown seaweeds are, in a sense, our ancestors, in the same way that trees are our cousins.

Today the invisible hordes still dominate the earth. From their viewpoint, we are a minority trespassing on their planet. It has been estimated that the total mass of microbial life on earth is approximately 20 times greater than the total mass of animal life. The products of its activities can be seen everywhere. Trees and flowers rise out of the nourishing brews that microbes mix in the soil. Myriads of invisible beings colouring its waters gave the Red Sea its name. The phosphorescence of ocean water is made by the jostling and tumbling of unseen hosts in the waves.

The invisible hordes are the water-wheel of life. By digesting raw elements, they lift them to a higher level of energy, so that they can be used as vitamins and enzymes by higher forms of life. By eating dead plants and animals, they cause 'decay', which releases locked-up elements. Thus they keep the three great cycles of life flowing—the carbon cycle for food energy, the nitrogen cycle for protein, and the cycle of minerals that spark off life. They live with us—and in us. Our whole world of visible plants and animals evolved from them and still depends on them. While our sub-microscopic ancestors could go on without us, *we* could not exist without them.

The Wondrous Inner Space of Living Cells

Rutherford Platt

Life's most basic form, the living cell,
is a complex community where needs are met
and responses made—just as they are in
the creature the cell helps to make

They saw cells walking—and it was a fascinating performance. Cells separated from their fellows floated around inert and helpless, until one happened to touch the container. Then suddenly it began to climb the wall.

The time was about 35 years ago, and what the scientists were watching were early experiments with tissue culture, a technique to keep cells alive outside the body by floating them in a nourishing fluid. From these experiments—and a host of more recent ones—came solid confirmation of what the scientific world had long suspected: that the billions of cells that make up a living body are far from being the simple, amorphous blobs of jelly they appear; they are vastly complex entities, each with a specific mission in life that it strives mightily to carry out.

A cell taken from the fresh young skin of an embryo, for example, bulges when it touches, say, glass. The bulge elongates—like an arm reaching out in the direction it wants to go. The tip of the arm flattens and glues itself to the glass. Then the arm shortens, like a contracting rubber band, and pulls the rest of the cell up to the spot. The operation is repeated as another bulge reaches out to another spot on the glass. Thus the cell creeps steadily onward, just as, in a body, it travels up to the surface of the skin from the inner layer where it is formed. It seems—even in a test tube—to be trying to reach its allotted location in the body.

Such experiments heightened curiosity about the living cell. Obviously no mere droplet of formless jelly could perform such deliberate movements. As ever more powerful microscopes plumbed the depths of the cell, vague shadows and specks were seen; slowly these were brought into focus, their geography was mapped and the cell's amazing structure came into view.

One of the most astounding discoveries is about the outer surface of cells. This used to be thought of as a 'semi-permeable' membrane through which foods and minerals dissolved in water could slowly seep, while harmful materials were held back. Now it is clear that a cell's surface is no mere film; it is the face of the cell. It acts as though it has chemical senses of taste and smell and can swallow what it chooses, when it chooses.

According to one theory, the cell surface has four layers, two of lipids (fat) sandwiched between two of protein. The two lipoid layers act like a rubber lining. Complex proteins on the outer and inner layers work together to see that the proper supplies get pulled through the lipids.

Using powerful electron microscopes, scientists have recently discovered that part of the outer protein skin will form a finger that reaches out and closes round a droplet of water or a nugget of needed chemicals. A dimple forms and elongates inwards as chemicals seized from the surroundings are forced through the fat layers inside a bubble. In this way a cell gulps nutrients.

Another fascinating discovery about cell membranes is that their outer surfaces are teeming with enzymes. (An enzyme is a catalyst, an agent that can cause a chemical change by its presence.) Some of these enzymes are probably created by the cell they stand on, but the majority are fresh arrivals from *other* cells.

These travelling enzymes are the voices of other cells calling across intercellular space, swapping information so that the millions of cells gathered to create body parts can act in concord in dividing and multiplying, taking their places and assuming special shapes. Many calls come from close neighbours, concerning local business in a lung, muscle or eyelid. Their effect can be seen when cells from heart tissue are separated in a tissue culture. The heart cells appear listless at first. But after a few minutes some begin to throb slightly. Then they start to move towards one another. After several hours, clusters are formed—and the cells in each cluster are pulsing in unison. The local messages carried by enzymes have apparently reminded the cells, in complex chemical ways not fully understood, of their original unity and of their basic assignment in life—to create a heart.

Long-distance calls are also handled by travelling enzymes. Among such 'pony express' enzymes are the hormones, which ride the bloodstream to and from distant points, with orders to step up or slow down growth, digestion or some other vital activity.

'Protoplasm' has been science's umbrella word for the jelly-like substance inside cells. About ten years ago it was considered to be just a kind of blob in which molecules swirled and collided at random. Then came the first hint that this was not so: a bit of netting was discovered near the nucleus of a cell. It was named endoplasmic reticulum, or 'netting in the protoplasm'. So dim and evanescent was it, even under the electron microscope, that its reality was questioned.

But then, five years ago, Dr George Palade, at the Rockefeller Institute, New York, reported that the inside of a cell contains a vast labyrinth of incredibly fine tubes and chains of minute bags. His discovery was a milestone. It showed that protoplasm has one of the most complicated and beautiful structures in the universe. So elaborate are cells that one can say that Nature had already done most of her job by the time she evolved them. After that it was merely a matter of putting cells together to build fishes, birds, horses, elephants—even human beings.

With the discovery of the nature of endoplasmic reticulum (ER), the 'mixing bowl' concept of protoplasm was overthrown. Molecules do not collide haphazardly in a cell; the elements of life are propelled unerringly, in disciplined, co-ordinated patterns, through the whole complicated ER labyrinth, whose tiny tubes and bags lead in all directions and connect every part.

The ER is not only a delivery system that carries supplies to every part of the cell. It is also a digestive tract. When the cell's membrane seizes food, it is pushed into the ER channels and brought to centres where proteins, carbohydrates and minerals are processed, stored or put to use. As it carries on the business of the cell, it is constantly expanding and contracting, tearing apart and reconstructing itself.

The ER system is continuous with the outside world. Its tubes lead directly to the cell's membrane —and out. The spaces between the ER channels are the true interior of the cell. Together they compose a large attic, used chiefly for storage, but with a hundred other uses.

This attic is a tortuous shape as it interlaces the ER labyrinth. Much of its space is occupied by vacuoles—reservoirs containing water, oil or liquid food. Also sprinkled throughout the interior area are many dark threads and grains called mitochondria, 'thread grains'. These grains have been prised open and found to contain high-powered generators that turn out a dynamic chemical fuel called adenosine triphosphate, or ATP, which powers all the cell's activities: the contraction of muscle cells, the constant building and rebuilding that keep the vibrant cell intact.

The vast, rambling attic of the cell is also the headquarters of the enzymes that facilitate much of the building work. Some of those in the cell are for home use, constantly peeling off from the lumps in which they are stacked and coursing off to special assignments in the cell's interior. They bear instructions for the personal activities in their cell.

One theory is that other enzymes are for export; they pass through the ER tubes—right out of the cell. These will be 'travelling enzymes', the voices of the cell talking to other cells.

What gives the enzymes their instructions? Enzymes, it seems, are at the business end of a long chain of command that leads back to a mysterious code of life in each cell's nucleus.

About 15 years ago, scientists blasted their way into the nucleus of the cell and pulled out a thrilling trophy called deoxyribonucleic acid. The nucleus of every cell was found to hold a rolled-up coil of

Model of a Generalised Cell

Mouse or man, earthworm or elm tree, each living thing is an intricate but orderly assembly of tiny cells. To meet the myriad demands of life, Nature has evolved an almost endless variety of specialised cells, but nearly all contain the basic equipment shown here.

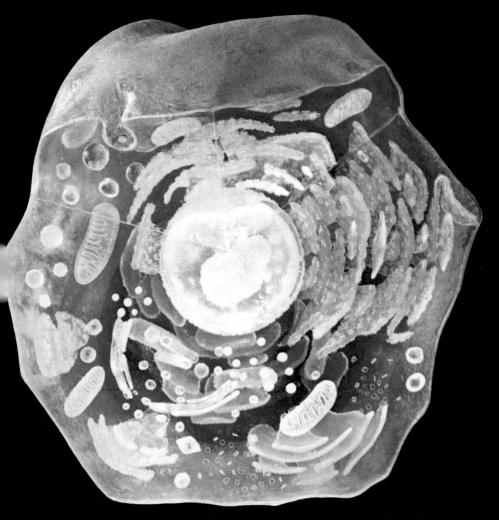

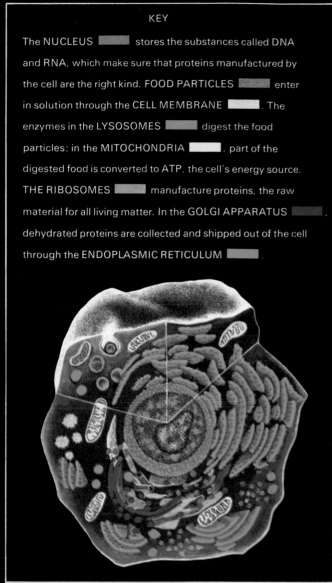

DNAs, the exquisite tape-like molecules that carry the code of life on them in the same way that a magnetic tape carries music.

DNA is the dictator of the cell. It regulates all the other chemicals in it, and all forms of life on earth, from bacteria to elephants, have DNA in their cells, directing all their activities.

DNA rules through a marvellous system of 'messengers' that create and guide the entire structure of the cell. Called ribonucleic acid, these messengers look and act very like DNA, except that they have an exit permit to leave the nucleus. First the master DNA and the messenger RNA intertwine—coiling their tapes tightly together. With electronic speed, DNA imprints a section of its code

on the RNA. Then the RNA rushes out into the far reaches of the cell, where its code is transferred to enzymes, one by one. To each enzyme the code spells out instructions for doing a particular job: to go to work building something in the cell, or to travel to other cells. It is through the RNAs that DNAs in all the cells talk to one another. Somehow they agree to co-operate so that a great mass of a billion cells looks and acts like a dog, a horse, an elephant or a human being.

These discoveries hold great promise. When future generations look back to our space age, they may well regard the exploration of inner space—the depths of the living cell—as far more important to humanity than the achievements of the astronauts.

PATTERNS IN NATURE

In all her realms, Nature makes use of certain basic forms. The circle, the spiral, the spinal or bilateral and the polygonal are repeated at will in plants, animals, minerals, liquids and gases. Of these forms, the circle is perhaps the most basic; planets circle around their sun, and things as diverse as flower heads and volcanoes are based on the circle. Spinal symmetry, in which a main stem bears symmetrical off-shoots, occurs in tree branches, leaf veins, feathers and river systems. Spirals can be found in water currents, clouds, galaxies and animal horns. Polygonal symmetry characterises crystals and beehive cells, and is also found in the scales of some animals.

These, then, are Nature's basic forms. But as curious as the way that they recur in apparently quite unrelated organisms and inanimate things, is the dominant place they occupy in the human mind. Long before microscopes were invented, Gothic architects built rose windows into their cathedrals, whose symmetry uncannily resembles the skeletons of microscopic creatures called radiolarians.

Even more strange is the way that certain numbers recur both in Nature and in art. These numbers, which form a sequence known as the Fibonacci Series, have many curious properties. Each number in the sequence is the sum of the two numbers preceding it: 0, 1, 1, 2, 3, 5, 8, 13, 21, etc. The relationship between any two adjacent numbers (after 3) can be expressed as a ratio of roughly 1:1·6 —the higher number in any pair of numbers will always be 1·6 times greater than the lower number. This ratio is the same as that which exists between the sides of the famous Golden Rectangle—a rule for ideal proportions which guided the ancient Greeks, and countless artists after them, in the design of their buildings. But as well as being the key to this ancient rule of design, the Fibonacci numbers also occur in Nature. The heads of sunflowers and daisies, for example, are composed of clockwise and anti-clockwise spirals of florets, and the numbers of these are always adjacent numbers in the Fibonacci Series. The same thing occurs in the spiralling scales of pineapples and pine cones. Moreover, each variety of pine cone has its own characteristic pair of numbers in the sequence.

Thus it is that flowers, fruit and men obey the same rules of design, and it may be that the creative impulse in mankind proceeds according to the very same laws that direct the bountiful creativeness of Nature herself.

꩜ Spiral Forms

Spiral forms, which are among the most vital and dynamic in Nature, are often characteristic of moving things: clouds, galaxies and water currents. The basic spiral movement may be thought of as a combination of two impulses: the circular impulse of radial symmetry, and the flowing or directional impulse of bilateral symmetry. Static examples of the spiral are also common, in flower heads and pine cones, for example. Sea shells are frequently spiral too—almost as if they were shaped by the same impulses that govern the waters they are found in.

A spiral current of muddy river water has shaped this bay in the Bismark Archipelago, New Guinea.

Nature had already perfected the spiral when these ammonites were fossilised about 150 million years ago.

This White Sheep ram, photographed in Alaska, has distinctive, spirally curved horns.

At rest, the common chameleon, from West Africa, coils its long, prehensile tail into a neat spiral.

The greatest of all collections of matter—the galaxies— often form spirals: above is the 'Whirlpool' Nebula.

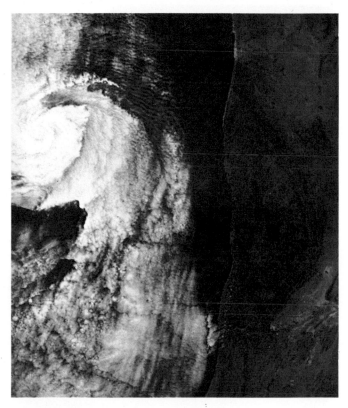

Spiralling storm clouds off the coast of Morocco, photographed from a Gemini spacecraft.

This fan-worm, Spirographis spallanzani, *lives in the Mediterranean, off the coast of northern Spain.*

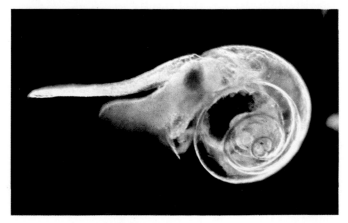

The transparent spiral shell of the swimming sea-snail, Spiratella retroversa, *reveals its internal organs.*

✳ Radial Symmetry

The basis of radial symmetry is the circle, an ancient symbol of perfection. Planets follow an almost circular orbit around their sun, and many flowers and sea creatures grow radially—in all directions from a central point. In three dimensions, the circle becomes a globe: the shape of the world itself, and the form which water, life's basic element, takes in a free state as water-drops.

Spore-disseminating gills radiate from the stem of Marismius rotula, *a small mushroom with an average height of 1 in. and a cap ⅜ in. in diameter.*

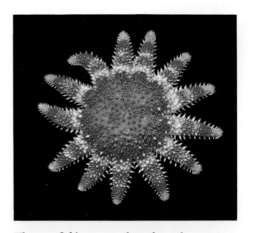

This starfish's arms radiate from the mouth in the middle of its stomach.

Tentacles fringe the mouth of the dahlia anemone, giving it a flower-like appearance.

Feelers are bilaterally disposed on the arms of this burrowing starfish.

🌿 Bilateral Symmetry

Bilateral symmetry is the most familiar kind. The forms of most living things—plants, animals and human beings—are symmetrical on either side of a line following the direction of their growth. In this lies the clue to the real nature of bilateral symmetry: unlike the symmetry of radial organisms, which grow in all directions from a central point, bilateral symmetry is the form taken by things whose growth is principally in one direction only. It also occurs in rivers and their tributaries which, seen from the air or on a map, resemble the veins of a leaf or the shaft and barbs of a feather. However, the symmetry of river systems is never perfect: only living things begin to approach that state.

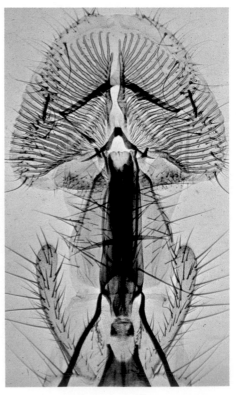

A blowfly's proboscis, greatly magnified; the mouth parts are modified for sucking.

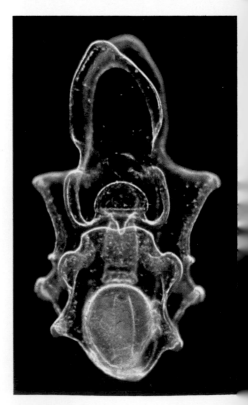

A starfish larva, magnified 20 times. The adult form is radially symmetrical.

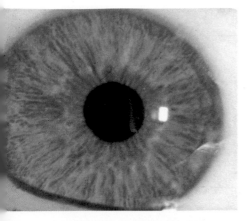

Streaks of coloured pigment in the iris radiate from the pupil of the human eye.

Flowers of the clematis 'Mrs Cholmondeley' have no true petals, but 4–8 elongated sepals.

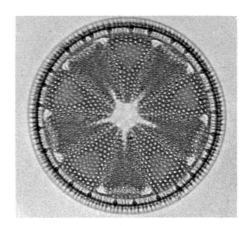

A photo-micrograph of a fossilised diatom, a unicellular alga found on the sea-bed.

The seeds of the dandelion form a globe, radiating white plumes in all directions.

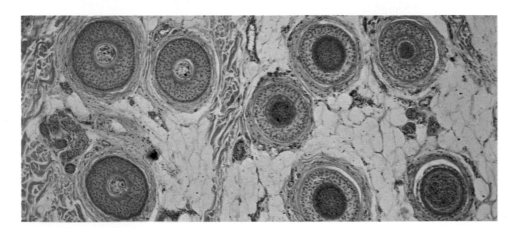

A photo-micrograph of a section of human skin, showing the concentric structure of the hair follicles just below the surface.

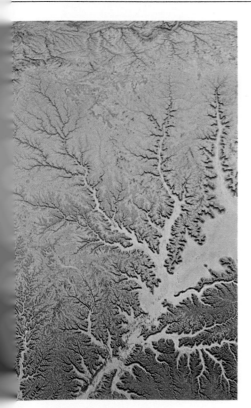

Wadi Hadramawt watercourse, in Saudi Arabia, resembles the veins in a leaf.

The plume-like sea pen, Pterolides griseum, anchors itself by the base in sand or mud.

Frost on a window-pane forms patterns as symmetrical as the ferns they resemble.

93

⬡ Polygonal Forms

Many-sided geometrical figures are not as rare in Nature as might be supposed; they occur mainly among inanimates, like crystals, and among the lower orders of life—plants, insects and reptiles. The character of polygonal symmetry is to be static, and when it does occur in animals, it tends to be mainly in scale formations. Scaled animals often rely on their immobility and armouring for defence, and they often have to moult their skins, which do not grow and expand with the animal.

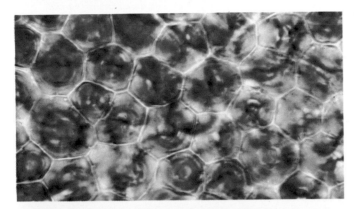

The petal of a common primrose, magnified 180 times, reveals the polygonal shape of its cells.

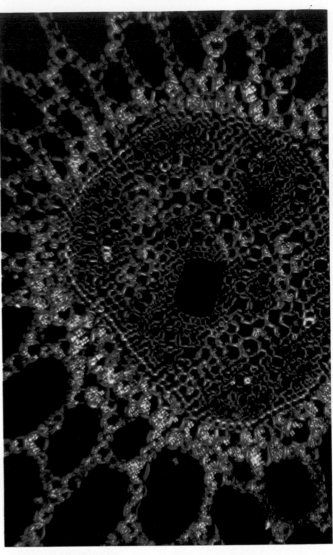

A cross-section of the stem of the floating pondweed. The air-spaces inside the stem help to make it buoyant.

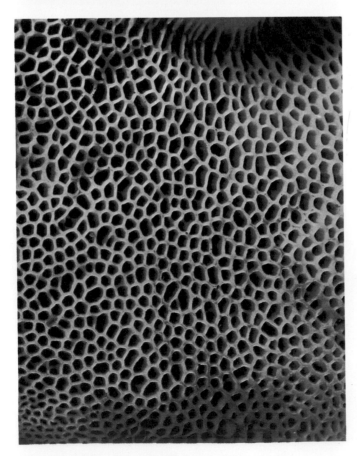

The undersurface of the velvet Boletus subtomentocus, *a fleshy fungus, is a mass of polygonal tubes.*

The deep-sea cushion starfish, Ceramaster placenta, *from the Bay of Biscay, takes the form of a perfect pentangle.*

The skin of the green-crested lizard, Calotes cristatellus, *has a horny surface layer of small scales. This skin does not expand as the reptile grows, and must therefore be periodically moulted.*

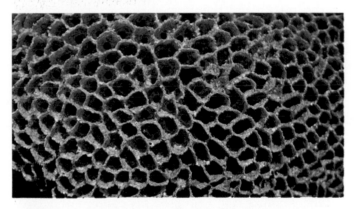

Part of a colony of the honeycomb worm, Sabellaria alveolata, *showing the mouths of the tubes which the worms build.*

Polygonal columns of basalt in the Giant's Causeway, Ireland, formed by fast-cooling lava about 30 million years ago.

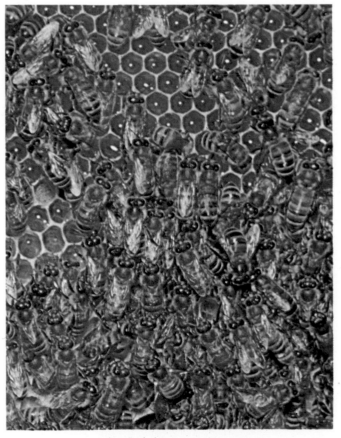

A close-up of the symmetrical cells in a honeycomb. The bees store honey in the comb to feed their growing larvae.

Green Magic

Green plants are the basis of all earthly existence. They work
the magic that transmutes sunshine, carbon dioxide and
water into food and replenishes the oxygen in
the air we breathe. Thus
our lives are intimately bound up with the quiet
miracle taking place in the very grass beneath our feet

The Marvels of Cross-Pollination

Rutherford Platt

An amazing system of accident
and mutual benefit ensures that plants
propagate and insects thrive

As you look across the land-
scape on a summer day, you see bees buzzing here
and there or butterflies fluttering, as seemingly aim-
less as leaves tossed on the breeze. Yet this apparently
capricious activity is part of a routine that is scientifically precise—the miracle of Nature known as
cross-pollination.

To the very last detail, a flower is designed for
one great purpose—reproducing its kind. Colour,
fragrance, form, the length and shape of each part—
all fit with perfection into that purpose. When
a flower finally reaches its full size and beauty, little
undeveloped seeds called ovules are to be found
in a swelling at the base of the pistil. Tiny
grains of pollen are held in a little box at the end
of the stamen.

By themselves, ovule and pollen have no future.
Only when the two unite can the cycle of reproduction be completed and a seed formed. But plants,
like animals, must obey the laws of eugenics, the
most inexorable of which is that inbreeding weakens
a race, while cross-breeding strengthens and perpetuates it. To fulfil its purpose, therefore, the pollen
must somehow find its way to another flower of the
same species, adhere to the stigma (the sticky tip
of the pistil) and then travel down and fuse with
the ovules.

Consider the problem. A target the size of a pin-
head (the stigma) must be hit by a microscopic
grain of pollen of the right kind at exactly the right
time. The brief life of most kinds of pollen requires
that it be launched, transported and at work in the
new flower within an hour or two. A fraction of an
inch or several miles may have to be traversed. The
way insects and flowers combine to accomplish this
almost surpasses belief.

One summer day I focused my camera on a two-
square-inch patch of a yarrow flower cluster. In this
tiny sector insects landed at the rate of about one
every five seconds—or 5760 visitors in an eight-hour
day. They scurried about, dipping here and there
with lightning strokes. Ants came at the rate of perhaps one per minute. A wasp zoomed in, looking like
a colossus next to the minute insects.

Bees are the chief engineers in cross-pollination;
if it were not for them, half of our most beautiful
flower species would disappear. The honey-bee,
which uses pollen as food for its larvae, does the
most work and covers the most territory; also, she
has better pollen baskets than the bumble-bee. These

Attracted by a daisy's colour, this American painted lady butterfly is drinking nectar through its long tube tongue. Highly sensitive taste organs in its feet indicate that nectar is present. The pollen that clings to the insect's body may be dropped on the next daisy it visits, to carry on the process of cross-pollination.

baskets consist of rows of stiff bristles on the hind legs; by packing pollen, moistened with honey, between these hairs the bee can accumulate a ball of pollen sometimes as much as $\frac{1}{4}$ in. in diameter and containing 100,000 grains.

Bees work at astonishing speed. On the head of a thistle a honey-bee, thrusting her proboscis into one flower after another, can pollinate at the rate of about 30 flowers per minute—theoretically more than 14,000 per day.

Usually a bee gathers pollen from only one kind of flower at a time. I have watched when there was every opportunity for a mistake. Vervain and heal-all, both dark purple, were growing so close together that bees working on them almost collided in mid-air. Not once did I see a bee touch the wrong flower.

The flowers lure insects with the promise of nectar—a sugar sap irresistibly attractive to them. When the insect arrives at the flower, Nature has made arrangements so that it will tread on precisely the right places to operate the pollinating gears. Many petals have nectar guides—white or yellow streaks, or bright dots—that converge at the entrance to the nectary. Sometimes the nectar guide is a bright circle, like the red centre of certain pinks and mallows, or the little yellow circle at the centre of cornflowers. The tiger lily has red glands that not only merge as nectar guides but also glisten deceptively, as though with nectar drops. In addition, many flowers have a matting of hairs to give the insect a good footing.

The insect must impregnate the stigma with pollen from another plant, and then pick up more pollen. To do this, his proboscis must slide in at exactly the right angle, the curve of his belly or back must be just right to pick up or deposit pollen, or possibly his legs are to be so planted that they will do the trick. All this is controlled with amazing accuracy.

The great blue lobelia offers one of the most vivid demonstrations. As the bee pushes in head-first, the whole flower stiffens and widens, and the top two petals fly apart. Between them a long, curving,

cylindrical arm nods up and down at just the right angle to touch the bee's back at the proper spot. From the tip of the arm pollen grains are forced out.

Each successive bee gets a fresh charge of pollen on his back. At length, when all the pollen is gone, the stigma emerges from the end of the cylinder and unfurls two fine, sticky branches to receive pollen from another flower. There is nothing hit or miss about this plan. The stigma in this second stage is in exactly the same spot formerly occupied by the pollen; it touches the bee's back exactly where it will pick up pollen from a previously visited flower.

Red clover uses another system. Its closely packed tubular flowers have nectar concealed at the bottom of each tube. To get his head inside, the bumble-bee must push the petals apart. As he does so, the pistil springs up, its stigma brushing his face and picking up the dose of pollen he acquired from his last clover. Then the shorter stamens pop up and dust his face with pollen to be carried to the next flower. The size of the bumble-bee's head, his weight and the pressure he exerts are all precisely balanced for this flower. The mechanism does not operate accurately for any other kind of insect.

The lady's slipper has a unique plan. Its gorgeous

Anthomyid flies (above), related to the common housefly, are feeding on the pollen of a blue columbine. After breaking the sacs on the stamen tips and eating their fill, the flies will be dusted with pollen grains, with which they may fertilise other blossoms.

This bumble-bee and thistle flower (right) are engaged in a partnership that is mutually beneficial. The thistle supplies the bumble-bee with pollen and nectar; the bumble-bee, by moving from flower to flower of the same species, fertilises the thistle with pollen.

bulbous sac has no apparent entrance, no stamens or pistil to explore. But on the front of this sac, the honey-bee sees a network of white veins converging on a vertical slit. She butts her way through it into a translucent chamber where she finds, scattered about the floor, drops of nectar. The bee swallows a few and prepares to be off—but that is not so easy. The edges of the sac have closed behind her and she cannot get out that way. Only at the upper end of the slipper can she exit—and it is a hole barely large enough for her. To squeeze through, she has to pass under an arching stigma that scrapes pollen off her back; and just above this stigma her way is partially blocked by a mass of pollen. This she squeezes under, bringing down a load of grains to be transported to the next lady's slipper.

98

These are just a few of the astonishing ways by which flowers achieve cross-pollination through insects. In the woods and the fields each kind of flower has its own blueprints and schedules; and as you study them you cannot help feeling that sense of incredulous awe which prompted Jean Henri Fabre to say of cross-pollination: 'Before these mysteries of life, reason bows and abandons itself to adoration of the Author of these miracles.'

Goliath of Seeds

Walter Henricks Hodge

*Before its island home was discovered,
the largest seed that grows, the coco de mer,
was believed to have miraculous origins
and possess magical powers*

People who live in temperate areas are generally unfamiliar with large seeds. When we plant garden vegetables, we know that a handful of average-sized vegetable seed should suffice for a row or two. In comparison, horse-chestnut seeds are really something to marvel at, as is shown by their popularity among small boys. Yet the seed of the horse chestnut is a puny thing compared to a coconut, and a coconut in turn is puny when set down beside a Seychelles nut, or coco de mer. For the Seychelles nut is the largest true seed, and is to the plant world what an ostrich egg is to the animal world. It is the Goliath of all seeds.

For centuries prior to about 1600, gigantic hard-shelled nuts, two or three times the size of an average coconut, were sometimes found washed up on the shores of India and other lands bounding the Indian Ocean. These enormous seeds looked like oversized coconuts, yet no one knew their origin other than that they were brought by the sea; in this way the name coco de mer (sea coconut) was given to them. Such marvellous flotsam was rare and, as was common in those days, its rarity was supposed to give it wonderful virtues.

At first, people were not sure whether the great floating objects were plants, animals or minerals.

Before long a number of wild tales had been invented to explain their source. One claimed that the nuts grew on submerged trees near the island of Java. Yarn-spinning sailors told that when they dived to pick these undersea seeds, the trees mysteriously disappeared. Another story was that in certain parts of the tropical ocean the trees, growing above the surface of the water, harboured a griffin, or vulture-like bird, which flew to the nearest land and fed on tigers, elephants and rhinoceroses. Unwary sailors were also devoured by the flying monster if their ships were inadvertently drawn in by the giant waves that supposedly surrounded the tree at all times.

Seeds obtainable only after passing such hazards must certainly be as valuable as the mythical golden apples. Kings and other potentates of the Orient coveted the strange nuts, and passed decrees that they might be acquired only by persons of high rank. The nut's chief virtue was thought to be as an antidote to poison, and at a time when royalty was under constant threat of poisoning, the possession of a coco de mer was almost a necessity for a successful and continued reign. No sum was too large to pay for a charmed life. In those days the nuts must have been hollowed out to form watertight receptacles, for it was believed that poison could be made harmless by adding to it water that had been stored in one of these containers. As the coco de mer became more widely known, its reputation grew to such a degree that it came to be considered a panacea, and a new name, *Nux medica*, was given to it in the 16th century.

Lodoicea maldivica, or coco de mer, is the biggest seed in the world. Before the discovery of the Seychelles Islands, where it grows, its origins were a mystery, since specimens had only been found floating in the Indian Ocean, or cast up on beaches.

The aura of mystery that veiled the coco de mer in its early contacts with civilised man was finally lifted in the middle of the 18th century. At about that time Praslin Island, one of the 29 islands included in the Seychelles group (lying in the Indian Ocean to the north-east of Madagascar) was discovered and in its extensive forests of palms was found one curious species, *Lodoicea maldivica*, bearing a giant nut. The source of the coco de mer was at last known.

Despite inroads by agriculturists and curiosity-seekers, groves of *Lodoicea* are still to be seen on this tiny island of palms. The trees form extensive colonies on the slopes and valleys there. Like many other interesting palms, it has wandered at man's behest far from its home, and several distant tropical gardens now boast living specimens.

The Seychelles nut palm is oversized not only in its seed but in most other respects. The straight, tough trunk, which is said to be 'as upright and unyielding as an iron pillar', sometimes attains a height of 90 ft and bears at its summit giant, rigid, fan-shaped leaves often measuring 25 ft from tip to base of the leaf stalk.

A peculiarity of the palm is a queer protective, socket-like bowl into which the bulbous base of the trunk fits snugly. As tough as the hard shell of the nut and apparently made of the same substance, the curious bowl is extremely resistant to decay, and half a century or more after one of these palms has been cut down, its socket may be found to be perfect in every respect.

But today, as in the past, it is the fruit that is the most spectacular feature of *Lodoicea*. In its homeland a female palm usually attains an age of at least 30 years before it produces its first crop of nuts; even then the tree is hardly out of its youth, and may not yet possess a true trunk. Clusters of the nuts, which require about ten years to mature, resemble somewhat the common coconut in every way except size (a single coco de mer may weigh upwards of 40 lb.), for they have a similar smooth, tough outer coat or husk which overlies the same sort of fibrous layer that one associates with the coconut bought at the market.

The big difference between them lies under the smooth outer husk, for the giant Seychelles nut, unlike a coconut, is bi-lobed, a fact accounting for its misnomer 'double coconut'. In its youth the jelly-like interior, or endosperm, is edible, like that of a green coconut, but at maturity most of it is as hard as ivory. The edibility of this bizarre nut is transient, but not its fame.

Look at Leaves

Donald Culross Peattie

Leaves respond to light and temperature;
they breathe and draw nourishment
into the plants that bear them.
Without them the world would be lifeless

It is an old trick of mine to think about leaves when I cannot sleep. I let my mind go first to the great oak outside my window, with its half acre or so of leaf-surface, all of it doing the tree, and me, a silent good. I listen to faraway foliage I have known, to the high seething of the silken needles of the pines above a woodland cottage, or to the heavy rustle of a chestnut tree; and I hear again the stiff rattle of palm leaves in the trade wind of a tropic shore.

Take any leaf and look at it closely. You will see that the two sides are not alike: the upper surface is darker, often glossy and waxen; the underside paler, sometimes with a protective coating of down. Because it is thus two-faced, a leaf can perform its two separate functions: respiration on the lower surface, work with the sun on the upper.

Trees must breathe oxygen to stay alive. It is oxygen, entering a man's blood, that kindles the fires of human energy. So with a leaf. It too must take in oxygen in order to release, from the sugars and starches packed away in it as stored food, the

The compound leaves of the horse chestnut play an important part in its growth. They breathe through their pale, sheltered undersides while in the darker upper surfaces, chlorophyll traps solar energy for the process of photosynthesis.

With the coming of autumn and fewer daylight hours, the production of chlorophyll slows down and the cells of the maple leaf form a scarlet pigment.

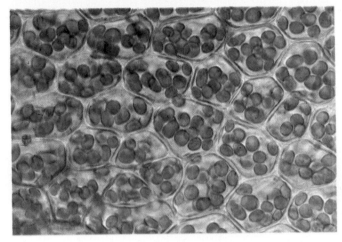

Magnified 500 times, these moss cells show the green, ball-like chloroplasts in which nutrients, water and air are converted to living tissue by chlorophyll.

energy to expand and, by the power of growth, to lift a sapling into a forest giant.

A leaf breathes through the pores on its sheltered underside—so many and minute that they average about 100 to an area the size of the loop in the letter P on this page. These pores are usually slit-shaped, like the pupils of a cat's eyes—and just as a cat's pupils expand in darkness or contract in bright light, so the pores of a leaf respond to atmospheric changes. On hot, dry days, to prevent the leaf from wilting by water loss through evaporation, its pores may almost close—but not completely, or it would suffocate. When the pores open their widest, the leaf, and therefore the tree, breathes more easily.

The pores of a leaf, even at the top of a tall tree, help to bring water up from the roots. Evaporation at the pores causes a partial vacuum within the cells, and this suction-like effect is communicated

from cell to cell back through the leaf-stalks and twigs, along the boughs and down the trunk. Boosted by root pressure from below, thread-fine columns of water are sucked up, like lemonade through a straw; and this goes on, against gravity, 100 ft up and more, to the crown of a great oak or elm.

Meanwhile, on the upper side of the leaf, the side exposed to the sunlight, a primal work of the world is going on. For aeons before this atomic age, the green leaf has been using solar energy to power the greatest industrial plant on earth. No wheel turns in it, no smoke pollutes the air around it; instead, leaves purify the atmosphere. This foliage factory—which first, of course, serves the tree itself, thus giving us timber, pulp and plastics—uses for machinery the green stuff in the leaf called chlorophyll; and with chlorophyll the leaf is able to capture part of that tremendous cascade of atomic energy that falls upon our planet from the sun.

As each tiny particle of solar energy (called a photon) collides with the green in the leaf, the energy leaps to the chlorophyll, setting it aglow. With this energy the chlorophyll smashes open the molecules of the water and carbon dioxide the leaf has taken in through its pores from the air; it re-assembles these atoms of oxygen, carbon and hydrogen into new patterns constituting sugars and starches, the basic foods in the leaf. Since it is with the energy from photons that the leaf synthesises its foods, the whole process is called photosynthesis. Throughout the sunlit hours all over the world, every leaf on every tree is doing this work.

No wonder chlorophyll has been called the green blood of the world. It is carried in minute green discs that, like the corpuscles in our own blood, can move about as if they led a life of their own. When the sunshine is too strong they can turn edge-on, or sink, or flee to the sides of the cells. When the skies grow grey, they may turn broadside to make the most of the light, or rise to the top of the cell, like fish coming up in cloudy weather to bite.

Leaves help to provide us with the very breath of life. For when the leaf breaks up those molecules of water and carbon dioxide by photosynthesis into their elements, there is a lot of oxygen left over that the leaf itself does not use. This it breathes out through its pores, in such quantities that our air is wonderfully freshened. When factory chimneys pour deadly gases into the sky, the oxygen exhaled by leaves helps to purify the polluted air. The winds of the world, storming around our spinning globe, thoroughly mix and distribute the leaf-breath. Without that gentle exhalation all animal life on earth would, like a candle lowered into a well full of carbon dioxide, long ago have flickered out.

Thus the man who has a fine old tree shading his roof lives under a sort of oxygen tent. Moreover, the foliage not only tempers the wind and shuts out the glare, but somewhat air-conditions his house. For the air around leaves is faintly cooled by the evaporation from them, just as a lake or river makes the nearby surroundings cooler. You feel this sudden coolness when, on a hot day, you enter a wood.

All through the summer, a green, serene benediction is upon us. In autumn every leaf seems to have put on a new colour. Not so; the reds and yellows are the natural pigments of certain foods stored by leaves that are merely masked by chlorophyll in the summer. We see orange in autumn foliage when red shines through yellow, and mauve when red begins to change chemically. Frost has nothing to do with it. It is the leaves themselves that end their own lives in this blaze of glory. Each leaf produces a growth of callous cells at the base of its stalk; this cuts off the water supply and makes a tear-line, like the perforations on a sheet of stamps, so that any breeze may pull the leaf off, or it may fall by its own weight. In the end, it will turn to mould, enriching the earth; or, raked into some bonfire, may rise again in a last blue twirl of pungent smoke.

Buds—Nature's Promise of New Life

Donald Culross Peattie

Packed to bursting point with
new life, buds are the ever-welcome signs
of spring's first awakening

When the pussy willows are out, spring has once again captured the world. Their furry tufts, silvery upon black twigs, are the signs of budding dearest to most of us; and budding is the everlasting reassurance, new each year.

Springtime is crowded with buds filled with leaf or flower or new twig shoots. Each bud holds its own kind of futurity: without buds no leaf would ever burgeon, no willow send out a withe, no flowering branch spread tenderly over some old grave. In our zone of winter-naked trees and shrubs you will find a bud at the axil, or base, of nearly every leaf-stalk. Buds are embryonic growths: on a great tree they may seem as superficial as your fingernails, but in fact they are deep-set in the twig that bears them, their fibres connected with the very core system of the old wood.

Slowly the buds begin to swell, the woods to wear green again. If you walk by a river and see the royal fern unrolling buds that look like the scrollwork on a violin, or if you go into the drier woods and look at the buds of bracken opening like the slackening of a clenched fist, you will be gazing at what is, perhaps, the oldest type of budding still to be seen among ferns—and ferns may be said to have invented leaves.

So characteristic are the buds of every kind of shrub or tree that the experienced walker learns to identify each kind either by the shape of the bud, the colour of the bud-scales—or sometimes by the total absence of scales. The beech is notable for the beautiful bronze overlapping scales that bring the bud to a slim, aristocratic point. Magnolia buds are covered by big scales, as silken as a cat's ears. The scales on the buds of the horse chestnut are gummy.

You might judge by these various coverlets that bud-scales are for protection against the cold. The fact is that winter buds *are* cold, cold as ice sometimes, for often ice crystals form inside them, without harming the sleeping bud. Rather do those gummed envelopes or hard scales protect the tender baby tissue from drying out. For wind, which can evaporate even snow—directly, without its first turning to water—may dehydrate the bud tissue. That is what makes an early thaw so dangerous, luring the tissues to unfold, then exposing them to the ravages of the wind.

If, just before spring begins, you slice a winter bud in two, you will scarcely need a magnifying glass to see how artfully Nature has packed next summer's foliage. The leaves are never telescoped in such a way as to crease and break the mid-rib, as this will become the spinal strength of the leaf and supply it with water. Instead, the careful folding is all done in the soft tissue between the mid-rib and other principal veins.

In the plum bud the leaf is simply rolled, lengthways. Leaves of cherry, peach, apple and elm are folded on each side of the mid-rib. Sycamore leaves, having numerous big ribs like fan sticks radiating from the base, are folded fan-wise between the ribs, to be flung out later on the summer breezes.

While the snow is still on the ground, the winter buds' temperatures are already mounting. This is because rapid growth has started, and rapid growth, like running, means quick breathing. Quick breathing signifies intensified oxidation, which gives heat. So certain buds may not have to wait for a balmy spell of spring; they may make it come—the heat they give off may melt the snow around them. In this way many alpine flowers bloom beneath a crystal dome of ice.

Why do some buds break into bloom in early spring, some in late spring, some only in summer or even autumn? Length of daylight is the governing factor. Modern experiments have shown that some plants are stimulated to flowering by relatively short days and long nights; these are the early bloomers. As the days lengthen and the nights grow shorter, the late spring flowers appear. Long days and brief nights give us summer flowers.

On a tree, what may count is the position of the bud upon the wood. Buds formed on old wood are ready to open in spring. If a bud is formed on new spring wood, it has no time to complete its embryonic life during the spring. At best it will unfold in autumn—like the witch hazel, whose green-gold flowers open after most leaves have fallen.

There are deep-set buds, sometimes under the tree's bark, which may lie dormant as long as the Sleeping Beauty. What gardener, nurseryman or fruit farmer does not know about their marvellous power to live and wait, sometimes for years? When a tree or shrub begins to run to long, sprawling shoots and barren leafage, the wise husbandman prunes back heroically to dormant buds. That is the way to stimulate flowering and fruiting, to put new life, vigour and shapeliness into a rose bush, an apricot tree or grape vine.

The vineyards of Bordeaux and Burgundy are cut back annually until the stock of the stem looks like an old, gnarled witch—all for the sake of the magic that is in dormant buds, forced into growth by the elimination of the others.

So the silver poplar may be cut back because it has become a beautiful nuisance, with its probing roots getting into pipes or under pavements. But even if the stump is levelled to the ground, the buds of those roots send up shoots.

This gift of perpetuity through the bud is exhibited in my own garden. I have a rosy-green little succulent which, I like to say, was given to me by Catherine the Great of Russia. In the impersonal way of plant life, this is truly so. For this neat rosette, by the process of budding, puts forth offsets all around it. Some of these Catherine dispatched to the most famous botanist of her day, Carolus Linnaeus of Sweden, who planted them in the botanical garden at Uppsala University. There, not long ago, one of the little rosettes was given to me. Transplanted, it seems quite at ease, continuing by budding to set around it ever-new little rosettes. Truly in a bud lies this year, next year and all the years to come.

Gaze in Wonder at a Tree

Donald Culross Peattie

Strength and grace are a tree's inseparable attributes: its roots can split rock or concrete, and its branches are miracles of harmony and balance

The greatest force in the natural world is growth; and the noblest example of that force is a tree. Springing from a trifling seed, it can split rock and soar skywards a hundred feet and more. It draws up water against gravity to its top, and spreads at last in an architecture of boughs and twigs as splendid as a Gothic vault, but living to the outermost leaf.

If a plant had a brain, said Darwin, it would lie in its roots. Deep in the earth they seek and find, they dodge and pry. Their delicate tips, wearing a sort of helmet called a root cap, penetrate the soil with a spiral motion like that of a corkscrew. Meeting an obstacle such as a rock, they may circumvent it, heave it aside, or even crack it open by dissolving it with acids that they can secrete.

If (as has been calculated) a single tuft of blue-grass may in one growing season produce 84,500 root branches and a million root hairs, what then must be the root system of a grand old oak? Like a mirror image of the tree above, the underground

The California redwood, one of the world's tallest trees, may exceed 350 ft. It is so resistant to decay that 500-year-old logs have been used for lumber.

growth has first a tap-root corresponding to the trunk, then huge primary branches, then more slender secondaries and slimmer tertiaries. From these slant off thousands of 'obliques', and these send out millions of hair-fine capillaries. Clustering near the tips of the capillaries are thousands of millions of even finer root hairs.

It is only through the root hairs that the tree can 'drink'. All the rest of it is practically waterproof. Even in a drought, a big tree will find water enough to keep alive in the film of moisture that clings to every grain of soil. As each soil particle is stripped of moisture, adjacent grains of soil are forced, by the law of capillarity (the blotting-paper principle), to yield up their moisture and send it towards the thirsty roots.

How does the water mount up the tree? Using tracer dyes, botanists have followed its course. Through the sapwood of the tree runs a sort of plumbing system consisting of very narrow cellulose tubes. These pipes run from the bottom-most root out into the veins of the leaves; and up these pipes goes the water which has been taken from the soil by the root hairs.

The force that pulls the water up is the evaporation (botanists call it transpiration) through the leaves and their pores. The pull that is felt in the tiniest veins of the leaf is communicated back through the sapwood of the trunk all the way down to the root hairs.

A 100-year-old beech with a quarter of a million leaves gives off by transpiration some 50 quarts of water daily. This creates a force strong enough to pump up, in six months, 10 tons of water from the soil, sending it all forth again into the air in quiet, freshening breath.

Far longer than our own is the life of a tree, and far stronger. We animals burn ourselves up with our living; trees hoard their power, calmly increasing it year by year. A tree has no set limit to its size or age. On the eastern slope of the Sierra Nevada Mountains in California stands a bristlecone pine that is estimated to be 4600 years old. It is the oldest known living thing.

Trees have a blessed power to repair injuries, and to grow over what they cannot thrust aside. Many a cannonball, a ploughshare, the antlers of a deer have been found embedded deep in the living wood.

All this power of growth in a tree resides in just one layer of cells, the cambium, which sheathes every part of the tree. If you scratch a bit of twig with your fingernail, you will notice, just under the bark, a thin band of green denoting the presence of the cambium. This paper-thin, fragile layer is perpetually dividing its cells lengthways; and the two halves of the cell have each a different destiny. For towards the centre of the tree the cambium lays down rings of wood, but towards the outside it builds new bark under the old.

The whole tale of a tree's growing can be seen in the end of a freshly cut trunk. Outermost lie the layers of bark, then the cambium with its tell-tale ribbon of green, then the pale sapwood with its life-giving water; and, at the centre of the trunk, the dark and ponderous heartwood, stained and clogged by resins and oils and solidified by the tremendous weight and pressure of the cells above and around it. Once, in the tree's youth, that dense heartwood was clear sapwood, but the pressures of living turned it into this pillar of strength at the tree's core. For the dead cells of a living tree still serve to hold up the whole marvellous structure, and to brace it against the torrent of the wind.

A tree is not only strong but amazingly supple. We have all seen how the wind bends saplings double. The same 'give' lies in the mightiest oak or beech, because of the structure of its wood.

Most of the cells making up that wood are like hollow tile bricks. They are made of cellulose, in double walls, and cellulose is flexible. This gives wood its flexibility and enables the living tree to 'roll with the punches'.

The pores with which the tree breathes are mostly on the underside of the leaf. Closing somewhat on dry, bright days, they cut down the escape of moisture from the tree; or, opening in the cool darkness, they let the tree breathe freely. The oxygen in that calm respiration has been released during the complex work done by the upper side of the leaf.

This work, called photosynthesis, is performed in partnership with the sunlight. The chlorophyll, the green stuff of the leaf, has the rare ability to use solar energy. With this it breaks up the molecules of water in the leaf, and of the carbon dioxide taken in through the leaf's pores. By rearranging these atoms of oxygen, carbon and hydrogen into other chemical forms, the leaf is provided with the sugars and starches it needs for food. Not even the mightiest factory on earth can compare in production with this silent industry.

The waters in the earth are to its trees not only drink. In them lie, in solution, all the elements that the tree needs: nitrogen, calcium, phosphorus, potassium, iron, copper, zinc, magnesium, and many more. Swept up by the transpiration stream to the living protoplasm, the growing cellulose, the functioning leaves, this vital nourishment goes to the making of a noble tree.

Only in water can the chemistry of its life take place—the making of its food, the building and growth of its cells, the greening and the glory, year by year, of its foliage. So every great tree is an invisible fountain, a verdant monument to life itself.

The 'Big Tree'—Forest King

Donald Culross Peattie

Some of California's giant sequoias were
seedlings before Christ was born;
now, 3000 years later, they are grown to
their full magnificence

The mightiest of living things is the giant sequoia, or California 'big tree'. After 30 centuries of growth, *Sequoia gigantea* is practically a geological phenomenon. Only its closest kin, the redwood of the California coast ranges, approaches it in both longevity and girth.

The home of the giant sequoia lies between 4000 and 8500 ft up on the western slopes of the Sierra Nevada. There, snow drifts among the titans up to 30 ft deep—a mere white anklet to such trees. The summers are dry; if rain does fall it is likely to come with violent thunderstorms and lightning bolts that have been seen to split a sequoia from crown to roots. Those who know the species best maintain that the tree never dies of disease or senility. If it survives predators in its infancy and the hazard of fire in youth, only a bolt from heaven will end its centuries of life.

The province of the giant sequoias extends for 260 miles. You will not find any single 'big tree'; they grow only in groves of five to a thousand. The Giant Forest, the Mariposa, North Calaveras and General Grant groves are perhaps the most famous and accessible. It is all too likely that Nature will never spontaneously create any more groves.

To see the 'big trees' you must travel far and climb high. It is a day's run by car from San Francisco or Los Angeles. After the red firs and the white of the upper forests come the Jeffrey pines, clad in great orange plates of bark like the leather shields of Homeric soldiers. Sombre Douglas firs darken the late afternoon as with oncoming night. At last the sugar pines with rugged purple trunks, the mightiest pines in all the world, close about you.

It will be dusk, no doubt, when you reach the giant groves, and the forest will be still, yet watchfully alive. A deer may put an inquisitive black muzzle in your outstretched hand. It will be a long moment before you realise that the vast shadow behind the little doe is not shade but a tree-trunk so gigantic that you cannot comprehend at first that this is a living thing. Were a cross-section of that great bole put down in a city street, it would block it from kerb to kerb. That mighty bough, the lowest one, is still so high above the ground that it would stretch out over the top of a 12-storey building. If it were cut off and placed upright on the ground, that bough would appear as a tree 70 ft high and 7 ft in diameter at the base.

Yet the trees conceal their true size by the very perfection of their proportions. Each part—breadth at base, spread of boughs, thickness of trunk, shape of crown—is in harmony with the rest.

On a second view, by morning light, the impression of the giant sequoias is not so much of size as of colour. The ruddy trunks are richly bright. The metallic green of the foliage is the gayest of all Sierra conifers. Unlike the misty dimness of the redwood groves with their over-arching canopy, the sunlight here reaches right to the floor. Instead of the hush of the redwoods, you hear among the 'big trees' the lordly racket of the pileated woodpeckers at their irreverent carpentry. The Douglas squirrels frisk familiarly up the monstrous boles and out upon the boughs, to cut the cones and despoil them of their seeds.

The General Sherman is usually considered the all-round exemplary giant sequoia. It is 272 ft high, has a basal circumference of 102 ft; at 16 ft above the ground it is more than 24 ft in diameter, and raises a shaft clear of any boughs for a height of 130 ft. In the North Calaveras Grove lies prone the tree called 'Father of the Forest'; inside its hollow trunk a man once rode on horseback without having to bend his head. Though the crown of this tree is gone, the taper of the trunk indicates that the Father of the Forest stood 400 ft high—which would have made it the tallest tree in the world.

The 'big trees' of North Calaveras Grove were discovered one spring day in 1852 by a miner, A. T. Dowd, who pursued a grizzly bear far up into tall

timber. When he encountered the 'big trees', his astonishment was so great that he allowed the bear to get away. His fellow miners came, incredulous, and beheld 50 acres of what was later to be called the North Calaveras Grove, covered with trees, many as tall as 330 ft.

In 1853, John Lindley, an English botanist, in a formal botanical publication named the mighty conifer *Wellingtonia gigantea*, after the Duke of Wellington, victor of Waterloo, who had died the previous autumn. Loud was the patriotic anguish of American botanists. But fortunately the generic name of *Sequoia* for the coast redwoods had been published in Germany some six years before *Wellingtonia*, and when it was realised that the 'big trees' too are sequoias, the Americans were satisfied. For the name had been bestowed in honour of Sequoyah, the great Cherokee chief who devoted his life to developing an alphabet for the Indian people and teaching others to read it.

General Grant Tree (left), in King's Canyon National Park, California. Sequoia are found only on the western slopes of the Sierra Nevada Range, and this Sequoia gigantea, *267 ft high and perhaps 3500 years old, has been designated the U.S. nation's Christmas tree. In Redwood National Park, also in California, groves of coastal redwoods,* Sequoia sempervirens *(above), rise from an undergrowth of lush green ferns.*

In the early 1850's a disappointed gold-seeker, G. H. Woodruff of New York, collected seeds from the 'big tree' cones in an empty snuffbox and paid 25 dollars to send them east to the nursery firm of Ellwanger & Barry in Rochester, N.Y. From those seeds sprang up 4000 tiny trees. They did not sell very well in the eastern states, but in England, where they were retailed as Wellingtonias, they sold rapidly. Botanical gardens in England, France and Germany wanted specimens. Cities planted avenues of them. Soon every man of wealth or title thought he must have such a tree for his grounds. 'The great event of the year 1864,' wrote Tennyson's son, 'was the visit of Garibaldi to the Tennysons, an incident of which was the planting of a Wellingtonia by the great Italian.' Eventually Ellwanger & Barry paid Woodruff 1036 dollars as his share of the profits on a snuffboxful of seeds.

Californians asserted that the 'big trees' were old when the pyramids were being built. John Muir counted the annual rings on the biggest stump he ever saw and claimed he had found over 4000. But accurate ring counts in recent times have not put the age of any logged tree at more than 3100 years.

Yet 30 centuries of life are awe-inspiring. There is something comforting about handling a section of sequoia wood that seems scarcely less living now than when it grew before the time of Christ. Somewhere about 2 in. inside the bark of a tree recently cut will be the rings laid down more than a century ago; and it is humbling to note that those particular rings may be 15 ft from the centre of the tree, the starting point of its growth.

Why, out of a world of trees, do these live longest? If there is any one answer, it lies in the very sap of life itself. The sap of the 'big trees' is non-resinous, hence only slightly inflammable. Though fire is a deadly peril to the thin-barked young sequoias, when bark has formed on the old specimens it may be a foot or more thick and practically as fire-resistant as asbestos. The only way that fire can penetrate is when some more inflammable tree falls as a brand against a giant sequoia and, fanned to a blowlamp by the mountain wind, sears its way through to the wood.

Even then fire seems never to consume a great old specimen completely. The repair of fire damage begins at once, even if the wound is so wide that it would take a thousand years to cover it. The high tannin content of the sap has the same healing action that tannic acid has on our flesh when we apply it to a burn. It is highly antiseptic, deadly to the spores of infecting fungus growth.

A giant sequoia waits 175 or 200 years before it first flowers, perhaps the most delayed sexual maturity in all Nature. When it comes, the trees are loaded with millions of male and female conelets from November to late in February. The green-gold pollen showers all over the giant's body and drifts in swirls upon the snow. A single tree will bear hundreds of thousands of cones when in the full vigour of its life.

The flaky seed which produces all these tons of vegetation is so small that it takes 3000 of them to make an ounce. There are from 96 to 304 seeds to a cone, and the cones themselves are almost ridiculously small—hardly larger than big leather buttons. They do not mature until the end of the second season; and not until the end of the third, at the earliest, do they open their scales in dry weather and loose the seeds which drift but a little way from the parent tree. Perhaps only 15 per cent of the seeds have the vitality to sprout, and long before they do they are attacked by squirrels and jays. Many are lost in the decaying vegetable matter of the forest floor. Of a million seeds on a tree in autumn, perhaps only one is destined to sprout when the snow-water and the sun of the late mountain spring touch it with quickening fingers.

The tiny seedlings are attacked from below by cutworms, from above by armies of black wood ants. Ground squirrels and chipmunks, finches and sparrows cock a bright eye at them and pull them up for a tasty salad. Deer browse on them by the thousands. If a seedling survives its first year, it may face the centuries with some confidence.

All the properties of sequoia wood save one are inferior to those of nearly every other tree. It is so brittle that when a big tree falls to earth the green timber often cracks both lengthways and across, into fragments fit only for lead pencils. Its only virtue is that it lasts for ever. In consequence, it was sought by lumbermen for shingles, water-channels, fence stakes and poles.

The giant groves seemed to promise ready fortunes. So logging railroads were hurried up the mountains, mills were set up, and the Lilliputian lumberjacks fell to work among these woody Gullivers. In this way was accomplished the destruction of the Converse Basin Grove, probably finer than any now standing, and the slaughter went on until there remained only a single great specimen. This the superintendent spared so that it might be named after himself, the Boole tree. Today in the Converse Basin there is not one seedling sequoia to give hope that this species will ever grow there again. Instead there are thousands of logs that were never utilised because they proved too big or too costly to handle, millions of board feet gone to waste because the wood smashed to bits in its fall. The whole enterprise ended in financial failure.

The long battle to save the 'big trees' was begun by Colonel George Stewart, a newspaperman of Visalia, California. He was joined by public-spirited citizens, and by newspapers and magazines in California and finally in the eastern states. Victory came in 1890 when Sequoia and General Grant national parks were created.

With other fine sequoia groves in Yosemite National Park and Tahoe National Forest, the future of the king of trees seems assured.

The African Baobab

I. M. Wright and O. Kerfoot

Although Bushmen believe that the first baobab was planted upside-down by the hyena—the force of evil—they still find many uses for the odd-looking tree

No tree gives as vivid an impression of the vastness, the variety and the magnificence of Africa as does the grotesque and unwieldy baobab. It is an integral part of African history and legend.

The baobab belongs to a family of thick-trunked trees that includes balsa and kapok. It is named *Adansonia digitata* after Michel Adanson, a French explorer-naturalist who, in a letter from Senegal in 1754, wrote:

'I perceived a tree of prodigious thickness which drew my whole attention. I do not believe the like was ever seen in any other part of the world.'

Although baobabs are not exceptionally tall, their trunks are enormous. One in Tanzania has a circumference greater than 130 ft. The smooth, heavily folded bark of the baobab is pinkish grey or coppery in colour, and closely resembles the wrinkled skin of an elephant. At the top of the trunk there is often a natural basin filled with water that supports large populations of malarial mosquitoes and other insects and provides a dubious water source for travellers.

In October the baobab's green leaves and beautiful white blossoms appear. The flowers, solitary and pendulous, with delicate filaments surrounded by fine waxy petals, have no scent, but when bruised they emit an objectionable odour reminiscent of decaying meat.

In December the tree produces a gourd-like fruit known as monkey bread. It consists of a woody capsule, up to 12 in. long, with a hard shell, and contains a mucilaginous, seeded pulp. Trees yield fruit after eight or ten years, but produce abundantly only after 30 years.

The baobab is irregularly distributed across Africa. Essentially a native of tropical Africa, it is found as far north as the Sudan and as far south as the Transvaal in the Republic of South Africa. It has an uneven distribution on the west coast, but is common in most coastal and thornbush areas of East Africa. In central Africa it thrives only below 4000 ft, being generally restricted to hot, low-lying areas of scant rainfall.

Baobabs are objects of worship in some parts of the African continent. In Rhodesia the tree is the totem of the Sebola tribe, who pray to it and believe that their ancestors lived almost exclusively on its fruit. Quite possibly they did, for virtually every part of the baobab is used somewhere for some purpose. Its soft and spongy wood can even be pounded into a fibre that is suitable for ropes and floor mats.

Much of the tree can be eaten. Although usually regarded as a seasoning or appetiser, it is used as a staple diet in times of scarcity. The fruit's cool-tasting, acidic pulp is refreshing when eaten raw but can also be mixed with water and boiled. The black seeds are pleasing to the taste and, when ground, make a passable substitute for coffee. But among the Ila people in Zambia they are taboo; anyone who eats them supposedly runs the risk of being bitten by a crocodile.

There is abundant food value in the baobab's vitamin-rich leaves, which resemble spinach, and the tender roots of young baobabs are similar to asparagus. In Nigeria the leaves are a common ingredient of fodder for cattle and horses.

Native doctors prescribe baobab roots, leaves, fruit pulp and bark for almost any ailment, from kidney trouble to toothache. The leaves are used as a cure for dysentery and respiratory ailments, and as a prophylactic against fevers; the bark serves as a

With their huge holes and stunted branches, the African baobab trees look like enormous carrots. Some of these 'upside-down trees' may be 2000 years old; one, with a girth of over 130 ft, is ranked among the world's thickest trees.

substitute for quinine. Although the medicinal qualities of the baobab are not acknowledged by modern medicine, they were once so famous that the Sudan exported parts of the tree to Europe.

Baobabs have numerous domestic uses as well. A red dye is extracted from the roots. The finely ground seeds are used for fertiliser and fuel. Ash from the burnt seeds is used by natives to make soap, as well as plaster for hut walls. The fruit's hard shell makes a receptacle for liquids or snuff and, when pulverised, is an ingredient of snuff itself. When the fruit pulp is burnt, it emits irritating smoke that keeps insects from cattle. Even the flowers of the baobab are used, since Africans extract a strong glue from the pollen grains.

It is the bark, however, that is the most valuable part of the baobab tree. It is used to tan leather and to make waterproof hats. Drinking cups and beer strainers are also made from it. It is used in ropes and in strings for musical instruments. It can also be woven into a clothing fabric, and it is exported for use as a component in the manufacture of strong packing paper.

Fortunately, baobabs have amazing vitality. They survive the repeated stripping of their bark and flourish even when their interiors have been burnt out. Enormous populations of wild bees frequently inhabit such hollow trees, and natives often suspend beehives in them.

Africans carve homes out of the boles of living trees. In one town the shelter at a bus stop is a hollow baobab that accommodates 30 people with ease. In another town, a baobab houses a bar, complete with counter and stools. Baobabs are used as

111

water cisterns in the Sudan, for they limit evaporation and keep water sweet and clear throughout the dry season.

Some tribes in central Africa believe that Resa, the Rain Lord, lives in a heavenly baobab tree that is the roof of the world. Others claim that there are no young baobabs at all, and that the huge adults are born fully grown. The belief is not unreasonable, for young plants, stately and slim, are striking contrasts to their bulbous elders—although, of course, they have the same foliage.

Many domestic uses have been found for the strange-looking baobab tree—soap, glue, fertiliser and insect-repellent are all derived from it—and its medicinal qualities, although not now acknowledged by modern medicine, were once so well renowned that parts of the tree used to be exported from the Sudan to Europe.

A Bushman legend claims that, when the first spirit gave trees to an early race, he gave everyone some tree to plant. But upon the arrival of the lowly hyena, the force of evil in Bushman religion, there was only one tree left, the baobab. Spitefully, the hyena planted it upside-down; and, indeed, its contorted branches do somewhat resemble tree roots.

The life-span of baobabs is unknown, since their wood shows no annual growth rings, but modern botanical research rejects any theories of vast age. Nevertheless, the trees are so much a part of the African continent that they seem inevitable and indestructible. Unfortunately, each tree's ultimate fate is oblivion. There is no majestic crashing down of a forest giant to remain in slow, still-vitalised decay on earth. There is only a crumbling subsidence, which in time forms a soft mound of bleached, powdery fragments to be scattered by the winds and devoured by termites until nothing of the tree remains.

Plants that Eat Insects

Jean George

Plants shaped like hunters' traps,
plants with digestive juices;
vegetable flesh-eaters have found many
ingenious ways to trap their prey

One summer day my small son brought home from a nearby marsh a strange but oddly familiar plant—a whorl of green antlers trimmed generously with tiny baubles. We put it in a bowl on the dining-room table. Presently my son announced that some small water fleas were rowing around in the bowl, apparently brought in on the plant's roots. I rushed to remove them.

As I reached for one sand-coloured flea, it flipped away into a bauble. I waited—but it did not come out. I began to wonder. Could this be the marsh plant that catches insects and devours them? Carefully I opened the bauble, and behind a tiny hinged door I spotted the entrapped water flea. At the same time a mosquito larva, caught by its tail, was slowly being sucked into another tiny trap.

Several days later a plant expert confirmed my guess. 'That is a bladderwort,' he said, 'one of the most amazing plants in the world. It is related to the famous pitcher plants and Venus's fly-traps that live in marshes and swamps.'

The botanist explained that carnivorous plants, usually considered rare and hard to find, are common throughout the world. 'Every section of the earth,' he said, 'has some kind of pitcher plant growing in bog and swamp areas, where the soil is poor. To survive, these plants catch and digest insects, and so receive essential nitrogen. The array of lures and snares they have evolved is amazing. To me, carnivorous plants are even more interesting than animals.'

As I studied and lived with these plants I understood what he meant. From a botanical supplier I bought some Venus's fly-traps and planted them in a terrarium in sphagnum moss and sand, wetted down with distilled water (they will not grow on a more nutritious diet).

Within a few weeks I had seven green bear-traps, each about $\frac{1}{2}$ in. long, complete with teeth. Slowly the traps opened and revealed vivid red, juicy-looking bait-cells. Then three thread-like triggers arose on either side of each open leaf, and the traps were set.

We put several houseflies in the terrarium and within four minutes one of them flew down to the bait. Instantly it was caught, for in entering the trap the fly touched the triggers that spring the hinge. In less than half a second the jaws snapped shut. With the fly safely enclosed, the trap slowly continued to tighten on the victim.

Ten days later the trap opened again. The fly had been devoured; only the hard bases of the wings remained. The plant tossed them to the ground and set itself again.

According to Francis Ernest Lloyd, who was an outstanding authority on carnivorous plants, the traps operate about three times before they turn black and die. By then they have done their work of providing food for the plant's development.

We experimented with our traps. On one we placed a tiny piece of glass. In five hours the trap closed; but instead of opening after ten days (the normal digesting time), the trap reopened, spat out the piece of glass and re-set itself within 24 hours.

Each species of carnivorous plant has invented a different kind of trap to catch its prey. But all have

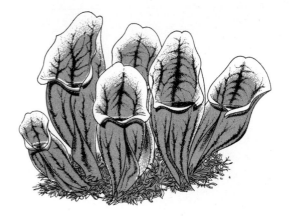

A jumping spider waits to seize any insect that may be attracted to this pitcher plant. A small web spun at the mouth of the pitcher keeps the spider from sliding down its slippery throat and into a pool of fluid so deadly that the plant's victims are not only drowned but dissolved.

one eerie thing in common; their 'stomachs' have much the same enzymes and acids as those contained in animal stomachs.

The trap most commonly used to get food to these stomachs is the pitfall evolved by the pitcher plants. It is designed to trap flies and moths that usually dine in the attractive corollas of flowers whose heads hang down. Pitcher plants look not unlike lilies or trumpet flowers; some have the same scent as violets or honey.

But there the similarity stops. For where the flower has steps for the insects to climb in and out, the pitcher plant has a one-way staircase that leads to the edge of the pitfall. Once there, the insect cannot return; stiff inward-bent bristles bar his exit. Lured by strong odours, the victim has no choice but to continue until he plunges into the pit. There he is drowned in an acid pool and then digested. Some pitcher plants add a refinement—a lid that closes on the prey and remains closed until the insect is devoured.

Ants are a great delicacy—but because they are skilled at walking on all types of surfaces upside-down, some plants have had to adapt their trapping devices. Brazilian plants have evolved a lobster-pot type of trap. The most beautiful of these is held within a miniature Chianti flask. Winding down towards the trap is a spiral staircase that grows smaller and smaller and is baited with scents irresistible to an ant. The ant follows the seductive trail until it cannot turn round. It goes on to the bottom, steps on a treadle, and stiff plant-bars close behind it to lock it irrevocably in the plant's prison.

Several carnivorous plants have evolved a quite efficient 'fly-paper'. Among them are the butter-worts, found all over the Northern Hemisphere in moist, mossy pockets. Lying flat on the ground, glittering like the points of honey-covered stars, the unobtrusive, ovate leaves wait until a moth or bee alights to feast. When the feet touch a leaf, the plant exudes a sticky mucilage to hold the insect. This flow is followed by a dose of acid containing a digestive enzyme that overpowers the insect. Then slowly, neatly, the edges of the leaf roll over and cover the victim. The butterwort takes 24 hours

This doomed wasp is held fast by a sundew's sticky spines. Like most insect-eating plants, the sundew grows in poor soil and obtains nutrients from insects and other small prey. But, like all green plants, it also manufactures food from non-living substances, and can exist for a while without a 'meat' diet.

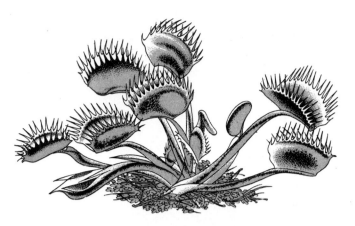

Lured by a compelling fragrance, this honey-bee has touched trigger hairs lining the outside of the Venus's fly-trap. With startling suddenness, the fly-trap has snapped shut and trapped the bee. Now enzymes and digestive juices which the plant secretes will convert the insect into nourishing substances.

to roll up, three to five days to devour the food, and one day for the leaf to uncurl. Then the 'fly-paper' is made ready once more.

Other fly-paper-type plants are the beautiful sundews that look like pin-cushions and grow in most swamps and bogs. These are sweetly scented—and sticky as glue. A wasp landed on one of these plants on four of its six feet, realised the texture was not right and tried to lift up the front two. In doing so, it put down the rear two, and was stuck on all six. It pulled and tipped. A wing went out; it stuck deep among the spines and pins. The wasp bit, and its jaws became stuck fast. Then the glittering heads of the pins began to curl over the wasp until the insect was still, and the plant tentacles, curled daintily over it, were dining.

One of the most deadly plant traps is the fungus that forms nooses to snare eelworms on their way to destroy wheat seedlings. The fungus grows on the damp ground, straight up like a pin, silver in the sunlight. Then a growing branch bends down and fastens itself to its own base, making a tiny noose. There may be many nooses in a group, so that sooner or later an eelworm, writhing over the ground, will get its head in one of them. Immediately the loop tightens. The worm tries to pull back. The noose grows tighter and tighter until the worm is dead. Then the loop sends out tiny runners to cover the worm—and eat it.

From Lloyd's book, *The Carnivorous Plants,* we learnt that the bladderwort could regulate water pressure, suck, and close doors. Through a magnifying glass we could see the green bristles that activate the trapping mechanisms. This tiny chlorophyll

trapdoor is set by water pressure; the change in pressure inside and outside the bauble sucks the insect into the chamber, the green cells working like a pump as they change the water level and draw the creature in and in. When the prey has been drawn into the chamber, the door swings shut and hairs bolt it; it is now leakproof, so that the enzymes that aid in digesting the victim cannot be diluted by outside water.

Charles Darwin wrote one of the first books on the insect-eating plants. He was intrigued by them and asked, with experiments of all kinds, 'What kind of intelligence is this?' As we gazed at our innocent-looking bladderwort one morning, my son echoed Darwin's question: 'Do you suppose these plants can think?'

'No,' I answered, 'but the fact that a single green plant *behaves* as if it can think is a miracle in itself.'

Life Between Land and Sea

Wherever land and sea meet—along a sandy beach, against a
rocky shore, across a mud-flat or at the edge of
a coral reef—a weird and wonderful array
of plants and animals
exists in a turbulent world that can
be breathtakingly beautiful and unyieldingly harsh

The Rockland

N. J. Berrill

Creatures and plants of the shoreline adapt
themselves in many ingenious ways
to the problems of their chosen environment

There was a time when the rocky shore must have been bare of all living things, a time when all life was still entirely confined to the water. The surf broke along the rocks and left them clean.

There is a rigid order of development of the shore—the plant invaders come first, looking for sunlit positions; when they have established their foothold, the second wave—animals—comes up the rocks, seeking food and shelter.

Seaweeds are plants of the sea edge where the rocks of the shoreline dip down into the sea, and those seaweeds exposed to the air between tides have migrated there from only as far away as those rocks that are permanently submerged. The low-tide mark is the dividing line—above the mark, the higher they go the more welcome sunlight the seaweeds get, but the greater danger there is of drying out from exposure to air or buffeting from wind and surf. Below the low-tide mark lies the greater protection of calmer water; however, the deeper seaweeds go, the weaker the light becomes, so that growth is increasingly difficult.

Below water are the red seaweeds, some of which look brown. These are the 'shade' weeds, and Irish Moss is one of them. There are also brown seaweeds such as the great kelps which form forests of the sea. All these weeds merely cling to the rocks, and what seem to be the roots are just holdfasts, for all the plants' requirements are taken direct from the water and not up through roots as with land plants. True seaweeds grow from the tips, not from the base. Each year the tattered fronds of the previous year's growth are thrown off and replaced by new growth from below.

Above the line the seaweed colonisation occurs in distinct bands, each kind thriving best at its own combination of exposure to light and heat and duration out of water. In general these shore weeds, most of them brown (though they frequently appear to be more olive-green or yellow), are inclined to be leathery and tough, and to resist evaporation; they are divided into narrow fronds capable of resisting the action of the waves.

At the highest level is the Channelled Wrack, with short, many-branched fronds curling along the

*Kelp, such as these beached Pacific varieties, grows
in a thick, tangled mass in low-tide zones.
Fish swim through the dense jungle of stalks; sea
otters float on the surface; and mussels anchor
themselves to the 'roots' at the base of the plants.*

116

A mole crab emerges from hiding, its long feeding antennae bent as they strain plankton from receding waves. Behind the shorter, breathing antennae are two jointed eyestalks which the crab uses to reconnoitre while still buried safely in the sand.

edge to enclose a channel. This is the most adventurous of them all, for it may be out of water for four-fifths of its life and may lose two-thirds of its water each time the tide goes down, to regain it when the sea returns.

Further down, the Flat Wrack is exposed for two-thirds to three-quarters of its life. Then comes the broad middle region of the shore, where the Bladder Wrack and the Knotted Wrack take over. Both have bladders filled with gas that buoy them up when the tide is in so that the whole region takes on the appearance of a small-scale submarine jungle. The two are not often found together—the Bladder Wrack can stand a lot of wave action, while the Knotted Wrack is a plant of sheltered waters.

Near the edge of low water, the Toothed Wrack finds its place, giving way to the short carpet of Irish Moss, which extends across the low-water line and several feet below.

A jungle, whether on land or under the sea, is more than trees and undergrowth. It is food for the animal world and shelter from its enemies, living and meteorological. As the tide leaves the rockland, the weeds hang like curtains, fold upon fold, and behind them lie crabs and starfish, awaiting the sea's return. Without this shelter, the drying air and sun would kill them, even if the gulls who walk the weeds watching for tell-tale movement did not get them first. Some sea animals—such as limpets and periwinkles—have come ashore to pasture on the rich meadows of weed-covered rocks.

The limpets have shell armour that rises to a low peak and is well designed to divert the force of a breaking wave. Its so-called 'foot' is a suction muscle that can hold the shell so tightly against the rock surface that the driving water can find no leverage to lift the animal, and so merely presses it down on to the rock. When the tide goes down, the same equipment prevents the soft tissues from drying out, and the gills remain moist along the inner edge of the shell.

Generally, there is no sign of weed where the limpets rule; so what are they doing there? These molluscs browse on the sporelings and filmy growths that continually strive to establish themselves on the rocks; they scrape off these minute forms of plant life as fast as they settle.

Periwinkles have coiled shells, and their shape is too close to being spherical for them to hold on to exposed rocks entirely by their own exertions. So they specialise in living on and among the large tangles of seaweed and within crevices, browsing on the weeds and scraping off what they can.

The seaweeds offer more than protection and food—they provide habitats. Some animals have little motive other than to find a smooth, soft surface on which to settle, fasten and build. One of these, abundant along the lower levels of a weedy shore and some distance below the shoreline, is the small plume worm.

It lives in a spirally coiled tube of lime stuck by one side to the weed. Each worm extends its pair of plumed tentacles to collect food and oxygen, while a modified tentacle forms a plug that closes the tube like a cork when the worm withdraws. With the cork in place the worm can stay wet and healthy until the tide returns.

Some animals flourish on exposed rocks where, in the violent surf, no weed can find a footing. The blue mussel is one of the most adept at this, clinging to the rocks in hundreds of thousands. When the water retreats, the two shells press close together, fitting so well that the mollusc within is almost hermetically sealed.

With good footing and clear water, the mussel spends many hours each day carefully filtering the

The ghost crab is a model of natural camouflage and defence. When it stands still, its sandy colour makes it invisible against the beach; when fleeing from an enemy, it scuttles for cover at a speed of over 5 ft per second; when another ghost crab approaches its burrow, it makes a rubbing noise to warn the intruder off; and when it retires to its burrow, it can close the opening to remove all signs of its presence.

microscopic plant cells out of the water drawn over its gill curtains, in the same manner as other bivalves. A single mussel passes several pints of water through its gill chamber every hour.

When a mussel is pulled off its rock, it comes away with a breaking of a cluster of strong threads, collectively called the 'byssus'. The mussel produces them by causing a sticky fluid to run down a narrow groove in its foot; this fluid solidifies on exposure to the water or the air. It is a true plastic, and the threads are used for anchorage to the rock surface, spreading out like the guy ropes of a tent. If some break, new ones are quickly formed.

Young mussels change their position by climbing with the aid of these ropes. Threads are attached and the mussel hauls itself up. The foot fastens new ones where it could not reach before, and by a slow, laborious method, the animal reaches a place of safety and good feeding facilities.

When it comes to sitting on a rock and gaining the necessities of life from a rising tide, the barnacle does as well as the mussel in its own way and with its own equipment. Looked at out of water, a rock barnacle has a shell of lime shaped like a miniature volcano, with ramparts along the rim. In the centre where the crater should be are the two valves, held together so that water within cannot escape.

Submerged, the two valves open and a ghost-like hand protrudes and fans the water urgently. In a second it is gone, but a moment or two later the valves open again and once more the hand comes out, as if its owner were casting a net through the water in the blind hope of catching some microscopic edibles, dead or alive.

The barnacle is no mollusc but a crustacean, whose ancestors swam actively in the sea and did not cling stubbornly to rocks. Its eggs develop into Nauplius larvae, typical of most crustacea, and change into another form after a certain amount of growth. This form swims about the sea as its ancestors did, by means of six pairs of swimming appendages protected by a pair of shells. In time these larvae attach themselves by their front ends to the rocks, feeling for a suitable spot with their antennae and then secreting a cement that will anchor them there for the rest of their lives.

Gradually more and more lime is produced around the animal until it is safely imprisoned in its own fortress. Inside, the crustacean, fastened to the ground by the neck, lies on its back with its six pairs of feet pointed towards the roof. When the two central shells are opened, the feet extend through the opening and fan away, pulling in a 'handful' of water, with or without food, towards the mouth.

The barnacle, lying on its back and kicking food into its mouth, is doing its best to live like a mussel; but it is, nonetheless, crustacean. Mussels and barnacles are without much doubt the descendants of molluscs and crustacea which were much more active and had brains of a sort. Heads and their accessories evolved to enable animals to sense and control where they were going. If they go nowhere, there is nothing left for a head to do. Briefly, mussels and barnacles have lost their heads.

The barnacles have been followed ashore by the dog whelks, which are small and look rather like periwinkles. Like all whelks and winkles, they have the shield-like cover, on the back end of the crawling foot, with which they seal off the opening of the shell when the animal withdraws. Its long breathing siphon has come from the ancestral habit of ploughing through sand and mud in search of food while simultaneously needing clean water for the gill chamber.

Dog whelks have the standard whelk equipment for boring holes in bivalves, but have less need of it since mussels and barnacles are relatively defenceless. Old mussels are drilled in the usual whelk manner, but young ones are eaten by forcing the shells apart.

No boring is necessary for feeding on barnacles. The valves are easily forced apart, the mouth tube inserted and the tissues within soon digested. When a dog whelk has been feeding on mussels, its shell is a dark-brown or pinkish-purple colour; when it feeds on barnacles its shell is white.

As a rule, dog whelks feed on barnacles until the supply runs low and then switch to a diet of mussels. When they do, they apparently have to learn new ways, which takes time. But it is significant that a dog whelk with its infinitesimal brain can accomplish something recognisable as adaptive learning. When you find a black dog-whelk shell with white bands running through it, you will know it is a mussel-eater that had to turn to barnacles once in a while and had some difficulty learning how to do it.

Through a Skin-Diver's Mask

Virginia Bennett Moore

Beneath the blue waters of
the tropical sea lies a magical world
of colour and excitement

Nothing in the world can really prepare you for what lies beneath the tropical sea. The moment my skin-diver's mask first broke through that cerulean surface in the West Indies, I was Columbus finding a continent—a new world of clear blue water, white sand and painted coral. As if the seascape were not enough, along came a paletteful of bright fish—silent, self-possessed, lively and even a little curious about the great finned Cyclops that swam among them.

I had seen fish before, but never like this. They were pattern, movement and colour. They staged their pageant in a bath of living blue, itself a stunning visual experience. It was a whole family of colours: cobalt, azure, ultra-marine, peacock, brilliant turquoise, sapphire and lapis lazuli.

As I eased into the water and lowered my faceplate that first day in the U.S. Virgin Islands National Park at St John, things began to happen in a series of images. There was the sand, a pale silken carpet. Lacy towers of coloured stone: the coral. Bare trees, outstretched: more coral.

Suddenly a welcoming committee of fish trailing angel robes appeared. Snowy 8 in. discs edged in black, they kept their calm gaze on me—alert, poised, darkly serene of eye. What were they? Palometas, or long-finned pompanos, explained a park ranger.

Reassured by the palometas, I kicked along. My mask was a window that framed the underwater world, while my body rested comfortably, half sunk into the lovely liquid cushion that was the sea. Suddenly something moved at the top of the window. Looking up, I thought someone had spread a coat of quicksilver on the surface, now seen from below as wrinkled and bubbled by the caprices of each crossing wave. Hung just this side of the pulsating silver surface like ornaments on the ceiling were half a dozen unmoving shapes watching me intently. They were thin 2 ft torpedoes of transparent green, with alligator jaws, and fins set so far to the rear that it looked as if the fish had tried to swim out of them. Barracuda? Needlefish, said the ranger.

What were those tracks on the sea-bed? To my surprise the small cowrie, on the beach a pretty shell, had become a living creature. Creeping under its shiny tan globe, it had cut a distinct furrow. Over here, the sand looked as if a pincushion had been rolled along it: that bunch of knitting needles, the spiny sea urchin, had come this way, stiffly using its bottom-most spikes as legs. Its long spines break off in your flesh if you knock against them and, since sea urchins cling to coral everywhere in the shallows, they are a constant reminder that you are touring an alien world and owe its inhabitants the courtesy of restraint.

Down there by a sponge called 'dead-man's-fingers' was a still shape—a foot-long 'Tiparillo', with a cigar-holder snout and fins at the tail like the feathers on an arrow: the trumpet fish. Only its bright, round eyes were moving: it seemed touchingly eager to pass for a frond. As I held my breath and swam down for a closer look, two shadows on the sand were suddenly fired with life. One was a smooth purple ray, about 2 ft across its diamond-shaped back; the other was a large flounder. The ray flew smoothly to the safety of deeper water. The flounder shot in the opposite direction; it had lain sprinkled with sand to deceive passing fish.

Just then the big reef came into full view. It was a castellated and battlemented undersea island, full of lively grottoes and tangled forests; it made one think of a pageant, a carnival, a busy medieval town. Here kings and queens, nobles, soldiers, pages, children and clowns all paraded in incredible finery.

Among the first fish I saw were damselfish, a family of square-cut little town-dwellers with diminutive faces. As with many reef fish, their sides are as flat as a pumpkin seed. A platoon of sergeant majors swam by, clad in white uniforms topped with vivid yellow, with smart black bars down their sides. A solitary beau gregory looked as if it had been dipped into two different pots of dye—its bottom half golden yellow, its top royal blue. A jewel fish was dotted every $\frac{1}{4}$ in. with single blue dots, like sapphires on a black velvet cloak.

Then there were parrot fish. Thick-bodied, thick-tailed, stodgy in demeanour, these otherwise dignified citizens come in red or blue, multiple tones of green, spotted, striped or streaked, with their tails and fins in yet another colour. The island name of one species, the black knight, evokes an image, but one still less splendid than the fish—a deep, stained-glass blue, with black streakings along the forehead and nape. Another wears black chain mail on a white ground and has a blood-red belly. Anyone who designed his own parrot fish might well see the matching reality swim by.

As I watched, enthralled, I was able to see that fish have personalities and even temperaments. Damselfish are among the most pugnacious landowners on the reef. A 4 in. fish will not hesitate to chase one four times its length. A 3 in. beau gregory tried to rout a 6 ft man by butting his faceplate. A blue parrot fish took a personal dislike to a particular black and white one and flashed to the attack every time it appeared.

Each day brought something new to look at. The sea, where life itself began, is still the mother of more kinds of living things than any other place on earth. Though the tropical Indo-Pacific is blessed with the greatest variety of fish, the Caribbean comes a close second. One incomplete count lists 340 species in the waters around Puerto Rico and the Virgin Islands.

Many species have colourful habits. Filefish, 18 in. long and wafer-thin, as if cut from sheet metal, feed standing on their heads. Wrasses often bury themselves in the sand at night to sleep. Many kinds of parrot fish sleep surrounded with a mucous

*Swimming above a Florida reef, a skin-diver surveys
this forest of brain and elkhorn coral—species
that can withstand the wave action in coastal shallows.
More delicate corals require deeper, calmer waters.*

balloon that may take them half an hour to blow up at night and another half hour to get out of in the morning. Some fish chatter, while others make so much noise grinding their teeth or strumming their swim bladders with special muscles that they play a symphony on ship's sonars.

Each fish is designed in some way for its environment and life. The translucent green needlefish is invisibly hung against a green surface; the white palometa might look like shimmering coral to a predator from the deep. The outline of the spadefish —a spectacular white disc with black bars—could fade against waving fronds and sea fans as a zebra's image would be broken on the hot plain. The Nassau grouper has eight different changes of dress to deceive the shark and its own victims.

Fish do not always use colour for camouflage. Some use it to express their feelings. A surgeonfish, chasing an irritating companion, was seen to turn pale with wrath on the front half and very dark on the rear. Fish may also blanch with fear. I watched a yellow fish covered with black polka dots swim into a clump of coral and, startled, come out clad in a blackish hood, his belly blanched light cream.

Sometimes the waters of the reef are filled with schools of tiny visitors. They are the fry, the plentiful young of fish of every description, almost too small and numerous to have a name. At times you can pass

around me like snowflakes on the wind. Then I saw two mackerel about 18 in. long. They were swimming up and down, holding the fry at bay or driving them back and forth with a gesture while waiting to take the first bite at their leisure—perhaps when I had gone. For the school, though too large to be entirely consumed, can never entirely escape.

Not all little things in the sea feel hunted. One day, not far from shore, I acquired a small school of white fish each the size and shape of a two-shilling piece, with yellow borders, a sharp yellow fin jutting out of their backs and almost no tail—probably baby yellowjacks. They were cheerfully swimming their hardest to keep up with me, dipping as I dived, rising and turning as I did, their little bodies shimmering with exertion. When I rested they peered in through my faceplate, as bold as brass, with big black button eyes. When I put my hand under one, it did not mind. When at last I climbed out of the water, it was with regret that I saw them run, hesitate, scan the sea, gather themselves and swim away. Theirs is a world that, having seen, I can never forget.

Shells of the Seven Seas

Donald and Louise Peattie

Wherever there is water—but especially
in the oceans—Nature has lavished some of her
most careful artistry on shells

With every tide the seas cast up on the beaches new treasure for those who come seeking it. Shell-collecting is now a world-wide hobby. Prized by man since prehistoric times, there are some 100,000 species to be found, not only in the seas but in ponds, rivers and meadows.

Their variety, in shape, tint and size, is dazzling. A shell may look like a petal frozen in stone; or like an ear, an egg, a screw, a butterfly, a turban, a lion's paw or a comb. Every one once housed a living creature—a mollusc, to which clan belong the succulent oyster and the garden snail.

The molluscs, one of Nature's oldest, and most successful experiments in animal structure, are

among them until they fill your vision—a gleaming mist of life whose droplets are sorted by sizes. They are pale, quick, hunted—and forever on the move.

Any day, but especially on days when storms kick up the water until it begins to look like milk, you may also share the water with great patrols—schools of amberjack, cavallas and Spanish mackerel. They swim in an easy blue-white glory, full of muscle, moving in unison, casting a wary eye on everything. These fish are predators. Unlike the calm, almost trusting reef-dwellers, when they see you they prefer to be gone. But on these murky days the dim visibility brings them closer.

One day, as I dipped into St John's Caneel Bay, I found myself among fry fleeing some unseen terror. Oblivious to my threatening bulk, they flittered all

Cast-up shells of clams, mussels, scallops, sea snails and sand dollars carpet the shore of Padre Island off the Texas coast. Other beaches on the island are composed entirely of lighter, smaller shells that have been pulverised by the surf.

spineless. But whereas the *internal* skeleton of an animal with a backbone usually appears unsightly when at last exposed, these *external* skeletons—the shells—keep their colour and lustre after death, each a monument to the passing beauty of life.

Just as our fingernails are products of our flesh, the shell is a limestone-like deposit of the animal living inside, secreted by the mollusc's mantle, the ruff-like fold you see on a snail as it 'comes out of its house'. The glands of the mantle regulate the rate of growth, the form and colour and pattern of the shell.

The outermost layer of a shell is a horny skin. The middle layer is the thickest—so thick in some of the giant clams of Zamboanga in the Philippines that each clam may weigh 100 lb. or more. The innermost layer is thin and has a porcelain sheen. This heart of the shell may gleam with a pearly lustre, glow with a delicate pink or shimmer with peacock greens and blues, as in the pearl mussel from the mountain streams of Scotland and Wales. From this layer comes the mother-of-pearl used in buttons, jewellery or inlay. Here the true pearl is formed when some irritating substance gets into the shell and is sealed off by the animal.

At a glance you can usually classify a shell as one-valve or two-valve. Bivalves, such as oysters, clams, mussels and scallops, consist of two halves connected by a hinge of ligament. The univalves tend to form a continuous spiral; these are the sea and land snails.

The spiral may be drawn out into a spindle in the distaff shells, flattened in the cone shells, hidden within the cowries—yet it is always present. Nowhere is this spiral more lovely than in the chambered nautilus, where it grows into a flawless logarithmic curve in which the width of the turns increases at a fixed ratio to their length.

The mollusc is not a simple or unfeeling creature. Within its armour the soft body has a heart, a stomach of sorts, a liver and kidneys. Sea molluscs breathe through gills, and if they live deep in the mud they send up a long siphon to reach clean water. Molluscs often have delicate senses. Some have compound eyes, like those of an insect; they may have a keener sense of smell than ours. The sense of touch, as with us, is distributed all over the flesh but is especially strong in the soft mouth parts, the folds of the mantle, and in the 'foot'.

This foot is the basic part of the snail that you are able to see when it is well extended from the shell. Using the muscles of the foot, the snail undulates along. Scallops, by opening and shutting their bivalves in rapid succession, bite their way forward, discharging water behind them through their siphons in a sort of jet propulsion.

Without dissecting these living creatures, you will not know 'the he-shell from the she-shell'. Yet molluscs have a sex life, and it is easiest to understand its oddities if we think of flowers—for flowers, too, are commonly male and female at the same time. Some flowers are wind-pollinated in chancy, extravagant fertility; others are economically self-fertilised. Again, flowers may be at one stage all male, or all female, or double-sexed. Molluscs may use any of these arrangements. Thus oysters never meet their mates, and many a snail is two-sexed.

The small fry get all varieties of maternal care or neglect, from being set adrift in the water, helpless as frogs' eggs, to being carried in a pouch, kangaroo-fashion. Some come neatly packaged in egg cases, from which they may emerge either complete, as tiny replicas of their parents, or in a free-swimming larval stage, like tadpoles.

Shells have had value since our earliest knowledge of humanity. As a medium of exchange, even in prehistoric times, they travelled far across the world. In the graves of Cro-Magnon man, who lived some 10,000 to 37,000 years ago in western Europe, have been found red helmet shells native to the tropic seas of the Orient.

Certain shells are so beautiful and rare that they are used like jewels for adornment; thus the golden cowrie of the Fiji Islands is worn only by the chieftains. Other shells are so coarse and common that we crush them up to surface roads or make mortar. On one little shell was built the wealth of the ancient city of Tyre, in Phoenicia. For the snail that lives within it exudes a fluid from which the Tyrians produced a dye ranging from rose to deep violet. So prized was this dye that it created a mighty commerce, and became a mark of distinction. Only senators of Rome were permitted to wear togas with this purple border.

The western Pacific is the richest of all sources of shell treasure, from southern Japan to Australia's Great Barrier Reef, from the Marquesas to the Malay Peninsula. In a fine collection there will be shells from the Caribbean, from Iceland, the Red Sea, Panama, Tasmania and the Indian Ocean.

The richest shelling ground in Britain is at the north end of the isle of Herm in the Channel Islands, where the beach is made up of more than 200 varieties of tiny, perfect shells. Because of its position, Herm exactly 'splits' the tidal stream, and the light shells are brought ashore in the slack water of the divide. There you may gather red spires and latticed spires, horn shells and pyramid shells and the larger, rare sea-ear, a lovely shell found only in the Channel Islands.

As daily you grow richer in your finds and your knowledge, no one is the poorer for it. The tides, indeed, have always more to give; and in this interest, shared by countless numbers throughout the world, you enter a happy fraternity. You come to understand that any shell, having held life, holds wonder—as a child knows, hearing against his ear that whisper like the sound of far-off surf.

The chambered nautilus uses its pearly shell (shown in cross-section) to alter its level in the water. Through a tube connected to its body, the nautilus fills the shell's chambers with gases so that it will rise in the water, and reabsorbs the gases to sink.

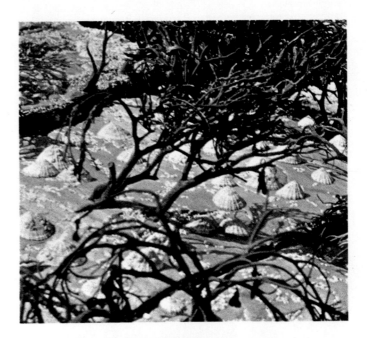

Limpets exposed by the receding tide on a Cornish beach. Their conical shells are perfectly adapted to life on the seashore, offering the minimum resistance to waves and the maximum suction area for clinging to rocks.

A TREASURY OF SHELLS

The jewel-like shells on these pages were gathered from the waters of the Pacific and the Caribbean, and from the seas around Australia and the Philippines. Despite their brilliant colours and subtle patterns, their porcelain-smooth finishes and—in many cases—the perfect geometry of their architecture, the function of the shells is both simple and homely: to protect the fleshy molluscs that spend their lives in them.

More and more people are becoming fascinated by the appeal of shells, and many amateur collectors hunt the beaches for them. But among some peoples —in the Fiji and Solomon Islands, and in New Guinea—shells have been prized from the earliest times, as a form of currency and as badges of rank. The most popular of the shells distinguished in this way are cowries, and a string of yellow money cowries (centre, this page) will still buy food, land or a wife in New Guinea. Western collectors, who will pay many pounds for a rare shell, are thus sharing a very ancient tradition when they delight in and value these jewels of the sea.

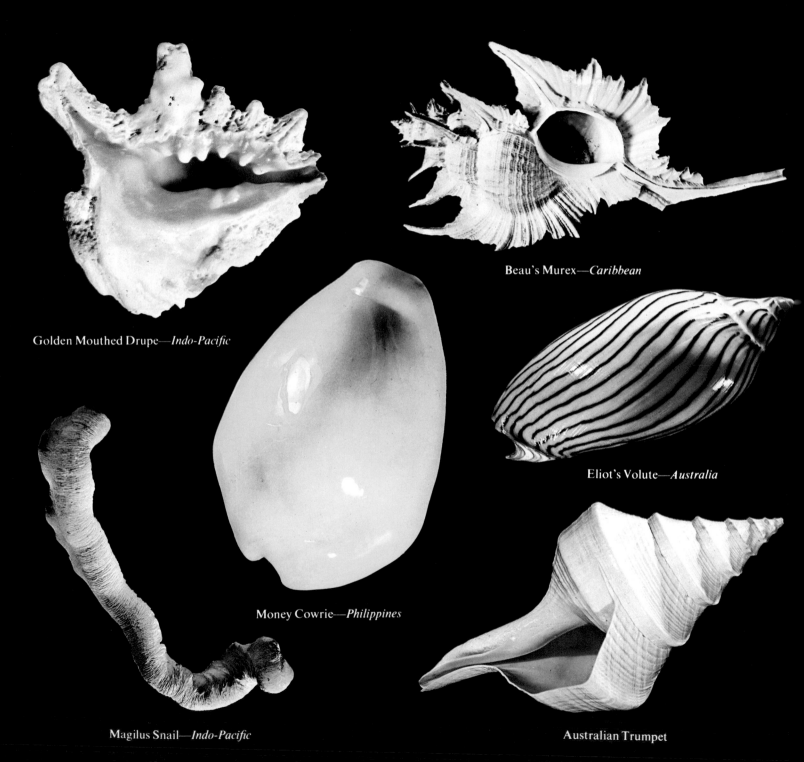

Golden Mouthed Drupe—*Indo-Pacific*

Beau's Murex—*Caribbean*

Eliot's Volute—*Australia*

Magilus Snail—*Indo-Pacific*

Money Cowrie—*Philippines*

Australian Trumpet

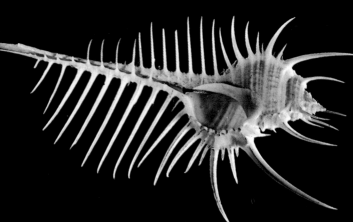

Venus Comb—*Philippines*

Perspective Sundial—*Australia*

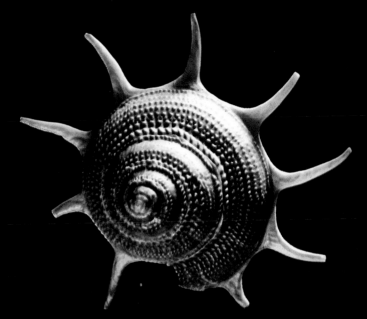

Triumphant Star—*Indo-Pacific*

Pontifical Mitre—*Indo-Pacific*

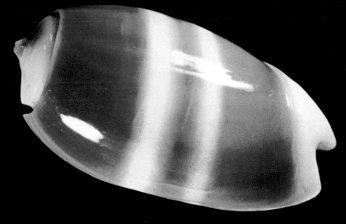

Carnelian Olive—*Philippines*

Australian Coral Snail

Spindle Shell—*Philippines*

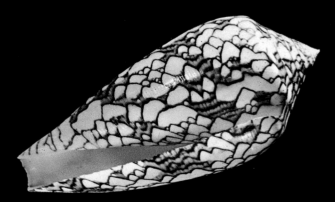

Textile Cone—*Australia*

Denizens of the Deep

Seals cavorting with obvious zest, men-of-war sailing before
the wind, sharks shaped like submarines—these are
a few of the innumerable creatures that
make their homes in the sea.
From the restless, wind-lashed surface to the
eternally black abyssal plains, the sea abounds with life

The Barber's Shop
of the Reef

Irenaus Eibl-Eibesfeldt

In the tropical seas
predatory fish suspend their hunting
instincts and submit to
the attention of busy 'cleaners'

I was sitting on an underwater coral block in the Caribbean, watching the brightly coloured fish, when an old grouper came swimming by. It moved slowly towards a coral growth, steering with the breast fins, and took up position above it. Then it slowly opened its terrifying mouth and, in a trice, small fish came swimming up. I could scarcely believe my eyes: some began to pick at the body surface of the huge predator, while others disappeared into its mouth and under the raised gill-covers. To my great astonishment, they came out again unharmed. When the grouper had had enough, it closed its mouth with a jerk—but not completely—and opened it wide again immediately. At this signal the 'cleaners' left the mouth of the grouper, which then shook itself a few times. When this happened the fish that had been picking over its body surface returned to their homes in the corals.

I observed this remarkable procedure again and again during the following months and eventually realised that the small fish were freeing the large grouper of parasites. They also ate pieces of dead tissue and thus cleaned the wounds. Various species of fish in the Caribbean belonged to this guild of cleaners: gobies, wrasse and damselfish. The many 'hosts' which appeared came from very different families: parrotfish as well as groupers, and the decorative butterflyfish.

When I went to the Maldive Islands in the Indian Ocean, I was anxious to know whether I would meet my old friends the cleaner-fish once again; it was on my second dive that I discovered them. They were blue cleaner-wrasse with a black longitudinal stripe. When I first saw them a pair were cleaning a sweetlips, which behaved exactly as the grouper in the Caribbean had: as a cleaner nudged it in the corner of the mouth, it opened its jaws and raised one gill-cover; when it had had enough, it requested its guest to leave by closing its mouth and shaking its body. I had discovered a barber's shop on the reef. The sweetlips were positively queuing up to be cleaned and a group waited to join the queue as one after another they were given a careful cleaning.

I now visited this place daily. The cleaners were always at work here. The sweetlips were regular customers but many others came too, even grey mullet from the open water. They came in shoals and took up position, waiting with heads hanging slightly down and gill-covers raised. The parrotfish,

This 2 ft-long squirrel fish, photographed in Cook's Bay, Morea Island, Tahiti, is having its skin cleaned of parasites and other nuisances by the 4 in.-long cleaner-wrasse, Labroides bicolor, *near its gill-cover. Other fish recognise the wrasse by its distinctive patterning and characteristic movements.*

by contrast, usually positioned themselves with their heads inclined slightly upwards. Each fish had its peculiarities. Some changed colour when being cleaned. The dark unicornfish became pale blue; the advantage was that the parasites then stood out more conspicuously from the skin.

The cleaner-wrasse showed some peculiarities which I had not observed in the Caribbean. For instance, it was much more agile and active. When inviting a large fish to be cleaned, the cleaner would dance up and down in front of its host with striking tumbling movements. One of the cleaners also repeatedly invited me to be cleaned, but as I could scarcely open my mouth under water, nothing came of it. In the invitation dance the cleaner spread its tail fin and see-sawed up and down with the hind end of its body. It seemed to me that when the cleaner approached the smaller fish or the sweetlips, with which it was familiar, it hardly performed a dance at all; on the other hand, it danced very actively in front of guests with which it was unfamiliar, such as the human diver. If it calmed down, one could immediately stimulate an intensive dance by frightening it. The dance evidently represented a conflict between the impulse to swim forwards and the impulse to dive down into the protecting coral.

When searching the surface area of a host, the cleaner flicked the host's body with its pelvic fins. In this way it indicated where it was working at that moment and the host righted itself accordingly, holding its fins in the appropriate position or raising its gill-covers. If the cleaner came to a folded fin, it nudged this with its mouth and the host then raised it; there was an excellent understanding between them. The cleaner-fish paid attention to every irregularity of the body surface. It would try to clean away every pale spot and every small wart, and in so doing it sometimes made a mistake. At one time we had a pufferfish in an aquarium; Nature has provided this fish with beautiful white spots, but the cleaners rushed towards the handsome object from all sides and did everything possible to pick away the spots. The tormented pufferfish finally hung gasping at the surface and tried to jump out of the tank. It was so desperate that it would even have crawled out on to the land if it could have done so. On another occasion we put in the tank a porcupinefish which had small pieces of tissue growing on its spines. The cleaners were once again deceived until they had been stung a few times.

In captivity, a personal friendship sometimes developed between cleaner and cleaned. We had a butterflyfish which had become accustomed to being cleaned by a medium-sized cleaner-fish. When, as an experiment, we added a somewhat larger cleaner, which chased the smaller one, the butterflyfish no longer allowed itself to be cleaned. We were obliged to remove the new cleaner before the butterflyfish allowed itself to be cleaned again.

I have often asked myself why it is that the large predator does not eat the small cleaner when it makes its first attempts at approaching the host. In many predatory fish, flight immediately triggers off the prey-catching reflex; the cleaner does not flee. We once saw a cleaner, which had just been released in the aquarium, take fright and flee, passing a snapper which, in fact, snapped it up. Another point is that when the cleaner-fish dances in front of the predator, the latter is apparently inhibited from eating it. But how does the predator recognise it?

I suspected that the striking uniform and the dance of the Indian Ocean cleaners were recognition signals. This was eventually confirmed in a very remarkable way. I had occasionally noticed that a host fish which was waiting to be cleaned would jerk back when the small fish touched it, and then flee rapidly; in such cases, the cleaner also behaved somewhat differently. It certainly did the correct see-saw dance, but then rushed rather strenuously at its host and appeared to bite it. For a long time I could not explain this; I thought it must be a degenerate cleaner, until one day I caught one of them. Then for the first time I saw that I had not got a cleaner-fish but a sabre-toothed blenny in my hand. It looked surprisingly like the cleaner-wrasse: it had a dark longitudinal stripe, and was also coloured blue; but I soon recognised from its teeth that I had caught a relative of the sabre-toothed blenny which I had observed in the Galapagos Islands. There, the blenny had attacked other fish and punched pieces out of their skin and fins with its sharp teeth. The sabre-toothed blenny which I had now caught behaved in exactly the same way, except that it mimicked a cleaner in order to deceive its prey.

Mimicry was not confined to appearance: the cleaner's dancing behaviour was also imitated by the mimic, and the host fish themselves were deceived by the similarity. Inexperienced hosts allow themselves to be bitten repeatedly before they notice the deception. As the mimics are far less abundant than the true cleaners, it is not easy for the host fish to gain experience of them.

The cleaner-fish try to drive away the mimic if it enters their territory. It is still not clear whether in doing so they distinguish it from members of their own species, because they chase off strange members of their own species in the same way. No other fish defends territory in the cleaning area and the barber's shops are common ground to some extent; fish which normally fight viciously can meet here quite peaceably.

There must be considerable competitive pressure for a species of fish to occupy permanently a role so unusual as that of cleaner-mimic. The mimic evidently adapts itself very quickly to any change in the fish on which it models itself. There are several races of cleaner-fish. Those in the Maldive Islands have a dark longitudinal stripe at the base of the breast fins; this detail is also present in the mimic. In places where the stripe is lacking in the cleaner, it is also absent from the mimic. The cleaner-fish of the Tuomotu Islands in the Pacific has an orange-red spot in the centre of the body, a characteristic

Moray eels are the most ferocious of the coral reef's creatures, but even they allow themselves to be cleaned by the tiny cleaner-fish. The eel in this photograph is characteristically lurking, half-hidden beneath a growth of coral, and will make a sudden attack on any living thing that comes by. Meanwhile, it is having its head cleaned by a juvenile wrasse.

Masquerading as cleaner-wrasse, these blennies tear pieces of skin from the fins of bigger fish who come hoping to be relieved of their parasites. Adult fish can usually distinguish these impostors from genuine cleaners, whose colour and movement are mimicked so closely, but young fish are more easily deceived.

which is also possessed by the mimic in this area. Evidently the mimic must always be very similar to its model, so that the host fish cannot distinguish between them.

It is interesting to speculate about the further development of this mimicry. One possibility is that the mimic will gradually slide into the permanent role of a cleaner; in this way it could perhaps attain greater numbers. I noticed, in fact, that the mimic frequently directed its attack against larger parasites which it definitely removed from the fish's skin; with its sharp teeth, it could reach those parasites which were inaccessible to the cleaner. In the barber's shop of the reef, some very stimulating problems still await further investigation.

131

COLOURFUL CREATURES OF THE CORAL REEF

In the underwater fairyland of the coral reef live fish and other sea animals whose colours are even more vivid than those of the coral itself. The layman, struck by the beauty of these animals, is usually content to admire them. The scientist, aware that Nature has a purpose for almost everything, wants to know what these colours are for. 'The loud colours of coral fish,' writes the naturalist Konrad Lorenz in his book *On Aggression*, 'call loudly for explanation.' Observing several kinds of 'poster-coloured' coral fish, Lorenz noticed that most of them establish territories which they defend vigorously against other members of their own species. His conclusion is that the coral fish have evolved these sharply contrasting patterns to warn or frighten potential intruders away from their territories. Most of the less brightly coloured coral fish do not establish territories and are not hostile to their own kind. When two poster-coloured fish of the same species meet, there is almost always a fight, the result of which is that the intruder is either driven off or killed. In only two circumstances do these fish strike their colours: some fish become so angry at the sight of another fish carrying the same pattern that the two sexes must fade to a duller shade in order to approach each other and spawn. Some of them change their patterns before sleeping, assuming a different 'night dress'.

Turquoise-striped and shaped like a torpedo, a 3 in. blenny lurks among the coral, ready to dart out and attack its prey—other fish. Blennies are able to leave the water and crawl from pool to pool on their ventral fins.

The clown fish has no need for camouflage, since it gets both protection and food from the sea anemone it lives with. Immune to the poisonous tentacles, the fish takes food from the corners of the anemone's mouth.

The blue hamlet, a member of the grouper family, stands out vividly against the subdued pastels of the coral.

The feather star catches plankton with its delicate silver-grey pinnules as it swims freely among the coral.

133

The brilliant banding on the clown angelfish makes it one of the most conspicuous of tropical fish. Its blue stripes are more iridescent than the yellow parts of its body and are outlined distinctively in black. Angelfish, with their majestic and stately movements, are a constant source of delight to skin-divers.

Bright markings on the blue-spotted stingray contrast with its dull body, enhancing its menacing appearance.

The red bigeye is a carnivorous, largely nocturnal fish which in the day hides among the coral.

The beautiful but deadly lion-fish has red and white striped dorsal spines containing a venom which is potent enough to kill a man who steps on them. The poison glands are situated at the base of these spines. The spotted pectoral fins with their curving white spines are shaped like exotic fans.

The harlequin tusk wrasse with its gaudy blue and orange vertical stripes hunts alone among the coral reefs.

The Squid—
Nature's Nightmare

Ronald N. Rood

The squid is one of Nature's masterpieces—an eight-armed predator with an astonishing life story

They have reached out and torn sailors from life rafts. They have reduced a huge tuna to head and bones before the hooked fish could be landed. Yet most people who know anything about the squid—one of the sea's most bizarre creatures—assume it is some sort of octopus, because it has snaky arms and tentacles at the end of a bullet-shaped body. This is like comparing a tiger with an alley cat.

A 50 lb. octopus with a 10 ft arm spread is a giant; the biggest squid weigh more than 1500 lb. Octopuses retreat singly into scattered holes on the ocean bottom; though one may occasionally maul a diver who surprises it in its den, most leave the scene when man appears. Some squid, on the other hand, may attack anything—even anchors, boat hooks or the hull of a ship. They work in ravenous mobs in open water. An attack by one may be the signal for a frenzied rush by others.

Like the octopus, the squid has eight arms with rows of suckers—but with the added touch of tooth-like horny rings around the edge of each sucker; and there are two more arms, called tentacles, which probably have no equal in all Nature. Like long rubber cables, they can stretch far beyond the reach of the other arms or snap back until they are nearly hidden. Armed at the tip with suckers, the tentacles shoot out towards a victim, clamp fast and pull the prey back into the squid's writhing nest of arms with the parrot-like beak in the centre.

Unlike the baggy octopus, most squid are long and thin, with two horizontal fins at one end. They travel by jet propulsion. Taking in water by opening the muscular mantle that surrounds its body like a loose overcoat, the squid squirts it out through a powerful siphon near the head. This shoots the squid backwards, slender rear section first. Rocketing through the water, it can overtake nearly anything that swims. By reversing the flexible siphon, it shuttles back and forth through a school of fish. The two tentacles whip out like living lassos,

catching fish after fish—killing far beyond its needs.

When I saw my first living squid in an aquarium, I had the uncanny feeling that I was being watched. The eyes are intelligent, alert, arrestingly human. Each eye has a movable lens to focus on objects at any distance, a refinement that is possessed by no other invertebrates outside the class. It has an iris and a pupil, just as the human eye has.

This would not be so surprising if the squid were close to us on the family tree of evolution. But squid are molluscs, with a history that stretches back 400 million years, far beyond that of man. As the ages passed, their ancestors—some with dozens of arms—developed shells like ice-cream cones, sometimes 12 ft long. Later types had coiled shells, like a ram's horn. Today they have no outer shells but are built around a cartilaginous internal rod called the 'pen'. It is the internal support of the cuttlefish—a member of the same class as the squid, and closely resembling it—which provides the cuttlebone that is often given to budgerigars.

The numbers of squid are fantastic. Ships sometimes get false bottom readings from echo sounders owing, some scientists say, to millions of squid suspended halfway to the bottom, feeding on plankton. Sometimes this layer is found on the surface. One ship sailed for two hours through a solid sea of squid stretching to the horizon in all directions.

The squid is a living kaleidoscope. Rob it of its prey, and it flashes an angry red. Frighten it, and it turns a pale, watery colour. It can be mottled like the sand or rippled like the surface. It has thousands of tiny colour cells, opening and closing like drawstring bags. One instant they are open, showing their coloured lining; a fifth of a second later they close. Deep-water squid may have hundreds of light-producing areas, sparkling like fireflies.

If camouflage does not work against a predatory enemy, the squid has an emergency measure—it shoots out a blob of black, gooey 'ink' through the siphon to form a smoke-screen. Squid from the depths even have luminous ink to make a flare in the water while the darkened owner sneaks away.

Only rarely does a really giant squid come up from the depths to be seen by man. An occasional specimen is vomited up by a dying sperm whale; and fishermen sometimes see an injured one floating on the surface.

Squid come in many sizes and have a wide array of adaptations. This squid is shown about 6 times its life size. The luminescent organs around its eyes and tentacles are probably lures for attracting plankton.

On March 25, 1941, the troopship *Britannia* was sunk in mid-Atlantic. A dozen men clung to a tiny raft. Only one or two could sit on it at a time, while the rest waited their turn in the water. Suddenly one of them cried out. Horrified, the others saw a great squid throw a tentacle around his body. Then the other tentacle clamped fast. Before their eyes, the unspeakable creature broke the sailor's hold on the raft and pulled him to his death.

Soon afterwards, another man felt a tentacle grasp his leg. For some reason, it let go again. But where the suckers had fastened, they left raw, bleeding sores. The scars, like the prints of bottle caps, were still visible two years later.

On October 26, 1873, near Portugal Cove, Newfoundland, two men and a boy were out fishing when they spotted a floating mass in the water. It hung limply, like a piece of wreckage. But, prodded with a gaff, it came to life, reared up and lunged at their boat. Its arms spread out, exposing a beak in the centre twice as big as a man's head.

It slipped one tentacle across the gunwale like a python, pulling the little craft towards that hideous mouth. It gouged at the planking, staring at the men with dinner-plate eyes. Then it threw an arm over the boat to secure its hold and sank beneath the water. Spellbound, the men watched their boat tip until water rushed in over the side.

Twelve-year-old Tom Piccot saved them all. He grabbed a hatchet and began to chop at the grisly creature. Not until he had hacked it free did it drop away. Then it lay alongside the boat and glared at them, its great cylindrical body pulsating and throwing out clouds of ink.

They raced for the shore. Their countrymen would not believe their tale until they showed the evidence —a 19 ft tentacle like a heavy rope, lying in the bottom of their boat. Beside it was another chunk, as big as a man's arm.

The longest squid actually measured was 57 ft, found on a New Zealand beach in 1888. No one knows how large squid may grow. Several authorities think they may reach 70 ft, including 50 ft tentacles. Such a creature would weigh well over a ton. There is an interesting point for further speculation, too. The suckers of a 50 ft squid leave circular rings on the skin of the sperm whale about 4 in. across. Yet whales have been found with round scars 18 in. across—more than four times greater than scars made by the largest squid known.

Compared with such giants, most squid are tiny— less than 8 in. long. These constitute one of the most important food items in the ocean. Schools of fish cut great swaths through their millions. (It is this fact, plus their own cannibalism, which keeps them from overrunning the ocean completely.) Porpoises and killer whales often gorge on them. Man has long enjoyed them, too—consuming about a million tons a year.

The mating procedure of the squid, which varies with the species, is extraordinary. Sometimes the male 'courts' the female, or fights with other males for her favour. At other times he merely seizes her abruptly in a many-armed embrace. Then, since he is a cannibal, he may forget himself. Many a squid romance ends as abruptly as it starts—with a squid dinner.

The sex organs of both male and female are hidden deep within the cavity of the mantle. The male squid's sperm are wrapped in small packets called spermatophores. With one of his arms he reaches into his mantle cavity, takes a few packets from the genital organ and places them in the mantle cavity of the female. The wrapping unravels, releasing the sperm. Later, as the eggs pass through the female on their way to the outside, they are fertilised by the waiting sperm.

The female gently blows the fertilised eggs out through the siphon and catches them in her arms. The eggs—from a few hundred to 30,000, depending on the species—are about the size of cooked tapioca. She presses them against underwater objects in foot-long, sticky strings, then swims away. The babies hatch in about a month. They are fierce little beauties with rainbow colours, looking like exquisite rice-grain editions of their parents. They spread quickly, but not before fish scoop them up in great numbers. So the chain of life continues.

Today, the squid has taken on scientific importance in the study of nerves and mental health. Biologists have discovered a giant nerve in several species that is 40 times thicker than the largest nerve worked on previously. Instead of working with fibres thinner than a human hair, scientists can now use one that approaches the diameter of a wooden match. Since nerve tissue is much the same no matter what animal it comes from, this should facilitate research in nerve action, vital body activities and hormones.

In this way scientists probe into 20th-century health and disease, aided by an extraordinary creature whose beginnings can be traced back almost as far as any living animal on earth today.

Some of the material in this article is taken from Frank W. Lane's book 'Kingdom of the Octopus' (published by Jarrolds, London, at 30/–) which is the major work on the subject and recommended for further reading.

Beware the Deadly Man-of-War!

Fred Warshofsky

One of the sea's most poisonous creatures
is a placid-looking jellyfish that
sails with the wind and dangles venomous
tentacles up to 60 ft long

*A wary swimmer surfaces a safe distance from
the bladder-like float of a man-of-war. By angling
its rayed crest in the breeze, this dangerous
jellyfish can drift along like a sailing boat.*

The Portuguese man-of-war—*Physalia physalis* (from the Greek word for bladder)—is among the most fascinating and least-understood creatures in the sea. Cruising the Gulf Stream, it ranges from the Caribbean northwards to Nova Scotia, whence it is swirled into the North Atlantic and drifts eastwards to the English Channel, the Irish Sea and even the Mediterranean. In the Pacific, a smaller version of *Physalia* ranges from the California coast to Australia.

Seen from the shore or from on board ship, a fleet of *Physalia* is an impressive sight: graceful ballooning floats shimmer like iridescent blue-and-purple Christmas-tree ornaments on the white-crested ocean. Three centuries ago, so the story goes, one such fleet was sighted by English ships off the Portuguese coast. To sailors on deck, the *Physalia* looked like miniatures of the Portuguese galleons that once ruled the seas, so they named the creatures 'Portuguese men-of-war'.

Like an iceberg, there is far more mass and menace to the man-of-war than meets the eye at the surface. Trailing away beneath each float like streamers of confetti is an array of murderous fishing tentacles that slowly writhe and reach as much as 60 ft below for prey. These deadly fishing lines are studded with thousands of stinging cells that contain a poison almost as powerful as a cobra's venom.

Unfortunately, it is impossible to keep *Physalia* in aquariums or other captivity for any length of time, so that much of its life cycle remains a mystery. Scientists have been able to identify the *Physalia* poison as a neurotoxin—a protein substance that deranges the nervous system. To the small fish (up to 6 in. long) and the larger planktonic animals which compose the man-of-war's main diet, the sting means instant death.

So powerful is the poison that even a stranded *Physalia* is dangerous—a false step on to one of the dried blue strings will cause an excruciating pain.

In the laboratory, *Physalia* venom has been frozen and stored for as long as six years without losing its potency. In the water, the venom acts with incredible swiftness. 'Within minutes,' explained Dr Charles Lane, marine-biology professor, 'as the neurotoxin goes to work, blood pressure drops alarmingly. Breathing becomes difficult, the pulse rapid and feeble.'

These symptoms were vividly demonstrated when a scientist ran foul of a *Physalia* while skin-diving. Writhing in pain, he was rushed to a hospital where he lapsed into shock. His breathing grew laboured; to save his life, doctors placed him in an iron lung. For two months he bore graphic evidence of the encounter—a trail of fiery red welts across his chest.

An underwater view of a Portuguese man-of-war, showing how the jellyfish, floating on the surface, trails its tentacles below it. Any small creature unlucky enough to swim too close to them is quickly immobilised by their poison.

There is no antidote for *Physalia* stings, but common rubbing alcohol seems to neutralise the poison and is used as a standard treatment. Natives on the Bimini Islands in the Bahamas have developed their own treatment—they wash the affected area with a strong detergent. If none is handy they use urine as a substitute.

Just under the *Physalia*'s iridescent float is its remarkable digestive apparatus, consisting of hundreds of stubby, vividly coloured red, orange and pink gastrozooids, or feeding polyps. When the tentacles reaching down into the sea have captured food, they contract and, like fishermen hauling in a net, raise the paralysed prey to the gastrozooids. Eventually the dead fish is studded with these polyps, which act like a communal stomach. Each of them secretes a potent enzyme that swiftly breaks down the proteins of the victim's body.

The *Physalia*'s float-like bladder, which ranges from 8 to 12 in. across, is topped by a graceful, rayed crest of flexible membrane. To keep the float

above the surface, where it can catch the breeze, it is filled with a gas (mostly carbon monoxide) supplied by a gland.

Like the lion in the jungle, the man-of-war has its own jackal, seeking scraps from the king's table. As the *Physalia* fishes through the heaving, plankton-rich meadows of the high seas, a bright, blue-and-silver-banded fish darts in and out among the tentacles, tearing shreds of fish and crustacea from the deadly lines. This is the *Nomeus*, or man-of-war fish. Often the small *Nomeus* will leave the *Physalia* and swim in ever-widening circles. Larger fish, looking for a meal, will start to chase after the *Nomeus*, which swiftly darts into what appears to be a forest of seaweed. Its unwary pursuer follows and is immediately overwhelmed by the lethal tentacles. Even as the fish is being hauled up towards the gastrozooids, the *Nomeus* is snapping at the man-of-war's tentacles for its reward.

For some years it was thought that the *Nomeus* was as vulnerable to *Physalia* venom as other fish, but was agile enough to avoid the writhing tentacles. A researcher recently disproved this theory: 'We took a group of fish the same size as the *Nomeus* and determined the amount of toxin needed to kill them. We then gave the *Nomeus* ten times that amount, and the little scavengers swam away as if nothing had happened.'

With its awesome weaponry and consorts of the food-luring *Nomeus*, it would seem that only violent storms or perverse winds could drive the man-of-war to destruction. But *Physalia* does have a natural enemy—the huge, lumbering loggerhead turtle. These giant sea turtles weigh up to 500 lb. and are armoured with a horny, brownish-red shell from which an immense beaked head rears out.

One observer reports seeing an enormous loggerhead ploughing through a fleet of men-of-war with its eyes swollen shut from a thousand stings, its mouth trailing broken strings of tentacles like blue streamers from a maypole. With great snapping gulps, the loggerhead tore through the fleet, in its wake a clear strip of water, on either side the bobbing blue floats, now quite defenceless.

It is not known by what strange chemistry Nature has rendered the great loggerhead and the little *Nomeus* partially immune to the lethal poison. Perhaps in time the answers will come, and with them possibly an antidote for the toxic venom. Until that time, the man-of-war will remain a deadly mystery, ghosting before the wind and spreading its tentacles to paralyse and devour any prey unfortunate enough to cross its course.

The Lobster—
an Ocean Oddity

David MacDonald

The common lobster is an upside-down, inside-out cannibal—but he has managed to survive unchanged for 100 million years

With his horny armour plating, spindly legs and menacing pincers, the common lobster might have resulted from mating a giant cockroach with a monkey wrench. Yet his bizarre design has enabled *Homarus gammarus* not only to survive for millions of years in a hostile underworld but also to remain uniquely himself— ugly, short-tempered and very, very odd.

To begin with, the lobster is both inside-out and upside-down. Besides crawling around in his bones, he carries most of his nervous system along his belly instead of his back. His brain consists of two parts, pinhead-size, above and below his throat. He listens with his legs, tastes with his feet and has molars in his stomach. His kidneys are behind his forehead.

Because of his flavour, *Homarus* has become one of the world's favourite seafoods. Fishermen from Land's End to John o' Groats catch about 2 million lobsters a year; almost half are exported and eaten by gourmets in Europe.

With his cousin *Homarus americanus*, the lobster is peculiar to the rocky north Atlantic coasts of Europe and North America. Peculiar is the right word.

'The lobster is as odd a creature as you'll find any-where in the world,' says Arthur Simpson, director of shellfish research at the Ministry of Agriculture's Burnham-on-Crouch laboratories. Scientists know the lobster as an arthropod—he is, in fact, a distant submarine cousin of the spider. His body is made up of a fused head and thorax and a flexible segmented tail, all encased in a lifeless cuticle called chitin. He has two pairs of antennae, sharp at detect-ing food or danger, but so insensitive to pain that he does not seem to notice if they are cut off.

He has six pairs of mouth parts. One pair, the mandibles, are food grinders which chew sideways. The others are used for tearing and shovelling in food. Starting behind the mouth, but held out in front ready for immediate action, are his menacing pincers, the heavy crusher claw and the slightly smaller sawtooth cutter.

Essex biologist Eric Edwards, demonstrating the lobster's speed with these cumbersome 'fists', slipped a small fish into the sink where his laboratory's 'tame' specimen is kept. The lobster shot out a claw and grabbed the fish before it could dart away.

The lobster's eight slender walking legs, which look hardly strong enough to carry his huge claws, bristle with tiny sensory hairs that pick up under-water vibrations. For lack of a better place, some of his 20 pairs of gills are located at the bases of his legs. Then there is the long, meaty tail, equipped with four pairs of swimmerets. His streamlining, typically, is all backwards.

Though *Homarus* walks nimbly forwards on his delicate legs, his heavy body buoyed up by the water, he flips his tail when frightened and clambers away in reverse, usually giving his adversary an unpleasant nip on the way.

The shell is usually a mottled bluish-black, which blends with his surroundings on the rocky sea-bed. But genetic accidents produce such striking excep-tions as scarlet and gaily spotted 'calico' lobsters. Whatever the original colour, all lobsters turn red when they are put into hot cooking water.

Beneath that crusty exterior is an even crustier personality. Wary, cranky and distinctly anti-social, *Homarus* spends most of his days in hiding, burrowed under rocks or in clumps of seaweed. Yet he is game to tackle anything that moves. In moments of fear or shock, lobsters may dismember themselves. If you grab a lobster by the claws, he is liable to snap them both off along a perforated seam. Many a crate of lobsters ends its journey as an assortment of bodies and claws, jettisoned after getting caught in the slats. Luckily, lobsters can always grow new claws, legs or other spare parts if they have the time.

In summer, *Homarus* gorges so ravenously that his shell finally splits a seam across the back, between the body and the tail. He then lies on one side, jack-knifes into a V-shape and squirms out through the crack.

This incredible moulting process may take about 15 minutes. The blood recedes from his big claws and they shrink enough to be pulled through joints only a ninth of their normal size. As the lobster backs out, his entire shell falls away in one piece, including the grinding teeth of his stomach, the film over his eyeballs, even the tiny crust on micro-scopic sensory hairs. Lying beside his old skin, the lobster looks as if he had suddenly become twins.

Defenceless, covered only by a jelly-soft skin, the freshly moulted lobster stays holed up in his burrow. Within a few hours, by absorbing sea water, he swells to his new size—an inch or two longer and half as heavy again. It takes several weeks for the new suit to harden. If he is replacing a lost part, the rest of the body's growth slows to let it catch up.

Every second year, after the female of the species has shed her tight corset, she takes a mate. They embrace and he deposits sperm in a sac between her last two pairs of walking legs. The female retains the live sperm for up to 15 months. Then she sheds her eggs through openings at the second pair of walking legs. The eggs are fertilised by the sperm and passed back to the underside of the tail.

The fertilised eggs, which look like dark green caviar, remain cemented to her body for almost a year. When they begin to hatch she stands on tiptoe and shakes off perhaps 75,000 tiny, beady-eyed larvae, which swim towards the sea's surface.

Lobsters are common in European waters, and such a popular food that laws once protected egg-laying females. Lobsters are scavengers—scouring the ocean floor for algae, eelgrass or bits of animal food. When they have moulted, or are growing new parts, lobsters crave shell-building calcium carbonate. They satisfy this need by eating crusty sand dollars, the shells of snails and, occasionally, even members of their own species.

Thenceforth the baby lobster's life is a constant fight against all but impossible odds: he has about one chance in ten thousand of growing up, one in a million of lasting to middle age—a good reason for his snappy disposition.

At the very outset, when baby lobsters swim and eat plankton—minute animals and plants living in the water—99 out of 100 fall victim to fish or to bigger baby lobsters. The few which survive, after moulting three times in as little as four weeks, then sink to the bottom and run for cover.

With luck, a European lobster can live for 30 years or more. The trouble is that by the time he is about five years old, 9 in. long and a pound or so in weight, *Homarus gammarus* has become fair game for his deadliest enemy, *Homo sapiens*.

We Europeans have been enjoying lobsters for as long as anyone can remember. Shore fishermen used to poke a stick into a hole in the rocks and, when an affronted lobster 'bit', pull him out. Since that time a variety of traps have been invented, the most successful being the type that has a basket-work pot with a funnelled entrance.

Today, another method of catching them has been discovered: aqualung diving. Skin divers in Cornwall and South Wales have almost come to blows with traditional fishermen anxious to protect their business. Now the Ministry of Agriculture has drawn up a new code for skin-diver fishermen, who may face legal action if they remove catches in nets, pots or traps: the use of spears or instruments likely to damage shellfish is forbidden.

In the 1870's, when exploitation seemed to be getting out of hand, laws were passed to stop fishermen from taking under-sized lobsters. Later, legislation was introduced to protect the egg-bearing—or 'berried'—hen lobsters, but fishermen evaded the ban by 'scrubbing' hens to remove the eggs. Recent scientific doubts about the value of protecting berried hens has led to the repeal of the measure.

Projects to farm lobsters in enclosed areas have failed; bred in such close proximity, the lobsters devoured companions which had just moulted and were consequently quite defenceless. The cannibals were eaten in their turn when they moulted, and the stock rapidly dwindled.

Until new methods of domesticating the lobster can be found, epicures will have to rely on Nature's own 'wild' product. Thanks to modern packing and transport methods, the market is world-wide. More and more people are sitting down, spreading napkins across their laps and asking themselves, 'How can something that looks so strange taste so good?'

Killer Whale

William Cromie

The fastest and fiercest thing that swims is the most terrible predator of all

Standing near the edge of the Antarctic ice, Herbert Ponting, official photographer of the British Terra Nova Expedition, was focusing his camera on a group of killer whales out in the bay. Suddenly the 3 ft-thick ice heaved up under his feet and cracked. There was a loud blowing noise, and Ponting was enveloped in a blast of hot, acrid air that smelt strongly of fish. Eight killer whales had come up under him, broken the ice with their backs and isolated him on a small floe. Now the floe began rocking furiously, and the whales shoved their huge black and white heads out of the water. One ugly, tooth-filled snout was within 12 ft.

The photographer leapt to a nearby floe, then to another and another. The killers followed him, literally snapping at his heels like a pack of hungry wolves. By the time Ponting gained the last floe it had drifted too far from the solid ice for him to make the jump. Then, by an extraordinary stroke of luck, currents pushed the floe back.

Still clutching his camera, Ponting made a life-or-death leap. His boots hit solid ice and he started running. He glanced back just once. He saw, in his own words, 'a huge tawny head pushing out of the water and resting on the ice, looking around with its little pig-eyes to see what had become of me'.

With his intelligence, speed, size and power, *Orcinus orca* is one of the most terrible predators on earth. Unchecked and unchallenged by any creature, including man, he roams every ocean and eats anything he can catch—fish, seals, penguins, walruses, porpoises. Porpoises can swim up to 25 mph, but killer whales have been clocked at 34 mph, making them among the fastest swimmers in the sea. They are primarily fish-eaters, devouring hundreds of them at a time, but they also enjoy warm-blooded animals. The stomach of one of these 21 ft killers was estimated to contain the remains of 13 porpoises and 14 seals.

In 1957 I went ashore in Antarctica as a member of an International Geophysical Year scientific group. I had seen killers on a previous trip to the Arctic, had watched them swim under floes on which seals were sunning themselves, tip the floes with their mighty backs and dump the unsuspecting creatures into mouths full of razor-sharp teeth. I had seen baby walruses, taking refuge on the backs of their mothers, butted off and tumbled to their doom.

Now, on a January morning, I had another example of killer voracity—plus their astonishing agility. A friend and I were studying a herd of Weddell seals on the ice. There was a large, solitary seal asleep near the edge, a fat fellow about 10 ft long and 6 or 7 ft around the middle. As we watched him, we saw a formation of sabre-like fins slicing through the calm water about half a mile out.

I ran over and kicked the sleeping seal as hard as I could. He did not stir. Seaward, six or seven killers broke the surface and spouted in unison—a low, bushy spout. I planted my heavy ski boot on the seal's sensitive nose. With that he awoke, staring and blinking at me in astonishment. I shouted at him and, gesturing towards the rapidly nearing fins, I turned and ran.

I was satisfied that I had saved the beast's life, but when I looked back he was still in the same position, sleepily unmindful of the menacing fins. Seconds later a head shot vertically out of the water a few feet in front of the ice. Hurling a third of its body length on to the ice, the killer sank its 3 in. teeth into the seal's hide and dragged the 1000 lb. animal over the edge as if it were no more than a stuffed toy. A few convulsive jerks of his body, a frenzied beating of his flippers and the seal disappeared.

Killer whales are from two to six times as large as dolphins and porpoises, reaching a maximum length of about 30 ft. Like porpoises, they are hairless and streamlined for rapid movement through the water. They have rounded snouts with 10–14 pairs of heavy interlocking teeth in each jaw. A killer's body tapers back to two broad, horizontal fins, or flukes, which with the fore flippers and co-ordinated body movements provide silent propulsion and great manoeuvrability at high speeds.

Orcinus orca can easily be recognised by his distinctive two-tone colouring. The adult's belly and throat are livid white, as is a lens-shaped area just behind and above the eyes, and the colour usually extends up on to his sides in a saddle shape. His back is midnight black. He is also easily distinguished by the triangular fin located halfway along his back. In the old males this fin is often 6 ft high. The females are much daintier in every respect, reaching only half the size of the males, or about 15 ft.

How do killer whales find their food? They cannot see more than about 100 ft and they lack the acute sense of smell that sharks have, but like all whales they can hear very well. They can hear sounds inaudible to humans and can pin-point the location of a sound source.

Like porpoises, they probably locate their prey under water by built-in sonar. Porpoises make sharp clicking noises producing sound waves that bounce off objects in their path, and they home in on their food by means of these returning echoes. Tape-recordings reveal that killers also make clicking sounds. And they 'talk' to one another in creaky-door sounds and high whistles.

Killers travel in packs or schools of from three to 40. When the pack is hunting or travelling, the females and young usually swim together in close company while the males travel alone, or in smaller groups, some distance away. They are often seen to leap clean out of the water.

An example of a co-operative attack by killers is given by a whaler, Frank Bullen, in his book *The Cruise of the Cachalot*. While on a whaling voyage in the North Pacific, he spotted a bowhead—a slow, big-headed whale. The whale was close to the ship and obviously in trouble. Bullen at first could not see what was the matter. Then a killer leapt completely out of the water and landed with its full weight on the bowhead's back. Again and again the aggressor cleared the water and fell on to the larger whale as if trying to flail it into submission.

The big whale did not seem to be able to swim away or fight off the leaping killer, and when it lifted its enormous head out of the foam, Bullen saw why. Two more 'furies' were hanging on to the bowhead's huge lips, as if trying to drag its mouth open.

The most active of the three kept up the tremendous pounding until the bowhead was exhausted. When its gigantic bulk lay supine on the surface, the leaping killer joined the others at its lips. After a short struggle they succeeded in dragging open its mouth, then devoured the defeated whale's tongue. 'This had been their sole objective,' Bullen wrote, 'for as soon as they finished their barbarous feast they departed, leaving it helpless and dying.'

Normally, a female gives birth to only one calf at a time, after carrying it for about a year. Since the killers are mammals, they suckle their young (the mammary glands are enclosed in a sort of pocket so that the calf can nurse without shipping sea water). The newborn calves are large and well-formed, and as soon as a baby is born the mother pushes it to the surface for its first breath of air. From that time on, it is able to swim along with the group.

Killers are splendid parents; they produce only a few young and are extremely solicitous of them, giving them the best of care and attention. Like wolves, killer whales have strong family and group ties: if a cow or calf receives an injury, the other females in the school will push the injured one to the surface or to safety.

These great predators are at the peak of the food pyramid. At the base of the pyramid are countless millions of microscopic plants floating on or near the surface of the sea. They are eaten by tiny animals like shrimps and copepods, which constitute one higher and narrower tier on the pyramid. It takes hundreds of pounds of these shrimps to keep 10 lb. of mackerel, herring or halibut alive. These are then eaten by large fish, sharks, seals and porpoises, which in turn become food for *Orcinus*. Since

The killer whale, Orcinus orca, *is the most savage thing that swims. It will attack anything that moves—including whales, and seals on ice-floes—and it has no natural enemies. Adult killers can reach a length of about 30 ft, travel at speeds of up to 34 mph, and often hunt in packs.*

killers have no natural enemies, it is well that they cannot reproduce at a high rate, or they would very soon eat themselves out of house and home.

Fortunately, killers pick the remote polar seas for their principal hunting grounds. But they also abound in the Gulf of Alaska and along the coast of British Columbia, and are occasionally seen from ships on Atlantic and Pacific crossings. They sometimes visit the North Sea, and in recent years have also been found stranded on the shores of Cumberland, Clare and Donegal.

Since everything in the ocean flees these piebald whales, it may be asked what purpose they serve. Actually, the killer whale fills an important niche in controlling the balance of Nature in the ocean. He is not a predator in the same sense that man is. As Dr Carleton Ray, associate curator of the New York Aquarium, points out:

'The most rapacious predator on earth is the two-legged one, man. But man seldom serves Nature's purposes. As a fisherman, he kills indiscriminately. As a hunter, he "takes off the top", usually slaying the prime animal. In contrast, the natural predator takes off the bottom. The wolf takes the weakling, the stray. The killer whale does the same in the sea, leaving the best and strongest to survive and breed.'

The Extraordinary Eel

Jean George

The eel's mysterious life cycle baffles
scientists; even the little
that has so far been discovered about it is a
triumph of biological detection

The eel caught by my son Luke was almost 3 ft long. She—it is believed that males never grow to that length—was curled gracefully with her small head on the long fin that ran down the centre of her back to her tail.

Little did I know that I would become hopelessly fascinated by our slender guest, or that my curiosity would eventually lead me to the Gulf Stream and to research laboratories in Europe,

tracking down fantastic stories of the eel—all of which turned out to be true.

The quest began when Luke and I put the eel in our land-locked garden pond. Slipping through our fingers, she slid purposefully around, lifting her head above water as if to take a bearing. In the morning she was gone. We searched under submerged stones to no avail. Finally Luke said, 'I suppose she walked away.' I stared at him. 'Everyone knows eels can walk,' he said. 'I've seen them walking about the marsh, hunting for insects.'

I hastened to a scientific reference library. My son was right: the eel *can* leave the water and wander overland. As it travels, it keeps its smooth, slippery, mucous skin moist by hiding under stones, wet leaves and grass. Some have been observed sliding as far as a mile from one lake to the next. A sight known to fishermen along the coast is young eels, or elvers, dancing and leaping over exposed tidal flats, moving not on belly scales like snakes, but by swinging their muscular bodies.

The eel, of which there are several freshwater species (congers, morays and snake eels are marine creatures; the electric eel is not an eel at all, but a relative of the carp and catfish), remains today one of the most mysterious animals on earth. Scientists have few explanations for many of its habits, because it goes through more transformations than any other vertebrate and accomplishes some of these deep in the sea, where it cannot be observed.

For most of its early life—usually the first five to eight years—the eel seems sexless. Then gradually it develops the organs of both sexes. Later one set of organs atrophies and the eel becomes either an immature male or female. Not until after the creature migrates from fresh water to the sea does it become capable of breeding.

Prevailing scientific opinion is that all American and European freshwater eels lay their eggs from January to March, 1200–1500 ft under the surface in the Sargasso Sea, an area in the south-western North Atlantic Ocean about equidistant from Puerto Rico and Bermuda. Almost as soon as it hatches, the eel makes its first startling change. As the eggs float slowly at middle depths, the pinhead-sized cases break open and release a creature that looks like a tiny, transparent ribbon. Millions of these sparkling, glassy sea gems float upwards and begin a migration that is so complex and vast—up to 3000 miles across open ocean—that it has no parallel.

The small creatures are carried northwards by the currents of the Gulf Stream. They have as much control over their destiny as thistledown on the wind, for they cannot propel themselves. As they move northwards, the crystal-clear bodies become cloudy. Now about 3 in. long, they are preyed on by fish and jellyfish.

The eel at this stage was first discovered in 1856 by Dr J. J. Kaup of the Paris Museum of Natural History. Kaup pronounced it a new species of fish, which he called *Leptocephalus brevirostris*. Its common name is leaf fish, because it resembles a large, veined willow leaf.

Some 40 years later, two Italian biologists watched *Leptocephalus* in an aquarium make another bodily transformation and its true nature was understood at last: it was the larval form of the eel, as the caterpillar is the larva of the butterfly.

And here is introduced one of the great eel mysteries: the American and European leaf fish, which hatch in approximately the same place, are somehow predestined for their respective continents. Somewhere these helpless slivers of life sort themselves out according to their ancestry. The European larvae, much slower to develop than the American, flow for two and a half years towards Europe, while the American larvae drift for a year towards the coast of the United States.

Few, if any, have erred in this disentanglement, thereby haunting marine biologists with the unanswered question: 'How do they know which way to turn?' Or is the answer simply that they are all of one species and that those which drift towards Europe develop more slowly because the food, temperature and mineral content of the water in that environment are different?

Unperturbed by the questions of science, the larval eels year after year find their way to numerous creeks and rivers—the Severn in England, the Waal in the Netherlands, the Potomac and the Mississippi in America. Approaching the coasts over the continental shelf, they undergo what may be the most violent change in their lives: they shrink in length from the 3 in. larval form and become cylindrical instead of broad and flat.

Still transparent, they are now called glass eels or elvers. After fasting for a few months, they haunt piers and wharves, the bottoms of pools and channels, eating everything they find—fish, insects, clams, crayfish and vegetable matter—dead or alive. They grow slowly, becoming immature yellow eels.

Active mainly in summer, the yellow eel spends the next 10 or 12 years swimming into lakes and farmland ponds, down ditches and up cascades, moving constantly inland as it eats and grows to a possible 40 in. for females, 24 in. for males.

Then, usually on a moonless autumn night, the moment of change occurs: the eel mysteriously turns and starts downstream. Past farm and city, harbour and ocean-going ship, it returns unerringly to tropical waters. As it travels, more changes occur. Its blunt, rounded nose becomes pointed and its colour changes to a glowing silver.

It is believed that the eel never eats again, for no silver eel has ever been caught with food in its stomach. Thus, with no nourishment at all, this extraordinary, deep-swimming creature goes swiftly and directly through thousands of miles of water back to the Sargasso Sea. Home again, and now sexually mature, the eel begins breeding.

It was the famous Danish marine biologist Johannes Schmidt who, in 1922, discovered the birthplace of the eel. He did it by following the leaf fish, tracing a trail over thousands of miles of ocean that led to smaller and smaller leaf fish until, after a search lasting 18 years, he found their source in the Sargasso Sea; but neither he nor anyone else has ever found a fully mature female with completely developed eggs.

The mystery of the life cycle of the eel persists. In 1966, Dr E. Bertelsen put another piece of the puzzle into place in the Sargasso Sea by trawling up some eel larvae in early stages, thus determining the eel's spawning season; but Bertelsen, too, failed to find a breeding mother. How do eels spawn? Do any of them survive? If not, what final change takes place before they die? The answers to these questions are still to be discovered.

On a recent visit to the Paris Museum of Natural History I learnt more of the wonders of the eel. For one thing, it has a marvellous sense of 'taste'; sensors in a band along each side of its body operate very much like taste buds on a tongue. It can thus sense food with its sides or head. A piece of beef dropped before a carp in a fish tank is likely to go unnoticed for several seconds, whereas a piece dropped near the tail of an eel is grabbed instantly. These extraordinary 'taste buds' may help the eel to find its way through the Atlantic to the Sargasso Sea. Just as a keen sense of smell brings the salmon up the river of its youth to the very stream where it was spawned, so a sense of taste, plus certain other factors, may lead the eel unerringly to the tropical home of its ancestors.

Even the partial unravelling of the story of the eel has been a great accomplishment for biological science. Whatever the final truths discovered about this changeling, it will always remain one of the earth's most provocative creatures.

The Ways of Insects and Spiders

Watch a garden spider weave an intricate web with easy precision,
or a leaf-bug mimicking the leaves it rests on. Observe
the bustling orderliness of a beehive or an anthill.
Intelligence at work?
No, it is the incredible, instinctive behaviour
that these many-segmented creatures have evolved

The Marvel of an Insect

Alan Devoe

Insects may look fragile, but for
their size they are the strongest, fastest, most
successful creatures in the world

A naturalist might conclude that God takes an exuberant joy in creating insects, for our earth so teems with the complex little creatures that no one knows how many different kinds there are. Some 900,000 species have been classified. About 4000 new varieties are found every year. Awed entomologists predict that when all our earth's insects have been discovered, the final tally may be in the millions.

The members of this vast and amazing group of living things have assumed countless strange shapes and habits which enable them to cope with life under almost any circumstances. One beetle thrives in red pepper; there are insects so tiny and so intensely specialised that they live on the tongues of horseflies. There are others whose shimmering lives under the sun are so brief that they have neither mouths nor stomachs and never eat at all.

Despite this immense diversity, all insects have certain things in common. The lovely giant moths with their beautifully patterned wings seem utterly unlike the pinhead-sized fleas hopping about in our dog's hair or the gauzy winged mayflies whirling in a lyrical dance over a brook pool in the dusk. But basically they are all a similar kind of living machine. To learn something of their make-up is to be introduced to extraordinary wonders.

An insect has no bones. It wears its skeleton externally. From man's point of view, it is built inside-out and upside-down. Its heart is on top, near its back. Its legs are tubular sections of its skin-skeleton armour-plating, with muscles, nerves and soft tissues protected inside. The engineering of an insect's leg makes it, for its size, the strongest supporting device possible. In a recent experiment in which an entomologist gradually piled tiny weights on a scarab beetle, he was able to get his little porter to move about under a load 850 times its own weight without buckling. An average man, straining, can lift a little more than two-thirds his weight.

This strong, pliable external skeleton provides even the most fragile-looking insects with astounding durability. Monarch butterflies, seemingly as insubstantial as blown thistle seeds, make migratory flights from Canada to Florida and back again. Painted-lady butterflies, marked for scientific identification, have made the gigantic journey from North Africa to Iceland; storm-tossed, lashed by rains and gales, they often reach their destinations with their wings in tatters.

With an outside skeleton there is no room for expansion. Growing insects must periodically moult.

Brush-footed butterfly caterpillar

Robber fly

The face of every insect is designed to suit the life the insect leads. Spines like those on the brush-footed butterfly caterpillar (top left) discourage predators; the beak of the robber fly (top right) is a weapon for impaling its prey. The mouth of the queen hornet (bottom left) is adapted for chewing up the woody material it uses for nest-building, and that of the plant-hopper (bottom right) for sucking plant juices (the red specks on the plant-hopper's legs are parasitic mites).

Queen hornet

Plant-hopper

149

A praying mantis feasts on a grasshopper that has strayed too close to its powerful, sharp-spined forelegs. Much superstition is attached to this big, gangly insect: in various areas, praying mantises are known as soothsayers, devil's coach horses and—in the mistaken belief that they carry a deadly sting— mule killers. Despite the folklore, mantises are harmless to anything larger than their fellow insects.

The horny casing splits and the insect creeps out in such a soft skin that for a brief period it is almost 'boneless'. To ensure that its new skeleton forms in a suitably bigger size, the insect swallows air or water. Gulping and swelling until it is the required new size, the insect waits, while its roomier skeleton hardens round it.

The insect's blood is not confined by any system of veins, as ours is. From its single great artery, which runs from the heart through the chest, the blood surges and seeps through the whole body. The blood is forced to the far tips of thread-fine extremities by little auxiliary hearts—pumping stations with sets of powerful muscles, located wherever there is a difficult booster job to be done. A cockroach has one in its head, to pump blood through its long feelers. Water insects have booster hearts to ensure perfect circulation in their legs.

For an insect, drawing the breath of life involves another remarkable process because it has no lungs, nor does it breathe by mouth or nostrils. Along its sides are symmetrical rows of tiny perforations. Each of these is an air-duct. Inside the body they link into two main trunk lines, which branch into hundreds of air lines running to every area of its body.

Thus the whole insect is continuously ventilated by a flow of air, which it controls by opening and closing its air-ducts as an organist pulls out stops.

Resting, an insect needs relatively little oxygen; but in flight it must breathe prodigiously. It must be able suddenly to call upon as much as 50 times the normal amount of oxygen. Its beating wings bring this about: as the wing muscles contract, they force out almost all the air in the system; as they relax, fresh air rushes into the ducts. The oxygenation provided to a flying insect is so complete that even in its wing muscles there occurs an almost complete change of air at every wing-beat.

No aspect of the dynamics of an insect's body presents more striking powers than its wings. A dragonfly, carrying its long body on wings thinner than fine paper, can reach a speed of about 36 mph. A mosquito, gorged on blood, performs the extraordinary aerodynamic feat of flying off carrying a load twice its own weight.

To do so, it beats its wings more than 300 times a second. Such a furiously rapid wing-beat is by no means a unique performance. When we hear the high, thin whine of a midge—so small that it is almost invisible—the midge's wings are beating more than 1000 times a second.

In insects which do not fly, the blaze of energy is concentrated in special adaptations that result in equally impressive displays of power. The little flea that hops aboard our dog is able to do so because it can make a leap of 100 times its own height. If man had the flea's jumping power, proportionately, he could jump over the GPO Tower.

Insects may look fragile, but their strength is as deceptive as the lacy engineering of a suspension bridge. In one experiment, bees and butterflies were sealed in a tube, after which the air was pumped out to make a vacuum. Even the insects' body moisture was sucked out of them. The 'fragile' little prisoners survived unharmed even when the tube was broken and normal pressure suddenly restored. The toughest elephant would have died instantly.

Insects have only rudimentary brains; they are guided through their lives by strange and lavish sensory gifts. They listen to life with two kinds of ears: delicate hairs sensitive to sound-waves, or tympanic membranes like our own eardrums; but these are distributed on many areas of the body, and are tuned to prodigies of special reception. Crickets have ears on their knees. Cicadas have ears in their abdomens. A water beetle is able to hear with its chest. Katydids, or bush-crickets, have been found to have supersonic hearing.

Acute human hearing seldom ranges above about 20,000 vibrations per second; katydids can hear 45,000. Many insects hear sounds outside our human range. Entomologists believe the whole outdoor world may be ringing with an insect chorus of mating calls and interchanged messages when we think there is only silence.

Insects see by small eyes (called ocelli) on top of their heads; by great compound eyes at the sides; and by a kind of all-over 'invisible eye', or light sense. With its eyes completely covered, a light-loving insect still moves unerringly towards brightness and a dark-loving one seeks the shadows. It literally sees through its skin.

With its compound eyes the insect sees a world of extraordinary composite vignettes. Several ingenious technicians have succeeded in taking photographs through an insect's eye. The world thus revealed is a landscape of finely patterned mosaic, each tiny piece of it caught by one facet of the eye. When fitted together, the pieces make a picture something like the stained-glass window of a church. The eye of a dragonfly is made up of more than 25,000 such facets.

With its capacities of taste and smell, an insect achieves perhaps the most remarkable sensitivity of all. It has taste organs in its mouth, but it also has the power of taste extended in other unimaginable ways and to an incredible keenness. Butterflies and bees are able to taste not only with their mouths but with their feet.

The insect's detection of even microscopically slight traces of edible material amounts to a sensory miracle. The extreme limit at which human taste can detect sweetness is in a solution of one part sugar to about 200 parts of water. Some moths and butterflies can detect the presence of sugar when it is one part in 300,000. As with taste, so with scent. An insect experiences the world as a 'smellscape' of titillating vividness. Some male moths are able to catch the scent of a female 9 miles downwind.

In addition to such sense powers—which, fantastic though they are, fall within our theoretical understanding—insects show signs of other sensings, the nature of which has not been fathomed. Experiments have been made with beetles, to try to discover how they find a hidden piece of meat. With every known sense organ put out of action, and with shellac applied all over their bodies, legs and feelers, the beetles still make their unerring way to the hidden treasure.

To know something of the wonder of insects is to contemplate a little of the miracle of life.

The Wizardry of Webs

Jean George

Spiders spin webs for flying,
fishing, courtship and catching—they are
their livelihood and speciality

From rock to grass blade, from twig to petal, the earth is strung with signal lines, traps, love nests, nurseries and railways, as some 40,000 species of spiders talk to each other, express fear and desire, hunger and anger through their complex and beautiful webs. Largely unnoticed by humans, thousands of spiders are working industriously on every acre of countryside.

The tons of spider silk, for which the earth is a mere spindle, comprise hundreds of varieties and weaves, to meet the multiple needs and crises in the spiders' lives. Where one thread suffices for dropping over a cliff, another tension, a different weave, is required to fasten webs to leaves; and still another to send warnings or receive messages from a stuck fly or courting male. Webs of spiders are, in fact, their eyes, ears, voice and fingers.

Spiders are such a different form of life that we cannot say they have a head and body; after all, their eight legs are attached to the front part, a head and thorax, while silk glands lie in their belly. Seven different kinds of glands, not all present in all spiders, lead out to the spinnerets. Most spiders have three pairs of complicated spinnerets tipped with many minute spinning tubes. These move like human fingers. They card, pull, weave and twist, as they turn the fluid silk coming from the glands into the right thread for the right situation.

The first need in a spider's life is to get away from home in order to prevent being eaten by parent or sibling. To this end, the spiderlings fly on a silvery thread over field and mountain, and they take off on this voyage like expert circus performers.

One spring I watched a hatch of grass spiders emerge from their egg-case and crawl down silken avenues to disappear in the garden plants. As they went they trailed behind a veil of threads that heaved and rippled between the leaves of the irises and ferns. One spiderling made its way to the top of a dried chrysanthemum stalk, where it circled until it faced the wind. Then it threw up its hind feet and stood on its head like an acrobat. In this position it spun out two or three feet of ballooning thread, a dry and wide strand. Then it let go of the stalk, grabbed the silk with its front legs, and in the best circus tradition went flying through the air. Aided by the wind, it guided itself round the elm in the garden by pulling in on the streamer and then letting it out. The wind bowed it. As it billowed away, it struck the edge of the house and was stopped. There the spiderling reeled in its slender balloon and hurried to the porch roof to take off again. In this splendid manner it sailed out of sight.

During the spring and autumn, when spiderlings go ballooning, the sky is filled with tons of dragline known as gossamer. In some places it will fall to earth with the rain in such abundance that the grass is swathed in white silk.

Gossamer and trapping threads are perhaps the best-known webs, but some of the lesser known are more exciting. There are the 'wild threads', for instance. These fine, almost invisible strands can surround a simple sheet trap—that flat, silver platform between grass blades—with a sunburst of trip-lines. As clear as air, these lines are nevertheless tough enough to trip a flying insect and send it tumbling on to the sheet below.

The swathing band is the most dramatic production of the spider because of its size and quantity. It rolls out in broad ribbons and is composed of strong parallel threads that come from the lower spinnerets, plus a criss-cross of finer silk from the upper spinners. So instinctive is the production of this band that anyone can induce a spider to produce it by tossing an insect on to its web. Before the thread appears, however, the insect must struggle on the web, a rhythm that impels the spider to rush forward and sink its poison fangs into the prey. It is the activation of the poison glands that sets off the spinners. Next the spider's feet turn the insect so that the river of silk is spread evenly until the prey is engulfed. Some spiders use their webs as trophy walls when the meal is done. Because they 'drink' the insect, by turning its interior into liquid with powerful digestive juices, the insect grows smaller and smaller as the feast goes on. Usually a mere dot remains, swathed in silk.

The most beautiful combination of threads is the famous orb of the garden spiders. Walking one day in a garden, I saw a spider among the phlox. She had just built a triangular frame for her web. Now she began the laborious task of constructing the orb. She walked to the middle of the top thread and dropped on a vertical line to the bottom. Back she climbed to the centre of this line and, establishing a hub, she spun out spokes, using a dry, hard thread. Then,

This delicate lacework, spangled with gems, is really the web of an orb-weaving spider hung with morning dew.
Its fragile appearance belies its strength: its viscous threads are so strong that they can easily stop a
grasshopper in full flight. Both male and female spiders spin webs, and each species has its own pattern.

A golden orb spider advances on her victim, a grasshopper trapped in her sticky web. Before killing it, the spider will roll the grasshopper in the web and spin strands of silk around it to prevent its escape. The intricate web, usually about 2 ft across, is repaired each time it is damaged or disturbed.

circling outwards from the hub, she built a scaffolding for her wheel. Next she spiralled back again, leaving behind a line with blobs of fluid on it. To space this shining glue perfectly, she gave the line a quick flip as she secured it. The line vibrated, spreading the fluid evenly. When the thread lay still, it was hung with droplets of equal size, nearly equally spaced. How, I wondered, had her race learnt and passed on this wisdom?

Spiders are predators, the best insect-killers known; in fact they will even kill one another if there is no communication between them. So spiders, too, must be careful of others' webs, for most of them work in the dark of night, are short-sighted and have no means of hearing except through their threads.

Under these conditions it is no wonder that their means of reproduction is the most complicated on earth. For the reason that every advance towards a female is fraught with danger, the males have evolved a strange, narcissistic love. They make love alone, to a web, before handing their cells of life to a female.

The tarantula's method is particularly spectacular. He spins a sheet in which there are two holes, one large, one small. Between the holes he leaves a narrow band of strong silk, different from anything else he spins. He steps through the large hole and, hanging below, strengthens its edges. As he does this, his body touches the exquisitely woven band. The sensation induces him to release a drop of sperm fluid. He crawls back to the top and, reaching round the weaving, draws the fluid into bulbs in leg-like attachments near his head, to be handed to his mate later.

The male spider then destroys the web and sets out upon the risky task of courting and mating. Almost invariably, the female, who matures later than the male and is usually larger, is not ready to receive his gift. She gives him a bad time, charging, threatening and sometimes eating him.

Because of the danger, the tarantula male uses caution. He approaches his mate. She rears in hostility. He jumps and pets her. She opens her fangs to bite and poison him; but he quickly grabs her fangs with hooks on his front legs and hangs on to them while he deposits the sperm in a pocket in her abdomen. Now he can walk away safely.

There are as many ways of subduing a female as there are kinds of spiders. One of the most intriguing ways is that of the crab spider. He ties his mate down with strong threads. Approaching her gingerly, he criss-crosses her body with threads until, when he is done, he has staked her to the ground with a veil of silver. This is known as the 'bridal veil' of the spiders.

With the renewal of the species—and it does go on, in spite of the dangers—the female spiders now weave the most important webs of the spider world: the cases for their eggs. Some are golden silk—tough, windproof, waterproof and resilient—while some are merely poorly constructed bags. The eggs are laid in the sac. Some species lay as many as 3000, some lay only one, but all of them spin around their precious offspring a beautiful thread that is carded and twisted by the last spinnerets. The egg-cases may be glittering baskets or dense whorls of hard thread.

The silk of a spider's egg-case is so beautiful that a Frenchman in the 18th century wove it into stockings and gloves. The gleam of the cloth impressed the Academy of Sciences of Paris, and it investigated the commercial possibilities of silk from spiders' egg-cases. It was found impracticable mainly because spiders, unlike silk worms, are solitary creatures. They could not be induced to live close enough together to produce easily gathered silk.

Most spiders spin certain traps and designs, then stop. But not the grass spiders. They continue to add to their webs all through the year until, when the frost falls, there may be yards of huge white sheets in the fields.

Of all the weavings and webs—the funnels and snares and trip-lines, the sperm webs, the draglines, the orbs—the one whose creator has the most faith in Nature is the fishing line of the bolas spider. It is a single line, ending in a sticky ball. It is swung from a tree limb, back and forth, back and forth, as the little spider fishes the vast night for a passing insect.

I met a bolas spider recently while sitting out at night under the apple tree. I was struck on the cheek by something sticky; and, as I tried to wipe it off, my finger became caught in the line. I turned my torch on, and at the end of the line was a fat bolas who looked more like a bud than a spider. She was balancing on a web trapeze and reeling up her line that had struck so noble a bite.

I jiggled her line again. She lifted her fangs and reeled in faster. Then I leant towards her, looming into her world. At that she crept off into the leaves, and I did not see her again. I often wonder how she felt, in the limits of her spider brain, about the 'big one that got away'.

Nature's Most Astonishing Creature—the Beehive

Jean George

When crisis strikes a beehive, social alchemy begins: sterile workers become egg-layers, foragers turn nursemaid and infants perform the work of adults

The tiny honey-bee dived on to a blue delphinium, braked on a petal and walked into the flower. Glistening on her back as she drank the nectar was a red dot, placed there by a scientist. After her drink the bee turned her eyes towards the sun, took a bearing on it and started home. At her hive a quarter of a mile away the scientist was waiting, for this honey-bee might well add another bright piece to an extraordinary mosaic of new bee research.

Today the beehive is no longer thought of as a mere collection of insects; it is considered a single organism of many glittering parts. An infant when it is swarming, the hive progresses from adolescence to maturity, gives birth to new swarms, finally subsides into the quietude of winter. A wounded, starving or plundered hive can actually suffer, moan in agony and then, in its drive to live, repair itself by a healing process like that of any other creature.

This concept is founded on a set of extraordinary discoveries. Any single bee, it is now known, can grow old quickly—or, more unbelievable, grow young. The sterile can lay eggs; the senile can rejuvenate glands that have atrophied. A single bee can, in short, do the 'impossible', in order to maintain the wholeness of the hive.

To understand the new bee research we should look into a typical wild hive that has lodged inside a hollow tree. There is always a main entrance with several combs of lustrous waxen cells hanging inside the door. Some combs contain honey, others hold pollen. A third type of comb, the brood comb, contains the larvae—unfledged bees in the wingless and footless state. Each hive has one queen, a large bee which lays up to 3000 eggs a day. There are also a number of drones who exist only to mate with the young virgin queens as they hatch, during the hive's sexually productive time of life.

Most of the other 20,000 to 40,000 bees in an individual hive are 'workers', who perform a variety of specific tasks. One is nursing: feeding protein-rich 'bee milk'—formed by special glands in the nurse bee's head—to the queen and the larvae. Making wax is another. In this process the bees eat honey, which is converted by special glands into beeswax. With the spines on their hind legs, they pick up wax scales protruding from pockets on their abdomens and pass them to their mouths. Then they chew and fashion the wax into six-sided cells which form the combs. The workers also forage for pollen and nectar. The nectar is fed to 'receiver' bees who convert it—by using the secretions of special glands—into honey and store it in the comb.

Some workers act as hive 'guards', admitting only foragers that belong to the hive—they are recognised by odour, scented through the 12,000 scent organs on the antennae. Strange bees are killed on the spot. Air-conditioning the hive (by standing inside the entrance and fanning their wings), building cells and cleaning the hive complete the list of duties.

As apiarists watched all these jobs being done year after year, they asked: how do bees know what to do? What intelligence tells them the hive needs more brood cells or a new guard detachment?

In 1925 a German scientist, G. A. Rösch, had a hunch that the age of the bees had something to do with their work. He daubed with paint a group of bees as they emerged from the brood comb. No sooner had their twinkling wings hardened than they started cleaning the cells, then moved towards the oldest larvae in the combs and began feeding them bee milk. Rösch examined one of the marked bees under the microscope, to see if her physical development correlated with her job. It did; she had enlarged pharyngeal or bee-milk glands that lie in front of the brain. She was physically a 'nurse'.

In a few days, the marked nurses abandoned their original charges and began to feed the youngest larvae. After repeated studies, Rösch was convinced that young nurses fed the older larvae, old nurses the younger.

As days passed the marked bees gave up their nursing duties and began taking nectar from the foragers and storing it. Examination showed that their bee-milk glands had begun to degenerate, and the honey sacs in their bellies were filled with nectar. Their mean age was 11 days.

Around the 15th day, these bees began making wax. The microscope showed that their bodies had changed once more to fit the job—their wax-making glands were highly developed. On the 18th day, the bees did guard duty; after the 21st day, their wax glands ceased to function. Now the bees became foragers. Rösch found that worker bees died when they were about 38 days old. With the publication of Rösch's findings, other scientists joined the investigation. In Munich, Dr Martin Lindauer noted certain variations in Rösch's time schedule—he had watched a marked bee stand guard duty for an unheard-of 9 days. In Russia, Mrs L. I. Perepelova announced that she had several precocious bees—one 2-day old was making wax, normally a job for the 15-day olds. Obviously a beehive was extremely adaptable. Jobs could be done earlier if the well-being of the hive demanded it.

Bee students everywhere set out to discover just how adaptable bees were. The most spectacular experiments were performed by Mrs Perepelova. She removed the queen, larvae and eggs from the hive and watched to see what the workers would do. For several hours the hive did not miss the queen. Then one of the attendants lifted her antennae and began to circle. She exchanged food with a nearby wax-maker, and the wax-maker drummed her wings. She approached and exchanged food with others. The cluster moaned. The moan spread through the hive, and the whole group began to throb as if besieged by fever.

Several weeks passed. Mrs Perepelova noticed some workers rushing over the empty brood cells and thrusting their heads far down into them. Then came the impossible, the supreme effort to heal the wound—a few 'sterile' workers began to lay eggs. Nurses clustered around the egg-laying workers, feeding them bee milk. Slowly, laboriously, the workers gave forth eggs—six to eight a day, as compared to the queen's 2000 to 3000. Mrs Perepelova's conclusion: 'When the queen is gone, some inhibitory factor that prevents the workers from laying is missing from the hive.'

Around the world, bee experts pressed on to find what else a hive could do to heal itself. Mykola Haydak, of Minnesota's Agricultural Experimental Station, removed the brood comb from a hive and isolated it. Then he put upon it newly emerged bees. There were no nurses, hive cleaners, guards, wax-makers, foragers. He waited.

The adjustment was violent. The entire development process was speeded up so dramatically that 3-day old bees took survey flights from the hive while others of this age built cells, a job normally reserved for the 16th day. On the 4th day the bees collected pollen. After a desperate week, the premature hive began to function as usual.

With the publication of Haydak's findings, experts wondered whether bees could also reverse their development. In Yugoslavia, Mrs Vasilja Moskovljevic placed 503 marked foragers, all about 28 days old and with dried-up bee-milk glands, on to an isolated brood comb with the queen. The bees would either have to produce bee milk or let the hatched larvae die. Days passed; no brood was reared. Then Mrs Moskovljevic noticed a forager leaning into a cell. The scientist looked closely. A glittering drop of bee milk was deposited near the mouth of a hatched larva. Quickly Mrs Moskovljevic placed the forager's glands under a microscope, and there was the proof. The old dried glands were swollen and filled with bee milk. The impossible had been achieved: youth had been regenerated.

Meanwhile, in Austria, zoologist Karl von Frisch discovered a 'language' used by foragers to tell others the distance and direction to sources of pollen. A bee which had found some flowers returned to the hive and performed a dance for her fellow foragers. A vigorous figure-of-eight dance meant

Although they prefer the shelter of a cave or hollow tree, wild honey-bees may build hives in the open, as in this mulberry tree. When a hive becomes crowded, the queen and most of the colony swarm near by while scouts seek a new site and report back by dancing. The swarm checks these reports, selects the best site and follows the scout to the new home.

that the flowers were near. A feeble tail-wagging dance meant that the flowers were far away (distance, near or far, could be spelt out explicitly in metres by the observer). If the bee's body was pointed vertically up on the comb, the flowers were in the direction of the sun. The body pointed down on the comb meant that the flowers were in the opposite direction to the sun. A bee dancing at a 60-degree angle from the vertical was telling her coterie to leave the hive at 60 degrees to the sun. The kind of flower was communicated to the other bees by a taste of the forager's nectar or pollen.

Next, Martin Lindauer discovered that this dance language was also used by forager 'scouts' to inform a swarming hive of the location of a new home—on several occasions he noted the angle and the rapidity of the dance movements and was able to get to the new location in time to observe the bees' arrival.

The final question to be answered was: what stream of intelligence flowed through the hive that told its separate parts what to do?

A British bee expert, Dr C. R. Ribbands, tackled this one. He noted an aspect of hive life that no one had seriously studied—the constant circulation of food in the hive. Food moved steadily from nurse to queen, from nurse to the wax-makers, to the cell cleaners, to the receivers, to the foragers, and back from the foragers to the receivers, the cell cleaners, the wax-makers, the nurses and the queen.

Ribbands became convinced that each stage of bee development contributed a distinct glandular secretion or an enzyme which, if all were present and in sufficient supply, would tell the individuals that the hive was in a balanced and healthy condition.

Dr Ribbands kept coming back to Mrs Perepelova's remark: 'some inhibitory factor', preventing workers from laying eggs, was missing when the queen was gone. He also saw that it took the hive several days to make the adjustment—the time necessary to circulate the food with the missing ingredient and lift the inhibitions. Could the food be a kind of circulatory system, a bloodstream of sorts?

Thus Ribbands conceived the idea of the hive-animal of many individually functioning parts, controlled by the essence of a hive—its golden food. Much study remains to be done; the chemical properties of the food ingredients, for instance, still need to be isolated and identified. But most bee researchers today agree that the concept is sound.

I realise now that many years ago I was present when a wild hive died. It had lived in the kitchen walls of our summer home, humming gently and giving birth to new swarms for 12 years. Then, one September day, there was a hum in the walls different from anything we had ever heard. We ran outside to see what was the matter. A few bees dropped from the hive doorway to the ground. Then silence.

Next spring the bees did not come out. A year later, when the walls were opened to make room for a window, my uncle described what he had found: 'A little dried queen in a circle of attendants, some of them close against her, as if to keep some vital life-blood going.' A beautiful golden creature had stopped breathing. We had always spoken of 'the hive' as a single thing, but none of us realised how close we were to the truth. Something with a thousand sparkling parts had lived and died among us—the humming, life-giving hive, without which the earth would be a poorer, less fruitful place.

War and Peace among the Termites

V. B. Dröscher

The social organisation and architectural skills of termites reach a sophistication that even man can hardly match

In the African veld, the vanguard of an army of ants reaches a termite fortress as tall as a man. Hundreds of the blood-thirsty predators swarm over the red-brown termite nest, while the main force, numbering tens of thousands, halts in an agitated throng immediately in front of it.

The walls of the fortress are as hard as concrete; nowhere is there the smallest hole through which they can penetrate. Nevertheless the termites within are aware of the approach of the invaders; the alarm signal has been sounded—a strange clicking sound lasting for minutes on end.

The termite nymphs and younger workers take refuge in the deepest parts of the structure, while older workers hastily wall up the entrances to the queen's palace and soldiers take up their positions in the outer forts, casemates, corridor galleries and other strategic points.

Meanwhile a reconnaissance party of the invaders has found a closed, chimney-like structure on the upper part of the fortress; its dark brown colour stands out against the lighter colour of the rest. This is a new storey added to the termites' skyscraper only a few hours ago, and here the concrete is still soft. In a flash the reconnaissance ant with its antennae 'trills' this information on to the head of its nearest fellow; in no time the news has been 'spoken round' to the great army, which promptly swarms up the hill and begins digging into the soft mass of the newly built structure.

Scarcely has the first breach been made than the intruders find themselves faced with numbers of little 'gun barrels'. In this case they are up against a particularly dangerous enemy, the nasute termites (*Nasutitermes*). These do not fight with the same weapons as other termites; instead of cut-throat nippers, they have a different kind of lethal weapon. Where their head ought to be, the soldiers of these tribes have a kind of glue-tube.

Through the 'gun barrel' of the proboscis they can spray the enemy with a foul-smelling, glutinous fluid

Termite nests in the Northern Territory of Australia. These nests are built by the 'magnetic' termite, Amitermes meridionalis, *so called because its nests are always aligned in a north–south direction, with their broad faces turned east–west. The purpose of this is presumably for the nest to catch the maximum amount of warmth from the sun.*

which glues them to the battlefield. The range of these 'glue-guns' is of course very short. Besides, the nasute soldiers, having no eyes, have to feel with their antennae everyone they meet before knowing whether he be friend or foe. In daylight this gives the invaders a slight advantage, as their eyes enable them to recognise an enemy (only if he moves, of course) at a distance of 2 centimetres, not more. So it often happens that after breaching the fortress they manage to pinch off the guards' glutinous proboscises before the glue is spurted.

The hunter, predatory or driver ants themselves increase their furious fighting spirit by means of a citral, aromatic substance secreted by special glands. They charge in a dense mass, swarming over and round each other, slaughter the guards and advance like shock troops into the labyrinth of passages and chambers inside the termite nest.

To be able to find their way out again, they leave a trail of pathfinder perfume with the points of their abdomens. Without this Ariadne's thread, they would be hopelessly lost in the labyrinth and would inevitably perish in it.

Through the breach a vast column of ants pours into the fortress. After some time the survivors of the battle reappear with their prey—dead termite soldiers, workers and nymphs—and drag them to a dumping-ground. Here the corpses are cut up into regular sizes by specialist butcher-ants and fed by 'nurses' to the ant larvae, which these creatures always take with them on their endless forays.

Only very rarely do they find the queen's palace, which lies roughly in the centre of the fortress. The passages leading to it are so confusing that the invading army is nearly always led astray. Moreover, around their queen the defenders fight with the courage of despair. Soldier termites fight on even after all six legs have been bitten off.

Round the queen even the workers are said to join in the battle. Observers have reported four small workers holding a Goliath of an ant by the legs until a big soldier arrived and glued it down in the middle of the passage with its nose-fluid. Gradually the aggressive spirit of the invaders flags, losses increase in the face of the enemy's numerical superiority, and suddenly the whole army withdraws from the nest as if at a word of command.

The vital thing is the survival of the termite king and queen. Even though hundreds of thousands of their 'subjects' perish in an invasion, even though on 'peaceful' days thousands of the dwellers in the stronghold are devoured by ant-eaters, ant-bears and woodpeckers, or by ground-beetle larvae, which lurk like ghosts in the wall recesses and seize termites passing in the dark—to the queen all these are trifling matters, for she lays one egg about every two seconds uninterruptedly, day and night.

A queen can lay up to 48,000 eggs in a day. In the course of her 10-year life her progeny numbers hundreds of millions. If the fertility of the latter is also taken into account, a queen and her offspring could, in the course of 10 years, populate the warmer latitudes so densely that there would be no room for a single human being or earth-worm. Fortunately the termites are highly prized delicacies.

At certain seasons, shortly before dusk, when the air is sultry and thundery, the termites open their

159

fortresses at the top. Soldiers post themselves round about in battle trim and 'smell' whether the coast is clear or not. If there is no cause for alarm, they give a scent signal and with explosive force hundreds of thousands of winged, sexual-form termites mount into the air like a rising column of smoke. Strange to say, they swarm out of all the neighbouring termite nests at the same time. They must have a kind of barometer in their antennae which tells them when the best conditions prevail for the nuptial flight.

The biological significance of this strange institution is that winged males and females belonging to different states meet in the air and subsequently mate. Thus the danger of inbreeding is reduced. Moreover, an innate time-sense in conjunction with this barometer tells them to embark on the nuptial flight only when the approach of night gives them protection from their enemies, and when the ground is about to be so soaked by an approaching storm that the mating couples will be able to dig themselves in.

But before that stage is reached the 'smoke-trails' of ascending swarms provoke a fierce assault by all the termite-eaters: birds, bats, hedgehogs, armadillos, ground-hogs, beetles, wasps, lizards, geckoes, chameleons and millipedes all come hurrying along to secure their share of the feast. Natives also appear on the scene and light big camp fires. These attract the swarming insects, singe their filmy wings and grill them as they fall. If fat is available, the natives fry the insects in big pans. They are said to be delicious done this way.

The relatively few survivors of the holocaust, after a brief courtship, mate in the hole they have dug for themselves and produce offspring. They are now king and queen; but for lack of staff or servants during the first weeks they have to do all the chores themselves—build the nest, search for food, fetch water if necessary, look after their eggs and feed the nymphs, when they emerge, with a milky fluid from their salivary glands. The nymphs look like tiny workers or soldiers and are soon able to take over 'fatigue' duties. After they have made further progress, one of their first tasks is that of immuring their parents in the so-called foundation chamber where, well protected from danger, they devote themselves entirely to the production of offspring. The only communication with the outside world is by way of small trap-doors through which nymphs, now fully grown workers, are able to slip.

As the population of the new termite state increases, the crenellated fortress which is its home grows too. The termite architects and builders perform fantastic feats in this respect. A comparable human achievement would be a building as tall as the Matterhorn.

The technique employed is as follows. After a heavy shower, workers open the top of the fortress from within. Soldiers then emerge and take up position in a circle some 12 in. in diameter round the hole.

Then workers appear, each dragging a small clump of earth, which (in the case of *Macrotermes natalensis*) it has fetched, not from the surface humus, which is unsuitable for building purposes, but from much deeper strata, and is so constituted that much harder concrete can be made of it. Each worker with his load makes his way in between two soldiers and begins mixing cement. His method is to squeeze out of his mouth a brownish sausage of half-digested wood and saliva, and he works this up with the clump of earth into a uniform mass. Single pillars begin to rise between the soldiers; when these pillars are finished they are joined by round arches. The walls are then completed and the structure closed in the shape of a dome. Thus these sightless creatures complete the extension to their home with a sleep-walker's assurance and after only a few hours' work.

The phenomenon surpasses our comprehension. How do these small, blind creatures, working without a plan, visualise the grand design they follow in building these great structures? The following experiment illustrates the nature of this baffling question.

Before the soldiers had, so to speak, drawn up the ground-plan by forming up in a circle, the 'building site' was divided in two by a thick steel-plate wall, making it impossible for the termites on one side to communicate by sight, sound, smell or touch with their fellows on the other. By human standards this should have led the little creatures astray. It seemed reasonable to assume at least that the building would be unsymmetrical, or that the dome arches would fail to meet. But the termites simply treated the steel plate as non-existent and incorporated it into the structure. This makes the phenomenon more baffling still; we are without the slightest clue to a plausible scientific explanation.

Termites are capable of still more extraordinary feats, in comparison with which those just described are quite elementary. They can, for instance, install an air-conditioning system in their fortress, by which they are able to regulate the temperature, humidity and the oxygen—and carbon dioxide—content of the air. This marvel was investigated by Professor Martin Lüscher, of Berne University, in the nests of *Macrotermes natalensis* on the Ivory Coast, which are up to 16 ft in height.

These termites require a tropical hothouse temperature of 86°F, with 98–99 per cent air humidity. If the humidity drops only a little, they die within five to ten hours. So it is essential that they stock themselves up with humidity in their home before they set out on their marches of several hundred yards through subterranean passages to such sources of food supply as rotting trees, houses, telegraph poles, railway sleepers, sugar-cane plantations and titbits of wood, wool, leather or ivory.

To keep their private climate as constant as possible and independent of outside fluctuations, they effectively insulate themselves within outer walls which are half a yard thick and as hard as concrete. But they also have to breathe: 2 million termites consume 26,500 pints of fresh air and exhale about 530 pints of carbon dioxide in a day. How do these waste gases escape, and how is the oxygen essential to life brought in?

The answer is a highly efficient ventilation system. Round the outside of the termitary there are a dozen ascending ridges. These are the 'cooling-fins' of the installation, which the termites 'invented' millions of years before man. In each of these ridges, about ten narrow air-shafts lead from top to bottom just under the surface. The hot, used air collects in the 'attic', passes down through the air-shafts where it cools, and at the same time unites with the outside air through microscopic pores in the walls, shedding carbon dioxide and absorbing fresh oxygen.

From these 'lungs' the revitalised air at the correct temperature passes into the spacious vaulted chambers which lie at a depth of about 3 ft underground. Here, on a number of supporting pillars constructed on mechanically sound principles, lies the real termites' nest, continuously supplied with fresh air from the vaults below.

In the hundred or so air-shafts inside the cooling-fins, termite 'mechanics' are continually at work contracting or widening air outlets on a valve principle, closing or opening shafts according to the time of day or season, depending on whether the temperature is too cold or too hot, or whether there is too much or too little oxygen.

The astonishing feature is that the ventilation is so regulated that the optimum temperature always prevails at the centre of the nest, and thus in the queen's palace, though the mechanics are at a distance of 3–4 yds in a bee-line from the queen.

Who or what keeps the mechanics informed about the atmospheric situation in the queen's palace? Do messengers come running to them? In view of the distances in the labyrinth, they would spend some hours on the way. Do the mechanics have an appropriate 'theoretical value control'?

In view of the different nest sizes and the constantly changing conditions inside and outside, this would be subject to such complicated fluctuations that such a hypothesis seems untenable.

Does the queen send signals with special aromatic substances reporting changes of temperature? That would be a phenomenon unique in Nature.

The ventilation technique is sufficiently sophisticated to be adaptable to climatic conditions in any part of Africa, and also enables them to survive in Central European conditions. They are not found in Europe for the sole reason that new colonies of *Macrotermes natalensis* can be founded only by swarming, sexual-form animals, and in the initial phase, when they are entirely dependent on themselves, they are not capable of surviving in the temperate zone, as their foundation chamber lacks the air-conditioning plant. If *Macrotermes natalensis* were able, like other species of termites, to found new colonies by digging underground galleries, all wooden buildings and objects in Europe would be threatened if not destroyed by them.

The Weirdest Orchestra on Earth

Jean George

To produce their amazing sounds,
the instrumentalists of the insect world
contort, modify and adapt
their bodies to an astonishing degree

The musician drew a thigh-bone against the teeth of a saw and began to play a six-beat phrase. Another instrumentalist came in on a drum, amplifying a low tattoo into a siren-like wail. A third snapped his head against a wooden board, and a fourth, lying on his back with his feet in the air, made music by arching his spine.

Most of this group can be heard during the summer in fields and hedges, for the musicians are

Two midnight musicians meet face to face. The katydid makes a loud chirping call by rubbing together two roughened areas of his front wings. The tiny tree frog produces a bird-like trill with his vocal cords and resonant throat sac. Both creatures have the same object: to attract females of their species.

a grasshopper, a cicada, a death-watch beetle and a click beetle—and they are all members of the weirdest orchestra on earth.

The conspicuous soloists of this orchestra are crickets, grasshoppers and cicadas, but you can listen to a fuller ensemble on any summer night on the stage they prefer—hot grass, dry earth and, for good measure, an August moon quivering in a sea of heat. Many of them (there are 900,000 kinds of insects in all, representing 80 per cent of all the animals on earth) reach a jazzy pitch that marks the high tide of their breeding season.

Familiar to nearly everyone are the crickets, with their fat bodies, long antennae, big heads—and their endearing habit of singing from the hearth and door-step. Crickets sing with a distinctive 'creeeak, creeeak', produced by rubbing a scraper on the left wing against a file on the right. Cricket songs have meaning. Some are love calls, others are danger signals and others simply announce 'here I am'.

The tree-cricket blasts forth one of the most shrill and persistent songs of all insects—a repetitive 'trill' that goes on endlessly. This is a mating call. However, it is a rather strange love song, because the female is deaf, having no sound-receptors on her body. But while the male rubs his left wing over his right in a series of harmonic frequencies, a small gland is exposed which emits fluid. The odour of this fluid *does* reach the female, who crawls up on the male's back to drink, and is then inseminated.

Grasshoppers use their thigh-bones as a bow. A grasshopper, standing on his 'hands', lifts his big back legs until the femurs rub against a line of small stiff pegs on each wing. The grasshopper also has a flight song. As he takes off, he snaps his two big top wings against the smaller inside ones and produces that familiar crackle of grasshopper jumps.

The loudest members of the insect orchestra are the 'drummers' that literally beat one object against another. The cicadas are the classical drummers. Those with the two-year life cycle are about $1\frac{1}{4}$ in. long, chunky, often with beautiful crystal wings. When the brood emerges from the ground, the cicadas leave their crisp brown coats on trees and plants. The sounds they make are courtship calls, a buzz-saw high in the tree tops that begins softly and rises to a frantic, ear-splitting climax.

S. W. Frost, the entomologist, calls the cicada's noise-making instruments 'the most complicated sound organs found in the animal kingdom'. The cicada not only has drumheads vibrated by powerful muscles, but also an amplifying system.

The sound organs are small pits on either side of the abdomen, just under the wings. Two large plates, which can be raised and lowered to control the volume, lie over them. The drumheads, or timbals, are in these cavities, together with the amplifier—a folded membrane, a so-called mirror or sounding board, and a pipe that lets in the air to be trembled. The muscles vibrate the timbals slowly at first and shake the air inside the cavity. The vibrations expand within the folded membrane, and then bounce off the mirror for more intense magnification. Meanwhile, the plates are opening, letting out a sound that is an air-cracking fanfare.

Of all the drummers, however, the death-watch beetle is the most astonishing; for this is the musician that hits its head on wood to beat a tune. He does this inside his burrow in woodwork and old furniture. These clicking concerts can go on for years. I recall the morning my father told me to listen to the top of his oak desk. I was amazed to hear snaps and clicks. Then he pointed to a little volcano of sawdust. 'The beetle's been getting closer to the surface for the last few days,' my father explained, 'and so I have been keeping an eye out for him.' Presently a slender, $\frac{1}{4}$ in. long beetle stepped out of the sawdust. 'I'll miss him,' my father said. 'He's been keeping me company for 12 years.'

In addition to the insects that sing deliberately to communicate, there is yet another group of noise-makers—the 'incidental musicians'. These are the flies, bees and mosquitoes that make sounds as they go about their daily chores of gathering food or defending the hive. They have not been ignored by the physicists. One study of the house-fly revealed that it whines the note F in the middle octave, by vibrating its wings 21,120 times a minute.

When I mentioned this to a friend who is a musician with perfect pitch, she listened to a house-fly and said, 'You're right.' Three weeks later, however, I had a phone call from her. 'Two flies in my studio are driving me crazy,' she reported. 'They're off-key. Flat!' I suggested she turn up the heat, for the warmer insects are, the more active they become. Later she rang to say that the heat had worked, stepping up the wings' vibrations. 'The flies are on pitch now,' she said happily, 'and I can work again.'

The 17-year cicadas require a long metamorphosis. After living underground for years as nymphs, cicadas crawl up plant stems and burst from their larval shells, winged and ready to mate. They die within a few weeks, after laying their eggs.

Bees and wasps also use their wings to create sounds, but the tones they make are an expression of their moods. They hum while peacefully gathering food, 'pipe' when calling to mates and 'roar' when attacked. But of all the fiddling, drumming, vibrating insects, the click beetle is my favourite musician.

I came upon one while I was working in the garden recently. He was a narrow, shiny beetle and he had fallen on his back as click beetles are wont to do. While I watched him, he suddenly arched his spine as he pressed head and tail against the ground. A section of his thorax pulled out of a groove in his abdomen, and he seemed done for. However, with a loud click he forced himself together again. This gave him such a jolt that he rose 18 in. into the air, where he turned over, and came down on his feet.

As I watched him scurry away, a passing bee hummed out the peace of nectar-gathering, and a grasshopper cracked out a ditty of flight. From near by came the drum and roll of a cicada. In the soft August sun, the band played on.

MASTERS OF MIMICRY

In the world of insects and spiders, things are not always what they seem. A katydid looks like the lichens on a tree trunk, a stick-insect like a twig, a grasshopper like a dried leaf. Such disguises, designed to deceive the eye of a predator, have played a vital role in these small creatures' evolutionary struggle to survive. Non-toxic insects and spiders are virtually incapable of protecting themselves from larger, more voracious forms of life, and this very limitation of size may be what has made them such masters of mimicry. Some have developed patterns and colours that help them blend into their natural backgrounds, and when an environment changes, insects which rely on camouflage must change their disguise accordingly. This happened to the pale-coloured peppered moth family, which became predominantly black when the Industrial Revolution turned trees around major cities in Britain black with grime.

Other insects have been able to alter their shape and coloration so that they closely resemble parts of the plants they live on. To scare off foragers, distasteful creatures tend to advertise their distastefulness, while more edible creatures try to imitate the distasteful ones. Thus a harmless caterpillar may look like a poisonous snake, and a defenceless moth like a sting-bearing bee. Mimicry is known among birds, reptiles, mammals and fish, but insects and spiders outstrip all other animals in the variety and effectiveness of their disguise.

The Indian leaf-bug mimics not only the shape and colour of the leaves it lives among, but also the way that they move. It clings to a tree or shrub, and rocks its body back and forth in a convincing imitation of a leaf blown in the wind.

When this caterpillar is threatened, its defence is to turn itself over, retract its legs into its body, and flash a pair of false eyes at its enemy. In doing so, it produces a convincing imitation of the deadly pit viper.

During the day, stick-insects rest alongside twigs,
which they resemble to perfection. After
dark, they crawl slowly about, feeding on leaves.

Treehoppers, which suck juice from plants, look like
thorns along the stems they feed on. This disguise
is good enough to deceive the birds, their enemies,
even when the plants they cling to have no thorns.

This hawk moth has the clear wings, fat furry body and
short black antennae of a bumble-bee. When a real
bumble-bee sees a hawk moth taking pollen and nectar
from a flower, it goes to search elsewhere for its food.

165

Perched among these lichens (above) is a cricket-like katydid. Though its long antennae seem easy to spot, they are camouflaged with alternate colours that obscure their outline.

Short-horned grasshoppers have protective coloration that blends with their environment. This one (left) looks like a dead leaf; others resemble green leaves or even pebbles.

The dune wolf spider is doubly safe. It lives in a tunnel, and when it emerges its markings so break up the contours of its body that it blends into the sand.

The pattern of this sphinx moth's wings makes it indistinguishable from tree bark. As added protection, the moth can startle an enemy by flashing bright-coloured underwings.

Cold-Blooded Creatures

It is not heartlessness but heatlessness that marks a creature
as cold-blooded. Lacking the built-in heating systems
of birds and mammals, all reptiles, amphibians
and fish, and the multitude
of lower animals, must regulate body heat by
physical activity (or inactivity) and by choice of environment

That Remarkable Creature the Snail

Oscar Schisgall

The snail's slow pace and humble appearance
give no clue to its strange
talents or newly discovered usefulness

It can exist on the tops of high mountains, buried in deserts or hidden in rain forests. Both constructive and destructive, it serves admirably as an item of food and in medical research, while producing havoc in vegetable gardens. Land snails originated millions of years ago and since then have made their way over most of the world, subdividing into some 18,000 species.

In many ways, the everyday snail is a phenomenal creature. It is without an internal skeleton and is practically all muscle. Although small and fragile in appearance, one species, *Helix pomatia*, which is the *Bourgogne* of gastronomic fame, can easily carry 12—and pull 200—times its own weight.

The *Bourgogne* has a predilection for sleep. In addition to several months of winter hibernation, it crawls into its shell at the least sign of hot sun, which dries it out, or heavy rain, which waterlogs it. The *Bourgogne* can take short naps or spend days huddled in its bedroom behind a thin curtain of mucilage. Desert snails carry the sleeping habit to miraculous extremes, dozing off for as long as three or four years.

In motion, a snail is a thing of graceful beauty. Its sinuous body—varying in colour from grey to silver —glides along without visible effort on its 'suction-cup' underside. Tiny muscles contract in a rhythmic succession of waves, and thus the fragile body is propelled forwards.

Wherever they go, snails lay a protective carpet under themselves, leaving behind a colourless, sticky discharge that sometimes shimmers silver in the light. So effective is this coating that snails have been induced to crawl along the sharp edge of a razor blade without a trace of a cut.

In the *Bourgogne*'s everyday life, moisture is the ruling factor—moisture to keep its body supple, moisture for its silver path, moisture to nourish the young shoots it dotes on. In mid-April, when temperatures turn milder and spring showers bathe the landscape, the *Bourgogne* wakens: its tiny silvery head appears, its horns dart here and there to learn what the world has to offer. The upper pair of antennae, which can be elongated to $\frac{3}{4}$ in. or more, are topped by the eyes; in the much shorter, lower pair are extremely sensitive organs of touch.

As the snail proceeds after its first meal, its body, which may be 3 in. long and $\frac{1}{4}$ in. thick, stretches out from the shell. The snail is woefully shortsighted, but its strong sense of smell guides it to new vegetation. Then its tiny mouth goes to work. Although no

The soft fruit of a blackberry is an ideal meal for a snail. With its tiny, tongue-like radula, covered with rows of hooks and horny teeth, the snail pierces the fruit and scrapes it into its mouth. The snail's eyes are on retractable stalks, shown here fully extended.

larger than a pinprick, it is equipped with 25,600 infinitesimally small but incredibly effective teeth. Put a snail in a cardboard box, and it will eat its way to freedom. If it wears down the teeth, the snail replaces them as easily as it repairs a broken shell.

Usually the snail forages for food at night, but cloudy and drizzly days become uninterrupted day-long orgies of eating. The rest of the time it hides from the sun's rays.

Twice a year, in spring and autumn, the snail suddenly stops eating and takes to wandering restlessly about. Its antennae reach out, probing here and there. Suddenly it sets out at top speed.

The snail is on a love quest which ends when it meets its chosen mate face to face. During the ensuing courtship, which may last for several hours, they first bite each other, then prod the right side of the neck, where the genital orifice is located. The two hermaphrodites—each snail possesses both male and female organs—unite at the neck and one leaves the other pregnant.

Some 12–15 days after mating, the pregnant snail picks a moist spot at the base of a tree or amid grass roots close to a potential food supply, and there digs a nest—a hole about 3 in. deep. For over 12 hours, it carefully drops as many as 26 tiny eggs, one by one, into the hole. It then covers up the traces and abandons the eggs to their fate.

In three or four weeks, the eggs hatch into near-perfect miniature *Bourgogne* snails, with paper-thin shells. As soon as they hatch, the young snails are fully able to cope with life—to crawl out of their nest, provide themselves with food and find shelter. They even inherit their parents' distrust of the sun, and circulate only at night.

Every year the snail adds about $\frac{1}{10}$ in. to its shell, depending on climate and diet. In France, where snails are regularly harvested, two years is the average life-span and thus size is limited. There are, however, giants that have been shipped to France from lands where they had been allowed to age much longer. Emile Dhumerelle, one of the best-known snail dealers in Paris, exhibits one shell as big as a tennis ball.

But big or little, the snail attains its greatest stature at the end of a fork. From the days when housewives had to spend tedious hours washing, cooking and elaborately preparing them, *les escargots* have become today one of the quickest and easiest dishes on the French menu. Some 40 large 'snail preparers' see to it that housewives can always find a ready supply of the two species of snails considered the most succulent by the discriminating palate—the tantalising *Bourgognes* and the slightly smaller *petits gris*. Some 250 million of them are swallowed every year in France alone.

But the snail may prove to be more than a gastronomic delight. Every spring the faculty of medicine at the University of Paris buys several hundred pounds of snails. These are kept alive at a low

169

temperature for the use of a staff of some 100 technicians. According to the scientists there, the gastric juices the snails secrete are invaluable in the study of sex and adrenal hormones, known as steroids, attached to other molecules in the human bloodstream. Thanks to a discovery made in 1952, the chemical properties of this secretion have made it possible to isolate steroids without damaging them. By studying their concentration in blood or urine, it is possible to detect the presence of certain types of cancer. There is no telling where the snail's silver trail may lead.

What Snakes are Really Like

Alan Devoe

Snakes live in the straitjackets of their skins—but they are among the most successful acrobats and killers known

Our fellow creatures on this abounding earth include about 2500 species of snakes. To understand a snake's life is to encounter some of the most amazing adaptations and specialised gifts in the world of Nature.

A snake never closes its eyes; it has no eyelids. A snake can engulf prey far bigger than its mouth; giant snakes such as Asia's pythons are capable of swallowing a deer. Some poisonous snakes, like the African mamba, are so deadly that men have died from a bite in less than a minute. Some harmless snakes have such odd endowments as a stomach that can digest bones and a yellow eye-lens that gives sharpened vision by filtering out ultra-violet rays.

It is hardly surprising that such curious creatures should be the subject of more myths and misunderstandings than any others under the sun—or moon, for many snakes are most active at night.

It is not true that snakes are 'slimy'; their skins are dry and exceptionally clean. No snake has a poisonous sting in its tail. No snake rolls like a hoop or hypnotises birds. Snakes' flicking, 'wicked-looking' tongues are harmless. Killing a snake will not bring its mate seeking vengeance. It is not true

that a mortally injured snake retains life until sunset. Nine-tenths of all species are harmless. Few are aggressive towards man. They do not suck milk from cows; and they are not charmed by snake-charmers' music—snakes are deaf.

The real facts about snakes are more remarkable than any fables. Everything about a snake is designed round the key fact that it has no arms or legs. Yet it is not a primitive or simple being like a worm (to which it is unrelated), but a highly developed, complex one. It breathes by a lung. It has a three-chambered heart. Its internal processes involve an intricate physiology of liver, gall bladder and kidneys. And it must catch prey, defeat or evade enemies and reproduce its race while confined inside its own elongated skin, like a man strait-jacketed and hobbled. To meet this unique problem, Nature has given it specialised equipment and peculiar skills.

A snake lives in a world of silence. Since it has no ears, it 'listens' with its sensitive underside for ground vibrations. The eyes can focus in delicate adjustment to near distances, like a precisely calibrated microscope. A night-foraging snake has eyes like a cat's, with vertical pupils.

A snake's tongue is both an exquisitely sensitive 'hand'—used for delicately touching and feeling every strange object it encounters—and a means of super-smelling. The fine forked tips pick up microscopic particles from the air, earth and water. Drawing in its tongue, the snake inserts the forked tips into two tiny pits in the roof of its mouth. These pits are lined with keen sensory cells, and they give the snake the precise scent and feel of its immediate environment.

From nose-tip to tail-tip the snake's body is covered with convex, overlapping scales, affording a tough covering so continuous that a portion of it, which is transparent, covers even the snake's eyes. The backbone is engineered for tremendous suppleness. Its vertebrae are articulated by perfect ball-and-socket joints. To each vertebra is attached a pair of ribs (some snakes have more than 300 pairs). There is no breastbone; instead, each rib is joined by a cartilage and a set of powerful muscles to one

Special adaptations enable this garter snake to swallow a cricket frog whole. The snake's mouth can expand enormously because its upper and lower jawbones are not joined and both halves of the lower jaw are connected by an elastic muscle. The snake's teeth point backwards, enabling it to grasp its prey firmly, and its stomach juices are so potent that they can even dissolve bones—which means that the snake has no need for chewing.

The water moccasin (above), a venomous snake found in North America, is one of the small number of species that give birth to living young.

The bull snake (below) illustrates the much more common form of reproduction: it is laying a clutch of from 10 to 24 tough, leathery-shelled eggs that will take about eight weeks to hatch.

of the scales on the snake's underside. This is the secret of its gliding ability.

In the glide a snake angles its ribs forward, hooks the ground with the attached scales on its underside, then gives a backward rib-push. The smooth-flowing glide of a snake is a beautifully synchronised, many-footed walking, all done from the inside. For faster speed, snakes supplement this action by undulating laterally in a wriggle that takes advantage of every projection in the terrain. Where purchase is poor, a snake may thrust its head forward, hold it firmly to the ground, and then pull up the rest of its body.

A snake usually becomes sexually mature in its second or third year. Only a few naturalists have been privileged to see the ritual of courtship. Among water and garter snakes, the male fondles his chosen female by rubbing his chin gently upwards along her back, in a series of gliding caresses. American black-snakes engage in a courtship dance. Weaving, bobbing, rearing with heads almost touching and then whirling in a new arabesque of challenge and response, the two courting snakes are whipped into a flashing crescendo of excitement.

About three-quarters of all snakes hatch from eggs; a minority are born alive, sometimes in immense broods. A garter snake has been known to produce 78 babies in a litter. Egg clutches, deposited by the mother in a sheltered spot such as an old stump, or buried in the sand, vary in number from a few to over 70 eggs.

A snake's egg is not brittle, like a bird's, but slightly malleable. An extraordinary fact is that it increases in size after being laid. It may grow as much as one-third before hatching. Some eggs hatch within four days, others take as long as 90. In temperate climates most snakes lay their eggs in early summer and the babies hatch in August or September. Research has disclosed that a mother snake may lay fertile eggs even though she has not mated for several years.

The baby snake gets out of its egg by means of a temporary egg-tooth, as a chick does. From the moment of hatching it is ready to cope with its world. Among poisonous species a newly hatched baby is already venomous and knows instinctively how to use its equipment. A rattlesnake two minutes old can coil and strike expertly.

During its first year a snake more than doubles its length and may treble it during the second year. Then the rate of growth slows, but it never stops entirely as long as the snake lives—and the life-span of a snake may be long. A water moccasin has lived to be 20, a boa constrictor 23. Even a little garter snake has lived to be 11 years old in contented captivity.

Since a snake grows steadily, it is obliged to change its tight and hampering skin, which does not grow, at an average interval of six weeks (except during hibernation in northern climates). New skin forms under the old. As the old skin begins to loosen and slacken, the snake rubs its head against a twig or rough stone until a hole is worn through the skin. It works its head free. Then, contracting its muscles rhythmically, pushing, pulling, thrusting against the ground, the snake slips the old skin off backwards, inside-out like a peeled glove, emerging gleaming in fresh colour and agile again in a fitted suit.

Because the snake may be able to catch prey only at undependable intervals, Nature has ensured that it can swallow a bulk that will keep it going through a fast of more than a year. A snake has six rows of teeth: two in its lower jaw, two above, two more in the roof of its mouth; they grow in a continual succession of replacements. Needle-sharp, the teeth all curve inwards, making it almost impossible for a small animal that has been seized to pull away.

All the movable bones of the snake's head are loosely articulated. The bones of its lower jaw can be separated from the upper. Each side of the jaw can be worked independently, the two halves being connected only by elastic ligament. As a result, a snake can perform eating feats that seem mechanically impossible. Some snakes can engulf large birds' eggs without breaking them. A slender garter snake has been known to eat 30 tree frogs in succession. To digest its big, unchewed meals, a snake is equipped with gastric juices potent enough to break down fur, feathers and even teeth.

In the venomous species, one or two pairs of teeth are lengthened into fangs, grooved or hollow, and connected with sacs of poison in the snake's cheeks. At the moment of biting, the snake gives a powerful squeeze to these sacs and squirts a jet of venom into the victim. The co-ordinated speed of a poisonous snake's lunging strike, bite, poison injection and return to normal stance is one of the most startling feats of agility in Nature. The whole operation may be completed in less than half a second.

Venom helps in the capture of food, making it possible for this limbless, handless hunter quickly to paralyse small creatures that might otherwise get away. A venomous snake employs its poison against big animals or human beings only rarely, and in self-defence. The rattlesnake basking on a sunny rock ledge, the adder stretched at ease on the moorland path, want nothing so much as to be left alone.

Nobody Loves a Crocodile

Gordon Gaskill

With snorkel nostrils and periscope eyes, huge jaws and deadly tail, the crocodile is one of the few animals which deliberately attack human beings

The most feared and hated beast in the world is its largest reptile: this is the crocodile, which kills more human beings than do lions, tigers, leopards and snakes put together. Each year Africa alone loses an estimated 1000 victims, mostly women and children.

The crocodile's domain includes central and southern Africa, the warmer parts of Asia, tropical

Pacific islands and northern Australia. He also inhabits the warmer parts of the Americas but is there far outnumbered by his cousins, the alligators. The differences between crocodiles and alligators are many and technical. The most obvious one is that, with jaws closed, the alligator's teeth are invisible, while in the crocodile the long fourth tooth on each side of the lower jaw fits visibly into a notch on the outside of the upper jaw. This gives the crocodile a deceptive 'grin'.

Except for a few tiny, chameleon-like lizards, the crocodile is the only reptile with a true voice. He can emit a loud, eerie roar, like distant thunder or the roll of a big drum. His dental arrangement is marvellous: if he loses a tooth, another one quickly grows in its place, and this goes on all his life. He will eat almost anything. His digestive juices are so strong in hydrochloric acid that they have dissolved, in a few months, iron spearheads and 6 in. steel hooks that have been swallowed. Even so, he does not seem to need much food. In captivity, crocodiles thrive on less than a pound of meat a day.

The crocodile has two deadly weapons—terrible jaws and a terrible tail. A murderous sideways blow of the tail can knock down and break the legs of the largest deer. But the crocodile's classic attack is to drift in unseen in the murky shallows and then, without a sound, to submerge entirely and make a final swift lunge to seize his prey in vice-like jaws.

Nature has equipped him well for this mode of attack. The crocodile, like a submarine, has a 'periscope' and a 'snorkel' breathing tube: elevated eyes and nostrils. They peep just above the water, almost invisible, while the rest of the body is submerged. Like a submarine, too, the crocodile has a system of valves that automatically close when he dives, to protect nostrils, ears and throat from water. Embedded in his eyes are thousands of tiny crystals that collect all possible light, giving him amazing sight under water, even at night.

The crocodile is one of the few animals in the world which deliberately and regularly attack human beings. In places where crocodiles are considered sacred and are fed, or in lakes that swarm with fish, they hardly ever attack. But wherever the crocodile's natural prey has been largely depleted, it soon acquires a taste for human flesh. Most victims are women who are bathing, washing clothes or drawing water, and children who splash in the shallows. Many Africans are careless because they rely on some witch-doctor's charm to protect them.

In Tanganyika some years ago, a tribal chief told an Englishman that crocodiles had, in one month, taken five women as they drew water. The Englishman suggested that the women should use large tins tied to long bamboo poles to draw water. The chief shrugged and said, 'Tins like that are hard to find and very valuable.'

When a crocodile catches a large animal, such as a deer or a cow, he keeps it off balance with savage sideways yanks of his head and pulls it into deep water to drown it. The crocodile can then feed at leisure—but he has problems. Impressive as his great jaws are, his teeth are not made for chewing. They serve mostly as clamps. He can therefore eat at once only something he can swallow whole: small dogs are among his favourite titbits. If his victim is large, he tows it away to rot and thus become soft enough to tear apart easily. Often he takes his prey to a tunnel-like den with a below-water entrance slanting up into the shore above the water-line, and an air vent in the roof.

Perhaps the strangest escape from a crocodile was that of a native who was seized and pulled under water within sight of friends. By enormous luck the crocodile's den was only a few yards away. The victim regained consciousness to find himself inside a dim cavern full of decaying carcases—and with the crocodile lying beside him. Soon the reptile went back to the water, and the African seized the chance to enlarge the air hole above him and escape. It was a long time before his family would let him into his own house; they were sure he was a ghost.

Most widespread of the several species of crocodile is the Nile crocodile of Africa and Madagascar. The Nile crocodile mother lays her 3 in. long eggs (averaging about 60 per clutch) near the water's edge in sun-warmed sand, covers them with more sand, and waits for them to hatch—a period of about three months. Her job is to protect the eggs from predators: mongooses, pythons, hyenas, monkeys and big monitor lizards. (People sometimes eat the eggs, too, despite their rather strong fishy flavour.)

At hatching time a miracle occurs. The baby crocodiles cannot dig away the foot or so of earth above them; therefore, while still inside their shells, they begin calling for mother, who has been listening for this SOS. At the first peep, she begins to dig away the earth. This instinct is so strong that, when scientists tested it by building a fence round a sand nest, the frantic mother tore it to pieces.

The newborn baby is about 10 in. long and, from the first moment of life, aggressive. It snaps at anything near it. With unerring instinct it makes for the nearest water to find shelter; for many animals, including storks, cranes and mature crocodiles, find

The crocodile (above), can be identified by its protruding teeth; an alligator's teeth cannot be seen when its jaws are closed. In water the crocodile is swift and agile; its limbs are held close to its body, and it swims by making sinuous movements with its powerful tail. Even on land, the sluggish-looking reptile is capable of quite startling bursts of speed.

the wriggling infants even tastier than the eggs. With all these hazards, some experts estimate that not more than 1 per cent of the eggs laid ever become mature crocodiles.

Recent wholesale shooting makes it unlikely that any crocodile will live to a great age—and thus to great length. Asiatic and Pacific species are said to reach nearly 30 ft, but in the past few years no Nile crocodile over 19 ft has been shot.

Since the war there has been a great feminine demand for crocodile-leather shoes, handbags and luggage. High prices lure men into shooting crocodiles almost everywhere they exist. In one seven-month period, some hunters in Australia made over £5000 each. Crocodile populations dwindle quickly under such pressure. Many lake and river spots which only a dozen years ago were packed with crocodiles are now bare of them.

Dr Hugh Cott of Cambridge University, an expert on the Nile crocodile, fears that the reptile may soon become extinct. 'It would be a grave loss to science and posterity,' he says, 'if these saurians, which have survived for over 100 million years, were to be sacrificed to the demands of fashion.'

Few others share this worry. There is a widespread belief that many crocodiles have retreated to places less accessible to hunters. 'After two or three days,' one hunter told me, 'they learn that a spotlight or an outboard motor means danger—and they move away.' Several nations have now placed some restrictions on crocodile shooting.

One of the largest concentrations of crocodiles in Africa—perhaps in the world—is at the foot of Murchison Falls on the Victoria Nile in Uganda. It is one of the most fascinating nightmares I have ever seen. The pools are alive with fish, and a hungry crocodile has only to open his mouth to have it filled. All shooting is forbidden here, and the crocodile has no enemy but old age. Consequently the shores are lined with shoals of big crocodiles, sometimes lying across each other like logs.

'The protection they receive in parks alone,' says one game warden, 'will preserve all the crocodiles that science would ever want—or that tourists would ever wish to see.'

Survivors of the Dragon Age

David Fleay

Dragons are still at large in the world—not as spectacular as their legendary counterparts, but still touched by something not quite of this world

The largest dragon in the world today is the Komodo dragon or monitor lizard. This giant reptile, often reaching 10 ft in length and 300 lb. in weight, is a plain creature, with none of the decorative embellishments usually seen on Chinese paper dragons. The monitor lizard is a native of the islands of Padar, Rintja and Flores in Central Indonesia and has relatives in Australia that closely resemble it.

Least known of these Australian creatures is a powerful 6 ft lizard known as the perenty, which inhabits the central and western parts of the continent. One such monster was observed catching and killing a partly grown kangaroo, and others have been known to knock aborigines off their feet with sweeping blows of their powerful tails.

The better known species is the common goanna, which makes its home in trees, and the sand or ground goanna, which spends practically all its time on the ground, using rabbit warrens as bases for hunting operations. The larger common goanna, known locally as the bungarra, often exceeds 6 ft in length and, when brought to bay, makes a most ferocious display.

There is a belief among aborigines that a goanna's bite never heals. However, I have an old scar on the back of my right hand that dates from the time when a particularly large one got hold of me and

The Komodo dragon or monitor lizard, Varanus komodoensis, is the largest species of lizard known. A savage, powerful reptile, it can grow up to 10 ft long, and can weigh up to 300 lb. It is strictly carnivorous, and will devour any kind of meat, carrion or freshly killed. Active by day, it hides at night in dens among the rocks.

hung on for several minutes, despite the fact that I twisted its tail to persuade it to let go. Eventually we parted company, although some of my flesh remained in its jaws.

When pursued, these big lizards spiral up the nearest tree, with a great clatter and rattling of claws on bark. When approached at close quarters with no chance of escape, they inflate their bodies until the slack skin along their sides disappears. This is accompanied by an enormous swelling of their throat pouches. Angry hisses are uttered, and the goanna's long, forked tongue flicks rapidly back and forth. The rough, whip-like tail is coiled, ready to lash about with powerful, stinging strokes. Finally, the goanna has an appalling habit of disgorging its latest meal, which may have been carrion, on anyone unwise enough to climb the tree in which it has taken refuge.

Of the five lizard families represented in Australia, one of the most attractive is the Agamidae, usually referred to by naturalists as the Dragon family. It includes the handsome water lizards, and the bearded dragon and its many smaller and more active relatives. Among these is the frightful-looking, though harmless, thorny devil of the arid inland regions.

Members of this family vary in length from 6 in. to 3 ft, with long, slender tails and well-developed hind limbs. Many of them, when pursued, race along with their forelimbs and head held high and clear of the ground. They can also change their skin colour according to the nature of their surroundings.

The bearded dragon is well known throughout most of Australia. On sunny days it frequently sits on fence posts or tree stumps watching for insects.

Varanus varius is an arboreal species of lizard common in the eastern districts of Australia, where the countryside is more heavily wooded. When frightened, the lizard usually runs to the nearest tree and rapidly climbs the trunk, spiralling to keep away from the observer.

The bearded lizard, Amphibolurus barbatus, *a common Australian species, has an array of spiny scales beneath its throat, extending to form a fringe behind the ears. When threatened, it changes colour and tries to frighten its enemy by distending its throat and opening its large mouth. The bearded lizard lives mainly on insects.*

When it spots one, the dragon swiftly runs down to snap up its victim. Its habit of flattening into a saucer shape, expanding its beard, lashing its tail from side to side and fearsomely opening its wide yellow mouth is a marvellous piece of bluff, well calculated to scare off the enemy. According to the background, it can change the colour of its whole body to hide from danger. Bearded dragons have been known to change from bright yellow to black in less than 15 minutes.

The little common or tree dragon of southern Victoria is called the bloodsucker by country people, although the origin of this formidable name is a mystery. When cornered, it generally limits itself to a display of bravado by snapping open its yellow mouth, although it is capable of a sharp pinching bite. Usually it will lie perfectly motionless and thus remain unobserved while awaiting a chance to dash for safety.

The range of the crested dragon extends over western, central and southern Australia. The low crest that runs along its neck and the middle of its back is responsible for its name. These pretty creatures often run on their long hind limbs. Referred to occasionally as 'racehorse lizards', they provide an amusing spectacle with their seemingly competitive sprints.

In dull weather, when the animal is sluggish, its general colour is a drab brown with rather indistinct tail bands. But on a hot, sunny day the alternate dark- and light-yellow rings on its tail become pronounced, its body turns yellow and its head becomes a mottled reddish-yellow and black. These lizards, like most of the Dragon family, are especially brightly coloured during the breeding season.

The thorny devil, which lives in the Nullarbor Plain, is the most harmless of the lizards, subsisting on a diet of small red ants. It has no weapons for offence and relies on its extraordinary appearance and colour camouflage for protection. Its head, body and tail are covered with ridges of short thorn-like projections that are fleshy and not nearly as sharp as they appear.

The vast continent of Australia is a living museum of fascinating Dragon Age survivors, from the large goannas down to the legless lizards, which closely resemble snakes. The attractive little bronze lizard is well known to trout fishermen along the banks of mountain streams. When handled, it frequently sheds its tail, which twists and turns and acts as a 'sacrifice lure' in encounters with birds. The lizard can soon regenerate a new one.

Blue-tongues are heavy-bodied lizards up to 2 ft in length. They make excellent pets, their bright Prussian-blue tongues lapping up bread-crumbs and milk in leisurely enjoyment. If they are approached in their native bush with no hope of avoiding detection, however, these lizards rely on gaping jaws and explosive hisses to scare the intruder. But their bite is no worse than the pinch from a pair of pliers. Baby blue-tongues are exceptionally pugnacious and, although only 3 in. long, they snap and hiss at all comers and even fight savagely among themselves. Fortunately for their species, they mellow with age.

Although many people recoil from lizards and other reptiles, there is much enjoyment in getting to know these small survivors of the age when huge reptiles dominated the earth. I, for one, share many of their likes and dislikes. Who, for instance, would not prefer to sleep through the cold and dreary winter and come out on lovely spring days with nothing more to do than loll blissfully in the sun?

The blue-tongue skink, Tiliqua scincoides, *takes its name from the startling colour of its tongue, which it darts in and out when threatened. The 2 ft-long skink, with its spade-shaped head and smooth skin, is a peaceful, sluggish creature which eats only fruit and earthworms.*

Like many desert-dwelling animals and plants, the Australian thorny devil, Moloch horridus, has developed an armour of fleshy spines. It is quite harmless and relies entirely on its camouflaging colours and bizarre appearance to protect it from predators. The thorny devil lives on red ants, which it catches with its tongue.

Gould's goanna, Varanus gouldi, is one of Australia's most common lizards. Although it looks ferocious, the creature is timid and flees to its burrow when frightened. The colour of the goanna varies according to its habitat; the yellow-brown markings on this specimen are associated with grassland areas.

Winged Wonder

What inner compass guides the Arctic tern each spring as it travels
to its nesting grounds across 11,000 miles of empty sea?
Why does a robin fiercely guard an invisible
line that marks its own home territory?
Science has yet to explain the mysterious migratory
instincts and nesting habits of even our most familiar birds

Of Spring and an Egg

Jean George

Each spring, in trees and hedgerows, on moors
and by lakes, along the sea-shore and
under the eaves of houses, the mystery of life
unfolds in countless birds' eggs

On pine bough and willow limb, in woven basket and ground saucer, hundreds of millions of birds' eggs lie hidden in springtime across half the earth. They vary in shape from the nearly round egg of the screech owl to the pear-shaped egg of the plover; in size from the ponderous 2 lb. egg of the ostrich to the 3/100th of an ounce egg of the humming-bird. All have two things in common: they start as a gold and crystal cell within the female, and they maintain a pattern of growth that has existed from the beginning of bird history.

This pattern is an amazing sequence of events that renders meaningless the question of which came first, the chicken or the egg, because a newly hatched female has already within her body the germs of more eggs than she will lay in her lifetime.

The real question is: what *is* an egg? In his book, *The Avian Egg*, Dr Alexis Romanoff, a professor of chemical embryology, has brought together many of the new findings. It has been established, for instance,

that both the process and the timing of egg formation inside the female are the same for wild birds and the ordinary domestic fowl.

An egg starts as a single cell, a spark of life. Still in the mother's body, it grows in size and complexity as layers of yolk, albumen, membrane and shell form around it. But it remains a single cell. It may or may not be fertilised by a male sperm in the process of its formation. If it is, it must still wait until it has been laid and incubated by the mother before a chick begins to form.

Thousands of closely timed microscopic studies reveal that the first coating of yolk is formed around a germ cell in the young chick when she is at least three months old. Moreover, they show that an egg yolk is made up of six rings, each having a white and a yellow layer, laid down to a strict rhythm determined by the position of the sun. During the day and up until midnight, the yellow yolk is formed; the white yolk forms between midnight and sunrise.

The final layer, however, requires a more subtle alarm than the passing of nights and days to set it off —it needs the presence of a male bird. His mere presence in a tree in spring triggers a hormonal change in the now mature female which creates the final layer. Most wild birds cannot lay if there is no mate, but this is not true of domestic birds—farmyard chickens, ducks and pigeons. One leghorn hen laid 1515 eggs in eight years, and never saw a rooster.

When the lustrous yolk sac is completed, the egg ruptures from its mooring and falls into the oviduct.

This heron chick has just used its egg-tooth, a small, temporary protuberance on its upper bill, to crack the shell of its egg. Having opened a window in the shell, the chick looks at the world outside. A young bird can take anything from several hours to several days to free itself from the egg.

This event is triggered by the courtship dances of the male bird. Each species has a different expression of affection. The pheasant jabs at the ground and fans his tail into a heart-shaped shield. The blue bird of paradise hangs upside-down and shakes his iridescent feathers into a blue mist. The egret displays his plumes and gives his mate a present of a stick.

Then mating takes place, and as the egg proceeds down the funnel-like oviduct, it encounters a male sperm. Immediately after fertilisation the egg goes on a precise schedule. It stops in the oviduct for 20 minutes while it gathers albumen or white. Like the yolk, the albumen is a series of layers. The first is a thin covering; the second is dense, elastic and tough, a shock absorber to protect the spark of life

in the centre during the plunge to the nest and the tumbling it gets during incubation.

The egg spirals down through the oviduct, and this motion forces the third layer of albumen—a light, watery fluid—through the denser second layer, up against the golden yolk. In this water-like fluid the yolk floats. The original tiny cell, which scientists call the 'blastoderm' (and which is the white speck you sometimes see in a fresh egg), rises to the top.

The spiralling serves also to twist the albumen at either end into the visible milky rope that every housewife recognises. These 'ropes' later break, in the incubation stage, and the mother rotates the egg in order to keep the yolk in the centre.

Next on the schedule is the formation of the two white sheets of tough membrane found under the shell of the breakfast egg. This takes an hour and ten minutes. Then the egg drops into the shell-secreting area of the oviduct and remains there for 19 hours while the shell accumulates in four porous layers.

During the last of these hours, the shell is coloured. (There are approximately 9000 bird species, and most have distinctively marked or coloured eggs.)

Eggs are always laid during daylight hours, usually between sunrise and noon. For ten minutes after it is laid, a bird's egg lies like a shiny gem in the nest. The shell is covered by a glistening film. This film hardens, and the egg waits for warmth. Air is entering the pores in the shell, and a breathing pocket is forming at the blunt end. Here, two weeks after incubation begins, the chick's head will lie.

The mother bird will lay more eggs—one a day, until she has filled her quota for this nesting. Then the eggs in her nest take complete control of her life, starting her on a schedule of brooding and turning. So delicate is the feeling of the mother for the eggs that some birds do not start to incubate until the right number of eggs lie in the nest. A female flicker, an American species of woodpecker, for instance, must sense four before she is triggered to brood. An ornithologist who removed one egg a day from a flicker's nest so detained the unfortunate female that she laid 71 eggs before she eventually gave up.

It is the heat of the mother's body that sets off the explosion of life within the egg. As soon as the temperature at the centre of the egg reaches 99·5°F, the cell development begins again. On and on the chain reaction goes until within the shell there are formed the lungs, the heart, the liver and eyes—all the exquisite organs of a living chick.

One Easter, in order to observe this miracle, I purchased six quail eggs and a globe-shaped plastic incubator. I placed the eggs in the incubator and turned on a seven-watt Christmas-tree bulb. I knew that after 12 hours at 99·5°F the germs of life would be racing round the centres of the gold and glass-like world, and that on the fifth day these germs would determine whether the embryos were male or female.

But it was the 23rd, the hatching day, that I waited for. Then, as I hovered over the incubator, a crack, like the beginning of a minuscule earthquake, shattered the side of one egg. I lifted the egg and heard a voice within—thin, high, fragile. During the night I watched as bits of shell were torn and knocked away. As the night passed, the other eggs cracked.

At dawn, when the sun illuminated the yellow-green buds of the apple tree and the white crocuses on the lawn, the first tiny bird fell out of the shell into spring. It rested for several hours while, one after the other, its brothers and sisters fought for freedom. Then dry, fluffy and bright-eyed, it got up on its feet, as though in a hurry to keep some mystical appointment with the eternal life it harboured.

The Miracle of Birds

Alan Devoe

Birds are a wonder of design,
whose every detail is immaculately planned
to make the air their element

The famous ornithologist Elliott Coues said: 'A bird is to me as wonderful as the stars.' To learn something about that winged marvel is to make the acquaintance of some of Nature's most breathtaking miracles.

In the making of a bird, every step was taken with a single thought in mind—flight. Here was to be a creature of incarnate air, a 'grace for the sky'. Here were to be lightness, buoyancy, arrowing strength; a sight to lift man's spirit as if on wings itself.

A bird is 'bird-brained' because it needs prodigious eyesight for flight. Because only a small part of a bird's eye is visible to us, we are not likely to realise what a gigantic organ it is. A bird's eyes are actually so big that there is barely room in its skull for them. Many hawks and owls have eyeballs bigger than yours and mine. These immense eyes force a bird's brain to be a relatively insignificant organ, squeezed to the rear of its skull. In many birds, the eyes weigh more than the brain. In some, each eye does; and for the eyes there is a third eyelid—to be drawn back and forth like a 'windscreen wiper' as the bird rushes through the sky.

Other marvels? An owl scans the dark woods with eyes 50 times as sensitive to faint light as ours. A hawk may have vision so piercing that as it perches on a lookout tree it can see small prey more than a mile away. To extract grubs from trees, a woodpecker has a tongue so long it curves over inside the bird's head and is rooted in front of its eyes. Many coastal birds have a built-in sense of time so precise that after inland trips they can return to the shore for feeding at the hour when the tide is right. The most common little finch in our shrubbery is such a fabulous quiver of life energy that its tiny heart races at 500 beats a minute. Some birds' body temperatures are as high as 110°F.

Ruskin was using only slight poetic licence when he spoke of a bird as 'but a drift of the air brought into shape by plumes'. A bird inhales draughts of air more deeply than just into its lungs. A bird's lungs connect with as many as nine additional air sacs, some of which have elongations extending into

*In flight, the American egret retracts its neck into an
'S' and thrusts its legs out straight for balance. Lazily
flapping its 54 in. wings, the egret achieves an effortless
buoyancy that seems to defy gravity. Even on the
ground, as it wades through quiet shallows in search
of food, this dazzling white bird has a regal dignity.*

the bones. A mammal bone is heavy, dense. A bird
bone is hollow, filled with a spongy network
engineered for air capacity. As a bird breathes, it is
flooded with air to its marrow.

Even the skull of a bird is designed to help this
airy insubstantiality. Skull bones become light-
weight plates and struts. To lighten the living flying
machine at its 'nose', Nature took away birds' teeth
—teeth need heavy jaws and muscles. For lightness
aft, tail feathers are all borne on one short bone.

Feathers are the strongest structures for their size
and weight known in Nature. A feather may seem to
be only a central shaft with projections on either
side. It is much more. Each projection (called a
vane) from the feather stem is composed of numbers
of parallel rods, the barbs. A barb is itself virtually a
complete miniature feather, with extremely fine
side-projections called barbules. Look still closer
with a lens and it is revealed that on these barbules
are tinier barbicels, and on these are almost infinitesimal hooklets. The hooklets mesh the barbs; thus
the whole vane is one light and perfect interweave.
A single feather may consist of over a million barbules and barbicels.

To make its streamlined body a perfect flight
machine, a bird's framework is the most rigid in the
animal world. Vertebrae of its backbone are fused
and united, to make an immensely strong axis. Backbone, ribs and breastbone form a 'cage' of incomparable strength. The bird's ribs are lashed together
by tough ligaments, fastened to both its backbone

*For a sea-bird, the puffin of the North Atlantic has
surprisingly small wings and an unusually plump body. It has
difficulty in taking off from either land or water but, once
airborne, flies rapidly. An excellent underwater swimmer,
the puffin collects several fish in its improbable bill
during one dive, possibly anchoring the catch with its tongue.*

and its breastbone. Its two powerful shoulder-blades
are braced together across the front by collarbones
that fuse in its wishbone. Down the middle of this
runs a tremendous ridge, for attachment of the great
pectoral muscles that work its wings. In many birds
these muscles constitute more than a quarter of the
bird's whole weight.

As a bird beats its wings in downstroke, it seems
to be pushing itself forwards, as if rowing through the
air. High-speed cameras show that it is not: a bird is
a natural miniature aeroplane. On the downstroke,
each wing moves forwards, the inner half held almost
rigid, its fore edge sloped like an aircraft wing, its
upper surface arched by a curve of feathers. The
outer half of the wing moves separately, activated
by the bird's 'wrist', located about halfway along the
wing's length. During wing-beat, the primary
feathers at the bird's wing-tips flare out almost at
right angles to the wing and become propellers. The
inner half of the wing, curved and tilted, is meanwhile the aircraft wing, providing steady lift. When
landing and taking off, the bird avoids the danger of
stalling by means of special feathers at the front
edge of its 'wrist'. It raises these to make a 'slot'
between them and its main wing, providing a perfect
auxiliary aerofoil.

A bird's flight feats can be nearly incredible. A big
Cooper's hawk is streaking in pursuit of a quail.
Suddenly the quail, from a height of only a few feet,
drops like a stone to a clump of bushes. Before it
reaches shelter, the hawk shoots under it, turns
upside-down in full flight, catches the falling body,
rights itself and zooms on without pausing.

A sparrowhawk, flying at top speed, saves itself from crashing into a sudden obstruction by performing a perfect Immelmann turn. An African eagle, swooping down at a speed of over 100 mph, brakes with such stunning skill—spreading wings and tail in an aerial skid-stop—that it comes to a dead halt in the space of 20 ft.

A bird cushions its landing with its legs, which consist of three single rigid bones with joints that work in opposite directions. This is probably the most effective of the shock-absorbing mechanisms devised by Nature.

As a male bird utters his song, to claim territory and invite a mate to it, he uses an extraordinary vocal organ called a syrinx. In this song-box is a bony band to which are attached structures of outstretched membrane under the control of intricate muscles that can precisely tighten or relax the valve as the ecstatic bird forces air from its lungs.

The songs of springtime lead into courtships stylised by instinct into some of Nature's strangest and most touching rituals. Courting lapwings hold a wing-waving fiesta, cranes dance, a woodcock climbs the sky in a spiral while he lets the air whistle through his outer primary feathers in an unforgettable love call.

Birds' nests are often so elaborate that it is almost impossible to believe such skill can be instinctive. But it is. Science has proved that for at least five generations the nest skill can survive in perfection, independent of experience. Four generations of weaverbirds were bred under artificial conditions in which they never saw a nest or nest material. Then the fifth generation was set free. At once the birds began constructing with unerring skill the complex woven nests of their ancestors.

After baby birds, using a temporary 'egg-tooth' that Nature provides, have tapped their way free of their shells, they become prodigies of almost unimaginable appetite. One infant robin eats as much as 14 ft of earthworms a day. A wren whose feeding trips to her youngsters were counted between sunrise and nightfall visited the nest 1217 times. A young black tern, weighing 31 grams, consumed daily 48 grams of food. To survive, every bird must eat at least half its own weight in food each day.

By late summer, bird families have been reared and the parents, withdrawing to deep woods, stilling their song, have moulted. Worn feathers are replaced in a change so delicately gradual that the first lost feather must be partially regrown before a second feather drops. The whole refeathering follows this pattern, so that in most birds flight is never impaired.

In autumn migration, birds fly at heights ranging up to 5000 ft or more above the earth, and cover distances nearly beyond belief. A tiny blackpoll warbler, nesting in Canada, wings 4000 miles to Brazil. A golden plover travels from the edge of the Arctic Ocean to Argentina, almost 8000 miles. Champion migrant is the Arctic tern, which summers at the north polar land limit and winters in Antarctica. Its annual round trip is 22,000 miles.

How do they find their way? Naturalists have recently proved that birds can expertly calculate geography, and probably time, from sun-slant. There is also increasing evidence that at night they are able to calculate their way through the trackless skies by using the complex star patterns.

The whole miracle of bird-life must remind us of what the great naturalist Charles Waterton put into four words of simple eloquence: 'We can but bow.'

The Continuing Mystery of How Birds Navigate

Max Eastman

Sun and star positions may help migrating birds to calculate their way across oceans, deserts and mountains

While physicists have been scheming how to navigate interstellar space, top scientists in another field have been trying to work out how birds navigate here on earth. How, for example, does an Arctic tern, born within ten degrees of the North Pole, leaving home at the age of six weeks, find its way to the Antarctic pack-ice 11,000 miles away and, after wintering there, fly back to the same northern nesting place for the summer? That its heart and wings are equal to it is miracle enough, but how does its tiny brain solve problems in navigation that stumped the human race for so many thousands of years?

The Greek philosopher Aristotle noticed that robins disappeared for the winter but redstarts did not, and concluded that robins turn into redstarts in

Against the silhouette of Mount Shasta, mixed flocks of ducks and geese rendezvous at Tule Lake. Literally millions of birds use Tule and other northern Californian lakes as resting places on their twice-yearly migrations. How birds navigate across thousands of miles remains one of Nature's intriguing mysteries.

the autumn and become robins again in spring. Pliny, the Roman naturalist, endorsed this general idea, and it became the expert opinion in Rome that swallows turn into frogs. The fact that gave rise to these wild ideas is that a great many birds, especially the small ones, migrate at night. They are here in the evening, and in the morning they are gone. Everybody knows that birds do not fly in the dark, so what becomes of them?

It was not until the 18th century that ornithologists began to realise that birds do fly at night, and in enormous numbers—one observer saw 9000 an hour fly past. This awakened scientists to the navigation problem involved in bird migration, and they never went to sleep again.

Closely bound up with it, of course, is birds' homing instinct, another hereditary gift which has

past century, it is only in the last 25 years that a determined effort has been made to find out how the birds do it. What do they steer by? The North Star? The sun? The moon? The winds? The climate? The earth's magnetism? Which of these, if any, gives them their sense of direction?

A step towards understanding bird navigation was taken by a German ornithologist, Gustav Kramer, who devised a way of testing the idea, casually suggested at the turn of the century, that birds guide themselves by the sun. Noticing that birds in a cage hop about restlessly when the time comes for migration, he put some caged starlings in a circular pavilion with windows through which only the sky could be seen. He then made a record of the positions the birds assumed and found them constantly orientated in the direction they wanted to migrate. When he darkened the windows, they lost their orientation and began hopping in all directions. Then he rigged up an artificial light to imitate the sun, but made it rise and set at the wrong place and time. The birds orientated themselves for migration again, but in a direction determined by this artificial sun. He thus established strong evidence for the sun theory and left only one unexplained mystery: how can a bird guide itself by the sun, day and night, in fair weather and foul?

The complexity of so using the sun, even in broad daylight, becomes apparent when you reflect that the sun's position changes with the time of day, with the time of year and with every stage of the journey. It would require a time sense in the bird's constitution almost equivalent to carrying a watch.

Professor G. V. T. Matthews, a former Cambridge University biologist, has set forth the difficulties of guiding a flight by the sun's passage through the sky. His demonstrations involve so much mathematical calculation that one would think only a computer on wings could get anywhere with such a shifting point of reference. Nevertheless, he is convinced that migrating and homing birds are equipped by instinct for such a feat.

The one thing he was unable to explain adequately, when he summarised the results of his enquiries in 1955, was how the theory applied to migration during the hours of darkness. 'The direction of the night's flight could be determined from the sun during the day,' he suggested, 'and maintained as well as possible throughout the darkness with possibly some guidance from the moon and star pattern.'

This rather hazy suggestion was unsatisfactory to another ornithologist, E. G. F. Sauer, of the University of Frieburg in Germany, whose prime interest is

been known and employed by man ever since Noah sent out a dove over the waters. Probably the world's record in finding the way home was established by a small seagull-like bird called a Manx shearwater. Many of these birds live in burrows in cliffs on the coast of Wales. One was ringed and taken by air to Boston, Massachusetts, then released there on June 4, 1952. On June 16 at 1.30 p.m., 12½ days later, it crept into its burrow on Skokholm, an island off the coast of Wales, 3050 miles across the trackless ocean.

While facts like these have been collected over the

in the tiny warblers that fly long distances, mostly at night. Sauer tried a series of night experiments. During the migrating season he placed a group of caged warblers where only the starry heavens would be visible to them. He found that at a glimpse of the night sky the birds began to flutter, and each would take up a position pointing 'like the needle of a compass' in the direction of its habitual migration. Even when he tried to turn the birds away by rotating their perches, they stubbornly turned back to the preferred direction.

Dr Sauer next placed his warblers in a planetarium—under a dome, that is, with an artificial replica of the starry sky. Again they took up the correct position for a flight to their winter quarters in Africa. When the dome was rotated, to put the stars in a false position, they made the corresponding mistake.

There is poetry as well as science in Dr Sauer's attitude towards the adventurous little birds he studied. 'When autumn comes,' he said, 'the little garden warbler, weighing barely three-quarters of an ounce, sets off one night on an unbelievable journey. Without being taught, all alone, never in the collective security of a flock, it unerringly wings its solitary way southwards to its distant goal in Africa, guided by the map of the stars.'

Dr Sauer had a favourite warbler, a lesser whitethroat called Johnny. From Germany the lesser whitethroat normally travels south-eastwards across the Balkans and then turns due south, flying along the Nile to its winter home in Central Africa. Johnny knew nothing of this, for he had been born and spent all his life in a cage. Nevertheless, when the migrating season came and his cage was placed in a planetarium showing him the German sky, he took up the normal flight position heading south-east. Moreover, as the planetarium was rotated to correspond to the flight route of his species, he shifted his position gradually towards the south, until in the region of the Nile he set his course due south. With Johnny's help, Dr Sauer has made it certain that warblers can guide themselves by the stars as well as by the sun.

How such elaborate instincts can be inherited remains a mystery—'one of the crucial mysteries of biology', to quote Professor Matthews. Moreover, as he reminds us, expert study and experiment in this branch of science are little more than begun. Dr Sauer has in mind to find out, by subtracting the constellations one by one from the planetarium sky, which stars are essential to the warbler's nocturnal migration. Suppose it should be, after all, only the North Star which guides the tiny migrant.

Scientists who have been studying bird navigation for the last 25 years are agreed about this basic fact. Some apparatus exists in each migratory bird's tiny brain from birth that, by putting him in complex relation to the lights that pass across the sky, makes him at home on the earth as man, with all his inventions, will never be.

Birds Live in Nature's Invisible Cages

John and Jean George

Nature has made birds the most mobile of all creatures; but she has also chained them by their instincts to rigid flightways and narrow areas of ground

Free as a bird, we say; yet nearly all birds and most bird-watchers know how mistaken that saying is. The conduct of birds is so rigidly fixed that they are prisoners to the land they fly over, slaves to the air they fly through. This territory fixation, which is strongest during the breeding season, serves to aid in the formation of pairs, to provide shelter for the young, and to ensure perpetuation of the species by spreading its population over a wide area.

Birds which are year-round residents tend to retain the same territory for life; migrants have both summer and winter properties. The birds that stay round your home all through the winter may seem to be in flocks, and therefore trespassing, but they are not. They are a well-ordered bird society made up of old-timers and young, complete with a leader or 'boss bird'. In these winter societies the defence of the breeding territory has given way, in certain species, to the common defence of a community territory against neighbouring groups of the same species. Birds will normally tolerate trespassers of a different species on their land, since they are not in competition with them. They will, however, put to flight any intruders belonging to their own species.

Birds' property lines are established by song. If a male bird, returning in the spring, can sing from a tree without being challenged by a neighbour, he has it as his own, to mark the limits of his estate. If, however, another male comes winging at him and puts him back a tree or two, he knows that this land is already claimed.

By taking the best land he can, and as much of it as he is able to defend, he ensures for himself not only a good food supply but also a mate. Female birds pick their mates by their attractive voices (each bird's voice is distinctive) and by the quality of the nest-sites in the land they have staked off. The weaker males and the late-comers, pushed into inferior territory, often remain bachelors.

Territory varies with different species from several square miles, as in the case of the horned owl, to only a square foot or so around the nest, as among the colony nesters such as terns and gulls.

Once boundary lines are settled, the feelings of the bird towards his territory mount with the progress of his nest, until he seems to do desperate things, particularly near the nest-site. Flying at windows and the shiny fittings of motor-cars is not bird hara-kiri; it is territory defence. His reflection in a window or hub-cap is another male on his property, and he will fight this adversary until exhausted.

Territorial disputes, though constant in the bird world, are normally resolved by singing duels, nearly always between males of the same species. Sometimes a disputed territory touches off a breast-to-breast battle in the air; the battlers seem to be sliding up and down an invisible wall. The fight will usually be brief, and afterwards each contestant will fly to a tree limb on his side of the property line and click in agitation. Usually there is a compromise and both birds will sing, in a full and exuberant song.

The female usually stays within the boundaries established by her mate, but occasionally a blundering or frivolous wife can cause trouble. One season we observed a tragi-comedy in a community of vivid indigo buntings.

A little female, a first-time mother, had by error built her nest on another male's property. She would fly happily to her nest, expecting her husband to usher her home, only to find that he had stopped at the edge of his territory. There he was, turning around in circles, torn between two powerful impulses: to follow his mate, and to stay off his neighbour's property. Apparently property rights proved stronger than family love. He never once crossed the barrier during the nesting period. When the young

hatched, the father would catch insects for the babies, call his mate and give her the offerings. Taking them eagerly, she would return to feed her ever-hungry young. We were all (including the frustrated father) greatly relieved on the day the little mother eventually coaxed her fledglings over the border to their waiting father's estate.

A territory boundary is not the only restraint in a bird's life. Even within their own property birds do not fly around their land on any random course, but stick to set routes. A bird will take the same path daily: from his night roost to his feeding spot and from his nest to a certain singing post.

Each night the bird returns faithfully to his bedroom, or roost, which he picks as carefully as his nest-site. In a world teeming with enemies, its loss can mean his undoing.

A woodpecker roosted in a hole in an apple tree outside our window. He went to bed at the same time every night, depending on the amount of light. As the days grew shorter, our clock showed him returning two minutes earlier each night, but our light meter registered exactly the same light value. On cloudy days he came to roost early.

One night a white-breasted nuthatch went into the woodpecker's bedroom a few minutes before he was due home. The woodpecker performed his nightly rituals according to his heritage. He squawked from the top of a maple. He defecated in the same spot he had used for months; he flew to the apple tree, spiralled up it and winged into his hole—where he hit the intruding nuthatch head on.

Out they both tumbled and fought briefly. The nuthatch departed, with the woodpecker in pursuit. Sometime later we caught a glimpse of the woodpecker. It was late, but probably he could still see to get into his hole. However, he had to repeat the rituals of retirement all over again and so he went back to the maple tree. The night grew cold but the woodpecker never returned. Now it was very dark, well below his accustomed level of light. He squawked but did not fly to the apple tree. One twilight a few nights later the nuthatch cautiously investigated the empty hole and moved in. He had won the contest, probably because he had upset the woodpecker's evening retirement habits, and the woodpecker, unable to change his routine, was literally left out in the cold.

Nearly all birds live and love and die behind the bars of Nature's compulsions. They are held captive in the cages of their own instincts, from which, with rare exceptions, they are unable to escape—and have no desire to.

Life in the Wilderness

Every wild plant, every free-born animal, is designed to fit some niche
in the wilderness community where it can find food, fend off
enemies, survive seasonal changes and produce young.
The dazzling variety of adaptations
that has evolved among the millions of
species on our planet is one of Nature's miracles

That Astounding Creator– Nature

Jean George

Hostile environments—deserts,
ice-fields and ocean depths—inspire some of
Nature's most astonishing inventions

A bird that eats feathers; a mammal that never drinks; a fish that grows a fishing line and worm on its head to catch other fish. Creatures in a nightmare? No. They are very much with us as co-inhabitants of this earth. Nature has fashioned most animals to fit the many faces of the land—moose to marshes, squirrels to trees, camels to deserts and frogs to ponds. Give Nature an environment or situation and she will evolve a creature, adapting a toe here, an eye there, until the being fits the niche. As a result of this hammering and fitting, however, some really unbelievable creatures circle the sun with us.

One summer I saw a sleek mother horned grebe herding her three bobbing young to eat among the green weeds. Suddenly I noticed through my binoculars that she was feeding her babies quantities of feathers from a deserted duck's nest. As she stuffed the dry feathers into the gaping mouths, she made

two or three pokes to get each one down. Finally she worked a dozen or so down her own throat, then, sailing low on the water, vanished contentedly among the plants. I later learnt that 60 per cent of the grebe's diet is feathers. When I asked why this was, a biologist answered, 'Because Nature finds a use for everything. Feathers seem to act as a strainer which prevents fishbones from entering and damaging the intestines.'

Australia has many strange beasts, one of the oddest of which is the koala. Perfectly adapted to one specific tree, the eucalyptus, this living teddy bear needs nothing else, not even a drink. The leaves contain just enough moisture for the koala, making it one of the few land animals that needs no water to supplement its food.

The creature with the fishing line on its head was created for the dark canyons of the sea. Here food is so scarce that the deep-sea angler fish, which preys on smaller fish, grew a line and an appendage on the end that wriggles like a worm. This catches the attention of the occasional passer-by and as the fish approaches the bait, the toothy angler swirls up and swallows it.

The gigantic ocean bottom creates other problems. A male angler fish could swim for years without meeting a female of his own species. Nature's solution to this problem is for the female to carry a dwarfed husband tightly fused to her body. Marine biologists believe that this nuptial begins when the eggs first hatch and there are many fry of both sexes.

Many creatures are specially adapted to elude their
enemies. The woodcock (above), which spends much
of its time probing the ground for worms, has eyes
set far higher in its head than most other birds. They
enable the woodcock to see clearly in all directions
and, even when its head is pointing to the ground,
the bird can see an enemy approaching from above.

The horned toad (right) also makes use of its unique
eyes when threatened—it squirts a fine spray
of blood out of them which can carry for several feet:
this distracts or alarms its attacker and gives
the lizard a chance to escape.

191

The whip scorpion defends itself by shooting a spray of acetic acid at its enemies. The glands that emit the spray, which can travel up to 2 ft, are situated at the base of the whip, and can be accurately aimed. They are so effective that the whip scorpion has survived more or less unchanged for some 300 million years.

A male then grabs hold of a female with his mouth and hangs on until he has literally become a part of her. His mouth becomes fused to her stomach and for the rest of his life he remains attached to his mate, making the most amazing union in Nature.

Sound has shaped the bodies of many beasts. Noise tapped away at the bullfrog until his ears became bigger than his eyes. Now he hears so well that at the slightest sound of danger he quickly plops to safety under a sunken leaf. The rabbit has long ears to hear the quiet 'whoosh' of the owl's wings; the grasshopper's ears are on the base of his abdomen, the lowest point of his body, where he can detect the tread of a crow's foot or the stealthy approach of a shrew.

Sometimes food determines an animal's appearance. Earthworms have shaped the woodcock, a snipe-like bird of the forest floor. This creature has a long, narrow bill that looks like a pencil and fits neatly into worm holes; but it has its disadvantages: with its bill buried deep in a worm hole, the woodcock is vulnerable to attack from above. To counteract this danger, the woodcock has eyes near the top of its head. This singular device permits it to scan the trees for danger even when its beak is buried: an arrangement which makes for longevity, but certainly creates an odd-looking creature.

The need to catch elusive prey has evolved some staggering biological tricks. The sea anemone, a flower-like animal of the shoreline, is usually riveted to one spot; yet it feeds on darting fish. A diabolically clever trap was necessary to catch them, so the anemone developed tentacles with 'bombs' in their ends. When a fish forages into these tentacles, the ends shoot a thin thread into the fish's body. This thread in turn explodes a paralysing poison. The stunned fish is then hauled in by the tentacles and shoved into the anemone's gullet.

Nature seems to have gone all out in creating preposterous gadgets for self-defence. The jacana, for instance, a bird found in the American tropics, has spurs that unfold like stilettos at the bend of its wings, with which it can slash its enemies to shreds.

Lizards are professionals in the art of warding off attack. The two-headed skink, whose tail is shaped like its head, confuses its enemy. A hawk, upon attacking this creature, anticipates that it will run in the direction of the lifted head and makes allowance for the movement. However, the bird usually strikes nothing, for he is aiming at the tail, and the real head has run the other way.

In order to be able to travel, the Portuguese man-of-war first mastered the art of floating. To do this, it evolved a purple bag and inflated it with gas from a special gland. As a crowning idea it also grew a sail. Once launched, the man-of-war can move away from enemies or approach food by raising or lowering its sail. When severely threatened, it forces the gas out of the float and submerges.

There is hardly any environment, however hostile, that some creature has not mastered. The land is, of course, fatal to fish. If they flop out on to it, they die. If their ponds dry up, they are helpless. Given this situation, it was almost certain that some fish would evolve a way to beat it; and so there is a lungfish. It breathes air, and must come to the surface every 20 minutes or so; otherwise it drowns. When ponds in Africa dry up during the arid season, the lungfish wrap themselves in mud and wait—sometimes for years. When the rains finally return, they resume their life in the water.

Just as Nature adds things to creatures that need them, so she occasionally takes things away from those that do not. The adult mayfly, for example, has no mouth or stomach. Last year I found myself amid hundreds of thousands of these insects. I told my companion that I was glad they did not bite. He replied that they have no mouths to bite with. 'Adult mayflies live only one day,' he explained, 'and that day is devoted entirely to pleasure. They do nothing but dance and mate all their short lives, and so they have no need for a mouth.'

With all this elaborate evolution, it is not surprising that some of Nature's inventions got out of hand. Into this category falls the reindeer's speedometer. A tendon snaps back and forth over a bone in the reindeer's foot, noisily tapping out the speed of his gait—a useless invention. And so is the nose on the stomach of the scorpion and the featherlike tongue of the long-beaked toucan.

Perhaps the most dumbfounding of Nature's extraordinary creations is the horned toad of the south-western United States. A herpetologist once invited me to observe one of these lizards just after it had moulted. In a sand-filled glass cage I saw a large male. Beside him lay his cast-off skin. The herpetologist began to annoy the beast with mock attacks and the old man of the desert, in his vulnerable new suit, became frightened. Suddenly his eyeballs reddened. A final fast lunge from my friend at the beast and I froze in astonishment—a fine spray of blood shot from the lizard's eye, like fire from a dragon! The beast had struck back with a weapon so shocking that it terrifies even the fiercest enemy.

Later I pondered the bizarre methods for survival with which evolution has endowed earth's creatures; sometimes comical, sometimes pathetic. I knew the biologists were right: if any adaptation is possible, we can be sure that Nature has tried it.

How Animals Help Each Other

Alan Devoe

In Nature, the struggle to survive is balanced by an equally vital urge towards co-operation and mutual help

A flash of bright blue in the green depths of the pine woods caught the eye of a wildlife biologist. Then a second spot of blue stirred, as another jay sailed on silent wings to the same branch. The newcomer, holding a morsel of food in its beak, hopped closer to the first bird. Turning eagerly, the first jay lifted its crested head and accepted hungrily the gift its visitor thrust down into its throat.

The man was astonished. In the fledging season, young birds often continue coaxing food from their parents even after they have grown up; in the courting season, birds often bestow gifts upon the females they are wooing. But this was not the season for fledglings, nor was it courting time. This was the dead of winter.

Hastily the wildlife expert raised his binoculars and got the answer. The recipient of the bounty was an adult jay, a grizzled veteran. The lower mandible of its beak had been broken off nearly at the base. It was unable to pick up food.

This impulse to share and co-operate is familiarly awakened in creatures of the wild by members of their immediate families. But here seemed to be something close to the human ideal of brotherhood.

Nature's creatures often exhibit impulses of self-assertion and competition. But all through life's vast range, these instincts are balanced by another kind of drive. Nature does not implant in her children just the single message: 'Take care of yourself.' There is a second ancient and universal injunction: 'Get together.' It is as vital as the breath of life.

Every creature has a need for companionship as biologically important as food and drink. Testing tadpoles, zoologists have found that even these humble creatures are so deeply influenced by social need that a solitary tadpole can regenerate an injured part of its body only slowly, but if it is given the comradeship of fellow tadpoles, its healing powers speed up almost miraculously. Scientists have discovered that mice reared in contact with other mice grow faster than those kept in isolation.

Animals often develop teamwork into active patterns of partnership. R. M. Yerkes, an authority on apes, gave a chimpanzee a heavy box of fragrant delicacies with a complicated lid-fastener. Sniffing delightedly, the chimp tried to drag away the box so that he could work at leisure on the task of getting it open. It was too heavy, so he sought out another chimp, tapped him on the shoulder and gestured for help. Together, the two easily moved the box, worked jointly at opening it, and shared the feast.

A chimpanzee, given food when apes in adjoining cages were left unfed, has been seen to pass a share of his delicacies through the bars. Sharing sometimes extends to giving help. An ape with a splinter in his finger goes to another ape, and the 'doctor' works as earnestly at the job as a human.

The coatis of Central and South America, long-nosed relatives of raccoons, swing through the jungle treetops in bands, hunting for small prey. A favourite delicacy is the iguana, the big arboreal lizard. But an iguana would be a tough customer for a small coati to tackle up among the tips of the twigs, so hunting coatis split into two groups. One band goes aloft and scares dozing iguanas out of the branches. As the lizards fall, they are quickly overpowered by the second contingent of waiting coatis deployed on the ground.

Bad temper, poor vision and formidable bulk make the black rhinoceros a highly dangerous animal. But in captivity, given the companionship of another animal, it will become more docile.

Eloquent of the bond of inner unity is the fishing art of the great white pelicans. The birds come swooping down and form a wide semicircle offshore. Then, as if at a signal, they start wading towards shore. Shoulder to shoulder, beaks poised just above the water, they advance as a living net. Now and again all the birds join in a tumultuous thrashing of the water with their wings, scaring the fish into a smaller and smaller area near the shore. This beautifully co-ordinated drive ends with a tightly penned haul of fish imprisoned in the shallows of the shoreline. Then the birds feast on a repast which none of them could have secured alone.

Crows and ravens demonstrate the rewards of joining forces. Frances Pitt, the naturalist, owned a raven pair, Ben and Joe, whose teamwork in dealing with visiting cats was characteristic. Ben would approach the cat from the front, parading nonchalantly close. Fascinated by what looked like an easy meal, the cat would fail to observe that Joe was mincing round to the rear. A moment later a black beak like a pair of steel pliers would close on the cat's tail. Meowing in outrage, the cat would whirl round, to see Joe waddling away, while Ben seized the tail now presented to him. If it was a very good day Ben and Joe could make a cat turn round and round like a frantic top.

Small alliances among animals grow into bigger ones. The spirit of the flock can result in such an amazing performance as the one reported by the great naturalist, Baron Georges Cuvier.

A pair of swallows had built their mud nest under the eaves. The naturalist, hoping to observe the fledging of babies, was watching one day when the nest was invaded and taken over by an interloping sparrow. The bullying sparrow sat defiant in the nest, thrusting its beak angrily out of the entrance hole, keeping the rightful owners at bay. Eventually the swallows flew off.

They returned with a noisy swarm of other swallows. With beakfuls of the wet mud they use for nest making, the birds converged on the invaded nest, deftly smearing and daubing. As they veered off, the watcher saw that the sparrow-held nest had been sealed. It had become its invader's tomb. Baron Cuvier felt that he had had an extraordinary look into one of the fundamental meanings of life itself.

Such group teamwork is not unusual among creatures of the same species, but scientists are discovering that the sense of brotherhood can be trained to cut across species lines. The elephants in Ringling Brothers/Barnum & Bailey's Circus and the circus cat, Midnight, were as devoted to each

White pelicans on Lake Naivasha. Pelicans are gregarious birds which sometimes fish co-operatively. They form a living net and herd the fish they prey on into shallow, confined waters from which the fish cannot escape.

other as if they were all kittens together. A few years ago zoo-keepers had a problem with a surly, unapproachable rhinoceros, until they gave him the only available companion they could think of risking in the cage; a domestic goat. Almost overnight the rhino's disposition began to change. Before long he would take all the high-spirited butting the goat cared to inflict and come back for more. He had discovered fellowship.

This innate urge can cut across even the lines of supposedly 'incurable' enmities. In a series of dramatic demonstrations a Chinese biologist, Dr L. S. Tsai, would put a cat and a rat in a cage adjacent to a food compartment that had a transparent shutter. This shutter could be opened by pressure on two buttons in the cage; but both had to be pressed simultaneously, one by each animal. Again and again, rats and cats learnt to put aside their wary distrust of each other and, faced with a common problem, worked successfully together to solve it.

This urge towards constructive co-operation touches first the individual, then expands to the family, widens to the flock, then at last in humanity becomes the shining ideal of universal brotherhood. Wherever naturalists have peered deeply into the mysteries of Nature's world, they have found the same message. Our human ideals are not visionary, not doomed. They are good biology.

A Tooth and a Claw

Jean George

Aggression in animals is often
as natural, necessary and harmless
as eating and sleeping

Once I watched two cows in a clover-spattered meadow cracking their heads together with such violence that I winced and asked the farmer why he did not separate the animals. 'Cow-fights,' he said, 'make for order and peaceful individuals. The sooner those two decide which is going to be the leader, the sooner I'll get a bucket of milk from both of them.'

In his lifetime with cattle this farmer had seen what science is now establishing: that animal aggression is creative. A tooth-and-claw encounter is a positive adjustment to an irritating situation, just as sleep is to fatigue, and eating to hunger.

Since the Second World War, psychologists and biologists have been prying intensively into the stuff that makes a fight. In man this can be expressed destructively in war and murder, or positively in murals in the Sistine Chapel. The human impulses that make a fight are also those that make a masterpiece.

One of the first clues that animal aggression has its constructive uses came to light in 1938, when psychologist C. R. Carpenter shipped several hundred rhesus monkeys from India to Santiago Island, off Puerto Rico, where he released them in order to study their natural society. When they were set free on the island, they swung into the trees—and fights started. Males battled until a leader emerged. Losers gradually took their positions under him. Now the females turned to the care of their young and to friendly relationships with other females. Once order had been established in the monkeys' society, they showed deeper feelings. Travelling groups went at a pace to accommodate the old and infirm.

Almost all lower animals use fighting only to create order. In his study of birds, the British ornithologist H. E. Howard found that the springtime song was actually a warning to other birds to stay away and avert a physical battle. Males sang from trees and posts to tell one another where their boundaries lay. Only rarely, when the warning song was ignored, did they clash physically, and then never to the death. More often a song was tussle enough. As the nesting season progressed and each bird became established in its territory with a mate, the loud songs died down.

There have been several recent experiments to discover what starts a fight. John Paul Scott, a research professor of psychology, discovered in testing mice that one of the primary ingredients of a mouse battle is pain. He had only to pinch a male mouse on the tail and it turned and slashed its nearest neighbour.

Emotional torches also ignite animal battles. For some animals conflicts may arise over females (although much less often than we have been led to believe), threats to their young and food scarcity. The most frequent battles, however, seem to relate to status and property. Every animal that has territory is aggressive against trespassers.

When status fights have established a hierarchy in a pack, herd or flock, fighting decreases. This can be observed in farmyard chickens, which are among the most pugnacious of all birds.

At an experimental laboratory a group of five hens was tagged alphabetically according to their previously established rank. Then a dish of food, big enough to feed only one bird at a time, was presented to them. All the hens ran towards it—but A stretched her neck, lifted her head feathers and threw up her comb: the others immediately stopped short of the dish and let her eat first.

The researcher then removed this strong leader. B stepped up to the tray. Only when all the birds except D and E were removed was there a fight. Wings batted, feet clawed and beaks descended on heads. 'They fight for status when the others are gone,' said the researcher. 'They need the dominance of the whole group to stop them fighting.'

Since the dominant animal, often the oldest and heaviest, is important to peace in some kinds of animal societies, the question of how dominance is achieved was studied by Dr Scott at Jackson Laboratory in Maine. It was found not only that the dominant animal is often a winner but that a winner is made by winning. Dr Scott and his co-workers placed two male mice in a small cage, where the animals had no choice but to fight after a tail pinch. The winner was then pitted against a series of weaker opponents until he became so confident that he did not even bother with the warm-up—tail rattling and hair raising—but simply charged and fought as soon as he was put into a cage. Fighters trained in this manner became so aggressive that they would tackle every mouse they encountered, including females and young—something that no normal mouse would do.

Bison have strong herd instincts, but during the summer mating season bulls paw the earth, bellow angrily and batter each other for the right to possess any cow in breeding condition.

Many wild creatures have a territory which, once it is entered by an intruder, forces them to make a decision—to fight or flee. Jack Couffer, a wildlife photographer, writes in his book *Song of Wild Laughter* about a lynx that was confined to a cage so small that the people who came up to it were within the cat's fight-or-flight perimeter. Unable to attack them and yet having no room to retreat, the animal, once a docile pet, turned viciously neurotic.

This is very important in keeping zoo animals healthy. When tigers and bears retire to that distant peaceable corner, they are actually removing the irritation of their human audience.

The ways an animal expresses anger are different in various species. In birds it may be a song. Some frogs will leap heavily upon the back of an intruding frog. An angry ram will lower its head.

Not knowing what animals respond to can sometimes get people into difficult situations with pets. Not long ago my usually docile Newfoundland snapped at a three-year-old child. I was perplexed, because the dog is accustomed to children mauling her. Then I noticed that the little girl approached Tonka from the rear and put a firm hand on her shoulder. Tonka instinctively turned aggressively, for unwittingly Patsy was going through the motions of dog aggression. Approaching from the rear, a paw on the shoulder, and a head higher than the other dog's is 'bossing' in the canine world. We solved Patsy's problem with a few counteracting suggestions: speak to the dog, let her see who is coming, and pat her gently.

When an animal is stimulated to aggression, blood rushes to its muscles, its heart beats faster and adrenalin flows. Violent action—fighting or running away—brings the body back to normal. But what happens if this body state cannot be worked off?

Knowing that in man long periods of suppressing aggression often contribute towards such disorders as heart disease, asthma and stomach ulcers, psychologists put animals under the stress of unresolved aggression. A number of mice—males and females —were crowded together in a small cage. Afraid and worried by constant threats, many died of fatigue. Some lost weight. The overcrowding interfered with the milk production of the mothers and therefore subsequent litters were smaller.

Where is all this research into animal aggression taking us? I had an answer recently while walking along a beach with a young psychologist. I picked up an oyster shell from the sand. 'There's a beast that knows no rancour,' I said. 'An oyster has nothing to fight with,' he replied. 'Give him a tooth or a hand, and even he will eventually use it. Weapons have a way of being used.'

I paused, thinking of the weapons we have. The young graduate tossed my shell into the water. 'That's why we are studying the nature of fighting,' he said. 'If we know what it is, we may be able to do something about it—before it's too late.'

Animals can be Almost Human

Max Eastman

Some forms of behaviour that we think of
as exclusively human also
occur in animals; our bond with Nature
is closer than we think

Hardly a week goes by that newspapers do not contain one or more stories about fabulous feats performed by animals. I have admired my animal neighbours all my life, but I confess that I find many of these stories a little too fabulous, others too sentimental, to suit me. I do not want animals to be supernatural; I want them to be natural. I am not half so much interested in tales of the intellectual prowess or moral heroism of some dog or cat or elephant as in learning about those traits of animals in general that are similar to ours and give us a sense of the kinship of life.

Take the giving of gifts and love tokens. According to Edward Armstrong, author of *The Way Birds Live*, even the custom of 'saying it with flowers' is to be found among certain birds and insects. The male empid fly, for instance, wraps up a flower petal or a bit of food in a web of fine silk that he weaves with his front feet, and presents it to his bride. 'Starlings,' says Professor Armstrong, 'carry flowers into their nesting-hole when the female is on the nest. A herring gull will pick up a shell or pluck a sea pink and, with great courtesy, lay it before the brooding mate.'

Other birds come so near to being human that they express their sentimental emotions by talking baby talk—a trick I cannot endorse in either species. According to Konrad Lorenz, an outstanding naturalist, 'Every delicacy the male jackdaw finds is given to the bride, and she accepts it with the plaintive notes typical of baby birds. The love whispers of the couple consist chiefly of infantile sounds.'

A more dignified example of similarity between humans and animals is the ceremony of betrothal. Long engagements always seemed to me an unbiological affliction that man in a state of puritanical super-civilisation has imposed upon himself. Among robins, however, extended engagements are an all but inflexible rule. They pair up in late December or January, but do not mate or start housekeeping until the end of March. Among jackdaws and wild geese betrothal occurs in the spring following birth, although neither species becomes sexually mature until a year later. Indeed, nearly all birds that marry for life are betrothed before they marry.

Another social custom commonly regarded as peculiarly human is the division of society into castes or classes, with the special privilege, oppression, cruelty and snobbery that go with it. You can see it in the hen-run, where a definite social hierarchy, or 'pecking order', is always established. Every bird has a wholesome fear of those above her in rank and also knows which ones are below her. It is not always by tests of strength that this order is established; energy, nerve and, above all, self-assurance, also play a vital role. Just as among men, this hierarchy of status and prestige is liable to culminate in dictatorship.

An equally human aspect of this ladder of prestige is the snobbery it entails. Dr Lorenz describes how a jackdaw of high rank fell in love with a young female among the lower orders. Within a few days the entire colony knew that this little low-class upstart, whom 80 per cent of them had been maltreating, could no longer receive a black look from anybody. She knew it, too, and made the fullest use of it. 'She lacked entirely,' Lorenz mourns, 'that noble tolerance which jackdaws of high rank should exhibit towards their inferiors. She used every opportunity to snub former superiors. In short, she conducted herself with the utmost vulgarity.'

Dr Lorenz warns us against the sentimental notion that animals are morally 'better' or 'worse' than man. Moral judgments, he insists, are irrelevant where life is instinctive. In explaining the all-too-human sins of animals, he relates the sad tale of the alienation of a swan husband's tender affections by a determined female. Swans are monogamous, and supposedly faithful to their mates for life. But one old male swan 'furiously expelled a strange female who came close to the nest where his wife was sitting and made him proposals of love—and then on the very same day was seen to meet this new female on the other side of the lake and succumb to her charms without more ado'.

Every autumn, Canada geese fly some 4000 miles from their northern breeding grounds—but keep their family ties. They mate when they are two years old, stay paired for life, and share the raising of their goslings.

Dr Lorenz is disposed to find 'human weaknesses' in nearly all animals. For instance, he says that his dog Bully was an accomplished 'liar'. Bully would always run out to meet him with exuberant affection at the front gate, but he would also run out there to bark savagely at strangers. In old age Bully's eyesight grew dim, and one day when the wind was blowing the scent in the opposite direction, recognition failed and Bully barked fiercely at his master. When he got near enough to perceive his mistake, he stopped short, then rushed past him and across the road, where he pretended to be barking at a neighbour's dog who was not there.

Cats, too, are exceedingly vain of their poise and dignity. If by some chance—perhaps a slippery floor when they are in a hurry—they slide sideways, they will instantly turn to examine some object in the new direction, giving a careful smell to each detail, as though that had always been their intention.

'Women and children first', a precept of chivalry not invariably lived up to by the human race, is an instinct that can be relied on absolutely in dogs. The most ferocious dog terrorising a neighbourhood of canine males will never touch a female or a young puppy. If a neurotic spinster bitch should attack him, he is completely nonplussed. His pride prevents him from running away, but he cannot bring himself to give battle. So he just stands about, shifting from foot to foot like a bewildered schoolboy.

Magnanimity to the vanquished, another high standard of conduct adhered to on occasion by

civilised man, is a law of Nature among wolves. When there is a fight between two timber wolves and the weaker is beaten, he stands rigidly still, turning his head in such a manner as to expose his throat deliberately, the primary point of attack. It is a gesture of surrender, a plea for mercy, and it renders the victor quite unable to attack. The victim, so long as he holds that position, is safe. This same instinct of magnanimity—as it may be called—is to be found among many kinds of dogs.

Pleasure in owning property is an instinct extending far down into the animal kingdom. It is this pleasure, most often, that birds are proclaiming when they sit on a high treetop and sing. They are shouting: 'This is my territory. Trespassers keep out!' Other animals deposit a proprietary scent along the borders of their private estates. The mongoose has a special gland that exudes a tiny spray which he uses for this purpose; if you wipe his markers away with a wet cloth, he will promptly come back and renew them.

A zoo director told me of his attempt to mate a pair of leopards. He kept them in two cages separated by bars until they had fallen quite madly in love. When, however, he admitted the female into the male's cage, the male's property sense overrode both love and lust. He snarled and struck her dead with one blow of his paw.

And so it seems that it was Nature, not man, who invented the delight of owning a little piece of this planet we live on.

Are Wild Animals Really Wild?

Andy Russell

The Canadian bighorn sheep is one of the wariest, most elusive creatures in Nature— but only as far as hunters are concerned

After 20 years as a guide for big-game hunters in the Canadian Rockies, I have learnt what I would never have believed before —that so-called wild animals are not really wild at all. Usually they do flee the presence of man, but only because they have learnt from bitter experience that he is the most dangerous creature they encounter. Offered friendly treatment and respect, they will respond in a most extraordinary manner.

The bighorn sheep, for instance, is reputed to be one of the wildest of all living creatures. Hunters, aided by guides, telescopic sights and long-range rifles, often spend weeks trying to collect a single trophy. Yet I recently sat in the midst of a band of 16 bighorn rams, the nearest ones less than 20 ft from me. The story of how Dick and Charlie, my two eldest sons, and I achieved this unheard-of friendship may add something to man's knowledge of natural history.

I received an assignment from a Canadian foundation to record the life history of the bighorn (*Ovis canadensis*). When my boys and I first began stalking them with cameras in the heart of their range along the Continental Divide, the sheep were wary and suspicious. Even with telephoto lenses, it is necessary to get close for good pictures—much closer than normal rifle-range. The usual sly approach of the hunter simply did not work, for if the sheep chanced to see us sneaking from one bit of cover to the next, we were left looking at mountain scenery where sheep had recently been. Even if we got within desirable range, our best shots were of startled bighorns leaving in a hurry.

One day when I was resting in a canyon and pondering this problem, under the watchful eyes of a bunch of rams bedded on a mountain shoulder half a mile away, it suddenly occurred to me that we might be going about it the wrong way. I remembered that once, years before, I had taken a hunting party into a remote valley cradled among 10,000 ft peaks in south-eastern British Columbia. We were rounding a cliff when we met a bunch of mountain goats face to face. Instead of running, they stood staring at us like children at a circus. Then, to our astonishment, three of them came towards us, obviously unafraid though nervous enough to stamp their front feet. My two hunters and I looked at one another, left the rifles hanging on their slings and began taking photographs. Hunting was one thing, but sheer murder was quite another!

So, I thought, perhaps the bighorn sheep would accept us in the same way, if we could convince them we meant no harm. Abandoning hidden stalks, the boys and I now resorted to patience and diplomacy, staying in sight of the sheep at all times. It was a slow, painstaking business requiring weeks of climbing. We schooled ourselves to move smoothly, for the sheep took instant alarm at any jerky motion. If, as we approached, we saw signs of nervousness, we turned our backs on the animals and wandered aimlessly about, admiring the flowers, as though bighorns were far from our minds. Above all, we avoided looking directly at them for more than a casual glance, for like all 'wild' things, bighorns do not like to be stared at. (Even the birds and squirrels in the parks of big cities, where people are a part of their daily lives, take alarm at a direct stare.)

In time, our new methods began to show signs of paying off. We found ourselves getting closer and closer to the sheep. Then one day I was able to work my way right in among a bunch of bedded rams and sit down. It was one of the greatest thrills of an adventurous life to look round and study the characteristics of individuals as they casually glanced my way or, better still, looked past me down the mountain in complete acceptance of my presence. No experience hunting with a rifle had ever matched this.

Either the news circulated along the mountain grapevine, or our technique had been perfected, for soon we were at home with the bighorns over their whole range. Out of the many sheep we encountered, we came to know about 40 individuals. These and many more seemed to recognise us and often let us approach to within a few feet, paying us no more attention than they would other sheep. Once I filmed a feeding ewe at exactly 12 ft. Charlie photographed a ewe's eye at less than 6 ft, obtaining a unique record of the rich, golden colour and the distinctive square pupil.

I remember watching Dick working with a bunch of ewes and lambs at the foot of a cliff. When they began to climb to the rims above, Dick fell in behind on all fours to climb with them. Then out of nowhere came a magnificent ram. He took a brief look at the procession and bounded up to take his climbing position directly behind Dick. I chuckled to think how Dick must feel with some 60 lb. of ram's horns so close to his hip pockets.

There was one huge patriarchal ram whose horns were the biggest I have ever seen, probably measuring 47 in. around the outside curls, and 17 in. in circumference at the base. He was about $3\frac{1}{2}$ ft high at the shoulder and weighed at least 400 lb. His head alone must have weighed close to 70 lb., and we often saw him take the load from his neck by resting a horn on the ground as he lay bedded. Time after time we climbed high, trying to come up to him, but he was too wary.

One day on my way down from a high peak I paused on a sunny ledge. At once, that sixth sense developed by chronic wanderers of the wilderness warned me that I was not alone. With infinite care I moved my eyes slowly to the side—to see the big ram not 20 ft away. He had let me climb down past him a little and now he was lying watching me with those magnificently keen eyes. For long minutes neither of us moved a hair. Then I saw a ripple rise in his throat and he began calmly chewing his cud— a sure sign that he was unafraid. I had been accepted by the king ram of them all. But I had used every scrap of film in my pack.

I am convinced that animals are not naturally afraid of human scent, for we found we could completely ignore the direction of the wind on approaching the sheep—though it was often noticeable that they did not enjoy our smell. The one thing the bighorns never would tolerate, no matter how well they knew us, was any quick movement. The accidental slip of a tripod leg or climbing-boot would trigger instant flight. Once when I was filming a group of rams with my cine camera, I dropped a glove. Instantly I was alone.

Perhaps the most fascinating of the habits we recorded were the bighorns' games—joined in by old and young alike. One evening after supper we were sitting in front of our camp when a mixed bunch of ewes, lambs and small rams appeared on the skyline high above us. Suddenly a dignified-looking old ewe ran down the ridge to a snowdrift pitched at a steep angle towards a formidable cliff. Without checking her speed, she launched into a reckless glissade straight down the icy drift. With the snow streaming over both shoulders, she seemed bent on suicide; but at the last precise instant she did a four-legged christie to run off on the naked rocks at the side. As she galloped back to the top the others followed her in turn, each making that hair-raising

A rutting-season duel between two Rocky Mountain bighorn rams. In such a charge as this, the two rams meet each other with a combined speed of about 45 mph. Bighorn sheep were once abundant from Mexico to western Canada, but their numbers have been reduced by hunters, disease and competition for grazing land from domestic sheep. These rams were photographed in the Alberta Rockies, Canada, at the height of the breeding season in early December.

swing on the brink of disaster. We watched until the light failed, while they went blithely round and round in a bighorn version of follow-my-leader.

They also play a replica of king-of-the-castle. Once we saw five young rams busy at this game. One stood on top of a loose pile of rocks and his companions took quick turns trying to knock him off, while he whirled and danced, meeting all-comers head-on, until he was dislodged. Then the victor took his turn at defending the castle.

Filming newborn lambs proved to be a problem, for the favourite lambing grounds are hardly chosen for their accessibility and the ewes are even more shy than usual. We followed one bunch for six weeks before we got close-ups. Yet before the lambing season these same mothers would allow us to come almost within reach.

Born in late May and June, the lambs weigh about 4 lb. at birth, and it would be difficult to find more attractive young animals. They can run when only a few hours old and we have seen them trailing behind their mothers before they were licked dry. In three days they can streak over incredibly rough ground like rabbits, and in a week they can jump clear over their mothers' backs, just for the fun of it. They are extremely playful and join in speedy games of follow-my-leader on cliff faces that would give human mothers nervous prostration to watch.

Throughout most of the year the rams stay by themselves in bachelors' clubs under the leadership of the oldest and wisest individuals. But in late November they disperse to mingle with the ewes, and all camaraderie is forgotten in competition for the females during the breeding season, which lasts through December to early January. Squaring off with dramatic dignity, the rams batter each other in head-on engagements that set the mountains ringing. These collisions often leave them temporarily groggy and permanently scarred. Nearly all mature rams have chips knocked off their horns, and their hallmark is the broken nose reminiscent of professional prize-fighters.

It was such a fight that I particularly wanted for the climax of our film. We had seen several battles from a distance, but our attempts at close-ups seemed fated to failure. Then, on a clear winter day, as I headed up into the sheep country, I had the feeling that luck was with me.

Stopping at a vantage point, I spotted a lone ram travelling across the front of a peak above the valley. Even at a distance of over a mile, he had that arrogance of bearing that is the unmistakable mark of a questing male. I climbed quickly up a side canyon to intercept him.

Near the top, I saw what I had hoped to see—another big ram escorting a single ewe. Scrambling on up the ice-draped rocks, I eased over the last edge just in time to film an epic battle.

The rams stood facing each other with heads held high and proud. Then both reared straight up with front legs hanging, to run towards each other on their hind feet. Two lengths apart, they hurled themselves forward to meet in mid-air, horn to horn, with a crash that rang for half a mile. The impact was so terrific that their bodies literally whiplashed and their ridiculous, short tails jerked straight up. For a few moments they stood staring into space, apparently dazed by the shock, before stepping back to resume manoeuvring for position. Again and again they collided with shattering slams. Once I saw splinters fly, and a new scar showed on a horn of the ram defending the ewe. Several times they came within 6 ft of me, paying me no more attention than if I were a tree stump.

Finally the defending ram had had enough; he broke off the engagement and headed down the mountain. The challenger followed him closely for a way, apparently to make sure he left for good. Then he turned back to claim his prize.

It would be nice to say that the proud victor returned triumphantly to the lady and that, together, they disappeared happily into the fastnesses of the peaks. But such was not the fact. The winner arrived back on the battleground just in time to see the cause of all the uproar disappearing over the skyline ahead of a young ram who had slipped in to steal her away. The victorious gladiator, too tired for pursuit, just threw a disgusted look in their direction and proceeded to feed. I passed him my unspoken sympathy and headed back down the mountain.

After 17 months of almost continuous living with the bighorns, I had completed my film. The job was done—now I could return to my guiding business. But somehow that prospect held small appeal. My experience with the sheep had opened up a shining vista of adventure with cameras instead of guns. I suddenly realised that I would never again be able to kill another bighorn.

So the sheep remain my friends. As a guide, I have been able to provide pleasure and thrills for the privileged few who could afford de luxe wilderness trips. Now, with camera and typewriter, I hope my sons and I can bring pleasure and a true knowledge of Nature to many others.

Heroes of the Wild

Alan Devoe

The human race is not alone in producing heroes: in the animal world, too, life is sustained by creatures able to meet the challenge of extreme circumstances

A tiny wren, hardly more than the size of a thimble, had been perched for an hour on an arbour post near the bird-box, pouring out such a tumult of cascading melody that I had been listening entranced. Abruptly the lilting rush of notes stopped. There was a second's silence. Then there burst forth a staccato chattering that among wrens means: 'Something wrong!'

I walked towards the arbour, watching. Father wren was dancing on the post in a spasm of agitation. Mother wren had poked her little head through the door of the bird-box, her bright eyes fixed on something below. Then I saw it. A milk snake as long as my arm was climbing in a steady glide up the arbour.

These snakes, relentless catchers of field mice and baby birds, can climb like a cat and clean out a bird's nest in seconds. Though not venomous they strike savagely, and when they bite they hang on viciously and chew. I grabbed a stick and hurried forward. I need not have bothered. This snake had had the misfortune to pick on heroes.

With a screaming cry, the father wren dived from the post and smacked the marauder just behind its head. The snake lunged, but its jaws hit empty air. In that instant the mother wren slipped from the bird-house door, plummeted, and caught him in the backbone with a lance-like thrust. The snake's body quivered and slackened. It took only about two minutes and some 20 furious blows before it was all over. The reptile lost its hold and dropped to the ground. But the tiny feathered defenders of their babies were not finished. Again and again they struck and flailed until the snake lay dead in the grass. And from a nearby post of the arbour there rang out a cascade of triumphant song.

That was last year. If this year there has been a throng of happy wrens to make my garden musical, there is no telling the extent to which this may be due to the extraordinary heroism I saw exhibited by that one pair of birds.

The great scientist Alexis Carrel once said that the whole human race is carried on the backs of a few heroes. Almost every one of us is alive today only because, somewhere along his genealogical line, there was a hero: someone who, in a tight spot, was brave beyond the call of duty, outstanding in patience or courage or the heroism of tenacity. And exactly the same thing is true among the creatures of the woods, hedgerows and fields.

Not long ago I asked a famous zoologist what had been the most outstanding action he had ever seen a wild creature perform. Casting around among his memories of valiant big-game animals, cunning coons and foxes, he suddenly smiled and said he thought his outstanding hero was probably an insect.

He had been standing on the bank of a small stream when he noticed a digger wasp on the ground near him. It had paralysed a huge spider and was trying unsuccessfully to drag it to its burrow. The wasp could not get into the air with its heavy load and the overland haul was also proving to be impossibly difficult.

Finally, the wasp dragged the spider the short distance to the stream and floated it on the water. Taking a firm grip on the now buoyant body, the wasp buzzed its wings at top speed. Slowly, like a helicopter towing a barge, the wasp towed the spider some 70 yds downstream, while the absorbed zoologist kept pace on shore. Suddenly the wasp turned inshore, and in a moment was heaving its sopping treasure up the bank. There, within a few inches of the water, was its burrow. Exhausted but triumphant, the insect at last dragged its hard-won prize into the doorway of its burrow.

'In that unforgettable glimpse into the insect world,' said the zoologist, 'I came to know that they too have their Columbuses and Galileos.'

I had never thought of heroism in connection with the slow, plume-tailed skunks that prowl around my woods, but one day I met a big fellow who had managed to get himself hung by the tail on a barbed-wire fence. He was dangling head downwards, his forepaws just clear of the ground. He had been there a long time and he was desperately spent and weak. I was tempted to help him but, remembering his effective weapon, I decided to watch.

The usual animal way in a strange catastrophe is to thrash and struggle in panic. What makes heroes is the capacity not to be usual. My skunk was acting with an unusual kind of heroic discipline. Instead of wasting his dwindling strength in a furious struggle, he would hang for long minutes as inert as a dead animal; then, in a wild swing contortion, he would whip his body up and around until he could grab the fence wire in his forepaws. Hanging so, bent almost in a circle, he attacked his tail with his teeth, just below where it was caught in the wire. He was intent on an amputation.

He could work only for seconds at the grim job; then his strength would fail and he would have to drop back to hang limp again, hoarding his powers for the next attempt. Then he was up and at it again, as controlled as a surgeon, not uttering a sound.

He made it. With a 6 in. stump of tail instead of a foot-long plume, he dropped to the ground, his legs buckling, and was off into the woods.

Heroism is contagious. To see it blaze up in one exceptional individual and spread from this leader to a group, sets a watcher's heart singing. An outstanding example was witnessed by Enos Mills, a naturalist who has made a special study of the American West. He was watching a band of seven mountain goats climbing a canyon in Alaska.

They had started up an almost sheer wall of rock, following a cleavage line in the rock face. Tiny ledges and root clusters afforded precarious footholds. Suddenly they stopped, only a few feet from the top. The cleavage line had petered out. In single file, hugging the rock face, they were trapped.

Mills turned his binoculars on the old billy in the lead. He saw how a hero acts. Slowly, with infinite care, the leader pawed with its front hoofs at the rock wall. He reared higher, higher, on stretching tiptoe, his front hoofs feeling and grappling until he found an infinitesimal hold. Then, with front hoofs hooked into it, he hunched and sprang straight upwards. Hind hoofs caught where front hoofs had been, and in that split second the big body hunched and sprang in a second upward leap.

The mountain goat had done the impossible. On the very summit of the cliff he whirled round, and stood there for all his comrades to see—a symbol of triumph. He had done it; they could too. One by one the others made the heroic leap, and joined the company of the heroes of the wild.

LIFE IN THE NEW WORLD RAIN FOREST

In the equatorial regions of the New World, aeons of torrential rains and hot, humid weather have nurtured a lush tropical forest. The interwoven branches of its trees form a canopy over 100 ft high, so dense that only occasional shafts of sunlight penetrate. Below the canopy, spindly young trees struggle upwards, and above it a few wide-crowned giants rise as high as 200 ft. Birds, monkeys, sloths, lizards and snakes live their entire lives in the branches; peccaries and tapirs forage on the floor; myriads of insects flit through the motionless air and crawl across the foliage. Everywhere woody vines, many over 200 ft long, hang from the trees. Countless orchids and other flowering plants grow on rotting logs and in the damp crannies of living trees. Acre for acre, the tropical rain forest harbours a greater variety of life than any other land area.

The harpy eagle (above) is king of the rain forest's birds of prey; it glides between the trees in search of sloths and monkeys.

A versatile predator, the jaguar (right) feeds on peccaries, fish and even alligators.

Anchored by its prehensile tail, a tamandua, a tree-dwelling ant-eater, tears bark off a dead branch with hook-like foreclaws and picks up termites with its long, sticky tongue.

The howler monkey (above), whose lion-like roar can be heard for a mile, never descends from the trees. When thirsty, it licks wet leaves.

The 12 in. golden conure (left) of eastern Brazil is one of the forest canopy's most colourful inhabitants.

A tree frog perches precariously on a Heliconia plant. This gaudy amphibian (shown about 6 times life size) sleeps all day and hunts insects by night.

Working their jaws like scissors, Atta ants (left), snip pieces from leaves to carry back to their nest. There the ants will chew the cuttings into a pulpy mulch, in which they grow an edible fungus.

Flowers abound in the rain forest, sprouting profusely from tree trunks and climbing vines. The butterfly orchid (top) grows on a long, thin stalk so well hidden by foliage that it seems to hover in mid-air. The passion-flower (middle) is the bloom of a woody vine. The petals of the ginger flower (bottom) catch water in which frogs and insects breed. In this photograph, the flower has attracted an inch-long Euglossid bee.

A foot-long giant anole lizard (below) preys on one of its small insect-eating relatives. Both of these tree-dwelling reptiles are related to chameleons.

PART THREE
MAN AND NATURE

The New Frontiers

Man has learnt more in the last 60 years than in all the rest
of his history. Yet even as the speed of discovery
increases, he becomes more and more aware
of what he does not know.
There will never be any shortage of new
frontiers in man's quest for knowledge of the natural world

Antarctica – the World's Most Fascinating Icebox

Ira Wolfert

Scientists and penguins live side by side
in an icy world which is only
now beginning to yield up its secrets

Exploring a continent is one of man's oldest adventures. Never before, though, has he had a chance to do it as it is being done in the Antarctic today. In 1961, 12 nations ratified a treaty agreeing to reserve Antarctica exclusively for scientific research for 30 years. As a result, scientists are now busily pursuing an intense programme of full-time research and exploration. It is a fantastic project, unique in history.

They are at work in an amazing land. The South Pole itself is in the midst of nothing at all—just flat, blank, snow-covered ice. But elsewhere on the continent there are jagged mountains, with all but their peaks buried in ice and snow; a lake—covered by more than 12 ft of ice—whose depths register a temperature of 80°F; violet and green ice; a smoking volcano; and penguins in rookeries of many thousands, sometimes hundreds of thousands. There were times when I felt that I was walking in the sky

because a sunset had encased me, the fields of snow reflecting the hues in the sky with breathtaking accuracy. At other times, when I exhaled, a bloom of tiny, exquisite ice crystals shimmered into the air and fell like a rain of diamonds.

The coldest temperature officially recorded on earth was −126.9°F at one of the Russian bases in Antarctica. The mean annual temperature at the South Pole is 56.7° below zero. Over much of the rest of the continent, it is 40° below or colder most of the time. In the words of one scientist, 'It's the world's most fascinating icebox.'

Weather permitting, never a day goes by when planes and helicopters are not giving aid to researchers. It is not unusual for eight aircraft to be aloft at once, flying supplies to the South Pole, doing aerial mapping, reconnoitring terrain for men travelling over land never before trodden by human feet, making touch-and-go landings to drop off or pick up field parties.

From October to March the daylight lasts 24 hours at McMurdo Sound; work goes on round the clock in 12-hour shifts. At two o'clock one morning, with the sun shining brightly, the nearby supply base was alive with typically varied and extraordinary activities.

A traxcavator (an excavating and forklift truck on tracks) lumbered by with a load of snow to melt for water. It was followed by another tractor vehicle hauling materials for the permanent housing (built to last 30 years) going up to replace plywood and

Mid-winter sunset at the American research base on Cape Hallet in the Antarctic. Here studies are being made of the homing instinct in penguins, and of Antarctic weather, which it is believed may provide clues to forthcoming weather throughout the world.

Ice particles in the atmosphere cause the sun's haloed appearance in this photograph of Britain's research base at Halley Bay in the Antarctic. The base stands on a floating ice-shelf 500 ft thick. The radio-sonde balloon is launched daily to study the atmosphere up to a height of 15 miles.

canvas huts constructed when exploration was on a maybe-never-again basis. The new housing has electric heating from a nuclear power plant, hot and cold running water from desalinated seawater pumped out from under the ice, plus refrigerators—to keep food from freezing.

There were more than 60 scientific research projects in the Antarctic during the 1967–8 season. One of the continent's attractions is that it is a landmass surrounded by an ocean, unlike the Arctic, which is an ocean surrounded by land. In the Antarctic, polar conditions and science meet on a stable platform, and prolonged studies are possible.

Seals, for instance, have become a subject of lively interest in fields as diverse as medicine, sonar and submarine design. Physiologists have found that seals are able to shut off the circulation in their outer surface and extremities to concentrate the blood in the vital organs so that they can conserve their oxygen supply. The Weddell seal can hold its breath for more than 30 minutes and can dive to the hull-crushing depth of 1500 ft. This seal is thought to navigate under ice by making sounds—one of which is hauntingly melodious—and reading the echoes.

A Weddell seal peers through its breathing hole in the Antarctic pack-ice. This half-ton creature can dive to 1500 ft and stay under for half an hour searching for squid, fish and small bottom-dwellers.

At the time I was there, a researcher was preparing to trap fish to study their metabolism. He attached one end of a net to a harness, the harness to a seal, then pushed the seal down a hole in the ice. The nearest hole was a quarter of a mile away. When the seal emerged, the harness was unhooked and what was thought to be impossible—spreading a large net under 10 ft of ice—was accomplished.

Four men took off in a helicopter. Two of them, who called themselves sea-cowboys, were on their way to brand seals in an effort eventually to gauge their ages and trace their wanderings. The other two, trying to determine how penguins are able to navigate so precisely over such vast distances in the featureless landscape, were carrying tiny radio transmitters to strap on to the birds so that their course could be tracked.

Meanwhile, at the South Pole, ten men were starting out in three tractors on a two-month, 900-mile zigzag traverse, through unexplored territory, towards the abandoned Soviet station at the Antarctic's furthest inland point, sometimes called the 'Pole of Relative Inaccessibility'. Hooked on behind the tractors were six trailers carrying scientific instruments, spare parts, explosives and 3 tons of food. The trailers rode on enormous tyres in which extra fuel for the trip was stored.

Biologists were amazed to find that the Antarctic Ocean supports larger numbers (although fewer kinds) of plants and animals than any other. (Among these is the biggest animal in the world, the blue whale.) Scientists worrying about feeding the world's expanding population are studying this phenomenon with interest.

The Antarctic also provides a window on unknown facets of Nature's mechanisms. For example, semi-tropical trees and plants once grew on the continent. In several places, petrified wood 270 million years old and coal-beds up to 25 ft thick have been found. The coal is hard, and ancient plant fossils are imprinted on many slabs of it; they record the past like the pages of a book.

Is the tropics-to-deep-freeze climate change temporary or permanent? Is it the result of a variation in solar activity? Or of the continent's breaking off and drifting from a previous position nearer the Equator? Or of an alteration in the earth's axis?

These questions are of moment to all of us, as about 90 per cent of the ice on earth is in the Antarctic. If it were ever to melt, the level of all the oceans would be raised some 250 ft, redrawing the map of the earth. Even a thaw too minor to make any significant change in ocean levels could, in the long run, affect the global weather pattern profoundly.

'Men haven't conquered Nature anywhere, here least of all,' said Major Hayter, commander of New Zealand's Scott Base. 'They've only found the terms under which Nature permits them to operate.'

The French reported winds reaching a speed of 200 mph before the instruments at their base broke. There is no overture of sound. Abruptly you are engulfed in the drumming and shrieking of a blizzard that goes on and on for days without let-up.

Nature has equipped every living thing in the Antarctic except man, who is an outsider, with boundlessly ingenious natural devices for enduring the harsh climate. The fish have certain chemical substances in their blood which, scientists think, act as anti-freeze and keep their body fluids from freezing. The insects, of which some 60 species have been discovered, are active only when the sun has heated their surroundings above freezing point. 'They have a practically instantaneous reversible hibernation,' said one entomologist. 'When in cold-stupor, they can be activated simply by breathing on them.' If ice forms over their resting place as they sleep, they can wait for it to melt—some insects have revived from hibernations thought to have lasted 70 years.

The Adélie penguins are also well adapted to the harsh environment. They spend most of their time on ice floes at sea, feed on shrimps and, though they cannot fly, swim at speeds of up to 30 mph. Every October they go ashore to breed, finding their way to the same spot in the same rookery. After the female lays her two eggs, she returns to the sea to restore her depleted body, and the male looks after the nest. He can go without food for six weeks.

On shore to nest, two Adélie penguins exchange ceremonial greetings. When summer begins, Adélies gather in great breeding colonies, called rookeries, around the rim of Antarctica. The eggs are brooded in simple pebble nests; the young hatch in December. In February the birds return to the food-rich pack-ice region further north.

The Adélies demonstrate emotion for one another graphically in what scientists call 'mutual display'. In each nest to which a female returned, the male jumped up from the eggs, stood on tiptoe facing his mate and, with head and neck swaying, let out repeated raucous 'ga-ga-ga' noises.

Afterwards, when the male had gone off to feed himself and the female had taken over the nest, I noticed that she would stand up every now and then, look at her eggs and go into mutual display again.

Once nations looked to their explorers for gold. Today, in the Antarctic or on the moon, men search for knowledge—which is, in the final analysis, the best and most enduring source of wealth.

First of the Microbe Hunters

Paul de Kruif

Antony Leeuwenhoek was the first man to look through a microscope and see miraculous new worlds beneath its lens

Three hundred years ago Antony Leeuwenhoek looked for the first time into a mysterious new world, peopled by a thousand different kinds of tiny beings, some ferocious and deadly, others friendly and useful. Unsung and scarcely remembered, he was the first of the microbe hunters. Other bold, persistent fighters of death followed him; some who were too bold died—killed by the immensely small assassins they were studying.

Today it is respectable to be a man of science. But in 1632, when Leeuwenhoek was born, the world had hardly begun to shake itself free from superstitions. Science was in its infancy; Galileo was put under house arrest for daring to insist that the earth moved around the sun.

Antony Leeuwenhoek was born at Delft, in Holland. His family were burghers of an intensely respectable kind; I say intensely respectable because they were basket-makers and brewers, and brewers are highly honoured in Holland. Leeuwenhoek's father died early and he left school at 16 to be an apprentice in haberdashery in Amsterdam. Think of a present-day scientist getting his training among bolts of gingham, being polite to an eternal succession of Dutch housewives who shopped with a penny-pinching exhaustiveness—but that was Leeuwenhoek's university, for six years.

At 21 he went back to Delft, married and set up a haberdashery of his own. For 20 years after that his life was inconspicuous. He had two wives and several children, was janitor of the city hall of Delft, and developed a love for grinding lenses.

There is no doubt that he passed for an ignorant man. Educated men talked Latin in those days, but Leeuwenhoek could not so much as read it. But this ignorance was a great help to him for, cut off from the learned nonsense of his time, he had to trust his own eyes and his own suspicious judgment.

Leeuwenhoek had heard that if you ground little lenses out of clear glass, things would look much bigger than they appeared to the naked eye; so he went to spectacle makers and learnt the rudiments of lens grinding. He then perfected a way to make a tiny lens, less than $\frac{1}{8}$ in. across, so perfect that it showed little things to him in fantastic detail.

He mounted the lenses in small oblongs of copper, silver or gold, and began to examine anything he could get hold of. He looked at the muscle fibres of a whale and the scales of his own skin; he peered for hours at the fine hairs of a sheep that were transformed into great rough logs under his glass; he delicately dissected the head of a fly and admired the clear details of the marvellous brain; and he wondered at the outlandish perfection of the legs of a louse.

He left his specimens sticking on his strange microscopes for months—in order to look at other things he made more microscopes until he had hundreds of them—then he came back to those first specimens to correct his mistakes. He never set down a word about anything, or made a drawing, until hundreds of viewings showed him that, under

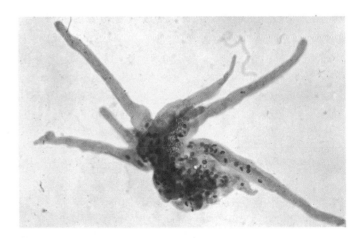

The giants of the microscopic world are the amoeba (above), with its characteristic extensions, or pseudopodia, by which it travels, and the paramecium (below) which moves by means of the hair-like cilla—visible here as a bluish line around each paramecium.

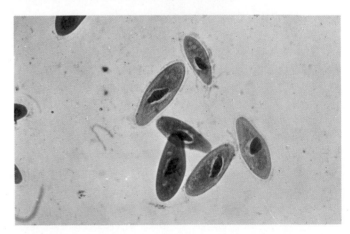

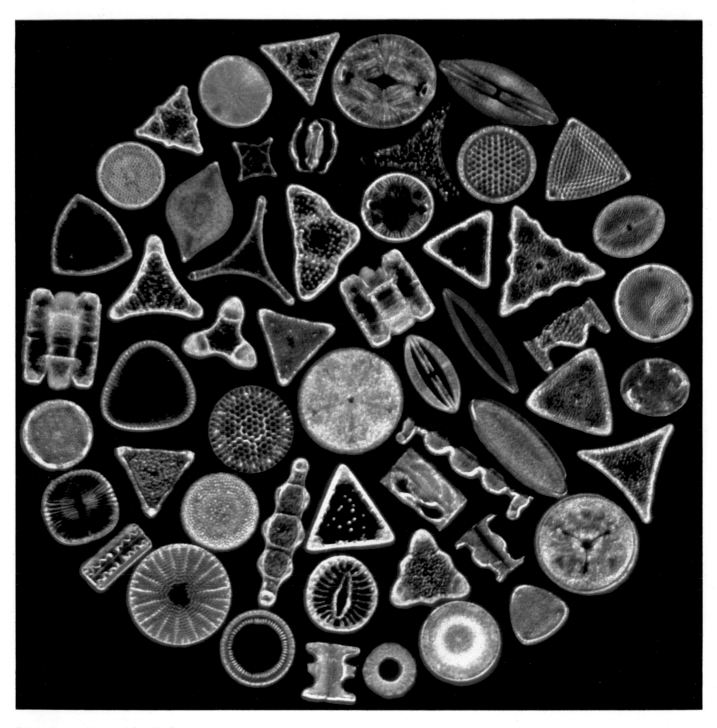

*It is to Antony Leeuwenhoek's discoveries in microscopy
that we owe our vision of the subvisible world and
its endless variety. This photograph shows a collection
of diatoms, one-celled organisms abounding in the sea.*

given conditions, he would always see exactly the
same thing. He worked for 20 years in this way,
without an audience.

By the middle of the 17th century great things
were astir in the world. Here and there men were
thumbing their noses at almost everything that
passed for knowledge. In England a few of these
rebels started a society called The Invisible College
—it had to be invisible because Cromwell might
have hanged them as heretics if he had heard of the
strange questions they were trying to settle. One of
the members was Robert Boyle, founder of the
science of chemistry, and another was Isaac Newton.
When Charles II came to the throne, this college
became the Royal Society of England; it was Antony
Leeuwenhoek's first audience.

One man in Delft did not laugh at Leeuwenhoek:
Reinier de Graaf, a scientist who corresponded with

217

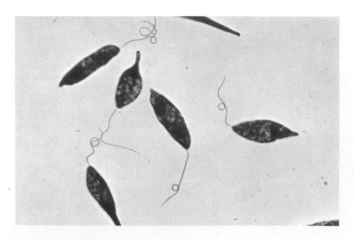

*Under the microscope, many protozoans—
one-celled animals with some of the characteristics
of plants—can be distinguished by the rapid
movements of their thread-like flagella.*

the Royal Society. Leeuwenhoek let de Graaf peep through his 'magic eyes', and what de Graaf saw made him write to the Royal Society: 'Get Antony Leeuwenhoek to write to you of his discoveries.'

Leeuwenhoek answered the request of the Royal Society in a long letter, written in conversational Dutch, the only language he knew. It rambled over every subject under the sun. The learned gentlemen were amused by the letter, but they were astounded by the things Leeuwenhoek told them he could see through his new lenses. They wrote to him that they hoped his communication would be followed by others. It was—by hundreds, over a period of 50 years. The letters were full of salty remarks about his ignorant neighbours and chatter about his own health—but sandwiched between this the Gentlemen of the Royal Society had the honour of reading accurate descriptions of Leeuwenhoek's discoveries.

Leeuwenhoek made better and better lenses, with the persistence of a lunatic, and examined everything with the curiosity of a puppy. One day he looked at a small drop of rainwater. Who but a maniac would have thought to turn his lens on clear, pure water, from the sky? What could there be in water but just—water?

You can see that absentminded, wide-eyed man take a glass tube into the garden, to an earthen pot kept there to measure the rainfall. He bends over the pot, goes back into his study and squints through his lens. Then suddenly he calls: 'Come here! Look! There are little animals in this rainwater. They swim! They play! They are a thousand times smaller than any creatures we can see with our eyes alone!'

This janitor of Delft had peered into a fantastic subvisible world of creatures whose lives had been completely hidden from man. These creatures were capable of ravaging and annihilating whole races of men 10 million times larger than themselves; they were silent assassins that murdered babes in warm cradles and kings in their sheltered palaces. This was Leeuwenhoek's day of days.

But where did these little inhabitants of the rainwater come from? Had they come down from the sky? Had they crawled into the pot from the ground? Or had they been created out of nothing by a God full of whims? There was only one way to find out. 'I will experiment!' Leeuwenhoek muttered.

He took a big porcelain dish, 'glazed blue within', and washed it clean. Then he took it out in the rain and put it on top of a box so that no mud would splash into the dish. He collected the water in one of his slender pipes, went into his study to examine it, and wrote: 'This water has not a single little creature in it! So, they do not come down from the sky!'

But he kept that water; day after day he studied it —and on the fourth day he saw those 'wee beasts' beginning to appear.

Did he write to the Royal Society to tell them of this entirely unsuspected world of life he had discovered? Not yet; he was a patient man. He turned his lens on to all kinds of water: water kept in the close air of his study, in a pot kept on the roof and from the not too clean canals of Delft. Everywhere he found those little creatures.

He then wrote to the great men in London, describing his astonishment to them. On page after page, in superbly neat handwriting, he told of his discovery of creatures so small that you could put as many of them into one drop of water as there were people in Holland. This letter, translated into English, was read before the learned sceptics. What? Nonsense! . . . Still, Leeuwenhoek was a confoundedly accurate man! So a letter went back, begging him to describe in detail how he had made his lenses, and his method of observation.

He replied, explaining his calculations and saying that many people of Delft had seen these strange new animals under his lens. But he would not say how he made his lenses; he was a suspicious man.

The Royal Society used the best microscopes available in England and found that Leeuwenhoek had not lied. A little later the Royal Society made Leeuwenhoek a Fellow, sending him a diploma of membership in a silver case. 'I will serve you faithfully during the rest of my life,' he wrote to them. He was as good as his word, for he mailed them those mixtures of gossip and science until he died at the age of 91. But he never sent them a lens.

218

Farming the Sea-Bed

James Dugan

Men may soon learn how to herd
fish and sow crops on the sea floor; in time, they
may even learn how to breathe water

Man is about to occupy the two-thirds of his environment that has so far been closed to him—the floor of the world's oceans. Before this century has passed man will have returned to the sea from which his species evolved. He will go back as a farmer, miner, artificer and researcher. The commercial fisherman and naval man will surrender mastery of the deeps to the *oceanide*, or man of the sea. Already the international free-diving movement has created a popular science of the sea. We have placed the first settlers in manned undersea stations. Shipyards are building scientific submarines, to follow the bathyscaphes, Cousteau's Diving Saucer and *Alvin*, which rescued the American atom bomb from the Mediterranean. Around the continents, on the continental shelves, stand thousands of Texas towers conveying petroleum, gas and sulphur ashore. They are a menace to navigation and their own crews. They will be superseded by safer and cheaper undersea stations, whose crews will work well-heads on the bottom at far greater depths.

The ocean hunt is concentrated in the North Atlantic, where Russia is conducting a massive hunt in the Great Banks from a floating cannery. Russia, with a far-sighted and well-financed oceanology, maintains the largest research operations on the world's oceans. France and the United States lead in sea-floor technology.

Man is looking down. The adventurous are gazing through masks and the conical ports of pressure hulls into the undiscovered world of liquid shadow. There the stars and nebulae are mirrored in living forms. Henri Matisse in old age used to be driven to an aquarium to marvel at its shapes and colours. Picasso sees the real thing through a diving mask.

The greatest undersea development of the last third of the century will probably be aquaculture. The sea is a stupendous culture broth waiting for experiments in cultivating food. Oyster and mussel growing are three centuries old in France and Japan. Britain, Australia and the United States have commercial oyster industries. In the Philippines there are market shrimp-beds as large as 25 acres. Of course, it was epicurianism and not economics that created shellfish farming; it means nothing to a billion marginal people who lack the protein that the sea might provide. The need is for pelagic farming, or ranching, after we have found the pigs, chickens and cows of the sea, the creatures that build the most protein, most quickly. Perhaps the popular edible species of today will not do at all. The pig of the sea may turn out to be a deep-water invertebrate that grows to 80 ft long. Observers in bathyscaphes report big mounds on the deep floor, indicating large burrowing animals not yet identified.

There is little future for ocean fishery. Of the estimated annual organic production of the world's seas—400 thousand million tons—fishery now takes only 52.4 million tons. Although the catch has doubled in the past decade, it is still trifling. Fishery has no effect on world starvation, and can have none in the future—it is merely hunting. Ashore we exchanged hunting for agriculture thousands of years ago. Now it is time to end sea hunting and begin fish farming; today's seafood industry must enter aquaculture.

Great things can happen in the Indian Ocean, a dense protein concentration surrounded by half-starved nations. In the Persian Gulf, many people have never tasted seafood. Yet delicious oysters teem undisturbed on the shallow floor, and rich shrimp grounds are being developed for export. In diving-saucer voyages on the continental shelf of the

The solution to the world's food problem may come from marine scientists studying such possible sources of food as plankton, the 'soup' of nutritious organisms, like this sea anemone larva, with which the sea abounds.

219

This sea-worm larva is one of the tiny organisms that make up plankton, upon which all animal life in the sea depends. Scientists are now trying to stimulate plankton growth in certain areas by 'stirring' the sea and bringing to its surface layers of the nutrients which help plankton to flourish there.

Indian Ocean, Captain Jacques-Yves Cousteau's men have found miles of crustacea almost obscuring the sea floor. A poor country like India, surrounded by productive ocean, might lift itself by diverting agricultural labour to piscaculture.

Today, seaweed is harvested to a limited extent for additives to processed food like ice cream. One of the more promising crops for sea farms is giant kelp. Off California it grows to 300 ft tall, its surface fronds spreading 200 ft wide. Kelp assimilates and stores iodine, potassium and other nutrients. It attracts many fish. It is the fastest-growing plant on earth, with fronds lengthening 2 ft a day. It is a cold-water lover, and thrives in man's filth: sewage, soda ash and starchy acids. Today floating reapers behead the California kelp forests to make cattle cake. By the turn of the century kelp culture may be a thriving branch of marine agriculture.

Ocean fish farming will have its own inverted form of irrigation, as nuclear-powered blowers on the cold, deep bottom force up nutrition into the poorer surface layers. Chemical nutrients will also be introduced to the fish ranch. The ranch hands will have sea jeeps, miniature submarines and remote underwater television to keep an eye on things. There are already a dozen underwater natural conservatories protected from fishermen, explosions and pollution. They can be converted into test farms now.

We need not look for radical departures in exploiting the sea; the models of aquaculture exist today, most of them in Japan. There, in the Inland Sea, oysters are cultivated in hanging farms. Cast and spun concrete floats—as many as 6000 in one place in Kesennuma Harbour—hold up oyster wires 6–25 ft long. There may be 200 wires to a float and 18 dozen oysters to a wire. The bivalves do not touch the bottom, where pollutants gather and predators, like the starfish, lurk. In Chiba there are abalone ranches, in Mutsu Bay scallop farms. In Okachi Bay the Japanese are raising salmon and trout in huge sleeves of pipe frame and netting, anchored 10 fathoms deep. They have feeding chutes from the surface and free divers as farm-hands.

The Seto Inland Sea Marine Stock Farms Association, incorporated in 1963, runs four large ocean farms, including one at Kamiura which comprises 753,000 square feet. Japan is training her commercial fishermen as divers, to make the transition from sea hunting to sea husbandry.

Farming fish will depend on a tremendous increase in basic research in marine biology. At the same time, water pollution must be curbed. The continental shelf, the best populated, most accessible area, is being poisoned at a quickening rate. Dr David Bellamy of Durham University has shown the catastrophic effect of pollution on seaweeds, which are at the base of the marine life pyramid, on the coast between Blyth and Middlesbrough. A hundred years ago 97 species of ocean vegetation flourished on this littoral. In a century of industry, filthy effluents from mines, furnaces, chemical plants and cities have killed off 56 of these. Of those that remain, only 11 useful species have survived.

220

Much that we regard as progress will turn out to be anti-progress. One example is nuclear-powered salt water conversion plants to meet the fresh water 'shortage'. Of course, there is no shortage; the same amount of water molecules as ever are circulating in the earth's respiratory system. The problem is merely that too many people are using too much water in the wrong places. The U.S. Government is financing more than 100 water conversion experiments for arid parts of the south-western states. By AD 2000 some of these areas must be allowed to revert to desert, for nuclear desalination plants leave embarrassing by-products in the form of radioactive waste and mountains of salt. Dumped at sea, poisonous atomic waste and super-salination could devastate the oceans.

In contrast to the interplanetary craze, underwater science is a social movement. The space industry has no popular base; but ocean scientists and engineers were preceded by thousands of laymen. Scholarly papers appeared long after a popular diving literature flourished in books and films. The Marine Technology Society was born at a convention of amateur divers. Undersea archaeology comes entirely from non-professionals—underwater research is the first pop science.

The deep-sea explorations that are now being made by divers are due to the discovery of The Saturated Man. The studies of the Royal Navy Deep Diving Committee in 1907, under Professor John Scott Haldane, showed that a diver becomes saturated with nitrogen on long and/or deep dives and that unless he returns by stages, giving his body a chance to pass off the heavy gas, he goes into an agony of embolism commonly known as the bends.

In recent years physiologists have asked why a diver should be brought up from great depths if he is carrying out a lengthy piece of work. There is a known limit to nitrogen saturation, beyond which the diver's body can contain no more; and, provided he stays at depth, this complete saturation does not bother him. He can redouble his working time and live in a house, breathing gases at the same pressure as the water round about. Engineering tests of the principle permitted John Lindbergh and Robert Stenuit to live and work 400 ft down for two days, and Cousteau's five oceanauts to labour continuously for a month in the dark zone 330–70 ft below. The saturated oceanauts worked four- and five-hour days outside in the water.

Undersea stations are taking men deeper and longer at an accelerating pace. A two-man Franco-German research team, Dr Cabarrou and Dr Arkmann, spent 100 hours in a dry chamber pressurised to the depth of 800 ft. Cousteau believes that in the early 1970's, soft-suited divers will be working 1600 ft down. The Royal Navy Physiological Laboratory at Alverstoke will soon have an experimental chamber that can simulate the pressure of 2500 ft down.

Captain George Bond is confident that most of us will live to see men diving to 3000 ft, and that they can be surgically altered to work as deep as 12,000 ft for two hours. That is half the average depth of the world's seas. The abyssal man would be prepared by a tracheotomy through which his lungs would be stuffed with a compound containing highly compressed oxygen and his sinuses packed with incompressible material. From his lungs the oxygen would filter to the blood and the carbon dioxide would become a harmless bicarbonate. George Bond, a doctor of medicine, philology and divinity, has led group escapes, without breathing gear, from submarines more than 300 ft down.

For 10 years Dr Johannes A. Kylstra, a young Dutchman born in Indonesia, has been inducing mammals to breathe water instead of air. I have seen dogs that survived several hours of breathing water. Within the next few years he expects to report on liquid-breathing divers. The respirational problem is not too difficult. Our body warmth is the problem. Cousteau's third round of oceanauts, working for hours in the open water 370 ft down, experienced Dante's hell of ice despite wearing the most advanced insulated diving equipment. The manfish of 1990 will probably be adapted physically to having cold blood in his veins.

At the Second World Congress of Underwater Activities in London in 1962, Cousteau proposed that man was evolving a marine species, *Homo aquaticus*. Sir Alister C. Hardy poses an intriguing theory that *Homo aquaticus* has already existed during human evolution.

The first mutants of *Homo aquaticus* may have already appeared: the oceanides who will occupy the ocean bed. In 1967 scientists at Queensland University, Brisbane, were intrigued by a visit from Terry Ridgway, a tanned girl of 18 with blue eyes and golden hair. She is the solitary inhabitant of Northwest Island in the Great Barrier Reef, where she studies the life of fish in mask dives to a depth of 60 ft. She lives in a lean-to and feeds herself from the ocean. 'I select a fish I want to know something about before I spear it,' she said. 'I can then do a gut slide, take a fin count, examine the teeth for identification and preserve the head. I eat the rest.'

Francisco Figueroa of the University of Manila found a sea boy. He was 13 years old, weighing 12 stone, and of limited speech. He spends more time in the sea than on land and is an astonishing swimmer. Without a racing start or flip turns in a pool, the boy swam 100 metres in the open water, recording a time which was only 5 seconds slower than the world record of 52 seconds.

To occupy the ocean a strong motivation is needed. The interest of the oil industry in manned undersea stations, and of the military in undersea vehicles, detection and weapon systems, has assured the growth of ocean engineering. When an air-transportable fleet of submarine diving tenders appears in the offshore petroleum business, many more uses will be found for the vehicles, if only to use idle time. When biologists are able to spend days and weeks in the depths, we shall learn marvels. When geologists make borings in oceanic rift valleys and archaeologists study deep wrecks, we shall know much more of the earth's history and of man's adventure upon it.

Seaweeds–
Harvest of the Ocean

Donald Culross Peattie

Scientists are discovering more and more
valuable properties in seaweed,
and there is an increasing demand for
the ocean's richest crop

In the doldrums of the North Atlantic—so goes the legend of the Sargasso Sea—lies a vast morass of seaweed, deadly in its sluggish power. Twisting in the spin of the currents, it winds itself about any craft unwary enough to venture there. Their ship held helpless, the crew become gaunt skeletons, the sails but wavering shrouds of mildew, until the rotted hull sinks through the suffocating mass.

Oceanographers long ago exploded this fantasy, only to be themselves mystified by the seaweed's behaviour. For there *is* a Sargasso Sea, bounded roughly by the Azores in the eastern Atlantic and the Bahamas and Antilles in the west; and there *is* a plant in it called sargassum, or gulfweed, a twiggy little thing looking something like holly, and kept afloat by air sacs. The first European sailors to see it were the sailors with Columbus, sailing west in 1492, and when they encountered seaweed in masses they feared that they were driving on to hidden reefs. So the Admiral took a sounding with a cannon-ball—and found no bottom at 200 fathoms.

While most other seaweeds grow on rocks, this one is wholly rootless, floating free in mid-ocean. But now you see it, now you don't. Some scientists in search of it have criss-crossed the Sargasso without finding any. Others a few months later have reported it abundant. When you do see it, it looks like an ocean meadow, the 'hay' rolled into long, yellowish wind-rows. When you don't, it is probably because the old plants, dying, have sunk, and the new ones have not yet developed air sacs to buoy them up into view.

Seaweed needs neither fiction nor a vanishing act, however, to make it marvellous. Off the Californian coast grow the largest giant kelps in the world, the sequoias of the ocean. They are rooted by suckers some 40–60 ft down; their stems, flaccid but tough, may reach 200 ft; their foliage is as ample and heavy as the leaves of a rubber tree. They are buoyed up by double rows of bladders or, sometimes, by a single float the size of a grapefruit. Some, like the trees of the earth, are perennials; in others, annuals, this leviathan growth is the work of a single season.

Furthermore, upon these towering, wavering seaweeds perch countless smaller growths, as lianas and orchids cling to the boughs of tropical forests. Others tremble on the ocean bed like moss and ferns. Such is the ocean jungle.

Of the smaller seaweeds that grow there, as numerous as wild flowers in the fields, some are brilliant in colour and exquisite in design. The most beautiful of all, looking like corals, are found in the Great Sound of Bermuda and in the Bay of Naples. Some, indeed, like corals, have helped to build the land we walk on. Their surfaces encrusted with lime, they have, by their endless living and dying, created reefs, atolls, islands and peninsulas. Animal corals get all the credit for such architecture, but the coral-line seaweeds have probably done half the work.

Stretching intermittently down the Pacific coast from Alaska to Mexico, a massive submarine forest of seaweed covers hundreds of square miles and weighs uncalculated millions of tons. The only boats that seek out the seaweed beds, plodding kelp

A dense bed of horsetail kelp, otherwise known as oar weed, Devil's aprons, or more formally as Laminaria digitata. *Horsetail kelp is a common European relative of the giant Pacific kelps; it grows mainly below the tidal zone, and sometimes just above the line of the lowest tide. This bed was exposed by a low tide at Wembury Church Reef in south Devon.*

barges, work back and forth like combine harvesters in a field of wheat. A 10 ft bar at the front cuts the kelp under water; the valuable weed is then carried by conveyor belt on to the boat, which has a capacity of 300 tons. The giant kelps of the Pacific are the only ones that can be harvested mechanically at present. If properly cut, harvesting makes them grow better. Old shoots are removed and vigorous young growth is given a chance to sprout. Kelp, rich in potash, also yields acetone and calcium acetate, necessary in the manufacture of gunpowder.

In the laboratory, seaweed, in the form of agar, helps to advance the frontiers of science and save many lives. About 85 years ago Dr Robert Koch, who discovered the tuberculosis germ, was seeking a satisfactory medium in which to cultivate bacteria. The wife of his associate, Dr Richard Hesse, suggested he try an ingredient she used in making jam.

The recipe had come from Dutch friends in Java, where *agar-agar* is the Malay word for a seaweed gelatine widely eaten in the Orient. Agar was just what science needed, for it keeps firm at the temperatures used for incubating bacteria and resists their liquefying action. Laboratories take only a small percentage of the agar-weed harvested today. It is used for such varied purposes as cake icing, artificial limbs, orchid growing and dental plates.

Like agar, the seaweed called Irish Moss slips into innumerable places in our daily lives; its smoothing, binding and stabilising properties give much of the goodness to ice cream. Because those who work with Irish Moss never have chapped hands despite the wetness of their job, chemists perceived in it a valuable base for lotions.

In the oddest ways, in things you handle or consume daily, you will find seaweed extracts turning up. One of them helped to make the electric-light bulb, as a lubricant in the hot wire-drawing of the tungsten filament. In a detergent another made washing-up easy. Your wife may use seaweed on her hair in one of the new setting lotions. You had it on your face in your shaving cream this morning. It is

223

a granulating agent in the aspirin you take. It is used in the sizing of cloth—some fabrics it makes waterproof, some fire-resistant. It can even be spun into 'seaweed rayon'.

Long ago people discovered that seaweed would give back to their hungry fields much that had been lost to the sea: the precious nitrates, phosphates, potash and manganese needed by crops. These rich fertilisers are constantly being swept into the sea, but the seaweeds take up great quantities into their wavering stems and fronds. So seaweed makes excellent manure. It makes good fodder, too, and in some European countries shore-dwelling people feed it to their stock. Denmark produces a seaweed meal for cows.

Some people are wise enough to make seaweed a staple part of their diet. The Japanese, the Chinese, the South Sea Islanders and the Greenland Eskimoes prize it as their principal vegetable. Certain seaweeds are rich in vitamins A, B and C, and in iodine. Yet it is not because it is good for me that a clear seaweed soup appears on my own table. I like the delicate taste of it, as I like the very names of the seaweeds on the shore—sea silk and mermaid's hair, laver and daber locks, wrack and tangle. Seaweeds are the harvest of the ocean, and offer mankind a bounty that is yet to be fully used.

Drugs from the Sea

Margaret B. Kreig

The world's oceans are an apparently
inexhaustible source of new drugs,
which medical science has only recently
begun to explore

The sea is the realm of Inner Space, a challenge to oceanographers and our last frontier on this planet. The oceans occupy about 71 per cent of the surface of the globe; some four-fifths of the animal life dwells there, as does the bulk of the vegetation. Aquatic plants, which grow at the prolific rate of 4000 tons per square mile, supply most of the oxygen in our atmosphere.

The new field of marine pharmacology—drugs from the sea—has just begun to receive the attention and financial support it needs. While vast expanses of water do not at first seem to offer much to medicine, a surprising number of important discoveries have come from this source.

In 1901, experiments with Portuguese man-of-war jellyfish stings unravelled the mystery of shock reaction, called anaphylaxis, and formed the basis of our present concept of allergies.

The process by which white blood cells protect the body from invading organisms was understood after studies of young sea urchins.

Work on the electric eel has resulted in the synthesis of PAM, an antidote for nerve gas.

Important vitamins concentrated in cod and shark livers showed the way to better nutrition for man.

The iodine in sea water and plants gave an early clue to thyroid function and goitre therapy.

Since the dawn of history, man has attempted to find medicinal uses for marine plants. In the most ancient Chinese writings, species of seaweed were prescribed for dropsy, abscesses and cancer. Primitive tribesmen in the South Seas and in America made seaweed extracts to treat skin diseases, stomach disorders and inflammations. The use of seaweed for treating goitre has been widespread: Peruvian Indians high in the Andes chew on compressed seaweed 'goitre sticks'; among the Irish, Chinese and Japanese, who today use mineral-rich seaweeds in their diet, goitre and other deficiency diseases are practically non-existent. It has long been known that seaweeds make good poultices for bruises and cuts. During both World Wars, when sphagnum peat moss was steam-sterilised and made into gauze-covered pads, wounds healed more quickly than with cotton bandages; the moss contains disinfecting substances in addition to its draining qualities. Old herbals mentioned Irish Moss, or Carrageen, for diseases of the lungs; these remedies were revived in the First World War to ease the throats of soldiers who were gassed. Carrageenin, derived from the sea, is valuable in treating peptic ulcers. Agar, a carbohydrate from algae, is indispensable in bacteriology, serving as a culture medium. Algin, first extracted in 1885, is still used in manufacturing delayed-action drugs, because alginates are not digested by stomach juices.

Is it not probable that drugs as diverse as those found in land plants might be available in the sea? Biologists have developed techniques whereby marine micro-organisms can be grown in the laboratory. These have been put to work as highly efficient

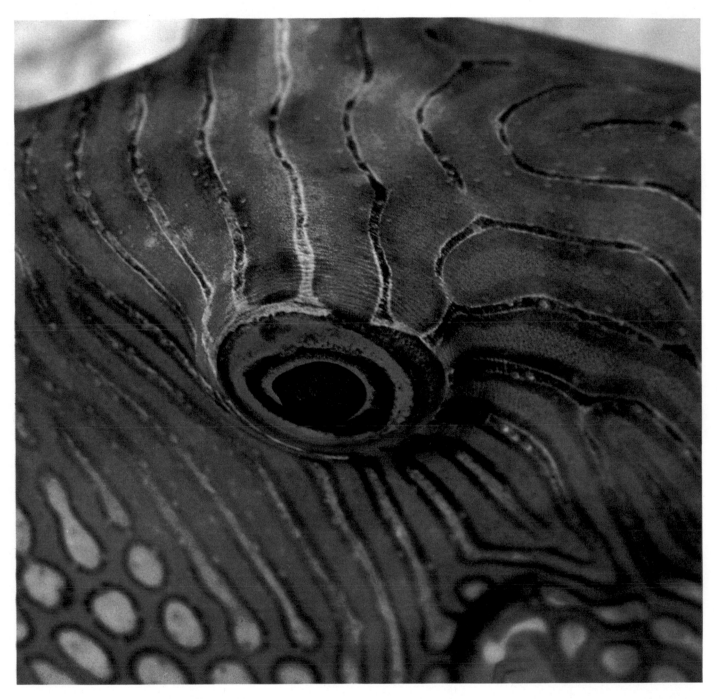

A close-up of the eye and head pattern of the long-nosed puffer. Puffer fish are among the most poisonous fish in the sea, and secrete a powerful nerve poison in their skin, liver and gall bladder. Despite this, they are served in Japan as a delicacy by specially trained chefs, who remove all the poisonous parts of the fish. The remaining flesh gives those who eat it a curious feeling of well-being; hallucinogenic drugs have been derived from other fish related to the puffer.

'laboratory assistants' to test for the presence or absence of substances in sea water; they are able to detect such dilute amounts as one part in one quadrillion. Such plants have nutritional requirements and need vitamins in order to grow. One of these 'laboratory helpers' is *Euglena*, an alga, which needs, but does not contain, vitamin B_{12}. This is one of the most complex naturally occurring nutritive elements of which the human body requires one-millionth of a gram daily. Research with *Euglena* may provide answers to some important nutritional questions that are related to resistant anaemia- and leukaemia-type disorders.

In the aquarium, researchers are making progress towards better understanding of heart and kidney diseases, cancer, mental illness and viral and bacterial infections.

During the First World War huge quantities of steam-sterilised sphagnum moss were used in wound dressings by the British army, and the traditionally known healing properties of the moss saved many lives.

Since fish suffer from cancer no different from the forms occurring in man, tissue cultures of fish cancer cells are being made. Fish can also have virus infections, tuberculosis and even cirrhosis of the liver. One research project concerns a Mediterranean sea-worm called *Bonellia*, the female of which produces a very powerful hormone. This hormone changes all *Bonellia* larvae that come in contact with it into males. Preliminary studies have shown that this water-soluble hormone can also affect the development of eggs in totally unrelated creatures. Its chemical structure is being studied with the idea of testing it on cancer cells.

A number of new drugs from the sea are currently being employed in the treatment of human patients. For some time doctors in Japan have been using the drug tetrodotoxin, a numbing chemical from poisonous puffer fish, to ease the terminal stages of cancer. It also helps to relax muscular spasms.

One of the strangest of all poisons in the sea is that connected with ichthyosarcotoxism—fish-flesh poisoning which comes after eating certain fish and produces symptoms different from any others known to medical science. The victim feels as if his teeth are loose and he experiences a weird reversal of hot and cold sensations.

Algae and fish toxins cause many other hallucinations or delusions. One hallucinogen obtained from a fish induces a deep depression with an aftermath of memories that are quite terrifying. It is hoped that drugs of this type can be used constructively in the study of mental illness.

In Japan special restaurants serve the flesh of fugu, a very toxic puffer. When prepared by trained cooks, who carefully remove the poisonous parts—the liver, skin and gall-bladder—this dangerous delicacy gives the diners a sensational meal. They experience a feeling of well-being and seem to be floating on air. Natives in the South Pacific seek a similar effect by eating certain goat fish which give them fantastic nightmares. Scientists have now catalogued more than 300 kinds of poisonous fish from the deep. These powerful agents must be useful somewhere, somehow, in medicine; already there are clues. In the poisonous weever fish and the equally venomous stonefish, anti-coagulant action on blood has been noted. The poison of the sting-ray slows down heart action. Toadfish venom burns up sugar in the blood and may eventually have some application in the treatment of diabetes.

In Scotland doctors report that brown and red seaweeds produce anti-coagulant action. Researchers in Venezuela are experimenting with pond scum as a possible therapeutic addition to the diet of lepers. An extract called peolin—one of the rare agents known to inhibit polio virus—has been isolated from abalone and oysters.

A certain water mould is an excellent test object for potential anti-cancer drugs. Serotonin, found in the blood, brain and certain tumours in man, is known to be abundant in clams, octopus, jellyfish and many other marine invertebrates; it may well become a capital clue to the biochemistry of sanity and insanity.

While almost in a science-fiction category, these phenomena are nevertheless being scrutinised by scientists with the idea of putting them to use in future space travel. Some researchers believe that when expeditions to distant worlds become commonplace, there will be a need for drugs that will relieve boredom or prevent conflict between passengers and crew. These emotional hazards could be greatly minimised if soothing sensations and pleasant dreams were induced by means of drugs —and these drugs may well come from the sea.

Problems of food and oxygen replenishment in space may also be solved by using marine plants. Experiments with algae and mice are being conducted to develop a system whereby astronauts could live in a sealed cabin indefinitely. Four brown mice were placed inside a small airtight 'space cabin' that also contained algae of the type found in green pond scums. The mice were able to live very comfortably: all the oxygen they needed was provided by the algae, and the carbon dioxide exhaled by them was in turn used by the algae in their life process, thus completing the cycle.

Scientists themselves have also spent many hours in sealed capsules breathing no other oxygen than that released by algae. It is calculated that in future spaceships each man will require about 45 gallons of water containing 25 lb. of algae. This will yield not only the oxygen required, but over a pound of food a day. While efforts to convert algae into mouth-watering planktonburgers have not proved successful—it looks unappetising and tastes like hay, with fishy overtones—biochemists have somewhat improved palatability and appearance by blanching the algae under fluorescent lights. When space stations are established on the moon, Venus, Mars and other planets, algal gardens may be the primary means of producing food.

As mankind reaches out towards space, drugs from primitive marine organisms could be key factors for maintenance of life.

Behold the Lowly Worm

Arthur Koestler

Recent research on flatworms
indicates that the theory of evolution may soon
undergo some far-reaching changes

One of the last joys of civilised middle age is to sit in front of a log fire, sip a glass of brandy and read the 'Worm-Runner's Digest'. Its full title is: 'An Informal Journal of Comparative Psychology, Published Irregularly by the Planaria Research Group, Department of Psychology, the University of Michigan.'

The editor of this journal is Professor James V. McConnell, an austere young experimental psychologist who, like many a good man before him, developed a passion for flatworms. Their fascination derives from the fact that they are the lowest creatures on the evolutionary ladder, with a brain of

sorts and a true central nervous system, but are at the same time the highest on the ladder among those which reproduce by fission. They multiply both asexually and sexually. In summer, they are liable to drop their tails and grow a new one, while the dropped tail will grow a new head. They can be sliced into five or six segments, each of which will develop all the missing organs and grow into a complete individual.

When fully grown, however (about $\frac{1}{2}$ in. in length) the delights of fission yield to those of mating. These are further enhanced by the fact that the worms are hermaphrodites; while young, they function as males, but after more mature reflection, as females, who lay eggs. In the adult animal both sets of reproductive organs are present, and though the male organs mature first, the two phases may overlap. To complicate matters still further, during the mating season the worms become cannibals, devouring everything alive that comes their way, including their own previously discarded tails which were in the process of growing a new head. Thus the previous state of affairs is re-established, by feedback as it were. The head itself, however, is rarely eaten, and never by its own tail (though technically this would be possible because the mouth of the creature is near the centre of its belly, and equipped with a retractable sucker). All of this goes to show that when the flatworms were created, evolution was in a rather confused state, as if trying to decide whether sex was really necessary for progress; and, if so, whether male and female should cohabit in the literal sense—that is, dwell in the same body—or be sorted out once and for all.

The latter idea won, for better or worse, but the Planaria were not informed of this and were left in confusion. As a result, we can tell neither whether the creature is male or female, nor whether the products of its asexual fission are its descendants or its doubles. This is an old philosophical teaser, but McConnell's experiments were designed to ask a new and crucial question: does the regenerated individual preserve a 'personal memory'? Is it capable of 'remembering' what happened to it before the fission—before the world split into two? Does the head which grew a new tail 'remember' more than the tail which grew a new head? The questions must not be taken lightly, because it is in the makeshift brain of the flatworm that the history of the mind originates.

That Planaria are capable of learning, and have a memory, was known for a long time. The experimental procedure designed by Thompson and

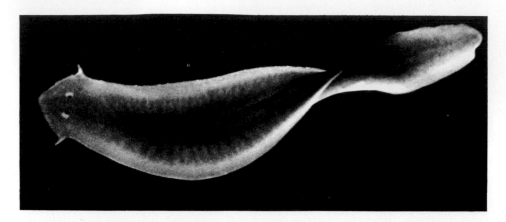

Recent research has shown that the humble flatworm, which reproduces both sexually and by fission, has an uncanny ability to inherit learning. This discovery has implications which may radically change our traditional ideas about the nature of evolution.

McConnell consists in putting the worm into a shallow plastic trough, $\frac{1}{2}$ in. in diameter and 12 in. long, filled with aquarium water. When the worm becomes accustomed to its new environment, it starts moving from one end of the trough to the other with its peculiar, snail-like gliding motion. Under the microscope its smooth and svelte body, with its algae-green and brown specks, looks rather pretty, though the squinting eyes are somewhat humourless—they are light-sensitive, but have no lenses and no pattern vision. Training the creature consists in suddenly flashing the strong light of two 100-watt bulbs on it, followed by an electric shock. In the untrained animal the light causes no reaction whatsoever, whereas the shock causes a sharp to violent contraction of the body. After a number of repetitions, the worm learns that the light is a signal heralding the shock, and contracts when the light is switched on. It has acquired a conditioned reflex.

The next step was to train the animal, then cut it into halves, allow both halves to regenerate, and to find out how much of its acquired learning each regenerated individual retained.

Here a slight difficulty arose. A severed head or tail will usually regenerate into a complete individual within a fortnight. To make sure that all internal organs had a chance to develop properly, an additional fortnight was allowed before testing began. Now, four weeks are a long time in the life of a worm, and it is to be expected that it will forget a considerable amount of what it has previously learnt—even if not distracted by being cut into two and having to build the missing halves. A control group was therefore trained and then kept idle for a month, to see how much 'brushing up' the worms needed to regain their former proficiency. The result was as follows: on the average a group of worms needs 150 'lessons' of light-followed-by-shock until it learns to respond to light alone. After

four weeks' rest, the same group will need a refresher course of 40 lessons to react reliably. Thus the 'saving' in the number of required lessons due to retention was $150 - 40 = 110$; that is to say, over 70 per cent, which is not bad at all.

Let us now turn from the normal to the sliced-up animal. Each half, after regeneration had been completed, was given a refresher course by the same method as the uncut animals. The astonishing result was that the 'tails' showed as much retention as did the 'heads'; and that both 'heads' and 'tails' showed as much retention—approximately 70 per cent—as the uncut animals. Similar results were obtained by other researchers, who taught flatworms to find their way through a simple maze. Again retention by 'heads' and by 'tails' was the same.

How is this possible? How does the tail retain memories of learning? And when the tail builds a new brain, how does it build the memory into it?

Confronted by this puzzle, the worm-runners went one step further. They trained a 'head', H_1, after cutting off its tail, T_1; they let H_1 grow a new tail, T_2; cut it off and let it grow a new head, H_2. This creature, $H_2 + T_2$ had anatomically not a single organ or mature tissue in common with the original $H_1 + T_1$, and yet it had still retained a significant amount of its learning. How was the information transmitted?

The latest experiments are even more surrealistic. I have mentioned that with the onset of sexual maturity, the worms become cannibals. In two experiments McConnell chopped up trained animals and fed them to untrained ones. The results seem to indicate, pending confirmation, that the cannibals fed on trained animals learnt quicker than the controls which were kept on a normal diet. In the jargon of communication engineering, information is always 'fed' into a computer or an organism; here the metaphor became flesh.

Since the flatworm's tail has as good a memory as the head, one might be tempted to believe that its brain plays only a subordinate part, but this is not so. The animal's brain, though primitive, is the centre of its nervous system in which the sensory impulses from the eyes and auricles converge, and from which motor impulses are conducted in two symmetrical nerve strands and their branches to other parts of the body. Moreover, experiments by Ernhart indicate, rather surprisingly, that two-headed flatworms (produced by a simple surgical technique) learn more quickly than others; while animals whose brain was removed were shown to be incapable of learning. Once, however, the animal has been trained, the tail alone is sufficient to retain the memory. One can only conclude that the brain is indispensable for the *acquisition* of learning, but not for its *retention*. This means that the memory of the animal cannot be located in its brain and nervous system alone; it must be represented by chemical changes in cells throughout the body. A leading American neurologist, Professor Gerrard, has suggested that, in the head of the flatworm, memory is retained by neuron circuitry, whereas in the rest of the body it is retained in the form of a chemical imprint. This, too, was confirmed by experiment: trained worms were cut in two and made to regenerate in a liquid which contained a chemical 'memory eraser'. The 'heads' were not affected by it; but the 'tails' forgot all they had learnt.

This is the point where the lowly worm acquires an unexpected significance for one of the basic controversial issues of our time. According to the orthodox theory of genetics upheld this side of the Iron Curtain, the progress of evolution from amoeba to man is entirely due to random mutations plus natural selection. The mutational alterations in the genes which determine heredity are said to be purely accidental, and natural selection is supposed to act as a kind of automatic sorting machine which perpetuates favourable mutations, and rejects the others. The negative implication of this theory is that no trace of what the parents have experienced and learnt in a lifetime is inherited by the offspring. The hereditary mechanism is deaf and blind to the requirements of the evolutionary progress which it serves. The genes—atomic units of heredity—are kept in the germ cells in hermetic isolation, sealed off from the rest of the parent body, and are passed on unchanged from one generation to the next—except for those purely accidental mutations on the evolutionary roulette board. Generations come and go, but their struggles exert no influence whatever on the hereditary substance of the race. Whoever defends the opposite view—that there may be an 'inheritance of acquired characteristics' which would invest evolution with a purposeful aspect—is considered to be guilty of the Lamarckian heresy, and is academically non-U.

The gentle flatworm is not the first animal to cause a breach in the battlements of orthodoxy. For the last five years or so, evidence has been steadily accumulating which does not seem to fit into the orthodox frame; the Planaria are merely the latest and most dramatic arrivals on the scene. They establish beyond any reasonable doubt the inheritance of acquired learning in *asexual* reproduction. (Up to now the worms have refused to reproduce sexually in captivity.) However, even this should be a sufficient shock to the accepted views on the mechanism of heredity, for asexual reproduction is after all *reproduction*. An English scientific weekly paid grudging tribute to McConnell's team, but at the same time reproached them because 'in reporting these experiments to the American Psychological Association, the authors have unfortunately described the worms which regenerate from halves of other worms as a second generation . . . [which might] suggest to the casual reader that here is evidence of the inheritance of acquired characters'.

And evidence indeed it is, semantic subterfuges apart. The Ann Arbor laboratory now has a whole tribe of Tigrina, all descended from a single individual. Whether one describes these animals at the fifth or sixth remove from the parent body as 'generations' or 'regenerations' does not alter the fact that all they have in common with that parent body is a biochemically inherited blueprint, transmitted by specialised 'regeneration cells'—the asexual equivalent of sperm and ova. These regeneration cells (also referred to as 'embryo cells' or 'formative cells') are scattered in the parenchyma, the loose meshwork between the Planaria's muscles and internal organs. When a worm is cut into two—or six—fragments, and each of these recreates all the complex organs of the whole individual, we are faced with a process similar to embryonic development. The regeneration cells which are responsible for this development must carry a chemical blueprint of the complete animal, as the germ cells do in sexual development (though the details of the chemical mechanism may differ considerably). The decisive fact is that these blueprints include the traces of memories and learning acquired during the lifetime of the ancestral animal; and that these acquired characters are built into the brain and nervous system of the new animal. The differences between sexual and asexual reproduction are many; but this basic fact is not altered by them.

Of special importance in this respect is the neat 'eraser' experiment. Here matters become technical and I must oversimplify a little. One of the two complicated 'blueprinting' substances which play a decisive part in the mechanism of heredity is ribonucleic acid, RNA. It can be broken up by another substance, RNASE. This was the substance used as a memory eraser. Worms which were made to regenerate in strong solutions of RNASE frequently grew into eyeless or headless monsters—proof that the 'eraser' interfered with the chemically coded hereditary potentials. Very weak solutions of RNASE, however, merely retarded the regenerative process without visible harmful effects—except for erasing the chemically impressed memories of acquired learning. It was an elegant method of proving that these memories had been incorporated into the blueprint; as the most recent and tentative additions to it, they were the first to be erased.

The flatworm studies are now being duplicated and continued in several universities. The results which I have described will probably be modified and reinterpreted in various details, but the basic fact of the transmission of acquired experience by asexual heredity is no longer open to doubt; whereas, as matters stand at present, its transmission by sexual heredity is passionately denied by orthodox science. This leads to the perversely paradoxical conclusion that the lower animals must have an incomparably *more* efficient evolutionary mechanism at their disposal than the higher ones. But if this were really the case, then the advantages of sexual reproduction—greater individual variety—would dwindle to insignificance compared with the enormous disadvantage of blocking the inheritability of acquired learning; and, through the process of natural selection, fissioning creatures would soon have gained the upper hand over mating creatures, sex would have been dropped as a bad bargain, and we would all multiply by budding.

In an excellent survey of *Darwin's Forgotten Theories*, in the 'Worm-Runner's Digest', T. H. Morrill writes that the present 'overwhelming preference for environmental selection of hereditary accident' might be due to a bias inherent in our extravert 'and accident-prone culture, causing its members to seek such an irrational rationale in the universe'. He quotes the orthodox view, according to which heredity can only be changed by 'high temperatures and energetic radiations which

intensify the molecular chaos' (Muller), and compares it to the ageing Darwin's views in the *Descent of Man*: 'The birth both of the species and of the individual are equally parts of that grand sequence of events, which our minds refuse to accept as the result of blind chance.' Confronted with the neo-Darwinist orthodoxy of our day, the old man would not fare very well. To return for a last time to the 'Worm-Runner's Digest': 'The later theories of Darwin are at base the last expression in Western science of those old, fond dreams of men—that in its largest aspect, beyond the misery, grime and cataclysms of earth, life is a "striving towards a goal, a far circuit and a sure coming home."'

Life in a Test Tube

Donald Gould

Eventually scientists
will be able to manufacture living
organisms in the laboratory

In the winter of 1967–8 Dr Arthur Kornberg and his colleagues of Stanford University, California, came closer than anybody before them to making the science-fiction fantasy of life created in a test tube come true.

They were able to 'manufacture' a living virus by joining together a large number of relatively small, simple and totally inanimate chemical compounds.

Chemists are rapidly uncovering the processes used by living cells for the assembly of the huge and complex molecules which make up the life machine. Moreover, the chemists are learning how to imitate these methods in the laboratory.

It is now at least conceivable that in the distant future they will be able to construct, from the liquids and powders they keep in their bottles, the prodigiously elaborate structure of the human fertilised ovum, which could then be artificially sustained until it has grown into a human infant.

All living things consist of an elaborate and precise arrangement of a large number of a relatively small variety of atoms. Carbon, hydrogen, oxygen and nitrogen are the principal atoms involved, and together these few elements make up the bulk of the cells and the body fluids. In other words, most of the raw materials of a human being would be contained in a piece of coal, a barrel of water and a large balloonful of air. Add a few salts and a pinch of sulphur, and you have pretty well got the lot.

The idea that living things are constructed from the common elements which make up the inanimate world of stars, stones and oceans has been commonplace for a very long time but, until comparatively recently, it was thought that some mysterious 'vital force', which only living things possessed, was needed for the assembly of the elements into the unique chemical compounds from which are formed the building-blocks of cells.

This idea was quashed in 1828 when a German chemist, Friedrich Wöhler, managed to make a compound called urea by heating a simple mineral salt. Previously, urea had only been obtained from living systems. It is a chemical which is manufactured in quite large quantities in the bodies of many animals, which excrete it in their urine. It is, in fact, a waste product of the breakdown of body proteins. Urea itself is quite a simple compound, being an eight-atom pattern of carbon, hydrogen, oxygen and nitrogen, but, before Wöhler's achievement, it had belonged firmly to the animate world.

The enormous significance of Wöhler's elementary test tube synthesis was the implication that if one compound previously peculiar to living systems could be put together in this fashion, then so could others, and the need to assume the agency of a 'vital force', or of some divine alchemy, had disappeared.

Organic chemistry (the chemistry of carbon-containing compounds such as coal, petrol, marsh gas, fats, sugars and so on, which are derived from living material) flourished during the remainder of the 19th century. Natural products were widely used in industry, so that there was profit to be had from discovering and exploiting the composition and chemical activities of useful materials obtained from animals and plants. Organic chemists determined the variety and the proportions of the elements present in most of the major constituents (such as fats, proteins and carbohydrates) of living things, but the detailed structure of the large molecules which are characteristic of the life machine evaded analysis. Their size and complexity is infinitely greater than any found in the non-living world, and the tools available to the scientists were not nearly powerful enough to penetrate their mysteries. A single molecule of a typical protein, for example, is constructed

from perhaps some 15,000–20,000 individual atoms. That is why the last secrets of the life machine have eluded understanding for so long, and why living systems have sometimes appeared to behave according to their own private set of chemical and physical laws, distinct from those which regulate the behaviour of earth, air and water.

In the past few years, new techniques have brought a flood of light to bear upon the intimate structure of the chemical machinery of life, producing knowledge which is an essential prerequisite to any attempts at creating life in the laboratory—since before you begin building something, you obviously need to know what you are trying to make.

One of the major new analytical techniques is crystallography, so called because it is applied to the investigation of materials which have a crystalline form—that is to say, materials which consist of an assembly of identical molecules, regularly related to one another. The principal materials found in living things can be prepared in a crystalline form. Haemoglobin, for example—the red, oxygen-carrying pigment of the blood—can be extracted in a pure form, and a sample large enough to be handled and analysed can be prepared. This sample will consist of thousands, or tens of thousands, of the large haemoglobin molecules, all lying in a regular relationship to one another. The handling and analysis of a single molecule is still beyond our capacity, but crystallography allows many of the fundamental features of a single molecule to be deduced from the study of a crystalline 'lump' of large numbers of identical units.

In crystallography a fine beam of X-rays is fired at a minute specimen of the substance you wish to analyse; behind your specimen you put a photographic plate. When you develop the plate you find a pattern produced by the X-rays which have reached it. The pattern is related in a highly complex fashion to the pattern of the atoms in the specimen. Putting it very crudely, the rays travel straight through the spaces between the atoms, producing an even background on the film, but rays which hit atoms are deflected, and form bright spots on the photograph. It takes some difficult mathematics and a computer to interpret the array of atoms through which the rays have passed.

The X-ray picture does not tell the whole story, but the patterns do reveal basic facts about the structure of a molecule; then the investigator, using his trained imagination, and taking into account all the other known chemical and physical characteristics of the material, can create a structure which fits precisely all the experimental findings. This is how Watson and Crick arrived at their concept of a double helix as the structure of DNA—the stuff of chromosomes—those massive molecules which carry in the pattern of their atoms the instruction manual for the chemical activity of the cells in which they lie, and which direct, for example, whether the chemical factory present in a cell shall manufacture the material and the form of an amoeba, or a daisy.

In this way (there are almost innumerable other techniques involved) we have been able to sketch out some of the finest details of the life machine. Even before the crystallographers began to work out the intricate structures of whole large molecules, we had been able to break many of them down into the simpler units from which they are built, and to establish the general composition of some of those which appear to be universal and essential components of all life forms.

We knew (before Watson and Crick) that DNA consisted of an arrangement of some thousands of units of only four varieties of quite simple molecules called nucleosides. We knew also that proteins were made up of equally large numbers of some 20 varieties of compounds called amino acids. The structure of these amino acids was known. Essentially they are made up of a dozen or so atoms of carbon, hydrogen, nitrogen and oxygen, some of them containing an additional element, sulphur.

The question then arose as to how these elements of the life machine had been formed out of the 'primeval broth' which existed in the hypothetical conditions of the primitive earth.

Many researchers have attempted to manufacture amino acids by manipulating mixtures of the chemicals known or thought to have been present when the earth first cooled. In 1955 Dr S. L. Miller found at least four amino acids in the broth produced after passing electric discharges through a mixture of hydrogen, methane, ammonia and water. Then, in 1962, two American scientists, Kliss and Matthews, suggested that only methane and ammonia were present in the primitive atmosphere, and that under the influence of solar radiation, these had combined to form huge quantities of the intensely poisonous but chemically simple gas, hydrogen cyanide (HCN). Molecules of HCN, they claimed, then joined together to form long molecules made up of H, C and N, which later settled in the new oceans, and gained oxygen to become not just amino acids, but structures called polypeptides, which are strings of amino acids—and the halfway house to proteins.

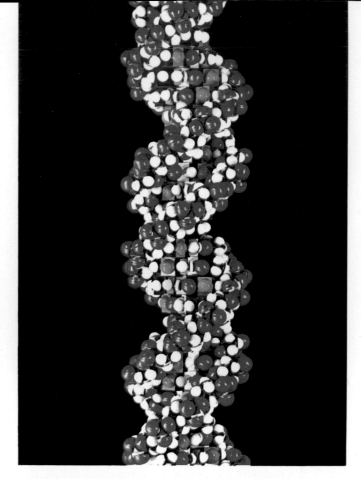

A model of the double-spiral structure of DNA—the substance which carries the code that directs the course of life itself. DNA gives cells the instructions that lead them to produce, for example, the material and form of an amoeba, a daisy or an elephant.

They were able to produce polypeptides by adding to water the products of spark-discharge experiments with methane and ammonia. Later they also produced polypeptides (containing at least eight common amino acids) by allowing HCN to react with ammonia; and by adding sufficient hydrogen to their mixture, they also produced traces of adenine —one of the essential building-blocks of DNA.

In 1968, Canadian scientists were able to synthesise a sulphur-containing amino acid by similar experiments, but with the addition of sulphuric compounds found in volcanic gases. The same year, an American team produced porphyrin in the same manner. Porphyrin is the major component of chlorophyll—the molecule in plants which can utilise the energy of sunlight for the synthesis of plant chemicals, which animals, in turn, burn to supply the energy for the synthesis of their own body materials.

There is now the possibility of producing complex biochemical molecules from the simplest chemical precursors, but there are great strides to be taken between achieving this, and actually putting these building-blocks together into a form which demonstrates the unique life properties of growth and reproduction. However, there is another approach to the business of creating life in the laboratory.

In December 1967, Dr Kornberg, using a mixture of quite small molecules as his raw material, managed to string them together into an exact and living replica of a virus.

A number of viruses consist—at least, at certain stages of their lives—of just a molecule of DNA, or a closely similar compound. DNA is the instruction manual for the chemical activity of cells. It consists of a long assembly of only four varieties of nucleosides. Each cell in all living things carries DNA molecules which are unique to their kind. The uniqueness consists of the *order* in which the four varieties of nucleoside are linked. Each group of nucleosides in a DNA molecule constitutes a gene.

We can call the four types of nucleoside A, B, C and D. Then, and this is a purely imaginary example, an A–A–C–D nucleoside sequence at a particular point on a DNA molecule might instruct the cell to manufacture the chemical which results in blue eyes, while a C–A–C–D sequence in the same position might result in brown. Another sequence in another position might make the animal produce a particular type of tail, or the plant a particular shape of leaf, and so on.

So the order of the nucleosides in the threads of a DNA molecule is of supreme importance, because this order determines the whole nature of the plant or the animal to which it belongs. Therefore, when DNA reproduces itself in order to provide the genetic material for a new cell, the replication must be precise; otherwise the 'daughter' cell would have a different nature to its parent. This precise replication is achieved by each nucleoside building-block attracting to itself a like block from the pool of unattached nucleosides floating around the parent cell. Then an enzyme—a biological catalyst—causes all these newly assembled nucleosides to link up, so that a complete new DNA molecule—the exact counterpart of the original—is formed.

By a series of further reactions, the new molecule detaches itself from its parent and goes on to lead an independent existence and, eventually, to act as the model for another molecule of the same kind.

Viruses are incomplete cells. They exist as parasites on 'proper' cells and, getting into them, instruct the chemical machinery of their hosts to produce the energy and the materials necessary for the assembly of new viruses, for which the original invader acts as a model.

What Arthur Kornberg did was to get some DNA from a virus, and put it into a test tube with some of the enzyme needed for zipping together new DNA molecules (he had managed to obtain this enzyme in a very pure form from other cells, and this was essential to the experiment). He then added a quantity of mixed nucleosides and found that these nucleosides, using the virus DNA as a pattern, and with the help of the 'zipper' enzyme, assembled themselves into complete DNA molecules. He was able to separate these new molecules from the mixture and to show that they were capable of infecting fresh cells, of reproducing themselves and of acting in all respects like the parent virus upon which they had been formed. He had, in fact (borrowing a living virus for the purpose), managed to manufacture quantities of new virus. So that if a virus is accepted to be a living organism, he had manufactured life.

Kornberg had started this line of research over a decade earlier, and had won a Nobel Prize in 1959 for reproducing, by similar means, molecules which were chemically close copies of viral DNA, but his earlier products had not been capable of pursuing an independent, *living* existence. Only a very small fault in the assembly line is needed to make the difference between a superb model and a working, indistinguishable replica—he had to get each one of some 6000 nucleoside building-blocks in exactly the right order. He achieved this by refining his techniques to the point at which the conditions in his test tube were an absolute imitation of the circumstances which the 'model' virus he employed would find in the living cell.

His triumph opens the way to experiments involving the introduction of chosen variations in 'natural' circumstances, which will undoubtedly lead to a greatly increased understanding of this most basic of vital mechanisms and perhaps to an understanding of how genetic faults arise which cause hereditary diseases, how cancer occurs, and of the means for correcting both these classes of hitherto mysterious and dreadful human afflictions.

His work may also produce the understanding which will allow chemists to assemble their 'life' molecules into a living machine, so that, in time, we may be able to create life from simple chemicals, in a chosen form and without recourse to templates. We shall be able to tailor our own DNA, and to use these molecules to supervise the manufacture of organisms of our own design.

This is an awesome and even horrifying prospect, but the step will be taken. J. D. Bernal, the British physicist and crystallographer, wrote in his book, *The Origin of Life*: 'Life is beginning to cease to be a mystery and becoming practically a cryptogram, a puzzle, a code that can be broken, a working model that sooner or later can be made.'

Man For and Against Nature

Sometimes men form strangely close bonds with other creatures.
If they sense that a bird or animal—even a tree or lake—
is somehow mysterious and unique, they will
take great pains to preserve it.
But to survive, men also impose themselves on Nature;
they herd animals, fell trees, destroy weeds and plant crops

The Great Flamingo Rescue

Katharine Drake

International co-operation and
dedicated hard work saved 130,000 flamingoes
from death in a Kenyan soda lake

In northern Tanzania, some 100 miles south of the Equator as it crosses East Africa, is an inaccessible lake called Natron. It is a weird soda lake, surrounded by steaming alkaline mud flats and quicksands; and for as long as anybody remembers, it has been the nesting ground of that strutting, crane-necked, stilt-legged, rose-plumaged bird called the lesser flamingo.

Several years ago an unprecedented drought dried up Lake Natron and killed half a million of the birds, perhaps a tenth of the world total, by cutting off their food supply. The following year floods buried the lake's mud flats under 5 ft of water, making nesting impossible. Driven by a compulsion to breed, the huge birds rose in a flaming cloud and flapped off in quest of other comparable nesting grounds. Weeks later, near exhaustion after their search, they finally dropped down—35 miles north of Natron, in Kenya—on an even weirder lake called Magadi. There disaster awaited them.

Lake Magadi has neither inlet nor outlet. It lies in a sprawl of volcanic rubble. Its sub-surface, nourished by piping-hot sulphur springs, gurgles and churns like a witch's cauldron, while above lies a motionless soda crust produced by evaporation—one vast, blinding deck two miles wide, 18 miles long, ranging in thickness from a mere film to 12 ft. So foul-smelling and noxious is Magadi that its wildlife consists mainly of vultures and rodents. Though only 510 miles south of the city of Nairobi, the area is uninhabited save for a chemical works, dredging mineral salts for export.

No one in Kenya was more delighted at first at the arrival of the lesser flamingoes—some 2 million of them—than a young British naturalist and wildlife photographer, Alan Root, and his wife, Joan.

For little is known of the lesser flamingoes' way of life. Almost all that was known about their breeding requirements was that the birds need privacy—the grimmer the heat and the wasteland, the better they like it; the alkalinity of the hot soda slush from which they build their nests must be neither too strong nor too weak. Surrounding mud flats are a necessity for fledglings to walk on; so are wide stretches of open water, for the blue-green algae that floats on most of the soda lakes is the principal food of the flamingoes.

Here at Magadi was a spectacle never before witnessed by human beings: a colony actually in the process of breeding. More than a square mile of Magadi's shimmering crust boiled with their motion.

234

Flamingoes on the safe waters of Lake Nakuru in Kenya.
Their beautiful plumage would certainly have put
flamingoes in great danger from hunters, were it not
that after death their feathers soon become colourless.
In captivity, unless their diet is carefully
controlled, they can also soon lose their colour.

Wherever the Roots turned their cameras, amorous birds swooped, soared, glided and flapped, belting out their noisy litanies of love, which are part honk, part squawk, part siren.

The nests alone were a revelation: acre upon acre of glittering, turret-shaped dwellings built up of the hot alkaline slush and baked dry in the sun, each about 18 in. high and from 12 to 24 in. across. They were jammed together, with as many as six and seven per square yard in the main concentrations. Later, when the goslings began to arrive—silvery bundles of fluff, equipped like small toys with pink beaks, goggle eyes and absurd squeaks—they stayed only on these turret tops a day or two, then with a hop and a skip they scuttled away in search of a pool.

It was near sunset on September 16, 1962, when Joan Root spotted the first hint of oncoming tragedy.

Head down in a shallow lagoon lay one of the chicks, dead, legs askew. Spread-eagled beside it lay another chick, barely alive, its still unformed beak ineffectually pecking at legs that seemed encrusted in plaster of Paris. Picking it up, Joan saw to her horror that the fledgling was sightless: soda splashes had dried over its eyes like a mask. A quick look round revealed more victims, all of them youngsters. Their frail, matchstick legs, wading through Magadi's supersaturated green slime, had picked up increasing deposits which the sun baked into crippling casts.

Before dusk the Roots, desperately trying to render first aid, rounded up 100 such casualties. These victims represented only the earliest hatches. Soon baby flamingoes would burst from their shells by the hundreds of thousands. Was there no way to stave off catastrophe?

It was well after midnight when John Williams, the ornithologist of Nairobi's Coryndon Museum, was awakened by two young people carrying in their arms some small, soda-frosted baby flamingoes. There was a conference in Williams's study; Tony

235

An aerial view of flamingoes massed on the saline waters of Lake Nakuru. Flamingoes have webbed feet and can swim, but they prefer to wade for their food—small plants and animal matter, which they sieve from the mud with their beaks.

Irwin, head of the East African Wildlife Society and editor of *Africana* (a periodical crusading for game conservation), joined in. The night hours produced just one lead: the shackles, they discovered, were soluble in fresh water; they could be washed off. The Magadi Soda Company, reached by radio-telephone, promptly offered to make available its freshwater tanks for a rescue attempt. It lacked a pipeline, however, to channel the water from the works to the nesting areas. By breakfast, the planners had drawn up a list of equipment needed for an enormous chick-washing operation. The minimum cost would be at least £1500.

Irwin grabbed the list and made for Nairobi's radio station. The story was broadcast out over jungle, mountain and bush. Within hours, collection boxes appeared in hotels, shops, cinemas, bars, even at street corners. Signs urged: 'Make a Splash—Help to Wash a Flamingo!' By the end of the first day the fund totalled £100.

Few Kenyans reckoned on help from the outside. But on Tuesday the heart-rending scenes at Magadi were shown on television screens in Britain, and a day later newspapers and radios gave the news to Western Europe, Australia and Asia. By midday on Thursday contributions and communications were pouring in from all over the world. With supplies loaded on a lorry and two Land-Rovers, Alan and Joan Root headed back for Magadi. For their preliminary task force, from the many who volunteered, they chose only two: Douglas Wise and Christopher Callow, British students on holiday. A more massive invasion, they felt, might scare away the parent birds and make them desert their chicks.

At Magadi that evening the four were greeted by a nightmare. Some 50,000 encrusted fledglings lay dead. Thousands more lurched around on cruelly shackled legs. Hyenas, jackals, vultures and marabou storks were all over the place, gorging on the dead and the dying. Everywhere sounded cries of distress. Parent birds frantically flapped wings and brandished bills, striving to create a diversion. Perhaps half the stupefied adult birds still clung to their turret tops, prompted by instinct to finish the hatching. There was only one cheering note: a dozen African youngsters, children of Magadi Soda Company employees, were standing by to help round up the crippled fledglings for bathing.

On the Friday, Operation Flamingo's first day, mishap piled upon mishap. The temperature rose above 130°F. The 500 yd hosepipe the Roots had brought turned out to be 200 yds short of the hardest-hit areas, meaning that chicks had to be carried to the watering terminal in canvas hampers, 40 at a time. The lake crust, deceptively sturdy to the eye, masked huge sub-surface holes gouged out by dredgers; by noon each team member had fallen through at least once, landing chin-deep in blistering-hot caustic. The terrified chicks squirmed, kicked and trampled one another in the hampers; at least half of each batch was dead on arrival. The work of dissolving casts and cleansing the soda-caked eyes and abrasions consumed more time than expected—five minutes per chick. Once free, the chicks scampered thankfully off, others simply collapsed and perished. By the end of the day only 200 chicks had been successfully liberated, and their rescuers were raw from soda burns.

The day had produced one ray of encouragement, however: discovery that the supersaturated, cast-forming seepage occurred only in the lake's north-eastern area, the densest area of nests. If other chicks could be kept from straying into the death-dealing lagoons, perhaps the number of prospective victims in need of wash-and-rescue might be reduced from hundreds of thousands to as few as 35,000.

That night Douglas Wise, a veterinary student, hit on a new approach to Operation Flamingo. If, in a hospital, plaster casts can be cracked off a child's leg without damage, why couldn't the soda casts be cracked off the legs of the baby flamingoes? The next morning, while Joan held a chick, Douglas gripped the cast and dealt it a quick hammer blow. The soda split in two. Another tap, and away sailed the other cast. With an incredulous headshake, the patient scampered away. The four rescuers were soon liberating a bird every eight seconds, while rubber-booted children nimbly shooed others away from the poison pools.

From then on, the ratio of chicks freed to new casualties improved steadily. Since results now warranted it, the British army sent in six 12-man teams made up of African and European volunteers. In the fierce heat and stench the soldiers tackled the bizarre operation with gusto. At the end of two weeks the score read: unshackled, 20,000 chicks; shooed away from danger, 70,000; victims still remaining, 15,000.

Meanwhile, with insufficient algae in Lake Magadi, the adult birds were faced with the arduous necessity of commuting twice daily to Lake Natron, 35 miles away, to fill their crops with food to keep their offspring alive. The sight of the airlift never failed to revive the perspiring rescuers; determination redoubled as the vast 'V' formations soared skywards, necks and legs ramrod-straight, wings indomitably beating, throats crying out a reassuring 'gurook-gurook' to inform left-behind youngsters that food was on its way.

A week after hatching, the chicks had lost their innocent, Easter-card look: matchstick legs thickened, beaks began turning downward, silver fluff gave way to dark, bristly hair. Mob-minded now, the youngsters began gathering in clusters, then in crowds. In a week or so whole armies, 40,000–50,000 strong, were pressed body to body. Soon, supervised by a handful of adults, the milling, squawking hordes began to move like a cloud shadow towards open water, 5 miles to the south. There the youngsters would soon learn how to fend for themselves.

It was this lemming-like action that called Operation Flamingo to a standstill at the end of its 21st day—a heart-breaking decision, since some 5000 chicks still remained shackled. But among these clamorous mobs, each new retrieve involved stampeding and endangering thousands of able youngsters. However, the ambitious mass rescue had succeeded beyond expectation. No fewer than 400,000 fledglings had survived the Magadi ordeal, 130,000 due entirely to human effort (30,000 unfettered, 100,000 saved from contamination).

The work had been punishing beyond belief. That last evening, as the Roots lay on their camp-beds, they were scarcely able to see through sun-swollen eyelids. Each was a stone lighter; they were incessantly sick; their skin was a lobster-red patchwork of blisters and sores, scars from which remain to this day. Yet exhaustion was not what was warding off sleep; neither could banish the thought of those 5000 doomed fledglings. They could still hear piteous cries of distress rising above the clamour of parent birds, the flapping of vultures' wings, and now and again the faraway roar of a lion.

Then another note crept into the bush symphony: an almost inaudible *plop*, light as a whisper on the tent-top. Then slowly another *plop*, another and another. The Roots started up, disbelieving. They leapt outside, necks craned back, palms outstretched, staring in amazement. Rain! Marvellous, wonder-working rain! In another minute sheer cloudbursts hit the lakeside—Kenya's autumn rains, ten days ahead of schedule. Alan and Joan, soaking wet, stood spellbound.

Within 26 hours not a chick remained shackled on the whole of Magadi. All the poison lagoons were diluted beyond further hazard.

After a rest, the Roots and the army put in two more weeks banding 8000 fledglings, so that other secrets of the lesser flamingo's life might become known. Thanks to worldwide generosity, enough money remained to pay for the bands. Operation Flamingo itself worked out at a penny per chick.

Last year the flamingoes returned to the ancestral nesting grounds on Lake Natron, their need for human assistance over. But skylarking around East Africa today are some 400,000 exotic, rose-plumaged birds offering proof that people everywhere share a sense of compassion for Nature's creatures.

The World's Most Exotic Nuisance

James Poling and John Barr

The beautiful water hyacinth
clogs waterways, suffocates fish, and defies
most of man's efforts to destroy it

Deceived by its lovely, pale-purple flowers, a romanticist once described the water hyacinth as 'a lavender symphony wreathing the world in beauty'. But the army of scientists who are battling against the ever-encroaching hyacinth in the waterways of Africa and Australia, Asia and America, know the plant more feelingly as 'the devil's lilac'. For the water hyacinth is not only one of the world's most widely distributed freshwater weeds; it is an aquatic plant whose ugly behaviour and unparalleled nuisance value are as striking as its unmatched splendour.

The water hyacinth multiplies with unbelievable rapidity. Its quite fantastic 'population explosion' is due to its dual method of reproduction: it spreads seeds and also sends out stolons on which daughter plants appear almost overnight. In the Sudan, Dr A. C. Evans, of the Commission for Technical Co-operation in Africa, has observed that in only

three weeks a pair of parent plants multiply to 31: in four months to 1200, forming a mat of menacing beauty that is 3 ft thick and so buoyant (because of the air-filled bladders the size of golf balls at the base of each leaf-stalk) that it can support a man's weight without difficulty.

Such a mat grows and spreads until it covers a body of water as a crust covers a pie, sealing it so tight that fish suffocate from lack of oxygen, and clogging it so that boats cannot fight their way through. Today, millions of acres of lakes, rivers, canals and swamps throughout the world are encrusted with this sinister weed.

Coupled with its fertility is an astonishing talent for survival. The water hyacinth's seeds can lie dormant for years in the dry mud at the edge of lake and waterway, germinating whenever the water level rises sufficiently. Though a freshwater inhabitant, the plant can live for days in sea water. It can move with the winds and currents over vast distances, and its tall, sail-like leaves give it enough mobility to travel even upstream if the wind is strong and the current is sluggish.

The invader causes immense economic waste. On the Congo River alone it reduces river traffic by an estimated 10 per cent—equivalent to an annual loss of £260,000. An entire hydro-electric system can be paralysed when the weed jams its inlet grids. The toll of human misery is even higher. The mats of the hyacinth are ideal incubators for malarial mosquitoes and perfect breeding grounds for disease-carrying water snails. The fish they stifle are sometimes the sole source of protein for the local people. The obstruction of slow-running channels may isolate whole communities. The clogging of drainage and irrigation ditches can threaten the very existence of farmers on the banks of the Nile and in the paddy fields of India.

Man has only himself to blame for the spread of the water hyacinth. The plant stayed in its native home of Brazil until 1884, when it was sent to a horticultural exhibition in New Orleans. Enchanted by its orchid-like, funnel-shaped flowers, a few gardeners took slips home to their ponds, and later tossed surplus plants into nearby streams. In six years the hyacinth had spread from Florida to Texas. By 1895 it had reached Australia, again probably transported by someone infatuated with its beauty. It was present in India by 1902, in Malaya by 1910, in Southern Rhodesia by 1937. In 1952 it was observed near Brazzaville and within three years had blanketed a thousand miles of the Congo River and its tributaries and made them all but impassable.

During this 80-year rampage, men have used every kind of mechanical, chemical and biological weapon to repel the water hyacinth. Pitchforks were being tried in the U.S.A. in 1899—but the weeds grew faster than men could move them. Later, dynamite was used—also without success. One scientist tackled the mats with a flame-thrower. The next growing season the burnt plants were not only the first to sprout; they also grew 9 in. taller than their unsinged neighbours. In Guyana, groups of men working with scythes found that their canoes had

The water hyacinth's beauty has earned it the additional name of water orchid; but throughout the world, wherever winter temperatures are not too cold, it long ago wore out its welcome. Chemical controls have been used against the thick, endless mats of the gorgeous weed, with varying degrees of success. Biological methods have also been tried, and the manatee, or sea cow, appears to be one of the few creatures able to eat enough of the plant to keep it under control.

only to penetrate the carpets of hyacinth for three-quarters of their length to become completely stuck.

In Australia mechanical dredges have had more success, dumping the plants on the river banks where they are burnt when dry. But such methods are costly. In Malaysia, where human dredges have tried the same technique by hand, monsoon rains swept the harvested plants back into the water. The current carried the heavy mats downstream until they crashed against bridges, seriously weakening or collapsing the piers.

The post-war development of chemical herbicides finally produced an effective anti-hyacinth weapon: 2,4-D. From Malaysia, a senior agronomist reports that spraying with 2,4-D 'has given satisfactory control . . . and been found to be virtually harmless to fish'. In the Congo, an 18-month campaign, using 2,4-D knapsack sprayers and water-borne pumps, cleared 5500 miles of infested streams and

rivers. Success with the chemical is also reported from Victoria State, Australia, where the weed has failed to maintain any foothold. The Government of the Sudan, where a 625-mile stretch of the White Nile became infested between 1958 and 1960, has some 800 spray-equipped hyacinth fighters in the field. So far, they have managed to hold the enemy south of the Jebel Aulia Dam, near Khartoum, and out of the Blue Nile.

Despite its widespread successes, 2,4-D is costly to apply—up to £8 per acre in strong doses. In 1963 alone, the Sudanese Government's bill for 2,4-D was more than £150,000, not counting labour. If the dose is too economical, the slowly dying weeds form mats as obstructive as the living plants. Even when enough of the herbicide is sprayed, the check is often only temporary and repeated applications are required. More serious, many crops, particularly cotton, bananas and cassava, are damaged by the 2,4-D mist which inevitably drifts over fields adjacent to the waterways. In the Sudan this problem is critical; cotton crops as distant as 30 miles from the Nile have been destroyed by herbicide drift. As a result, spraying times had to be limited. One solution may be a 'Bi-fluid' spraying technique developed by Shell International Chemical Company and tested in the Sudan. The new 2,4-D is mixed in the nozzle of the sprayer and has a mayonnaise-like consistency which has been found to reduce dramatically the risk of the spray drifting on to cotton crops and destroying them.

A cheaper and safer method of halting the spread of the water hyacinth is most likely to be found in biological control. In India, Dr V. P. Rao of the Commonwealth Institute of Biological Control is experimenting with a grasshopper and two species of caterpillars which, he says, may prove to be natural enemies of the water hyacinth. Another ally is the huge manatee, a 7 ft long, bosomy mammal with a boundless appetite for aquatic plants. The Food and Agriculture Organisation of the United Nations reported an experiment in Guyana where two manatees cleared a canal 22 ft wide and 1600 yds long in 17 weeks. If the manatee can be persuaded to breed in man-made waterways, it may prove to be an invaluable ally.

Even if man should finally rid the world of the water hyacinth, his rejoicing might be short-lived. For the natural law of plant succession decrees that when one species of plant dies or is destroyed, another shall immediately rise to take its place— with no guarantee that the new plant will not be equally or even more troublesome.

240

Spectacle of the Skies

Joan Parry Dutton

The U.S. Fish and Wildlife Service has found a new answer to the problem of crop damage caused by migrating wildfowl: they look after the birds

Klamath Basin, an expanse of rich upland on either side of the California—Oregon border, is the scene of one of the world's most spectacular air shows. Located at the centre of a huge 'Y' in intercontinental bird travel, and hemmed in by high mountains, forest and desert, the Basin's marshland and lakes offer the only area within 150 miles where migrating birds may stop for food and rest. In spring, on 121,000 acres, songbirds by uncounted thousands, wild duck, geese, herons, egrets, grebes and bitterns—more than 160 bird species—nest and raise their families here. From September, when the migrating hosts begin exploding out of the northern skies, until early November, the Basin seethes with the bustle and noise of 5–7 million waterfowl.

Legions of duck—pintail, mallard, canvasback, green-and-blue-winged teal, goldeneye—arrive in mile-long columns. The Basin feeds one of the largest white pelican flocks in America. Platoons of snowy-white whistling swans wheel in from remote Arctic tundras. Canada geese in 'V' formation, and flocks of snow geese, some from Siberia, swing down to nest on the lakes. The sound of the beating of millions of wings is like a mighty surf.

Yet just a few years ago this awesome spectacle seemed doomed to extinction. That it has been preserved in all its primeval splendour is the result of a remarkable alliance between man and Nature.

Early this century the draining of four shallow lakes and marshes created rich farmland. The deep black soil yielded from 60 to 100 bushels per acre of the finest grade of brewers' barley. Potato crops were also prodigious.

Further drainage, irrigation and power projects reduced the bird refuges. The remaining areas of water could no longer provide adequate food and resting places for the birds.

The feathered armies, starving and riddled with disease, became pillagers. To protect their valuable crops, farmers put live scarecrows in the fields to blaze away at marauders with blank shells. At dawn

A man-made paradise for wildfowl. This is the view of Lower Klamath Wildlife Refuge, on the California—Oregon border, which tempts millions of migrating wildfowl to land there for food and rest during their spring and autumn migrations. Before the refuge was made for them, the hungry birds played havoc with crops on the neighbouring rich farmlands.

and dusk, the main feeding hours, aeroplanes buzzed the hungry flocks and huge searchlights flashed beams of light skywards as keep-off warnings. These measures were effective, but they were costly. No one was satisfied.

At this point, there came into being an almost unique conservation project. In 1948, the American Congress appropriated $500,000 for adequate development of Lower Klamath and Tule Lake National Wildlife Refuges. The idea of the U.S. Fish and Wildlife Service was to provide such an appealing resting-place for birds that they would not be tempted to forage neighbouring farmlands. This operation has been so successful that today

only 10 per cent of the former acreage supports almost as many wildfowl as flourished when the white man first came. Farmlands occupy the other 90 per cent and although some farmers still lose a small percentage of their barley to the birds, their losses are at least partly compensated by the fertilising droppings that the vast winged hosts leave scattered on the land below.

To see how this transformation was made, I have visited the Fish and Wildlife men at work on the refuge at various times of the year. In midwinter—while the duck and geese are taking their ease in their southern resorts—a 24-man crew starts work with bulldozers and other earth-moving machinery. During the past decade these men have turned the remnants of the two big lakes into a maze of dikes, marshes, water channels and islands. They have built pumping stations and other controls to keep water levels at the right height to provide the maximum aquatic vegetation for the migrating birds.

241

The 25,000–45,000 muskrats which live in the marshes demand attention, too. For it is their part in Nature's scheme to maintain water spaces among the reeds and grasses—spaces that provide cover for the wildfowl but allow them to move freely. In their foraging for food the muskrats trim out the thicker growths, allowing the pondweeds and other water plants favoured by the birds to thrive.

Too many muskrats would mean too great a denuding of the cover; too few, an excess of rank growth. So the refuge men take a muskrat census—by counting the muskrat burrows and multiplying by seven, the average number in a muskrat household. Contracts are then let to professional fur trappers. A percentage of the profits from the sale of the pelts

White pelicans, dyed yellow at Lower Klamath Wildlife Refuge as part of a plan to trace migratory movements and study the effects of pesticides on wildlife. The pelicans are in a pen, awaiting their release.

is paid to the government and goes towards helping to support the refuge area.

In mid-April the planting season begins: 5000 acres, widely scattered, are ploughed, harrowed and sown, mainly with choice barley. To make it easy for the birds to get at the grain, 12 ft-wide landing strips are rolled flat at intervals of one-eighth of a mile when the barley has ripened.

The birds respond by consuming 250,000–300,000 bushels of the barley every year. There are now about 650 farmers in the area that the birds used to ravage. Probably less than a dozen of them have any complaint against the birds.

A major task during spring and summer is to seek out sick or injured birds. This the refuge men do with a special ambulance—a flat-bottomed 'air-boat' which can skim over water 6 in. deep. They pick up as many as 4000 birds in a season and take them to a special hospital which restores 80 per cent of the birds to flight again.

During the summer, the Fish and Wildlife crew conduct a census of nesting birds by counting nests and taking aerial photographs. They also band some of the birds to study the flights of wildfowl. The birds to be banded are caught in a net fired from a remote-control mortar, or are herded by airboat into a closed channel when they are moulting and flightless in late summer.

At the beginning of August the first birds migrating from the north arrive. Their view of the chessboard of barley, aquatic plants and clear water must be a wonderful invitation to land and rest.

Meanwhile, preparations are being made for the autumn shooting season, which coincides with the great bird show. About 16,000 acres of the Klamath Basin area are open to hunters, to keep the mighty flocks in balance with their food supply. On an autumn visit three years ago I saw regiments, divisions, armies of wildfowl manoeuvring in formations that darkened the sky, while from boats and hides lines of hunters shot at them. Some 60,000 duck and 22,000 geese fell that season—but since the refuge's nesting season had added more than 90,000 ducklings alone to the flocks, the winged legions gained in numbers.

In fact the hunters helped to make the gain possible. Each hunter must purchase a Federal Duck Stamp if he wishes to shoot migratory waterfowl. Since 1935, when the stamps were introduced, their sale has provided support for the Klamath Basin Refuges and for other American waterfowl refuges. Thus this great spectacle of the skies almost pays for itself.

Martyr for a Species

Darwin Lambert

The story of how the earth's
oldest living thing was casually killed
in the name of science

Fewer than 50 people saw earth's oldest known living tree alive. Among those of us who did, none knew its great age until too late.

In the summer of 1956 I wandered by chance among the bristlecone pines of eastern Nevada's 13,063 ft Wheeler Peak. As I made my way over jumbled boulders without benefit of a trail, seeking a glacier which had recently been discovered, I watched quaking aspen and Engelmann spruce shrink to bush-size as I neared the timberline. Then I saw—stooped as under a burden, with roots like claws grasping the ground—a magnificent monster standing alone. It grew in my sight as I approached. Four spans of my outstretched arms were needed to encircle the mis-shapen trunk. Not far away were more colossi, some still larger and more grotesque.

Forgetting the glacier, I spent hours paying my respects to these amazing trees which had remained hidden for so long, even from personnel of Humboldt National Forest, in which they stood. They looked like abstract sculpture produced by an artist imbued with feeling for the persistence of life in the face of incredible hardship. Most of them were squat and gnarled, only 10–30 ft tall, yet their twisted branches reached skywards as though proclaiming victory over death.

At the time I was editor of the nearest newspaper, the Ely (Nevada) *Daily Times,* and I wrote of what I had found. Soon I was introducing friends to the arboreal patriarchs on the state's second highest mountain (only the 13,145 ft Boundary Peak, astride the California line, stands taller). Or, more often, we visited other bristlecones on nearby Mount Washington (11,676 ft), which was easier to reach.

Few people knew much about the bristlecone pine, *Pinus aristata,* and we sought additional information. The species, we learnt, was first identified in 1853. A botanist named Creutzfeldt, travelling with Captain John Gunnison's Pacific Railway survey, had collected a twig in Colorado and had sent it to an Eastern herbarium—shortly before he and seven of his associates, including Gunnison, were massacred by Ute Indians.

The popular name comes from fragile bristles on the cone scales. The young cones are blue; mature cones are brown, and 3–3½ in. long; their winged seeds sail on the wind, sometimes from mountain to mountain, starting new colonies.

The needles of the bristlecone pine are 1–1½ in. long in bundles of five, massed along the twigs for as much as a foot. David Brower, of the Sierra Club, who helped me to measure one Wheeler giant with a 35 ft 8 in. circumference, nicknamed the species 'bottle-brush tree' after the long, dense clusters which distinguish its foliage.

The size of a bristlecone pine is no reliable indicator of age, but if a tree is extraordinarily old its trunk has generally been eroded—sculptured—by windblown ice crystals and sand and is bare of bark except for a strip up the leeward side, connecting with the persistent foliage.

Many of the branches are dead or half-dead. The wood is striking in colour and texture, from pale silver to rich yellow and tawny red-brown, polished to a high gloss which you want to caress. Dave Brower warned that this very sculpture of Nature—the dead remnants or branches—would be in danger from novelty collectors if it were not closely guarded.

The wood of the bristlecone is heavy for pine, 35 lb. per cubic foot. Too brittle for good lumber, it resists decay so well that samples have been found intact as long as 2000 years after death.

We soon learnt that scientists were probing the secrets of the bristlecone pine 300 miles westward on the White Mountains, just beyond the California border. Edmund Schulman, of the University of Arizona's Laboratory of Tree-Ring Research, had found living trees more than 4000 years of age. One, which came to be called 'Methuselah', was 4600 years old, exceeding by more than a thousand years the maximum age of *Sequoia gigantea,* the redwoods of the Sierra Nevada, long considered to be earth's oldest living things.

This research, we found, had practical objectives. Conifer growth on arid sites is especially sensitive to fluctuations of moisture, and Dr Schulman was reading in the tree rings the precipitation records of the past. Such data would reveal climatic cycles and help foresee future weather patterns, a matter of particular importance in the dry West, as it would be in any arid area. The work involved twisting a Swedish increment borer into the trunk to secure ¼ in. cores, a technique which does not endanger the tree's life. Since as many as a hundred annual rings were frequently found crowded into an inch, the cores had to be studied under magnification.

243

In addition to probing the climate of the past, Dr Schulman was dating archaeological sites by matching wide and narrow rings from living trees with similar patterns in timbers used by prehistoric Indians, such as those in ancient cliff-dwellings. He believed that the long-lived bristlecones might also cast light on the general problem of longevity, and other institutions were already helping to extend the studies into such fields as ecology, geology, genetics and plant physiology.

Interest in the Wheeler country grew. The state's congressional delegation asked the National Park Service to study the area. There was a preliminary reconnaissance in which the National Park Service and the U.S. Forest Service joined. Then months went by with nothing being done. When my friends and I prodded, we were told there were no funds to allot for detailed investigation.

By now, however, those grotesquely beautiful trees had an enthusiastic group of admirers. At a public meeting in the grounds of Lehman Caves National Monument in the foothills below Wheeler Peak, a Great Basin National Park Association was organised. When the then Secretary of the Interior, Fred A. Seaton, planned to visit the West, we invited him to break his journey for an excursion on horseback into bristlecone country. He declined, but invited us to his hotel room, where we showed him photographs. 'I believe,' he said after studying the pictures, 'we might be able to do something.'

His department found part of the needed funds, and our association and the Sierra Club contributed the rest. I had the privilege of guiding federal experts on some of their explorations. In a report recommending that a national park be established, one of them wrote: 'A day among the bristlecones is an unforgettable experience. Their weird, hobgoblin shapes, with arms reaching and turning at all angles like the illustrations in the Wizard of Oz, give one the feeling of being in a strange world. Each tree is a character to meet.'

In the spirit of Adolph Murie's reactions, we began naming the most distinctive personalities—'Buddha', 'Socrates', 'Cliff-clinger'. We called one 'the Money Tree' because a local photographer sold so many portraits of it that he recovered part of the cost of his excursions. Another was called 'Storm King', because its foliage sheltered a group of us through hail and rain, while its wood, where bark had been weathered off, presented a surprising show of colour, turning red with moisture.

We called the tree that was soon to be destroyed 'Prometheus', after the mythical Titan who gave fire

and arts to mankind, and who was chained to a mountain crest for thousands of years, being fed upon each day by a vulture, yet always growing whole again, and who was finally freed by Hercules. But the thought, perhaps, is no longer appropriate. What name could capture the essence of a tree which started life when the Sphinx was created at the dawn of civilisation, which was a vigorous giant in the heyday of Greece, which was showing signs of age at the time of Christ, yet which lived on into the 1960's only to be destroyed by modern man?

Whatever the name, that tree and its fellows and surroundings were drawing me from ordinary existence into a unique adventure as president of the park association, bringing me into contact with eminent scientists, conservationists and political leaders. While the Department of the Interior was studying its findings, we worked to make the bristlecones and other attractions nationally known. The late Weldon Heald, the association's vice-president, wrote articles for conservation and travel magazines, bringing membership and financial support from more than half the states of the U.S.A., as well as from several foreign countries.

In co-operation with the state's publicity agency, we produced a pamphlet and a colour film with a sound-track for distribution throughout the nation. More organisations joined the movement. Fred M. Packard, of the National Parks Association, visited the area, and then when he returned to Washington publicly declared that 'the Wheeler country has more variety of outstanding scenery than any existing national park'.

Victory seemed just around the corner, but then grazing, prospecting and hunting interests mobilised opposition to the scheme. Nevada's only congressman disagreed with the senators, and Congress failed to pass legislation for the park.

For several years I was too far away to help, since my newspaper career had taken me to Alaska; but when I returned, I began to pick up the threads. Bills were again pending, as they had been in four previous Congresses. Bristlecone research had advanced, too.

By supplementing the records from living trees with those from long-dead trees, C. W. Ferguson,

One of the oldest trees in the world, a bristlecone pine in the White Mountains of California. Centuries of wind and weather have eroded the trunk, and stripped the bark on the windward side of the tree. Many bristlecones have reached ages of well over 4000 years: they were young when the pyramids were being built.

continuing the programme of the Laboratory of Tree-Ring Research at Tucson, has reached back to 5150 BC, thus establishing a continuous bristlecone pine chronology covering just over 7100 years. More recently, analysis of a small piece of dead wood has indicated an age of about 9000 years, and Dr Ferguson sees 'great promise for the extension of the tree-ring chronology further back in time'.

But a shock was in store. A brief clipping from a University of North Carolina newsletter started me on the trail of an event which had escaped the notice of conservationists and the public. During the summer of 1964, Donald R. Currey, a geography student working on his doctorate, had been studying Little Ice Age glaciation in the mountains of the South-west. The glacier and related phenomena on Wheeler Peak attracted him, rather as they had lured me eight years before. He and his associate found the bristlecone pines near the timberline. To help date glacial features, he cored several old trees.

Then, in coring another patriarch, he found indications that it was more than 4000 years old. As excitement built, the coring tool broke. He sought permission to chain-saw the tree—and, incredibly, obtained it from the national forest's supervisor. After cutting through the trunk at a convenient level more than 8 ft above the original base, he found, after counting under low-power magnification, 4844 annual rings.

The oldest living thing had been killed in the process of discovery.

Scientists at the heart of bristlecone research eventually agreed that 'Prometheus' (Currey called it WPN-114) had been approximately 300 years older than any other living tree whose age had been verified. It was, indeed, probably older than 4900 years, allowing for missing rings and the distance of counted rings from the tree's base. While deploring the unnecessary cutting, they saw that the hypothesis that the oldest trees were in the westernmost stands had been significantly weakened.

The maximum known ages of bristlecone pines were now 1200 years in Colorado; 1600 years in Arizona; 4600 years in California; and, finally, 4900 years in Nevada.

The killing, when news of it finally spread in 1966, shocked people throughout the country into an awareness that something unique was being lost for ever. Storms of protest raged, and the head of the U.S. Forest Service declared a keen interest in bristlecone security.

Both the importance and the difficulties of protection became evident. Those responsible for tree research tightened the already strict conservation standards of the projects under their supervision, but a major threat continued to come from people cutting branches or gathering fallen wood to decorate their homes, or—sometimes by the jeepload—to sell. According to Dr Ferguson, fallen wood was even more valuable to science at present than the living trees.

Observing that the spotlight was on Wheeler Peak's bristlecones at last, a member of the park association commented that 'Prometheus might become widely enough known as a martyr to save other ancients', and indeed the feeling has grown that there should be a memorial to the tree to accent the value of all ancient bristlecone pines. Cross-sections of 'Prometheus' are to be found at the University of North Carolina, in several Forest Service offices, and on public display in a Nevada hotel, but the stump remains unprotected and unsung on the rocky moraine of Wheeler Peak. Hopefully, the forces that are now in motion may be able to accomplish something to atone for the tragedy of its death and seek ways to safeguard the rest of these irreplaceable marvels of Nature.

The opportunity must remain for everyone to visit the bristlecone pines where they grow, and receive their message of the grandeur and persistence of life.

The Elements

Antoine de Saint-Exupéry

A solo pilot's life and death battle with a cyclone above the mountains of the Patagonian Argentine

I had taken off from the field at Trelew and was flying down to Comodoro-Rivadavia, in the Patagonian Argentine. Here the crust of the earth is as dented as an old boiler. The high-pressure regions over the Pacific send the winds past a gap in the Andes into a corridor 50 miles wide, through which they rush to the Atlantic in a strangled and accelerated buffeting that scrapes the surface of everything in their path. The sole vegetation visible in this threadbare landscape is a series of oil derricks looking like the after-effects of a forest fire. Towering over the round hills on which the winds have left a residue of stony gravel, there rises a chain of prow-shaped, saw-toothed, razor-edged mountains stripped by the elements down to the bare rock.

For three months of the year the speed of these winds at ground level is up to 100 mph. We who flew the route knew that once we had crossed the marshes of Trelew and had reached the threshold of the region they swept, we should recognise the winds from afar by a grey-blue tint in the atmosphere, at the sight of which we would tighten our belts and shoulder-straps in preparation for what was coming. From then on we had an hour of stiff fighting and of stumbling again and again into invisible ditches of air. This was manual labour, and our muscles felt it pretty much as if we had been carrying a longshoreman's load. But it lasted only an hour. Our machines stood up under it. We had no fear of wings suddenly dropping off. Visibility was generally good, and not a problem. This section of the line was a stint, yes; it was certainly not a drama.

But on this particular day I did not like the colour of the sky.

The sky was blue. Pure blue. Too pure. A hard, blue sky that shone over the scraped and barren world while the fleshless vertebrae of the mountain chain flashed in the sunlight. Not a cloud. The blue sky glittered like a new-honed knife. I felt in advance the vague distaste that accompanies the prospect of physical exertion. The purity of the sky upset me. When you are flying very high in clear weather the shock of a blue storm is as disturbing as if something collapsed that had been holding up your ship in the air. It is the only time when a pilot feels that there is a gulf beneath his ship.

Another thing bothered me. I could see on a level with the mountain peaks not a haze, not a mist, not a sandy fog, but a sort of ash-coloured streamer in the sky. I did not like the look of that scarf of filings scraped off the surface of the earth and borne out to sea by the wind. I tightened my leather harness as far as it would go and I steered the ship with one hand while with the other I hung on to one of the struts that ran alongside my seat. I was still flying in remarkably calm air.

Very soon came a slight tremor. As every pilot knows, there are secret little quiverings that foretell a real storm. No rolling, no pitching. No swing to speak of. The flight continues horizontal and rectilinear. But you have felt a warning on the wings of your plane, little intermittent rappings scarcely audible and infinitely brief, little cracklings from time to time which sound as if there were traces of gunpowder in the air.

Then everything round me blew up.

In the first place, I was standing still. Having veered right in order to correct a sudden drift, I saw the landscape freeze abruptly where it was and remain jiggling on the same spot. I was making no headway. My wings had ceased to nibble into the outline of the earth. I could see the earth buckle and pivot—but it stayed put. The plane was skidding as if on a toothless cogwheel.

Meanwhile I had the absurd feeling that I had exposed myself completely to the enemy. All those peaks, those crests, those teeth that were cutting into the wind and unleashing its gusts in my direction, seemed to me so many guns pointed straight at my defenceless person. I was slow to think, but the thought did come to me that I ought to lose altitude and make for one of the neighbouring valleys where I might take shelter against a mountainside. As a matter of fact, whether I liked it or not, I was being helplessly sucked down towards the earth.

Trapped this way in the first breaking waves of a cyclone—which, 20 minutes later, I learnt was blowing at sea level at the fantastic rate of 150 mph—I certainly had no impression of tragedy. I found myself imprisoned in a valley at the wheel of a ship that was three-quarters out of my control. Ahead of me a rocky prow swung to left and right, rose suddenly high in the air for a second like a wave over my head, and then plunged suddenly down below my horizon.

Horizon? There was no longer a horizon. A hundred transversal valleys were muddled in a jumble of perspectives. Whenever I seemed about to take my bearings a new eruption would swing me round in a circle or send me tumbling wing over wing. I was wrestling with disorder, wearing myself out in a battle with disorder, struggling to keep in the air a gigantic house of cards that kept collapsing despite all I could do. Scarcely the faintest twinge of fear went through me when one of the walls of my prison rose suddenly like a tidal wave over my head. My heart hardly skipped a beat when I was tripped up by one of the whirling eddies of air that the sharp ridge darted into my ship. If I felt anything unmistakably in the haze of confused feelings and notions that came over me each time one of these powder magazines blew up, it was a feeling of respect. I respected that sharp-toothed ridge. I respected that peak. I respected that dome. I respected that transversal valley opening out into my valley and about to toss me God knew how violently, as soon as its torrent of wind flowed into the one on which I was being borne along.

What I was struggling against, I discovered, was not the wind but the ridge itself. Despite my distance from it, it was the wall of rock I was fighting; it was against this that I was butting my head. Before me on the right I recognised the peak of Salamanca, a perfect cone which, I knew, dominated the sea. It cheered me to think I was about to escape out to sea. But first I should have to wrestle with the wind off that peak and try to avoid its down-crushing blow. I had been granted a second of respite. My whole plane seemed to be shivering, spreading outwards, swelling up. Horizontal and stationary it was, yet before I knew it, it was lifted 1500 ft straight into the air. I who for 40 minutes had not been able to climb higher than 200 ft off the ground was suddenly able to look down on the enemy. The plane quivered as if in boiling water. I could see the wide waters of the ocean. At that very moment, without any warning whatever, half a mile from Salamanca, I was suddenly struck straight in the midriff by the gale off that peak and sent hurtling out to sea.

There I was, throttle wide open, facing the coast. A lot had happened in a single minute. In the first place, I had not flown out to sea. I had been spat out to sea by a monstrous cough, vomited out of my valley as from the mouth of a howitzer. When, what seemed to me instantly, I banked in order to put myself where I wanted to be in respect of the coast-line, I saw that the coastline was a mere blur, a characterless strip of blue; and I was 5 miles out to sea. The mountain range stood up like a fortress against the pure sky while the cyclone crushed me down to the surface of the waters. How hard that wind was blowing I found out as soon as I tried to climb, as soon as I became conscious of my disastrous mistake: throttle wide open, engines running at maximum, which was 150 mph, my plane hanging 60 ft over the water, I was unable to budge.

In this latitude the South American continent is narrow and the Andes are not far from the Atlantic. I was struggling not merely against the crushing winds that blew off the east-coast range, but more likely also against a whole sky blown down upon me off the peaks of the Andean chain. For the first time in four years of airline flying I began to worry about the strength of my wings. Besides, there was a chance that I should find myself out of fuel and simply drown. I kept expecting the petrol plungers to stop priming, and indeed the plane was so violently shaken up that in the half-filled tanks, as well as in the feed pipes, the petrol was having trouble coming through and the engines, instead of their steady roar, were giving forth a sort of dot-and-dash series of uncertain explosions.

I hung on, meanwhile, to the controls of my heavy transport plane, my attention monopolised by the physical struggle and my mind occupied by the very simplest thoughts. I was feeling practically nothing as I stared down at the imprint made by the wind on the sea. I saw a series of great white puddles, each perhaps 800 yds in extent. They were running towards me at a speed of 150 mph where the down-surging wind-spouts broke against the surface of the sea in a succession of horizontal explosions. The sea was white and it was green—white with the whiteness of crushed sugar and green in puddles the colour of emeralds. In this tumult one wave was indistinguishable from another. Torrents of air were pouring down upon the sea. The winds were sweeping past in giant gusts as when, before the autumn harvests, they blow a great flowing change of colour over a wheatfield. Now and again the water went incongruously transparent between the white pools, and I could see a green and black sea-bottom. Then the great glass of the sea would be shattered anew into a thousand glittering fragments.

It seemed hopeless. In 20 minutes of struggle I had not moved forward a hundred yards.

Fear, however, was out of the question. I was emptied of everything except the vision of a very simple act. I must straighten out.

There were moments of respite, nevertheless. I dare say those moments themselves were equal to the worst storms I had hitherto met, but by comparison with the cyclone they were moments of relaxation. The urgency of fighting off the wind was not quite so great: I could tell when these intervals were coming. It was not I who moved towards those zones of relative calm, those almost green oases clearly painted on the sea, but they that flowed towards me. I could read clearly in the waters the advertisement of a habitable province; and with each interval of repose the power to feel and to think was restored to me. Then, in those moments, I began to feel I was doomed. Then was the time that little by little I began to tremble for myself. So much so that each time I saw the unfurling of a new wave of the white offensive, I was seized by a brief spasm of panic which lasted until the exact instant when, on the edge of that bubbling cauldron, I bumped into the invisible wall of wind. That restored me to numbness once again.

Up! I wanted to be higher up. The next time I saw one of those green zones of calm it seemed to me deeper than before and I began to be hopeful of getting out. If I could climb high enough, I thought, I would find other currents in which I could make some headway. I took advantage of the truce to essay a swift climb: 300 ft, 600 ft. If I could get up to 3000 ft I would be safe. But a swift blow sent me rolling over and over and the sky became a slippery dome on which I could not find a footing.

One has a pair of hands and they obey. How are one's orders transmitted to one's hands?

I had made a discovery which horrified me: my hands were numb. My hands were dead. They sent me no message. Probably they had been numb a long time and I had not noticed it. The pity was that I had noticed it, that I had raised the question. That was serious.

Lashed by the wind, the wings of the plane had been dragging and jerking at the cables by which they were controlled from the stick, and the stick in my hands had not ceased jerking for a single second. I had gripped it with all my might for 40 minutes, fearful lest the strain snap the cables. So desperate had been my grip that now I could not feel my hands.

What a discovery! My hands were not my own. I looked at them and decided to lift a finger: it obeyed me. I looked away and issued the same order: now I could not feel whether the finger had obeyed or not. No message had reached me. I thought: 'Suppose my hands were to open; how would I know it?' I swung my head round and looked again: my hands were still locked round the wheel. Nevertheless, I was afraid. How can a man tell the difference between the sight of a hand opening and the decision to open that hand, when there is no longer an exchange of sensations between the hand and the brain? How can one tell the difference between an image and an act of the will? Better stop thinking of the picture of open hands. Hands live a life of their own. Better not offer them this monstrous temptation. And I began to chant a silly litany which went on uninterruptedly until this flight was over. A single thought. A single image. A single phrase tirelessly chanted over and over again: 'I shut my hands. I shut my hands. I shut my hands.' All of me was condensed into that phrase and for me the white sea, the whirling eddies, the saw-toothed range ceased to exist. There was only 'I shut my hands'. There was no danger, no cyclone, no land unattained. Somewhere there was a pair of rubber hands which, once they let go of the wheel, could not possibly come alive in time to recover from the tumbling drop into the sea.

High above the mountains of the Argentine a propeller-driven plane makes steady progress through the calm air; but when air currents from the Pacific rise over the Andes and whip the sky into cyclonic fury, a pilot can become involved in a grimly terrifying battle with the elements.

I had no thoughts or feelings, except the feeling of being emptied out. My strength was draining out of me and so was my impulse to go on fighting.

The thermometer on the wing, I happened to see, stood at 20 below zero, but I was bathed in sweat from head to foot. Later I was to discover that my storage batteries had been jerked out of their steel flanges and hurtled up through the roof of the plane. I did not know then, either, that the strips on my wings had come unglued and that certain of my steel cables had been filed down to the last thread. I continued to feel strength and will oozing out of me. Any minute now I should be overcome by the indifference born of utter weariness.

In 80 minutes I had managed to climb to 900 ft. A little to the south I could see a long trail on the surface of the sea, a sort of blue stream. I decided to let myself drift as far down as that stream. Here where I was, facing west, I was as good as motionless, unable either to advance or retreat. If I could reach that blue pathway, which must be lying in the shelter of something other than the cyclone, I might be able to move in slowly to the coast. So I let myself drift to the left. I had the feeling, meanwhile, that the wind's violence had perhaps slackened.

It took me an hour to cover the 5 miles to shore. There in the shelter of a long cliff I was able to finish my journey south. Thereafter I succeeded in keeping enough altitude to fly inland to the field that was my destination. I was able to stay up at 900 ft. It was very stormy, but nothing like the cyclone I had come out of. That was over.

On the ground I saw a platoon of soldiers. They had been sent down to watch for me. I landed near by and we were a whole hour getting the plane into the hangar. I climbed out of the cockpit and walked off. There was nothing to say. I was very sleepy. I kept moving my fingers, but they stayed numb. I could not collect my thoughts enough to decide whether or not I had been afraid. Had I been afraid? I couldn't say. I had witnessed a strange sight. What strange sight? I couldn't say. The sky was blue and the sea was white. I felt I ought to tell someone about it, since I was back from so far away! But I had no grip on what I had been through. 'Imagine a white sea . . . very white . . . whiter still.' You cannot convey things to people by piling up adjectives, and by stammering.

There is nothing dramatic in the world, nothing pathetic, except in human relations. The day after I landed I might get emotional, might dress up my adventure by imagining that I who was alive and walking on earth was living through the hell of a cyclone. But that would be cheating, for the man who fought tooth and nail against that cyclone had nothing in common with the fortunate man alive the next day. He had been far too busy.

I came away with very little booty indeed, with no more than this meagre discovery, this contribution: how can one tell an act of the will from a simple image when there is no transmission of sensation?

I could perhaps succeed in upsetting you if I told you some story of a child unjustly punished. As it is, I have involved you in a cyclone, probably without upsetting you in the least. This is no novel experience for any of us. Every week men sit comfortably at the cinema and look on the bombardment of some Shanghai or other, some Guernica, and marvel without a trace of horror at the long fringes of ash and soot that twist their slow way into the sky from those man-made volcanoes. Yet we all know that together with the grain in the granaries, with the heritage of generations of men, with the treasures of families, it is the burning flesh of children and their elders that, dissipated in smoke, is slowly fertilising those black cumuli.

The physical drama itself cannot touch us until someone points out its spiritual sense.

Barro Colorado— Tropical Noah's Ark

J. P. McEvoy

Sixty years ago a high peak became an island refuge for innumerable wild creatures. Now scientists gather there to study one of the world's richest tropical nature reserves

When, in the year 1909, the Chagres River was dammed to create Gatun Lake for the Panama Canal, every living thing fled before the rising waters. The largest concentration of these creatures found refuge on the highest peak in the lake—Barro Colorado.

Here, in 6 square miles of jungle, was a wealth of plant and animal life: pumas, ocelots, peccaries, toucans, capuchin monkeys, black howling monkeys, coatis, coral snakes and the deadly fer-de-lance. It was a tropical Noah's Ark, and it was readily accessible to scientific study.

Fortunately an alert scientist named James Zetek, who had been working on malaria control in the Canal Zone since 1911, recognised the importance of this island sanctuary. He was largely responsible for getting it set aside in 1923 for tropical research. During some 40 years of devoted toil in the Tropics, Zetek was fairy godfather of the island's exotic fauna and flora. Guide, philosopher and host to distinguished scientists who came to the island from all over the world, he was also the dogged money-raiser whose efforts helped to keep this modern Noah's Ark financially afloat.

Hundreds of scientists have prowled this open-air laboratory and have taken home new-found knowledge to enrich natural history textbooks, educational films and classroom teaching.

On Barro Colorado, year after year, the murderous campaigns of army ants were followed by the noted authority Dr T. C. Schneirla. Here Zetek himself, with Dr Thomas Snyder, pioneered invaluable research in termite control and continued to report new findings on the creatures' voracious appetites.

This tropical island paradise is a unique zoo-in-reverse, where animals roam as they please through the primordial jungle while human visitors warily walk the narrow trails by day and lock themselves in at night.

A three-toed sloth peers at the world through myopic, sleepy eyes as it labours up the branch of a Cecropia tree, its habitat and primary source of food. The sloth rarely leaves the tree; much of the time it hangs upside-down, with its claws hooked over a horizontal branch. During the rainy season, green algae grow in its fur, providing camouflage for the sloth and food for small moths that also live in the fur.

When I sat down to my first meal in the dining-room, also used as the laboratory, I was fascinated by the shelves of canned goods and pickled vipers, and I envied the aplomb of my companions—all famous scientists—who looked upon the life-in-the-raw around them with professional detachment.

'I hear the wild pigs are quite vicious,' I volunteered offhand to no one in particular. My neighbour said, 'The white-lipped peccaries, the more vicious of the two species of wild pigs on the island, have been known to charge, especially if you happen to get between the female and her young, in which case . . .' His remark trailed off as if the outcome was of no importance.

I made a mental note to observe the traffic rules of the peccaries and pointed to a large glass jar containing, tastefully coiled in alcohol, a 6 ft fer-de-lance, the deadliest serpent in this Eden.

'How about snakes?' I asked. 'Like that?'

Another scientist replied: 'Oh, that one. I killed her last year with a matchet. When I dissected her she had 47 little ones in her. They are born alive, with venom and fangs, you know.'

He turned to discussing the fertilisation cycle of army-ant queens with the lady scientist across the

Toucans, like this Swainson's toucan in the Barro Colorado rain forest, use their brightly coloured beaks to pluck fruit. Being honeycombed with air spaces, the beaks are strong but surprisingly light for their size.

table. 'But those pumas,' I said, during a lull, 'they're pretty big, aren't they? Do they really run wild out there?' I pointed up the hill to the trail that I had promised to walk with Dr Schneirla after lunch.

'Oh yes! Fellow here last year collecting fungi suddenly saw a puma right in front of him on the trail. Not more than 20 ft away. Zetek made rules for visiting scientists: "Don't panic. Don't run. You can stare your puma down."

'This fellow kept thinking about his wife and children and how they would miss him. But he stared his best and seemed to be holding his own, when all of a sudden there was a second puma, about the same distance away, but off to the right. So now he had two pumas to stare down. He says he became so cross-eyed that he must have frightened them, because suddenly they were gone.'

Many miles of narrow trails criss-cross the wild and rugged island, all named and marked every 100 metres, starting with nought at the laboratory. I followed a trail with Dr Schneirla, who was looking for one of his army-ant colonies. 'They are not easy to find,' he said. 'And even when you find them it's easy to lose them.' I asked him how you could possibly lose 60,000 ants on the march and he said, 'Do you see any ants on that vine?' I looked carefully and said, 'No.'

'That's what I mean,' he said. 'Look closer and you'll see a single file of them. They come to a ravine like this and cross on one of these long lianas like a suspension bridge. They don't make any noise, and a single file of ants, unless you've had experience of seeing them, can disappear right under your eyes.'

'How do you know one colony from another?'

'I mark the queens,' he said. 'Snip a little nick in the back of their necks. I kept track of one queen for five years. That's a record.' He went on to say that army ants are blind and rather stupid. They follow a scent laid down by the scouts and each queen has a scent of her own. 'I've learnt to distinguish different queens by their smell.'

'How about the popular notion of army ants cutting a wide swath through the jungle and killing everything as they go?'

'An army-ant colony on the march will travel less than one mile an hour on a front up to 50 ft wide; and it is true that everything gets out of their way. They bite viciously and will overwhelm the largest victims by sheer numbers and ferocity.'

Barro Colorado is ideal for studying army ants. They cannot get off the island, so you can keep track of them and build up a year-to-year record. Schneirla had studied ants in other tropical countries but always came back to Barro Colorado. 'In no other place,' he said, 'can the scientist find such perfect conditions for tropical research. Here you are close to modern transportation and communications. Food, shelter and sanitation are cared for and you can spend your time and energy doing research instead of hacking out trails, carrying supplies, cooking and just keeping alive.'

Schneirla told me that all the big cats of the tropics follow the Barro Colorado trails, including the jaguar, which does not live on the island but swims over to poach. Automatic cameras with trip wires across the trails have taken flashlight shots of nocturnal prowlers, and occasionally ocelots and pumas have been detected taking parallel strolls with the scientists. 'Just curiosity, I would say,' remarked Schneirla.

Capuchin monkeys, once favoured by organ-grinders, are the most intelligent of American primates. In captivity they exhibit a remarkable ability to solve practical problems and to use and improvise tools. Some of them have been able to paint pictures; others have watched films attentively.

When Zetek first came to Barro Colorado, he paddled across the lake in a native canoe and camped on the bare ground. Later he cut trails and built termite test-houses, combining shelter and research.

'After more than 20 years of continuous research we are still learning about termites,' Zetek once said. 'We have 59 species on the island. They not only eat practically every kind of wood, but will chew their way through wire insulation, inferior concrete and even lead sheathing.'

Thomas Barbour, the great naturalist, was the first patron saint of the island, according to Zetek. 'He contributed generously out of his own pocket and came to our rescue time after time. Since our job is conserving and understanding life instead of thinking up new ways to destroy it, we are down at the end of the table when it comes to financial support. We have survived precariously through the years by passing the hat among our friends. But I feel optimistic for the future. Here on Barro Colorado scientists can continue to do valuable work, as they have in the past, when they were happy to contribute time, experience and knowledge at no expense to the government.

'Years ago a simple Chiriqui Indian, who had never worked with concrete before, made, single-handed, the 198 steps you climb from the quay to our laboratory. He proudly signed the last step: "Made by Donato with all possible economy." You might say that is the motto of Barro Colorado.'

Underworld of the Fungi

Donald Culross Peattie

These gangsters of the plant kingdom are shifty, fertile and, all too frequently, murderous

In days gone by when Britannia ruled the waves, many of her oak-hearted ships were sunk by a secret enemy. In 1782 such a saboteur caused the bottom of the flagship *Royal George* to drop out off Portsmouth, drowning the admiral and several hundred of his crew.

The killer was dry rot, a fungus that works under the surface of the wood, so that before danger is suspected it may already have eaten out a ship's timbers. No ship then was expected to last more than a few years.

Another fungus changed the history of Ireland. That was in 1845—'the year the praties had black hearts'. The potato had become the national crop of Ireland—easy to grow, easy to cook, belly-filling.

Then the crop failed. One after another the potato beds were invaded by a fungus pest that left blackened leaves, withered plants, rotten tubers. Famine set in. Nearly 2 million Irish—a quarter of the population —fled to America in ten years.

Fungi have ruined many a business. For instance, when coffee was England's favourite drink, Ceylon

was one vast coffee plantation. But in 1869 the bushes with crimson berries began losing their glossy leaves; each season the leaves dropped earlier and the bushes grew weaker.

Ten years too late, a specialist, Henry Marshall Ward, was called to the scene. He showed the planters how the wind carried the fungus spores, and how nothing could kill these hard-shelled spores unless they were attacked with fungicides at the one weak point in their life cycle: when they started to germinate, well before the bush showed sickness.

The planters tried his preventive chemical sprays; but the infection was too widespread by then to be controlled. Their coffee was totally destroyed. The Ceylon planters began again, this time with tea, and the coffee empire passed to Brazil.

Fungi may be microscopic, or visible to the naked eye as a blue-green cast on fruits, or a powdery mildew on leaves; or they may stand boldly forth as toadstools, which are just big spore-disseminating bodies. All fungi lack any real woody tissue; they have none of the green chlorophyll found in plants that earn their living honestly in sunlight. Instead of making their food, they steal it. They have no leaves, genuine roots, flowers or seeds. They all grow at a fantastic rate, and seem to spring up overnight; their powers to spread are terrific.

Some fungi live by theft and assassination; these are the parasites. Some are saprophytes: ghouls that feed off dead material such as house timbers, fallen leaves and the like. Occasionally a fungus plays both roles. Such is the honey-tuft mushroom, named for

In late summer, Russula *mushrooms (above) sprout on the forest floor. Young russulas have rounded caps that gradually unfold as they mature. The taller mushroom on the left has reached the final stage of growth.*

The shaggy ink cap mushroom (right) can grow up overnight and be gone by morning. As the cap opens, its white gills turn pink, then a purple colour, then brown; finally they dissolve into an inky black fluid that drips to the ground. The cap disappears within hours, leaving only a stem.

Looking like an orange flecked with snow, a fly agaric mushroom (left) sprouts beneath a fern. The 'snowflakes' are tiny spores, which usually vanish in the rain. Though poisonous, this toadstool is not fatal to man.

its golden colour, which as a parasite will attack a tree with its sucking strands and, when it has killed it, proceed as a saprophyte to devour the dead wood. Most baffling are those fungi which live upon alternate hosts. For instance, the fungus that causes the spotting on barberry leaves called 'the yellows' also produces the red rust on the wheat in a nearby field—a dangerous enemy to farmers. One way to fight this fungus is to break its life cycle by destroying one of the hosts—in this case the barberry.

Fungi must also take the blame for the destruction of the chestnut trees which once lifted their richly flowered crowns in the eastern states of the U.S.A. In 1899 a species of Chinese chestnut tree arrived in the United States bearing a fungus blight. Its spores infected the American chestnuts, leaving gaunt

skeletons in the forest. Millions of dollars were allotted to combat the foe. Quarantine lines were drawn—but never adequate, and always too late. When total loss of the American chestnut became certain, lumbermen moved in to cut while the timber was still sound enough.

Not all fungi are enemies to man, however. Penicillin comes from the kind of fungus called mould; other kinds give us streptomycin, aureomycin, terramycin. Cheese, beer and the bread leavened by yeast all come to us through the fermenting work of scarcely visible fungi. Others help in the curing of tobacco, the tanning of leather and in the fodder in the farmer's silo.

Some soil fungi are friends of our finest plants in a partnership called symbiosis. Many members of the beautiful heath family—heather, azalea, rhododendron—live intimately with a fungus which can supply them with moisture more efficiently than can their own root-hairs. Some of the tree-perching orchids are dependent on their symbiotic fungus allies to satisfy their thirst.

From wet earth or sodden log the fungi spring, their colours ranging through eerie tints of sulphurous crimson, violet, palest yellow, Carrara white. Their shapes are impish or fantastic, and their names seem to come from folk tales: 'shaggy cap', 'earthstar', 'witch's butter', 'horn of plenty'.

Most enchanting is the 'fairy ring', made by toadstools that spring up each year in an ever-widening circle. Botanists have estimated that some fairy rings may be 350, 400, even 600 years old. The belief that these are the places where 'the little people' danced in the moonlit dew is even older. Science and fantasy meet in the magic of fungi.

Confessions of a Tree Surgeon

W. E. Matthews

Especially in towns and cities, trees often need skilled care to make them safe and keep them healthy

Few people realise that trees are another part of wild life which is rapidly becoming extinct; many seem to regard them as inanimate objects, screwed into a socket, which can be abused regardless. To learn that there is as much again below the ground takes them by surprise. (Someone once described a tree as being a large beast with only its tail showing.)

In fact there is a very exact science of tree care, and those who imagine tree surgeons to be sandal-and-nut fanatics engaged in a crusade to romanticise trees, are wrong—though we are as irritated as anyone else by foresters who want to blanket the countryside with funereal conifers. Those who believe us to be hired assassins with sharp axes and a hatred of trees are wrong, too—though we are irritated by romantics who think trees dead on their feet are sacred just because they are picturesque.

There are many, and often disturbing, parallels between tree care and the human situation. The tree surgeon's patients are also very much alive. They need nourishment, they absorb enormous amounts of liquid, they breathe, they need light and air and room to develop properly. They can be strangled, smothered, starved, drowned or otherwise neglected. Their wounds bleed and need protection. They can be racked with various diseases. Heredity also influences their potential, and selective breeding can produce far better specimens.

The tree should be dealt with from its infancy, when it is selected according to its situation. This precaution can prevent enthusiasts planting 80 ft forest trees with a 40 ft spread on pavements, planting oaks actually touching kerbstones on the edge of dual carriageways (our local one kills several people each year), planting cedars outside front room windows in suburbia, and planting poplars at the bottom of the garden, where, unlike fairies, their activities can cause distress if the neighbour's house starts to fall apart.

When the monster is reaching maturity most of our problems are a question of: 'Here it is—preserve it, and all of us round about it.' This can actually be done providing the circumstances are not too unfavourable. Most trees are destroyed as a result of damage caused by decay, climatic conditions or unnatural interference; very few die naturally in their beds. The trouble is that most trees are in an artificial environment and probably not even in the country of their origin. So some care to keep them healthy is not unreasonable. This opens up a very wide field involving all the techniques of tree surgery. However, the tree surgeon is usually not consulted while the tree is still in good shape.

The business of diagnosis can be very difficult. Not only must one know all the natural hazards to which the tree might be susceptible, but also (as is often the case) the unnatural ones. These vary from the cunningly malicious to the innocent (and often nearly forgotten) alterations around the tree. But although these patients cannot put out their tongues and say 'ah', a good deal can be told from a routine examination—yes, you can tap their chests.

The examination begins by standing well away from the tree. By far the best time is in the early spring or at least when the tree is in leaf. The most obvious and visible signs can be seen on the extremities of the upper branches. They give the first indication of a decline in the tree's vigour. At its worst this condition is known by the very descriptive title of 'stag-headed', the dead pieces appearing very much like antlers. It is heralded by a thinning of the foliage at these points. The leaves are small and late developing; they fall early in the autumn and the tree starts to look generally miserable. This is where good observation is important. If 'going off' can be spotted in its early stages, it is far more likely that it will respond to treatment.

The next thing to examine is the trunk of the patient. Not only does it support the tree mechanically, but it also acts as a vital supply link between roots and crown. A common misconception is that the tree takes up liquid rather like a pipe—through the centre. In fact, the porous outer inch or two channels liquid to the leaves, where, having been processed by sunlight and converted to nutriments, it is fed back to the tree. This delicate plumbing system can be easily disrupted by a disease or mechanical damage, or a combination of the two.

A core is usually taken out with a small auger, which can reveal a great deal. The first and most obvious point is to see if the tree is hollow. This is not as easy to detect as might be supposed. Some of the most common heart-rots creep quietly into the centre of the tree by way of the root system with little or no external signs. A sharp look-out must also be kept for any fruiting body or fungi. These could take a form similar to a mushroom or, when on the bole, be bracketed to the tree, like a hoof.

Despite peculiar rumours about injecting trees or giving them pills in bore-holes, no effective way has been found to eliminate fungus in live tissues once it is established. There are very sophisticated chemicals for dealing with this problem on sawn timber, but similar preparations applied to a living tree would not only kill the fungus but probably also the tree.

The outer bark can also reveal a great deal. The things that can happen to tree trunks cover almost the whole sphere of human activity. Even in the most respectable gardens they can be accidentally bashed by mowers, or used as targets for guns (air gun pellets can carry in decay to a surprising degree), or as targets for junior knife- or hatchet-throwers.

In the inhospitable outside world they are irresistible to the vandal who finds it essential to leave his mark. Perhaps we are fortunate that the effort involved in engraving a tree usually keeps the text to a minimum. Tree guards (an expensive and unsightly protection) are often forgotten for so long that they quietly strangle the tree as it swells into them. The bole is often mistaken for a fencing post and is wired round and wounded by nails. Iron rails are secured to it, park seats are placed against it and cemented in. Clothes lines are wound round it and, in a crowning indignity over recent years, television aerials are fastened to its top.

The tolerance of the tree to these injuries depends a good deal upon its condition. The young, healthy tree growing fast will engulf these artificial encumbrances with a lava-like flow of natural callous, and eventually absorb them completely. Here they remain digested until the post-mortem by some unfortunate timber man whose first knowledge of their presence is when his saw disintegrates.

In older or less vigorous specimens serious rot can follow, often destroying the whole tree. Whatever the age, strangling by complete encirclement of the bole by any kind of band will inevitably kill it. Some ancient forms of bracing (still practised, alas) support the limb with an iron collar which, like an unrelieved tourniquet, starts to strangle the tree from the day it is put on. It is still possible to see trees completely dead from this ring upwards.

The next thing is to look up inside the crown. The problem here is to keep it intact. Heavy branching, especially when it is out of balance with the tree as a whole, is always regarded with great suspicion. Water and rubbish accumulate at the junctions with the main stem which turn to slush and decay and can eventually cause branch shedding. Multi-stemmed or heavily forked trees are always prone to this.

Assessing the strength of the crown and its probable resistance to stress depends a great deal upon the type of tree in question. The wood of the plane tree, for example, is very durable, while chestnut is one of the worst timbers known to man— it breaks easily and rots at an alarming rate, characteristics which are aggravated by its natural tendency to form large lateral branches. The village blacksmith was in far greater danger than he realised as he exercised his brawny arms beneath these monsters. Those who were aware chopped the tops off—which was probably a greater evil. Elm, of course, scare most laymen, not without some justification; although more durable than horse chestnut, they can also shed large branches without warning; and they have a nasty habit of falling over. Beech can sometimes break up, especially in the spring, which seems to be branch-shedding time.

Many trees brought to Britain from other countries grow very successfully, but the extremes of climate encountered here are often inconsistent and can have disastrous effects on them. Cedars, for instance, have thrived here, but their dense, flat

The tree above was continually battered by a corporation lawn-mower, just above its base. Where the bark was damaged, fungal rot penetrated the trunk, and so weakened it that the tree was blown down.

Oak trees in Bradgate Park, Leicestershire, where Lady Jane Grey was born. On the day that she was beheaded, February 12, 1554, the Park's oak trees were also beheaded, or 'topped'. Most of them still survive— striking evidence of the resistance that trees sometimes have even to the most adverse treatment.

branches hold snow so well that the whole thing snaps off. The Douglas fir, when grown in isolation, breaks up rapidly in the exposed conditions which are more than its slender, heavy-ended branches can stand. The giant sequoia or *Wellingtonia*, a tree with similar characteristics, loses branches in storms, and although these are not enormous they can be dangerous in a confined space.

All these factors are very important and should be carefully considered when incorporating these trees into developments such as new towns. But even assuming that the tree is of a vulnerable type, there is no need to rush out and cut the top off. Modern bracing, with enormously strong cables of thin, flexible steel, can prevent much damage.

Many purists are against bracing as they imagine it means the conglomeration of ironmongery which has passed for bracing over the years. Others imagine their tree is being trussed up like a turkey and will look artificial and unnatural. In fact, properly applied bracing is usually hardly detectable.

Equally, where restriction of light is involved, there is no need to pollard the tree drastically, or chop the ends of branches off. Careful thinning by modern methods can remove as much as one-third of the weight carried by any lateral branch which, apart from contributing towards the general safety of the tree, allows light to filter through the crown whilst keeping the tree in its natural form.

This business of lopping and topping, lumped together under the ugly word 'pollard', has been a source of friction for years. In some instances bad planting—forest trees put in a confined situation—

leaves no alternative. In other cases skilled crown-thinning can achieve the same object without the expensive mutilation of the tree.

Excessive dead wood is another danger sign. Some dead branches are inevitable where lack of light in the crown has killed off superfluous live growth. Careful pruning early in the tree's life could prevent a good deal of this trouble, particularly with crossing branches. In any event, dead wood of all kinds (be it faulty pruning, a legacy of storm damage, or a natural die-back) should be removed. It is one of the most common sources of decay and festers gradually into the tree until the whole is weakened beyond repair. Unless it is removed in its early stages, flush-cutting cannot get back to the sound wood and the remaining cavities will need further treatment.

Cutting close to the bole or branch is the golden rule of all pruning. This enables a natural callous to form which will heal cuts far more effectively than any artificial sealant. It is, however, vital to cover all wounds immediately after pruning to prevent the access of fungus spores until the natural process has taken over. Modern bitumen compounds not only seal the wound, but encourage rapid callousing. Creosote or tars must not be used: their burning action destroys the delicate tissue on the outer bark and retards the natural process of healing.

Some trees die for no apparent reason. As with all things living, they will fade quietly away. But sometimes an overall decline can be traced to impoverishment of the surrounding soil. This is understandable when you consider that this huge plant takes a great deal from the soil and cannot draw nourishment from any further than it can reach. Bearing in mind that it can sit in one place for sometimes hundreds of years, it is reasonable to suppose that it may exhaust the available supply of nutriment.

Some people are aghast at the suggestion of a tree needing artificial nourishment. If the tree were, as Nature intended, in a natural forest, there might be no need. In a forest the fall of leaf builds up into a layer of leaf mould which in turn feeds and keeps the surface of the soil damp by its mulching effect. Contrast this with the tree on a lawn where even the grass is carefully taken away. The surface floods in winter and bakes in summer, causing havoc among the fine feeding roots of the tree which are just below the surface. Trees in parks and public places fare even worse; soil is compacted over their roots to a shiny pan impervious to air or moisture.

Trees in these circumstances respond very well to an applied stimulant, particularly if coupled with aeration of the surrounding soil. In time to come, the fertilising of large, broad-leaved trees will be accepted as a normal part of tree maintenance, as it is gradually becoming accepted in commercial forestry practice for nursery work.

The tree surgeon also has to protect his charges from all the other mischiefs that could befall them.

Trees can be gently dozing in a pasture which one fine morning becomes a new town. How can their interests be respected enough to ensure their survival? In an existing town, apart from the process of preserving the trees already there, there is the question of things to come: suitable trees for suitable places, and they need not be cherries. Trees can fruit quite prettily, but the fruit must not fall on the pavement and make a mess; they can be deciduous, but the leaves must not fall in the roadway and put the skids under motor cars; they must not obscure street lamps, road signs, put leaves in gutters, roots in gardens or throw shadows on bedroom walls to frighten babies.

Another problem, particularly in urban areas on heavy soil, is the question of root trespass. Both poplar and elm have rampant root systems. I have seen roots from an insignificant pollarded elm stump disappearing under the footings of a house 90 ft from the tree and still as big as broom handles. They cracked the walls so that the doors would no longer fit, and caused in all £4000 worth of damage. Another nasty habit they have is to burrow into drains—their fine hair-like roots go through a crack and swell up inside until they eventually choke the whole passage. This is an instance where more

care should be given to the initial planting to ensure that trees are not put in which will become a menace to adjoining property.

Shading and overhanging branches are another sore point in urban areas. Most people know that an offending branch from a neighbouring tree can be cut to the level of the property line, provided the wood and fruit arising are returned to the person who owns the tree. What is not realised is that skilled tree surgery can often do a great deal to alleviate such difficulties. There is no need either for belligerence (the owner refuses to touch the tree at all), or for panic measures in which branches and tops are lopped off indiscriminately—which anyway causes the tree to blossom out far more densely than before. Careful pruning and thinning can leave both parties on speaking terms.

The responsibility of an owner for a tree's safety is another difficult problem. The law says that any tree that, to a layman, is obviously dangerous, renders the owner liable for any damage that may be incurred in its collapse. However, a layman is not expected to have technical knowledge. But since prevention is a good deal better than cure (and probably a good deal less expensive), get an authoritative opinion in advance about any aspect of tree work which causes concern in whatever situation.

This goes for everyone. If some of the ladies who chain themselves to trees to protect them, or form delegations, or wrestle with the workmen in a flurry of public-spiritedness, made the effort to find out the facts, it would save a great deal of trouble. (The idea persists that most borough surveyors dispatch their lads to chop down a few trees·when things are a little slack.) The irony is that only a minute part of this enthusiasm goes to care for trees which are standing and not obviously threatened.

Even the excellent tree preservation orders are little more than anti-destruction orders, a legal means of keeping the tree upright. No provision is made to get it into good condition and preserve it for as long as possible. People can cheerfully call the most neglected tree 'picturesque', claiming that they love trees and would not dream of touching them.

But still, when an unknown—and unqualified—man knocks on the door and says the tree is dangerous, madam, gullible to the last, takes his word for it and watches the tree's expensive assassination. If the same stranger wanted to dismantle her car or take out her appendix she would be most offended, but this prize possession, which has taken decades or even centuries to grow, will be sacrificed to any casual caller with a good story.

IN NATURE'S FOOTSTEPS

We shall never know if man, in a world without birds, would ever have learnt how to fly, or how much longer the discovery of flight might have taken without their example. All we can be sure of is that man has found endless clues in Nature to inventions that have shaped his way of life.

In the last few years, recognition of this debt has taken the form of a new science, bionics, in which living systems are studied for the light they may throw on technical problems. This is a new way of regarding Nature, which brings together scientists in many different disciplines—zoologists working with engineers, chemists with botanists. The present development of bionics may mark a change in human civilisation as great as that which was brought about by early man's transition from hunting to farming.

Already man has learnt much from many creatures. He has learnt about echo-location from bats, about sonar and underwater streamlining from dolphins and about the rattlesnake's incredibly delicate heat-sensing mechanism. As he continues to unravel Nature's secrets, there is no telling what new inventions may arise.

The long-eared bat's ears catch the echo of his high-pitched squeak as he flies at night; thus he 'sees' obstacles and finds his prey. Radar engineers hope to solve problems of interference by learning how the bat distinguishes its own signals from those of other bats.

The electric ray generates an electrical charge for attack and defence. Some electrical fish may detect their prey by sensing the distortion it makes in their electric field. Studies of these fish could lead to submarine detection by underwater electric fields.

In the pit between its eye and nostril, the American rattlesnake has a heat-sensing mechanism capable of detecting temperature variations as small as 1000th of a degree. The rattlesnake uses this mechanism to locate the warm-blooded creatures it preys on. Man has invented heat-detecting equipment which is even more sensitive, enabling a rifleman, for example, to locate an enemy at night solely by his body heat.

The head of a male silk moth, showing the antennae with which it senses the odour of a female silk moth. These antennae are so sensitive that a male is able to detect the presence of a female more than 6 miles away. When man understands the principles governing such a feat of detection as this, there is little doubt that he will make widespread use of them—in areas as varied, perhaps, as criminology and farming.

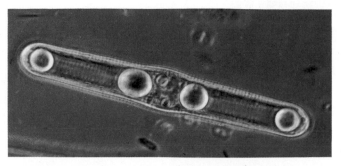

To overcome the problems of life under water, the water spider, the microscopic diatom and man himself have arrived at similar solutions. The water spider (left) constructs an air-bubble diving bell in which it lives and breathes. The diving saucer (below) enables man to explore the oceans, and protects him from the pressure of deep water. The diatom (above) contains tiny oil bubbles for buoyancy and stability, and some deep-sea diving vehicles contain oil tanks for the same purpose.

Dolphins (above) have given engineers many valuable insights into marine design. Everything about the dolphin equips it for life at sea: its shape is perfectly streamlined for speed through water, and studies of its skin structure have been basic to the design of an anti-drag skin for submarines and torpedoes. Dolphins are also equipped with an amazingly accurate underwater sonar system—another characteristic which has led the U.S. Navy to subsidise scientific research on them.

The Bond with Living Things

Man has worked with, and pitted his wits against, creatures
many times stronger and faster than himself. He has had
both success and failure. But the real bond
with living things begins when
we start to understand them. When that happens
we discover our true relationship with the natural world

Augusto Ruschi's Jungle Paradise

Allen Rankin

*A self-trained naturalist has turned
the Brazilian forests into his laboratory,
and shown science a new
way of learning about living creatures*

The little boy was six years old when he made his first all-day expedition into his vast back garden—a Brazilian forest. Entranced, he gazed wide-eyed at the towering jacaranda and *paraju* trees, the myriad orchids hiding in their shadows and the swarms of humming-birds like tiny jewelled darts on speed-blurred wings. 'It's wonderful there. Marvellous!' Augusto told his family that night. 'When I grow up, I'm going to spend *all* my time with the birds and flowers!'

To his parents, leading citizens of the little village of Santa Teresa in the State of Espirito Santo, this sounded anything but practical. Yet Augusto Ruschi, now over 50, has done just what he said he would—and is probably South America's greatest all-round naturalist.

In satisfying his insatiable curiosity, Dr Ruschi has become the leading authority on the ways of humming-birds. He is also an internationally recognised expert on other exotic forms of life, from the beautiful wild orchid to the hideous vampire bat. His discoveries of previously unknown species or sub-species of flowers, birds and mammals have added appreciably to the science of biology and to the pleasure of millions of nature lovers everywhere.

Ruschi was tall, lanky and physically tough; his eyes still glowed with a childlike enthusiasm. 'I call this my Eden,' he told me, as we strolled through the forest park surrounding his boyhood home, where he lived with his wife and two sons. Orchids of every hue flamed along the garden paths; parrots and gaudier birds flashed and screamed in the pavilions; and dazzling humming-birds zipped or hovered around us.

The area is a public wildlife museum which draws some 30,000 people a year, although it is 45 rugged mountain-trail miles from the nearest town, Vitória. 'All I ask,' said Ruschi, who developed it largely at his own expense, 'is that people look at things closely enough to enjoy them. Because the longer and harder you look at *any* living creature, the more marvellous you find it to be.'

Ruschi's own life is a case in point. At 12 he was staying in the forest for as long as two weeks at a time, living off wild fruit and the meat of small animals he bagged with a rifle. His closest friends were not schoolmates but the creatures in the woods. His favourite books were tomes on botany, biochemistry, ornithology and other natural sciences, which he learnt to read not only in his native Portuguese, but in French, German and Latin.

Augusto's first great teenage love was the wild orchid, After combing about 400 square miles of wilderness, he numbered, mapped and indexed the locations of 90,000 orchid plants of scores of different species. He kept elaborate records on each of the choicer specimens: what kind of tree or rock it lived on; at what elevation and in what degree of sun and shade; when birds and insects arrived to pollinate it; its size and colour at various phases; its peculiarities. Many of the plants literally burst into bloom, with a glorious and quite audible puff. The boy kept track of these, and even when a flower blossomed in the small hours after midnight he was often on hand for the event. Sometimes a series of blossomings would keep him running from plant to plant all night. He found it all marvellous.

That is what the professors at the National Museum in Rio de Janeiro thought, too, when they received one of the most startling documents ever written by a boy of 15. Hand-penned in scholarly Latin, it revealed that the young prodigy had discovered two new genera of orchids and at least 19 new species. More important, it contained 'A. Ruschi's simplified formulas' for the conditions under which many species of the plants flourish best. They have helped naturalists, and amateur and commercial gardeners in South America and elsewhere to produce healthier, lovelier orchids.

Augusto's father, who had 11 other children to provide for, could not afford to send his nature-obsessed son to college. The boy, left to roam the woods, was delighted. From orchids his interests turned towards humming-birds. The elusiveness of these minute feathered acrobats, flashing all colours of the rainbow, offered a special challenge to him—especially when he learnt that no one knew enough about their habits to get them to live and breed in captivity. At 19 he embarked on studies that would greatly change that situation.

First, he set up an observation post near the nest of a tiny emerald-crowned lady humming-bird. There he kept watch for 35 days and nights, sleeping or dashing home for food only when the mother bird slept. Ruschi saw the mother lay her two eggs and, 14 days later, saw the eggs hatch.

Often, when the mother flew off to get food for her young, he gently borrowed the little ones from the nest. He weighed them (on a pharmacist's scale) and took their temperature. With an eye-dropper thrust down their throats, he even took samples of their stomach contents, which—with his remarkable

Hovering like a bumble-bee, a royal wood nymph humming-bird probes deep into a fuchsia blossom to suck up nectar and tiny insects through her tongue—which is shaped like a drinking straw and works like a suction pump. Humming-birds must eat every 10 or 15 minutes.

self-taught knowledge—he chemically analysed. In this way, Ruschi began to learn precisely what humming-birds must eat to survive—exactly the kind of proteins (insects) and carbohydrates (flower nectars) they must have at various ages.

Through this technique and others, he gradually revealed some of the best-kept secrets of humming-birds (called *beija-ôres*, 'flower-kissers', in Brazilian

263

Portuguese). He learnt the exact amount of space that certain species of the birds require to 'pair off' and mate in proper privacy. He discovered what flowers the birds need for nutrition, what plants for shelter, what materials—down to the last wisp of spider's web—they must have for nest-building.

Putting this knowledge to use, he began to build aviaries and stock them with the finicky little creatures. Soon they were reproducing. Today, in Ruschi's *viveiros* (flower-filled enclosures), some 400 humming-birds of 95 different species live, breed and perform their sensational aerial stunts almost as freely as in the wild state.

More and more zoos are now providing the 'natural' conditions under which even the most exotic humming-birds can live. Ruschi has freely given thousands of rare birds—and plants, animals and insects, too—to parks and museums. 'I do what I do for the love of it,' he explained simply.

Though the gifted young man did not go to college, the college at nearby Campos came to him. It gave him a scholarship and allowed him to do his 'classroom work' in his beloved woods, requiring only that he turn up at school for examinations. About the same time, Professor Cândido de Mello Leitão, a leading naturalist at the National Museum in Rio, urged young Ruschi to work for the museum and get some of his college credits there. Ruschi lasted only a month before he resigned, explaining: 'I cannot be pent up by walls. I must go back to my forests.'

But the museum directors refused to accept his resignation. Instead, they made a government biological field station of his home in Santa Teresa and paid him for managing it—a job Ruschi has held happily ever since. He also practises law occasionally—a profession he mastered on his own at 35.

Dr Ruschi still spends much of his time in the wild. To catch a really rare humming-bird, he may camp for three months in the South American mountains or jungles. Finding a creature smaller than one's thumb on a largely unexplored continent of more than 7 million square miles requires the most knowledgeable kind of detective work.

Consider, for example, the case of the missing *Loddigesia mirabilis*. No specimen of this gorgeous fancy-tailed humming-bird had been recorded since 1933. The species was feared to be extinct, but Ruschi thought it was not and in 1962 set out to try to rediscover it. Because he knew that the bird had lived at an altitude of over 6500 ft, he selected an appropriate area in the Peruvian Andes. Then, reckoning that the *Loddigesia* would prefer foliage thick enough to hide in, but thin enough to avoid the

Unique among birds, the male Loddigesia mirabilis *has only four tail feathers: two inner spike-like feathers and two outer paddle-like feathers attached to long filaments, which the humming-bird manipulates to attract a mate.*

danger of snagging its elaborate tail, he narrowed his search to areas with relatively sparse undergrowth. It took two months of hunting, but suddenly, hovering before a bright flower, a female of the missing species appeared.

Then, to Ruschi's delight, the cock bird showed up, his long twin tails spinning and interlacing like the blades of an ethereal egg-beater to impress his lady. *Tat-tat-tat-tat!* drummed the tails and wings in rhythm as the bird performed his courting dance. Ruschi was so enthralled that he waited until the half-hour wedding ceremony was over before catching the two lovers.

Dr Ruschi's great curiosity about all phases of nature has led him to astonishing bits of knowledge. Once, for example, he followed a single ant for 30 hours just to see where the insect was going. At long last the ant—a giant *Toçandira*—reached its home colony and joined its fellows there. Until then it had been generally believed that this ant was non-gregarious and spent most of its life alone. Subsequently, Ruschi became an expert on the *Tocandira's* busy home life.

To observe the nesting habits of a marsh bird called the small diver, Ruschi hid neck-deep in swamp water for three days and nights, his head and face masked by a hollow gourd in which he had punched holes to peer through. He watched the bird dive to feed on something at the lake bottom. What was it eating? Ruschi later sieved the mud and brought up some 5000 tiny frogs of a kind he had never seen. No wonder, a zoologist told him later; this animal was a primitive frog that gives birth by opening up its back. The species had never been found so far south before.

For his contributions to the natural sciences, Ruschi holds six major decorations, including the Brazilian Government's highly prized Award of Dom João VI. He has lectured at scientific conferences all over the world. But he is still happiest when coaxing yet another secret from his forests.

'Isn't it marvellous,' he asks, 'that this is such a great world that we can never begin to solve all its mysteries, and that the secret of an exciting life lies not in finding wonders but in searching for them?'

Assignment with an Octopus

Arthur Grimble

Catching an octopus is literally child's play
for the Gilbert Islanders; for a
European, it can be more like a nightmare

The old navigators of the Gilberts used to talk with fear of a gigantic octopus that inhabited the seas between Samoa and the Ellice Islands. They said its tentacles were three arm-spans long and thicker at the base than the body of a full-grown man—a scale of measurements not out of keeping with what is known of the atrocious

monster called *Octopus apollyon*. There were some who stated that this foul fiend of the ocean was also to be found in the waters between Onotoa, Tamana and Arorae in the Southern Gilberts. But I never came across a man who had seen one, and the biggest of the octopus breed I ever saw with my own eyes had tentacles only a little over 6 ft long. It was a member of the clan *Octopus vulgaris*, which swarms in all the lagoons. An average specimen of this variety is a dwarf beside *Octopus apollyon*: laid out flat, it has a total spread of no more than 9 or 10 ft; but it is a wicked-looking piece of work, even in death, with those disgusting suckers studding its arms and those bulging, filmed eyes staring out of the mottled gorgon face.

Possibly, if you can watch objectively, the sight of *Octopus vulgaris* searching for crabs and crayfish on the floor of the lagoon may move you to something like admiration. You cannot usually see the dreadful eyes from a water-glass straight above its feeding-ground, and your feeling for crustacea is too impersonal for horror at their fate between pouncing suckers and jaws. There is real beauty in the rich change of its colours as it moves from shadow to sunlight, and the gliding ease of its arms as they reach and flicker over the rough rocks fascinates the eye with its deadly grace. You feel that if only the creature would stick to its grubbing on the bottom, the shocking ugliness of its shape might even win your sympathy, as for some poor Caliban in the enchanted garden of the lagoon. But it is no honest grubber in the open. For every one of its kind that you see crawling below you, there are a dozen skulking in recesses of the reef that falls away like a cliff from the edge where you stand watching. When *Octopus vulgaris* has eaten its fill of the teeming crabs and crayfish, it seeks a dark cleft in the coral face and anchors itself there with a few of the large suckers nearest to its body. Thus shielded from attack in the rear, with tentacles gathered to pounce, it squats glaring from the shadows, alert for anything alive to swim within striking distance. It can hurl one or all of those whiplashes forward with the speed of dark lightning, and once its scores of suckers, rimmed with hooks for grip on slippery skins, are clamped about their prey, nothing but the brute's death will break their awful hold.

But that very quality of the octopus that most horrifies the imagination, its relentless tenacity, becomes its undoing when hungry man steps into the picture. The Gilbertese happen to value certain parts of it as food, and their method of fighting it is coolly based upon the one fact that its arms never change their grip. They hunt for it in pairs. One man acts as the bait, his partner as the killer. First, they swim eyes-under at low tide just off the reef, and search the crannies of the submarine cliff for sight of any tentacle that may flicker out for a catch. When they have placed their quarry, they land on the reef for the next stage. The human bait starts the real game. He dives and tempts the lurking brute by swimming a few strokes in front of its cranny, at first a little beyond striking range. Then he turns and makes straight for the cranny, to give himself into the embrace of those waiting arms. Sometimes nothing happens. The beast will not always respond to the lure. But usually it strikes.

The partner on the reef above stares down through the pellucid water, waiting for his moment. His teeth are his only weapon. His killing efficiency depends on his avoiding every one of those strangling arms. He must wait until his partner's body has been drawn right up to the entrance of the cleft. The monster inside is groping then with its horny mouth against the victim's flesh, and sees nothing beyond it. That point is reached in a matter of no more than 30 seconds after the decoy has plunged. The killer dives, lays hold of his pinioned friend at arm's length, and jerks him away from the cleft; the octopus is torn adrift from the anchorage of its proximal suckers, and clamps itself the more fiercely to its prey. In the same second, the human bait gives a kick which brings him, with quarry annexed, to the surface. He turns on his back, still holding his breath for better buoyancy, and this exposes the body of the beast for the kill. The killer closes in, grasps the evil head from behind, and wrenches it away from its meal. Turning the face up towards himself, he plunges his teeth between the bulging eyes and bites down and in with all his strength. That is the end of it. It dies on the instant; the suckers release their hold; the arms fall away; the two fishers paddle with whoops of delighted laughter to the reef, where they string the catch to a pole before going to rout out the next one.

Any two boys of seventeen, any day of the week, will go out and get you half a dozen octopuses like that for the mere fun of it. Here lies the whole point of this story. The hunt is, in the most literal sense, nothing but child's play to the Gilbertese.

As I was standing one day at the end of a jetty in Tarawa lagoon, I saw two boys from the village shouldering a string of octopuses slung on a pole between them. I started to wade out in their direction, but before I hailed them they had stopped, planted the carrying-pole upright in a fissure and, leaving it

there, swum off the edge for a while with faces submerged, evidently searching for something under water. I had been only a few months at Tarawa, and that was my first near view of an octopus-hunt. I watched every stage of it from the dive of the human bait to the landing of the dead catch. When it was over, I went up to them. I could hardly believe that in those few seconds, with no more than a frivolous-looking splash or two on the surface, they could have found, caught and killed the creature they were now stringing up before my eyes. They explained the amusing simplicity of the thing.

'There's only one trick the decoy-man must never forget,' they said, 'and that's not difficult to remember. If he is not wearing water-spectacles, he must cover his eyes with a hand as he comes close to the *kika* (octopus), or the suckers might blind him.' It appeared that the ultimate fate of the eyes was not the thing to worry about; the immediate point was that the sudden pain of a sucker clamping itself to an eyeball might cause the bait to expel his breath and inhale sea-water; that would spoil his buoyancy, and he would fail then to give his friend the best chance of a kill.

Then they began whispering together. I knew in a curdling flash what they were saying to each other. Before they turned to speak to me again, a horrified conviction was upon me. My damnable curiosity had led me into a trap from which there was no escape. They were going to propose that I should take a turn at being the bait myself, just to see how delightfully easy it was; and that is what they did. It did not even occur to them that I might not leap at the offer. I was already known as a young man who liked swimming and fishing and laughing with the villagers; I had just shown an interest in this particular form of hunting; naturally, I should enjoy the fun of it as much as they did. Without even waiting for my answer, they gleefully ducked off the edge of the reef to look for another octopus—a fine fat one—*mine*. Left standing there alone, I had one of those visions...

It was dusk in the village. The fishers were home; I saw the cooking-fires glowing orange-red between the brown lodges. There was laughter and shouted talk as the women prepared the evening meal. But the laughter was hard with scorn. 'What?' they were saying. 'Afraid of a *kika*? Why, even our boys are not afraid of a *kika*!' A curtain went down and rose again on the Residency; the Old Man was talking: 'A leader? You? The man who funked a schoolboy game? We don't leave your sort in charge of Districts.' The scene flashed to my uncles: 'Returned

A common octopus crawling over the rocks to which it anchors itself by its suckers when lying in wait for prey. Gilbert Islanders in the Pacific kill such octopuses by biting them between the eyes.

empty,' they said. 'We always knew you hadn't got it in you. Returned empty . . .'

Of course it was all overdrawn, but one fact was beyond doubt: the Gilbertese reserved all their most ribald humour for physical cowardice. No man gets passed for a leader by becoming the butt of that kind of wit. I decided I would rather face the octopus.

I was dressed in khaki slacks, canvas shoes and a short-sleeved singlet. I took off the shoes and made up my mind to shed the singlet if told to do so; but I was wildly determined to stick to my trousers throughout. Dead or alive, said a voice within me, an official minus his pants is a preposterous object, and I felt I could not face that extra horror. However, nobody asked me to remove anything.

I hope I did not look as yellow as I felt when I stood ready to take the plunge; I have never been so sick with fear before or since. 'Remember, one hand for your eyes,' said someone from a thousand miles off, and I dived.

I do not suppose it is really true that the eyes of an octopus shine in the dark; besides, it was clear daylight only 6 ft down in the limpid water; but I could have sworn the brute's eyes burned at me as I turned in towards his cranny. That dark glow—whatever may have been its origin—was the last thing I saw as I blacked out with my left hand and rose into his clutches. Then, I remember chiefly a dreadful sliminess with a Herculean power behind it. Something whipped round my left forearm and the back of my neck, binding the two together. In the same flash, another something slapped itself high on my forehead, and I felt it crawling down inside the back of my singlet. My impulse was to tear at it with my right hand, but I felt the whole of that arm pinioned to my ribs. In most emergencies the mind works with crystal-clear impersonality. This was not even an emergency, for I knew myself perfectly safe. But my boyhood's nightmare was upon me. When I felt the swift constriction of those disgusting arms jerk my head and shoulders in towards the reef, my mind went blank of every thought save the beastliness of contact with that squat head. A mouth began to nuzzle below my throat, at the junction of the collar-bones. I forgot there was anyone to save me. Yet something still directed me to hold my breath.

I was awakened from my cowardly trance by a quick, strong pull on my shoulders, back from the cranny. The cables round me tightened painfully, but I knew I was adrift from the reef. I gave a kick, rose to the surface and turned on my back with the brute sticking out of my chest like a tumour. My mouth was smothered by some flabby moving horror. The suckers felt like hot rings pulling at my skin. It was only two seconds, I suppose, from then to the attack of my deliverer, but it seemed like a century of nausea.

My friend came up between me and the reef. He pounced, pulled, bit down, and the thing was over—for everyone but me. At the sudden relaxation of the tentacles, I let out a great breath, sank, and drew in the next under water. It took the united help of both boys to get me, coughing, heaving and pretending to join in their delighted laughter, back to the reef. I had to submit there to a kind of war-dance round me, in which the dead beast was slung whizzing past my head from one to the other. I had a chance to observe then that it was not by any stretch of fancy a giant, but just plain average. That took the bulge out of my budding self-esteem. I left hurriedly for the cover of the jetty, and was sick.

268

Dogs and Men— the Covenant

Konrad Lorenz

Dogs hunt and herd on man's behalf; they guard and guide him, give him companionship, and serve as a symbol of lasting fidelity

There is no faith which has never yet been broken, except that of a truly faithful dog. Of all dogs which I have hitherto known, the most faithful are those in whose veins flows, beside that of the golden jackal (*Canis aureus*), a considerable stream of wolf's blood. The northern wolf (*Canis lupus*) only figures in the ancestry of our present dog breeds through having been crossed with already domesticated Aureus dogs. Contrary to the widespread opinion that the wolf plays an essential role in the ancestry of the larger dog breeds, comparative research in behaviour has revealed the fact that all European dogs, including the largest ones such as Great Danes and wolfhounds, are pure Aureus and contain, at the most, a minute amount of wolf's blood. The purest wolf-dogs that exist are certain breeds of Arctic America, particularly the so-called malemutes and huskies. The Eskimo dogs of Greenland also show only slight traces of Lapland Aureus characters, whereas the Arctic breeds of the Old World, such as Lapland dogs, Russian lajkas, samoyeds and chows, certainly have more Aureus in their constitution. Nevertheless the latter breeds derive their character from the Lupus side of their ancestry and they all exhibit the high cheek-bones, the slanting eyes and the slightly upward tilt of the nose which give its specific expression to the face of the wolf. On the other hand the chow, in particular, bears the stamp of his share of Aureus blood in the flaming red of his magnificent coat.

The 'sealing of the bond', the final attachment of the dog to one master, is quite enigmatical. It takes place quite suddenly, within a few days, particularly in the case of puppies that come from a breeding kennel. The 'susceptible period' for this most important occurrence in the whole of a dog's life is, in Aureus dogs, between 8 and 18 months, and in Lupus dogs round about the sixth month.

The really single-hearted devotion of a dog to its master has two quite different sources. On the one

In the light of dawn a man and his trained truffle hound hunt for truffles. These underground fungi are prized delicacies, and the search for them usually takes place at night, to keep secret the places where they grow.

side, it is nothing other than the submissive attachment which every wild dog shows towards its pack leader, and which is transferred, without any considerable alteration in character, by the domestic dog to a human being. To this is added, in the more highly domesticated dogs, quite another form of affection. Many of the characteristics in which domestic animals differ from their wild ancestral form arise by virtue of the fact that properties of body structure and behaviour, which in the wild prototype are only marked by some transient stages of youth, are kept permanently by the domestic form. In dogs, short hair, curly tail, hanging ears, domed skull and the short muzzle of many domestic breeds are features of this type. In behaviour, one of these juvenile characters which has become permanent in the domestic dog, expresses itself in

the peculiar form of its attachment. The ardent affection which wild canine youngsters show for their mother and which disappears completely after they have reached maturity, is preserved as a permanent mental trait of all highly domesticated dogs. What originally was love for the mother is transformed into love for the human master.

Thus the pack loyalty, in itself unaltered but merely transferred to man, and the permanent childlike dependency resulting from domestication, are two more or less independent springs of canine affection. One essential difference in the character of Lupus and Aureus dogs is attributable to the fact that these two springs flow with different strength in the two types. In the life of a wolf, the community of the pack plays a vastly more important role than in that of a jackal. While the latter is essentially a solitary hunter and confines itself to a limited territory, the wolf packs roam far and wide through the forests of the North as a sworn and very exclusive band which sticks together through thick and thin and whose members will defend each other to the very death. That the wolves of a pack will devour each other, as is frequently asserted, I have strong reason to doubt, since sled-dogs will not do so at any price, even when at the point of starvation, and this social inhibition has certainly not been instilled into them by man.

The reticent exclusiveness and the mutual defence at all costs are properties of the wolf which influence favourably the character of all strongly wolf-blooded dog breeds and distinguish them to their advantage from Aureus dogs, which are mostly 'hail-fellow-well-met' with every man and will follow anyone who holds the other end of the lead in his hand. A Lupus dog, on the contrary, who has once sworn allegiance to a certain man, is forever a one-man dog and no stranger can win from him so much as a single wag of his bushy tail. Nobody who has once possessed the one-man love of a Lupus dog will ever be content with one of pure Aureus blood. Unfortunately this fine characteristic of the Lupus dog has against it various disadvantages which are indeed the immediate results of the one-man loyalty. That a mature Lupus dog can never become *your* dog, is a matter of course. Worse, if he is already yours and you are forced to leave him, the animal literally becomes mentally unbalanced, obeys neither your wife nor children, sinks morally, in his grief, to the level of an ownerless street cur, loses his restraint from killing and, committing misdeed upon misdeed, ravages the surrounding district.

Besides this, a predominantly Lupus-blooded dog is, in spite of his boundless loyalty and affection, never quite sufficiently submissive. He is ready to die for you, but not to obey you; at least, I have never been able to extract implicit obedience from one of these dogs—perhaps a better dog trainer than I might be more successful. For this reason, it is seldom that you see, in a town, a chow without a lead walking close beside his master. If you walk with a Lupus dog in the woods, you can never make him stay near you. All he will do is to keep in very loose contact with you and honour you with his companionship only now and again.

Not so the Aureus dog. In him, as a result of his age-old domestication, that infantile affection has persisted which makes him a manageable and tractable companion. Instead of the proud loyalty of the Lupus dog which is far removed from obedience, the Aureus dog will always grant you that servitude which, day and night, by the hour and by the minute, awaits your command and even your slightest wish. When you take him for a walk, an Aureus dog of a more highly domesticated breed will, without previous training, always run with you, keeping the same radius whether he runs before, behind or beside you and adapting his speed to yours. He is naturally obedient: he answers to his name not only when he wishes to and when you cajole him, but also because he knows that he *must* come. The harder you shout, the more surely he will come, whereas a Lupus dog, in this case, comes not at all but seeks to appease you from a distance with friendly gestures.

Opposed to these good and congenial properties of the Aureus dog are unfortunately some others which also arise from the permanent infantility of these animals and are less agreeable for an owner. Since young dogs under a certain age are, for members of their own species, 'taboo'—that is, they must not under any circumstances be bitten—such big babies are often correspondingly trustful and importunate towards everybody. Like many spoilt human children who call every grown-up 'uncle', they pester people and animals alike with overtures to play. If this youthful property persists, to any appreciable extent, in the adult domestic dog, there arises a very unpleasant canine character, or rather the complete lack of such a commodity. The worst part of it lies in the literally 'dog-like' submission that these animals, who see in every man an 'uncle', show towards anyone who treats them with the least sign of severity; the playful storm of affection is immediately transformed into a cringing state of humility. Everyone is acquainted with this kind of dog which knows no happy medium between perpetual, exasperating 'jumping up', and fawningly turning upon its back, its paws waving in supplication. You shout, at the risk of offending your hostess, at the infuriating creature that is trampling all over your person and covering you from head to foot with hairs. Thereupon the dog falls beseechingly upon his back. You speak kindly to him, to conciliate your hostess and, quickly leaping up, the brute has licked you right across the face and now continues unremittingly to bestrew your trousers with hairs.

Yet my affections do not belong entirely to Lupus dogs, as the reader might conclude from this little canine characterology. No Lupus-blooded dog has offered his master such unquestioning obedience as our incomparable Alsatian—an Aureus dog. But both sets of qualities can be combined. It would, of course, be quite impossible for the dog-breeder to make the predominantly Lupus dog catch up, in one stride, with the Aureus dog which has been domesticated for a few thousand years longer, but there is another way.

Some years ago my wife and I each possessed a dog, I an Alsatian bitch, Tito, my wife a little chow bitch, Pygi. A son of Tito's, Booby by name, married the chow bitch Pygi. This happened quite against the will of my wife who, naturally enough, wanted to breed pure chows. But here we discovered, as an unexpected hindrance, a new property of Lupus dogs: the monogamous fidelity of the bitch to a certain dog. My wife travelled with her bitch to nearly all the chow dogs in Vienna, in the hope that one at least would find Pygi's favour. In vain— Pygi snapped furiously at all her suitors; she only wanted her Booby and she got him in the end, or rather he got her by reducing a thick wooden door, behind which Pygi was confined, to its primary elements. And therewith began our crossbred stud of chow and Alsatian.

At the moment, our breed contains very little Alsatian blood, because my wife, during my absence in the war, twice crossed in pure chows; this was inevitable, for otherwise we should have been dependent on inbreeding. As it is, the inheritance of Tito shows itself clearly in the psychological respect, for the dogs are far more affectionate and much easier to train than pure-blooded chows, although, from an external point of view, only a very expert eye can detect the element of Alsatian blood. I intend to develop further this mixed breed, and to continue with my plan to evolve a dog of ideal character.

My Duel with Moby Don

Donal Heatley

The story of a man's
record-breaking battle with a giant fish—
a monster, black as ink
and armed with a murderous spear

I was looking forward to a lazy week-end of fishing when we set out from Tauranga, New Zealand, that Friday morning in January 1968. My companions, Les Deasy, Leo Devlin and Dick Meredith, were all experienced deep-sea anglers. This was my first big-game fishing trip and I was more keen on relaxing than on breaking any records. Even if I did not get a fish, just floating around on the ocean would take my mind off work.

We had collected our boat, the 40 ft launch *Abalone*, and its crew of two, and were heading out across the fabulous Bay of Plenty on New Zealand's Pacific coast. Here, at what Maoris call 'The Well of Fish', anglers gather from all over the world in pursuit of the fighting black marlin swordfish, the fierce mako and thresher sharks, and occasionally the game fisherman's dream, the true swordfish known as the broadbill.

Our plan was to cross to Mayor Island, 22 miles offshore, and make our base there at the fishing lodge. Our skipper provided all the equipment; we brought enough food for lunch each day.

Our method of fishing was to drift with live bait— 18 in. Kahawai fish—which carried the hook and swam well below the surface of the water. Some 50 ft up the line from the bait was a float which bobbed under when a fish struck. We had three lines out, two forward and one aft, and there were two chairs in which we took turns each half-hour. When we had a strike, the other two lines were hastily pulled in.

We fished all day Friday, with a few strikes but no fish. On Saturday we went back to Mayor Island with the best catch in port; but I had yet to get a strike. The next day was my thirtieth birthday, and we celebrated at the lodge that evening. At six o'clock on Sunday morning, we weren't very enthusiastic about getting down to the boat.

For seven hours we floated about with little action. After lunch I took the chair from Meredith and, since I was now the only one who had not yet landed a fish, I was in for some teasing. 'What's the use of giving you the chair, Donal?' my friends said. 'The fish don't like your looks!'

'I'm not interested in those little 200- and 300-pounders you chaps have been catching,' I retorted. 'It's my birthday and I'm going to show you what a really big fish looks like.' I was thinking about a black marlin—they weigh as much as 800 lb. and put up a long, rough fight.

I had been in the chair about five minutes when my float gently slipped beneath the surface of the water. I did not feel anything on my line. Skipper Ces Jack left the wheel, strode over to my chair and tested the line with his hand; then he let out an oath and told me to put on the canvas fighting harness. The straps of the harness went round my back and clipped on to either side of the reel.

'He's taking the bait down to taste it before he eats it,' Ces said. 'He's not hooked yet. Give him line. You'll know when he's hooked.'

A minute later I felt my line snap taut; then it went screaming off the reel as my fish charged away. He tore off diagonally from the boat, swimming well under water where we could not see him. Over half the 400 yds of line had peeled off the reel when he suddenly arched out of the water into the air and crashed back into the sea. I caught my breath in disbelief. His enormous black body, suspended for that breathtaking second against the sky, seemed to obliterate the horizon.

Unfortunately, only the mate, Dougal, and I caught that brief glimpse of the monstrous fish, and neither of us could identify him. We only knew he was enormous and black as ink. When we described him to Ces, he said, 'Must be a big black marlin.' He sized me up appraisingly. 'We landed a big marlin not long ago. It took 16 hours.'

Sixteen hours! I wondered if I had the strength to fight the fish all night. No one could relieve or assist me at the reel, according to International Game Fish Association rules. I was on my own. 'Fight the fish with all you've got,' Ces advised me. 'The quicker you tire him, the quicker we'll bring him in.'

So I put my back into trying to reel in the monster. You brace your legs and, leaning into the harness, pull back in the chair as far as you can, then bend forward and reel in whatever line you have won from the fish. When he runs, you give him back the line; when he pauses you try to reel some of it in again. You use all the muscle in your back, your arms, your hands. You use muscles that you did not know you had.

From 3.30 that afternoon, the time of the strike, until darkness closed in, the great fish headed out to open sea with *Abalone* in pursuit. I fought him, but I was never able to get in more than half of the line before he would take off again. I wore a cotton glove on my left hand to protect the skin on my fingers as I guided in the line. By dusk it had worn through.

Dougal brought me a canvas glove. I kept fighting the fish but he was so strong I could do little against his runs. Before daylight my canvas glove had worn through, too. The skipper told the mate to bring me a leather glove.

While the fish was not actually towing the boat, he was dictating our course, and a crazy course it was—circles, figures of eight, zigzags, leading us away from the waters of Mayor Island, north towards the Alderman Islands, 22 miles away.

'He's a powerhouse,' Devlin observed. 'Let's call him Moby Dick.'

'No,' Meredith corrected. 'Moby Don. He is Donal's birthday fish.'

At dawn on Monday, I managed to get Moby Don reeled in to within 60 ft of the boat. I had the brake set on hard to hold what gains I had won, when suddenly he rushed off in the opposite direction. I could not get the brake released fast enough. The rod pulled right out of the socket, taking me with it.

The fighting harness yanked me into the air, then dragged me over the side of the boat. I felt hands grabbing my back and legs, hauling me on board again. While two men hung on to me, a third got a rope and tied me into my chair.

By 7.30 on Monday morning I did not seem to be any nearer landing the monster fish. Ces told me I had broken the local endurance record. The big fish *must* be beginning to tire. I certainly was. The harness cut into my back; my arms and elbows ached. It was becoming increasingly difficult to wind the reel, and the fingers on my left hand were so numb it did not matter whether I wore a glove or not.

At about nine o'clock my line began playing out slowly and I felt Moby Don going very deep—a new tactic. The fish rested on and off for about five hours. He swam around a few times, but there were long quiet spells in between when I was able to catnap. Then, at about two o'clock, he suddenly charged up from the depths and swept out to open sea again, the quarter-mile of line screaming out behind him.

I experienced my first feeling of despondency—Moby Don had apparently regained all his strength, but my naps had done little to restore me. My eyes were swollen with fatigue. My body cried for sleep.

For the next four hours there was no thought of trying to bring in the monster fish. As fresh as though he had never felt a hook, he ran free, taking his captive boat and passengers with him. (Ces estimated later that the giant fish had piloted us nearly a hundred miles.)

We ran the entire day under a burning sun. Since I was wearing shorts, the boys had given me a towel to protect my knees, but I had to brace my legs against the sides of the boat when I was playing the fish and there was no way of keeping my shins covered. They were burning badly. (When the ordeal was over I was treated for third-degree burns.) My back was also burning, not from the sun, but from the constant chafing of the canvas harness.

By late afternoon I was close to exhaustion. I had to reel in Moby Don. I got him within a few yards of the boat, when suddenly he veered off sharply and dived underneath it. There was nothing I could do. You have to stop reeling in the line when a fish goes under the boat, otherwise you will cut it on the sides of the boat or the propeller. The only thing the angler can do is to let the fish have the line back.

This was just what Moby Don had been waiting for. When he felt the line slacken, he promptly struck out for open sea. When he eventually slowed down, I started once more, agonisingly, to reel him in. By now, darkness had overtaken us for the second time, and Dougal was holding a searchlight on the line. As I brought Moby Don close to the boat, under the glare of the searchlight, the skipper got a look at the monster's head for the first time. He saw the shape, the size, the murderous long spear.

'It's a broadbill swordfish!'

A broadbill! I felt a prickle of excitement. The fiercest fighting fish in the sea, every angler's dream catch! The world's record broadbill, captured off Chile in 1963, weighed 1182 lb.

'He's a giant!' Ces gasped. 'A minimum of 1000 lb., and I would guess closer to 1500. He's the biggest fish I've ever seen.'

'My God!' Meredith whispered to me in an awed voice. 'His eyes are 2 ft apart!'

Still the battle continued. Moby Don had learnt a simple trick, so he kept on using it. Each time I worked him in near the boat, he dived underneath so that I was forced to give him back the line. Four times that night I brought him up close; four times he went under and won back the line.

Ces tried to give me heart. 'You've already passed the world endurance record for fighting a fish— 30 hours and five minutes.'

It did help a bit, and I started reeling Moby Don in close for the fifth time. Then I heard a shout. My friends were pointing to a bronze whale shark that had surfaced between Moby Don and the boat. In that instant the broadbill dived. But my reflexes were at a standstill; my paralysed fingers moved too slowly to release the brake. The line snapped taut with a *zing*. Then suddenly it went slack.

I fell back into my chair, my head slumped on my chest, and waited for the torrent of disappointment to flood over me. Around me I could hear my friends commiserating with me, their voices bleak with dejection.

'It must have been that shark, Don, he must have cut your line as he swam past——'

'Or else it chafed in two against the side of the boat when your fish went under——'

'My God, the fight you've put up—to think he's got away!'

It was 11.30 on Monday night—32 hours since Moby Don had first struck my line.

I looked at the line now, hanging limp and empty. And I suddenly realised that I was not disappointed. Instead, I felt a curious sense of relief, then of elation. Moby Don and I had waged a great battle. I had fought him with everything I had, but he was too much for me. As he deserved, he had won. Yes, he had won the right to be out there in the ocean, swimming free—and he had taught me that some things in Nature are still unconquerable by man.

The Husky— Hero of the Arctic

Laurie York Erskine

The husky's boundless vitality and unshakeable devotion have helped to make life and civilisation possible in the frozen North

Of all the creatures on earth, one of the hardiest is the Eskimo sled-dog, commonly called the husky. There is no other breed of dog which has perished in such great numbers in the service of mankind.

Until recent years, the husky provided the only means of overland transportation throughout the 2 million square miles of North America that stretch from the 60th parallel to within 500 miles of the North Pole; and in the largest part of that area he is still man's sole means of locomotion. Without the husky, explorers, pioneer traders, prospectors and engineers could never have developed the rich fur and mineral resources of the North. Today doctors, missionaries and the Royal Canadian Mounted Police still depend almost entirely on the traditional method of dog-team transportation.

Among the first necessities flown in to the chain of weather stations now being jointly maintained by the United States and Canada in the Arctic were teams of sled-dogs, so that the weather crews can hunt fresh meat and reach help if they need it.

This dog is called a husky not because of unusual strength but because early traders coined the name as a short form of the word Eskimo. Today it is loosely applied to any kind of dog that draws a sled, but it rightly belongs to only three breeds: the malemute of western Alaska; the Siberian husky, which was taken to North America by the Russians when they occupied Alaska; and the pure strain of the original breed which lives in northern Canada.

A typical husky of this original breed stands about 25 in. high and is about 44 in. long from the tip of his nose to the base of his bushy tail, which curls proudly over his back. His weight ranges from 60 to 100 lb. The female is slightly smaller and lighter, but both are built for hard pulling, with deep, wide chests, thick, muscular necks and iron-hard legs. Their tough, padded feet can take punishment on jagged rock and broken ice that would split the hoofs of a horse. The husky's coat is a dense growth of coarse hair 4–6 in. long. Under it is another coat of oily wool 2 or 3 in. thick. This double covering enables the husky to endure great cold, even 50 degrees below zero, without needing shelter.

The true husky never barks, but gives an eerie, long-drawn howl which, combined with his shaggy coat, sharp face and slanting black eyes, makes people think he is a domesticated wolf or a half-breed 'wolf-dog'. Actually, although the wolf and the husky spring from the same family tree, they branched off in different directions thousands of years ago. Today the wolf is the husky's bitter enemy. So great is this aversion that, even when starving, the dog will not eat wolf flesh.

However, huskies will mate with wolves. Sometimes a wolf bitch will lure a male dog to break away and follow her; but she always leads him back to the wolf pack, which promptly kills him. The female husky is more fortunate. If male wolves court her, they invariably let her return to camp unharmed.

A husky may come into the world at any time of the year as one of a litter of from six to eight pups. In winter the mother pulls her weight in the traces up to the day her puppies are born, and from her warm body they emerge into a temperature that hovers between 20 and 60 degrees below zero. As a rule the Eskimo will build the mother a snow kennel. If she must nest in the snow, only a few of her litter survive.

Most huskies pull a great deal more than their own weight. Loaded for the start of a trip, the average Eskimo sled weighs about 1100 lb., and is usually drawn by a team of from 12 to 15 dogs. As long as he can move from one good hunting ground to another, the nomadic Eskimo lives well. If he cannot move, he perishes, so his life depends on the faithfulness and efficiency of his dogs. He will seldom part with them at any price, and will frequently risk his life for them. Many an Eskimo has died trying to free his dogs when thin ice has broken under a heavy sled.

The Eskimo trains the pups by putting them, one or two at a time, into a team of veterans. The novice pup will be about eight months old, and he finds that the seasoned old-timers are tough teachers. For years they have toiled together as a team, but all will fight fiercely for a lion's share of the food, and they carry on an unending competition for the favours of the females.

This hard-bitten crew is harnessed to the sled in what is known as the 'fan hitch'. From the front of the sled runs a stout walrus- or seal-hide pull-rope about 6 ft long. Each dog is hitched to this separately by a raw-hide tug line about 12 ft long. Thus, when the team starts pulling, the dogs at the ends of their tug lines are abreast of each other in a fanwise formation. Compared with the single tandem hitch, which we generally see in pictures, this seems clumsy, but it has sound practical advantages. For one thing, it is the only method by which more than eight animals can be handily controlled.

The young husky will probably first find himself hitched beside a cantankerous veteran. This is the 'boss dog'. He can outfight any other member of the team and is always ready to prove it. His job is to see that every husky pulls its full weight and obeys the driver's commands, and he runs tirelessly back and forth behind the formation, bounding over the tug lines and unmercifully nipping shirkers.

The lead dog, chosen for character and intelligence, works with a quiet determination that holds the rest of the team together. Some of the best lead dogs are bitches, for the female often shows a keener intelligence than the male and gets better support from the boss dog. A good leader reacts to its master's voice with almost human understanding and will frequently make wise decisions of its own. It will often feel out thin ice before its master does and veer the team away from danger. Sometimes it can lead the team back to base when the driver has completely lost his bearings.

Food is the dog's greatest incentive because it is always scarce. The dog needs rich fats, muscle-building meat and many vitamins, all of which are concentrated in the flesh of the Arctic seal—the Eskimo's staff of life. A tired team will often dash forward without any visible reason, only to arrive

A team of huskies basking in the summer sun near Thule in Greenland. An Eskimo, whose life depends on his dogs, will risk his life to save them. They are normally affectionate and friendly, but can be ferocious when hungry; their sense of smell is so sharp that they can detect a seal hole—and hence food—several miles off.

at a seal hole several miles away. A veteran Hudson's Bay trader declares that once, when his food had run out and he was following the coastline in search of fresh meat, his dogs veered inland against all he could do to control them and led him to a herd of caribou 12 miles away. This ability to discover food is probably due to a keen sense of smell, aided by the Arctic atmosphere, which will sometimes carry a scent for miles.

In the two months of Arctic summer, when the Eskimos turn their dogs loose to fend for themselves, the huskies range along the shoreline eating shrimps, mussels, birds' eggs and dead things cast up by the tide, or they scatter inland and run down hares and lemmings. This scanty diet reduces them to such a state of starvation that they gladly come back to camp when the weather turns cold, knowing they can count on a feast of rich walrus meat.

Much of the husky's reputation for ferocity is due to his generally famished condition. Well fed and well treated, he is affectionate and friendly. Goaded by hunger, however, huskies put up a fearsome show of snarling and snapping at feeding time, and have a dangerous habit of hurling themselves upon any human being who stands between them and their food. This can be fatal, for a fur-clad human being flopping about on the snow can be easily mistaken for a seal by a famished and excited dog. Then the whole pack may set upon the victim. The wife of one of the Canadian Mounties was killed in this way.

The husky more than makes up for his occasional lapses by extraordinary devotion and self-sacrifice. Under ordinary conditions he will cover 25 miles a day at the rate of six or seven miles an hour, and hardly feel it. When the sledding is really tough, he will outstrip almost anything that can be imagined in the way of endurance.

Sub-zero gales that lash the dogs with drifting sand and snow will sometimes freeze their faces so severely that the dogs have to be destroyed. When the thermometer falls under 50 below zero, the lungs of a panting dog become frost-bitten if he is driven too hard, causing haemorrhages that choke him. If the snow is slushy it packs between the dog's toes and forms hard balls of ice that cripple him. Thoughtful drivers make him boots of raw-hide or canvas, but while these protect his feet, they hamper his footing, making the pulling much harder. In spite of such hardships, a team of 15 huskies travelled 1300 miles in 85 days, bringing home a rescue party of the Mounted Police and hauling the last ten days of the journey without any food at all.

Realising how greatly the development of the North depends upon this indomitable dog, the Canadian Government now sends animal patholo-gists into the Arctic to study the huskies' needs and combat epidemics of rabies and distemper that used to kill them by the hundred. Closely co-operating with the Canadian Government's Northwest Terri-tories Administration, the Royal Canadian Mounted Police and the Hudson's Bay Company are teaching the Eskimos to feed their dogs a full ration all year round, to breed them for strength and intelligence, to have them inoculated against disease, and to isolate them when they fall sick.

In many settlements throughout the Arctic hundreds of white men and women are pioneering in a country which, 25 years ago, most people con-sidered uninhabitable by any but Eskimos. Steadily they are turning it into a new stronghold of civilisa-tion. But the first credit for anything they achieve must go to the faithful husky. By his boundless vitality and his unstinted devotion, it was he who first made it possible for white men to enter that land of long winters and hard sledding.

My War with the Ospreys

John Steinbeck

They stole his garden tools,
scattered debris about, and spurned the nest
he built for them; then the battle
between the author and the ospreys began

My war with the ospreys, like most wars, was largely accidental—and it is not over yet. The winter caused an uneasy truce, but hostilities may soon reopen, although I can find it in my heart to wish for peace, even friendship. I hope the ospreys, wherever they may be, will read this.

I shall go back to the beginning and set down my side of the affair, trying to be as fair as I possibly can.

Three years ago I bought a little place on a beauti-ful point of land near Sag Harbour, Long Island. Sag Harbour is a fishing town, inhabited by people who have been here a long time. Though we are not natives of the village, I believe that the people have accepted my wife, my two sons and me as citizens. With the ospreys, however, I have not only failed to make friends; I have, on the contrary, been insulted, have thrown down the gauntlet and had it accepted.

In the upper branches of a half-dead oak tree on the very tip of our point, there was, when I took possession, a tattered lump of rubbish which looked like an unmade bed. 'That's an osprey's nest,' a native of the village told me. 'They come back every year. I remember that nest since I was a little boy.'

'They build a messy nest,' I said.

'Messy, yes,' he said, 'but I doubt if I could design something the winds wouldn't blow out. It's darned good architecture from a staying point of view.'

Towards the end of May, to my delight, the ospreys came back from wherever they had been, and from the beginning they fascinated me. They are about the best fishermen in the world. They would coast along, hanging on the breeze perhaps 50 ft above the water; then suddenly their wings rose like the fins of a bomb and they arrowed down and nearly always came up with a fish. I soon became a habitual osprey watcher.

In time, two of my ospreys were nudged by love and began to install new equipment in the great nest on my point. They brought unusual material—reeds, pieces of wood, rake handles, strips of cloth, swatches of seaweed. One of them, so help me, brought a piece of two-by-four pine 3 ft long to put into the structure. They were very untidy builders; the ground under the tree was strewn with excess stuff that fell out.

I mounted a telescope on the sun porch and even trimmed some branches from intervening trees, and from then on those love-driven ospreys did not have a moment of privacy.

Then one morning the ospreys were gone. I walked out to the point and saw, sticking halfway out of their nest, the shaft and feathers of an arrow. Now Catbird, my younger son (he was eight at the time), is the archer of the family. I ran him down and gave him what-for in spite of his plaintive protests that he had not shot at the nest.

The birds did not come back. They were across the bay. I could see them through the telescope building an uneasy nest on top of a power transformer on a pole where they were definitely not wanted.

I took a ladder and climbed up to the nest on our point, and when I came down I apologised to Catbird. For in the nest I had found not only the arrow, but my bamboo garden rake, three T-shirts and a Plaza Hotel bath towel. Apparently nothing was too unusual for the ospreys to steal for their nest-building.

Now I must admit that I had been pleased and a little proud to have my own osprey nest. I had planned to observe the nestlings when they arrived. The empty nest on the point that summer was a matter of sorrow and perplexity to me. I went to my Audubon, and it told me the following:

'Osprey (fish hawk), length 21–24 in., wingspread 4½–6 ft, weight 3½ lb. . . . Provided they are not molested, ospreys will nest wherever there is a reasonably extensive body of clear water and some sort of elevated nest site. The birds are excellent watchdogs, driving off crows and other birds of prey. For this reason platforms on tall poles are often erected to encourage them to nest about homes and farmyards.'

It was in February 1956 that I asked myself: if people put up platforms on poles, why not build a nest so attractive as to win back my own birds? (The electricity company had meanwhile torn the nest off the transformer.)

In late winter I went to work. Climbing the oak tree, I cleaned away the debris of the old nest. Then I firmly wired in place, horizontally, a large wagon wheel. I cut dry pampas grass stalks and bound them in long faggots. With the freezing blasts of winter tearing at my clothes, I reascended the tree and wove the reeds into the spokes of the wheel until I had a nest which, if I had any oviparous impulses, I should have found irresistible.

After that I had trouble with the novel I was writing, since I had to rush constantly to the telescope to see whether my prospective tenants had returned. Finally, June 1 came and school broke up, and I put my boys on watch.

One morning Catbird charged into my study. 'Ospreys!' he shouted. 'Come running—ospreys!'

I rushed for my telescope. There were the ospreys, all right. But they were not settling into my beautiful nest. They were tearing it to pieces, lifting out the carefully bound reed pads, carrying them across the bay and propping them clumsily on top of the electricity company's transformer.

Of course my feelings were hurt. Why should I deny it? But on the heels of injury came anger. Those slipshod, larcenous birds, those ingrates, those—those ospreys. My eyes strayed to the shotgun that hangs over my fireplace, but before I could reach for it, a Machiavellian thought came to me.

I wanted to hurt the ospreys, yes. I wanted revenge on them. But by using number-four shot? No. I ached to hurt them as they had hurt me—in their feelings, psychologically.

I am an adept at psychological warfare. I declared the garage out of bounds to everyone. My novel came to a dead stop. Daily I worked in the garage, using pieces of chicken wire and a great deal of plaster of Paris. Then I asked my neighbour, Jack Ramsey, a very good painter, to come to my workshop. At the end of two days we emerged with our product: a life-size replica of a nesting whooping crane. It is my belief that there are only 37 of these rare and wonderful birds in the world. Well, this was the 38th.

Chuckling evilly, I hoisted the plaster bird up in the tree and wired her firmly in the nest. Her white body, black tail and brilliant red mask stood out magnificently against the sky. I went back to the sun porch and turned my telescope on the ospreys, who

Too young to leave its nest, this osprey flaps its wings to test them. Catching fish is as natural to ospreys as flying, but young birds often miss the first few times that they plunge for prey.

pretended to go about their nest-building on the transformer as though nothing had happened.

I knew what must be going on over there, though. Mrs Osprey was saying, 'Lord Almighty, George! Look who has moved into the place *you* didn't want. Why did I listen to you?'

I laughed to myself. These are the wounds that never heal; this is psychological warfare at its best.

Two days later my son Thom came running into my study. 'The nest!' he cried. 'Look at the nest!'

I bolted for the door. The ospreys in jealous rage were dive-bombing my whooping crane; but all they could accomplish was the breaking of their talons on the hard surface of the plaster. Finally they gave up and flew away, followed by my shouts of derision.

The ospreys have not attacked any more, but we have had other visitors. One morning I looked out of the window to see a rather stout lady in khaki trousers and a turtle-neck sweater creeping across my lawn on her hands and knees. Field glasses dangled from her neck, and she held a camera in front of her. When I went out to question her, she angrily waved me away.

'Go back,' she whispered hoarsely. 'Do you want her to fly away?'

The Coconut Palm—
Nature's Most Bountiful Tree

Gordon Gaskill

Like the proverbial horn of plenty,
this beautiful tree
bursts with the essentials of life

One night in the Philippines, I stood in a grove of great coconut palms with an old man who had spent his life tending them. 'If you could count those stars,' he told me, pointing to the sky, 'then you could count all the ways that coconuts serve us.'

Many people call it the tree of life, and indeed this strange palm is by far the most useful of all trees. What other tree is there that provides not only material to build an entire house, but most of the furnishings: chairs, beds, mattresses, carpets, brooms, cups, saucers—even soap and toothbrushes? That not only heats a house with fire and cools it with fans, but also lights it, with a coconut wick burning coconut oil in a coconut lamp?

The coconut palm provides clothes for the whole family. It gives a fisherman materials to build his boat and to equip it with sails, ropes, fishing lines and nets. It not only cooks food but provides the actual food to be cooked—as well as a variety of drinks. (A single good nut has as much protein as a 4 oz. steak.) You could live indefinitely on the tree's products. In industrialised nations, people use coconut-palm products every day—in factories, kitchens, cars and the manufacture of cigarettes— and new uses are constantly being found. Nearly 11 million acres are currently planted with these trees and some 25,000 million nuts are used every year.

Some argue that the coconut palm is not really a tree at all. It has no branches and no proper bark. In normal trees, the bark carries the vital sap; the coconut palm's sap rises through the whole trunk. While most tree trunks taper, the coconut's is the same diameter almost all the way up—though it always seems to have some curve or leaning. It has no growth rings either, but its age can be reckoned by a spiralling row of scars left by leaves that have fallen away—one scar a month. Most trees bear fruit only once a year, but at any given moment the coconut has 12 different crops on it, ranging from the opening flowers to the ripe nuts.

'But you don't understand . . .' I began. '*Will* you keep your voice down?' she rasped. 'Do you know what this is? The club will never believe me. If I don't get a picture of her, I'll kill you.'

Yes, we have had bird-watchers—lots of them. You see, our whooping crane can be sighted from a long way off. After a time they discovered the nature of the thing, but they would not listen to my explanation of the ruse. In fact, they became angry; not at the ospreys—where the blame rests—but at me.

No one can say I am unforgiving, though. I have taken my whooping crane down and restored the nest to its old beauty. Let us see whether this year the ospreys are big enough to let bygones be bygones.

279

The graceful coconut palm is one of the most bountiful trees known to man. With only a little ingenuity most of life's necessities can be derived from it—and some of life's luxuries too.

High at the top of the tree is its growing bud, its 'heart': a bundle of tightly packed, yellow-white, cabbage-like leaves the size of a man's forearm. If this is cut or even slightly damaged, the whole tree dies; but if the tree can be sacrificed, the heart makes a tasty treat, a 'millionaire's salad'.

The unopened flowers are protected by a canvas-like sheath. From this natural cloth, many rugged products are made: shoes, caps and even a kind of pressed helmet for soldiers. If the flowers are left to open, bees visit them, producing honey with a special tang; then tiny button-like nuts appear which ripen about 12 months later.

If the flowers are prevented from opening, many strange results can be obtained. Bind a clump of unopened flowers tightly, bend the clump over and bruise the tip, and it soon begins to 'weep' steady drops of sweet juice—up to a gallon a day. The cloudy brown liquid has no coconut taste at all. It is easily boiled down to a good syrup, then crystallised into a rich, dark sugar; or, left standing, it ferments quickly into a robust 'beer' with an alcoholic content of up to about 8 per cent. Called *toddy* in India and Ceylon, *tuba* in the Philippines and *tuwak* in Indonesia, it is a popular drink. After a few weeks it becomes a fine vinegar.

The nut itself has round it a thick husk, a packed mass of fibres called coir. Soaked in salt water, these fibres can be woven into strong twine or rope. The natural fibre is also used in padding and upholstery.

The shell of the coconut is a hard, fine-grained substance which can be carved into all kinds of lovely, intricate objects. Half a shell makes a good glass; with a handle it becomes a jug. Cut in various other ways it becomes a spoon, a knife handle, a toy, an ashtray, a button, a buckle, a lampshade—or even a teapot. From the shells a superb charcoal is also made, used not only for cooking-fires but in air filters in gas-masks, submarines and—recently—cigarette tips.

Carefully cut the nut open. A good five-month-old nut yields about two glasses of 'water'. Crystal clear, cool and sweet, it contains about two tablespoons of sugar, plus minerals and vitamins. It is also wonderfully pure and sterile. During the Second World War both Allied and Japanese military doctors found that in an emergency they could drip this coconut water, instead of sterile glucose solution, straight into a patient's veins.

As the nut ages, a jelly-like substance—the nutmeat—begins to form inside. At about 12 months, this meat becomes firm. It is possible to eat a little of it raw, but it is too rich for a steady diet.

In coconut country, the nutmeat is scraped into a pulpy mass and squeezed through a cloth. The 'milk' or 'cream' that comes through is used for sauces and other food. Heated, it yields oil for cooking, lamp fuel and lotions or, treated with ashes, soap.

For commercial use, the rounded nutmeats are cut in half and dried. Shredded, the meat is used in sweets, cakes and pies. But the vast bulk—$3\frac{1}{2}$ million tons a year, called 'copra'—is processed for its oil. The cake residue is used for cattle fodder.

There seems to be no end to the uses of the oil. Rich in glycerines, it is used in quick-lathering shampoos and soaps, shaving cream and toothpaste, lotions, lubricants, hydraulic fluid, paints, synthetic rubber, ice-cream and plastics. One of its greatest markets is in India. Along the Malabar coast, where coconut palms are abundant, people have cooked with the oil for centuries.

For the rest of the tree, too, there are numerous uses. Thin strips of the fronds are woven into furnishings and clothing. The stiff midribs of the leaves make cooking skewers, kindling, arrows, or, bound into bundles, brooms and brushes. The trunk provides timber. It is somewhat fibrous inside, but the outer portions season into hard, dark-coloured 'wood'. Even the roots are used—for a dye, a mouthwash and a medicine for dysentery.

The coconut's life cycle is curiously human. Although it can begin bearing fruit at seven or eight years, it is usually around 12 or 13 (roughly the time of human puberty) before it reaches full production. Then it bears heartily until about 60, when the tree begins to fail, eventually dying at 80 or 90.

With improved growing methods, a coconut palm can average between 70 and 120 nuts a year, but most small farmers do not bother and get only 10–40 nuts a year per tree. Some do not even pick the nuts, but wait until they fall off by themselves. (Such people argue, with good reason, that tree-ripened nuts have more oil.)

The coconut palm demands plenty of sunlight and rain. South-east Asia seems to have been its original home, but today it grows on islands in the Pacific and Indian oceans, in the Caribbean, in East Africa and even further afield. How did it spread so widely?

Doubtless, man planted most existing palms, but they can spread themselves, too. Nuts fall from overhanging palms into the sea and float until they are cast up on some friendly beach. Some years ago, volcanic action threw up a new little island in the East Indies. When it cooled off enough for men to be able to visit it, they found 41 coconuts cast up on the virgin beach—and sprouting.

The palm can grow inland, but it has a mysterious affinity with the sea. Nearly all the coconuts on earth grow on islands, coasts or peninsulas.

Before the Second World War, Indonesia was the greatest single producer, but today the Philippines is the largest exporter, growing enough to give almost two nuts a year to every man, woman and child in the world.

In listing all the gifts we receive from this giant of the vegetable kingdom, I have omitted one: the gift of beauty. As wind stirs the feathery coconut fronds, they rustle overhead with a drowsy, pleasant murmur and make ever-changing patterns against the sea or sky.

When the air is still, the palms become tall ballet dancers, arms poised in a swirl of graceful curves. A tropical sunset with white beach and blue sea is always a scene of great beauty, but doubly so when coconut palms frame the picture. No tree on earth is so useful, none more beautiful.

PART FOUR
WORLDS WITHOUT END

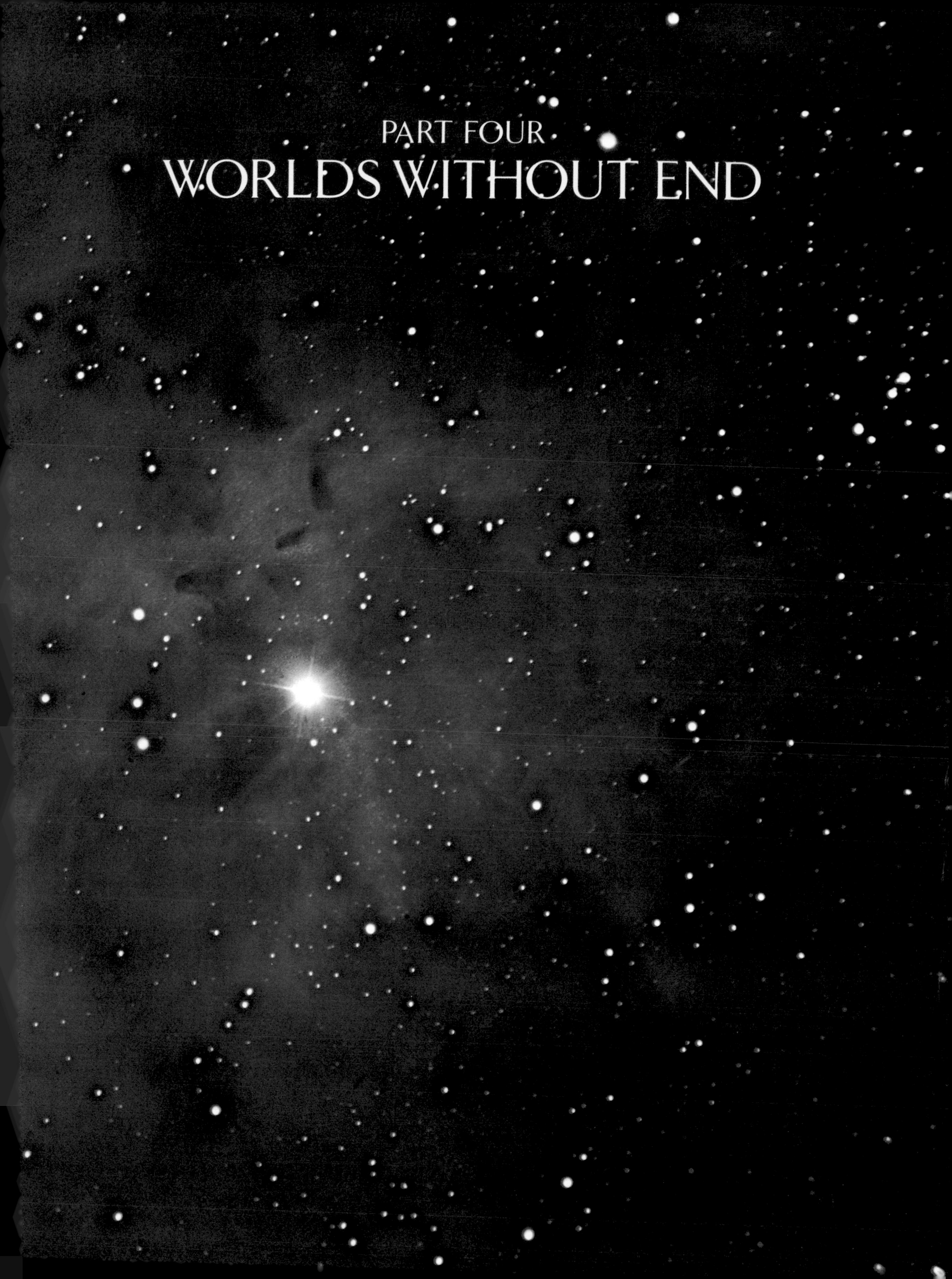

Sun, Moon and Planets

We stand on the threshold of a great new age of exploration, as one of
mankind's oldest dreams is fast becoming a reality. Freed at last
from the shackles of gravity, men and machines
from Earth are setting forth to
explore neighbouring worlds in our Solar System.
Yesterday's science fiction is today's accomplished fact

The Thing that hit us from Outer Space

Wolfgang Langewiesche

*Most meteors entering the Earth's atmosphere
burn up in it. Only the biggest reach
the Earth—sometimes with dramatic results*

On the high plains of Arizona near the Grand Canyon, just south of the Painted Desert, there is a strange wonder to be seen: the Meteor Crater, where the Earth was hit by a thing that came from space.

A 6 mile access road runs from U.S. route 66 over the dry, empty plain, and there it is: a hole in the ground, almost a mile across and 570 ft deep—nearly deep enough to hide the GPO Tower.

Something came from space, hit here, and in one second made the hole. The thing was nickel-iron, and it was huge: perhaps about as big and heavy as an ocean liner filled solidly with iron.

It did not simply drop; it *flew* in. It came out of the northern sky in nearly level flight, more orbiting than falling. Then it dipped down. Some think the thing hit as one solid mass of iron. Others think it may have travelled through space as a cluster of iron boulders, flying in close formation. Certainly it pushed ahead of itself a mass of white-hot glowing air, a 'plasma' several thousand degrees hot, more brilliant than the Sun; and when it hit, it *hit*. The hole it made, through layer upon layer of solid rock, was originally more than 1000 ft deep. Some chunks of the iron probably went 1500 ft into the Earth. It happened perhaps 20,000 years ago. Since then, the hole has partly filled up with loose rock fallen from the steep walls.

But where is all the rock that used to fill this hollow? Where is the alleged huge mass of iron?

When the iron mass hit (at several thousand miles per hour) and was instantly stopped, it just as instantly got hot all through; so hot that much of it may have vaporised, just as a high-speed bullet does when it hits armour-plating. It turned into an iron-steam, you might say. It did not merely squash the rocks down or push them aside; it was a bomb, it exploded. The iron went down into the ground and then blew everything sky-high, itself included.

By atom-bomb standards, it was a $5\frac{1}{2}$ megaton bomb. There was certainly a mushroom cloud. It consisted in part of vaporised iron, and as it cooled off there fell from it an iron rain. Drops of this have been found by dragging magnets over the desert. It looks like caviare. Substantial chunks of meteoritic iron, some weighing half a ton, have also been found.

And some of the iron did go on into the ground and stay there. In 1902 a mining engineer from Philadelphia, Daniel Moreau Barringer, heard that there was an amazing hole, and that the country

A mass of iron 200 ft in diameter and probably weighing a million tons may have punched this enormous meteor crater into the desert near Canyon Diablo in north-east Arizona. Some 30 tons of meteoritic iron have been unearthed within a 6 mile radius of the crater. The largest single piece, with a heat-blackened crust and silvery interior, weighs 1400 lb. and is now displayed in a museum at the crater's north rim.

around it was strewn with rock and meteorites. At that time, meteor craters were unknown on Earth; any crater was considered volcanic. But Barringer jumped to the correct conclusion that this one at least was meteoritic. He dug holes just outside the crater and found chunks of meteoritic iron containing 7 per cent nickel. Convinced, he filed mining claims on the land and spent much of his life and fortune trying to lift its treasure.

Barringer started by sinking shafts from the bottom of the crater. Water and quicksand stopped him. He drilled. The drill found solid rock, but no

iron. Up to that time he had assumed that the object had fallen straight down from the sky; 'orbiting' was not thought of in those days. But now he reasoned: if the meteorite had come in on the slant, then its iron would be lodged not under the crater but under the rim. In 1919 he had another hole drilled, down from the rim. The drill found meteorite fragments; but at 1376 ft it got stuck in a cluster of meteorites and could not be moved. In 1928 he founded a company that sank a shaft half a mile south of the crater. It was stopped by underground water. Barringer, deeply depressed, died in 1929.

With what remained of the money, his sons had geophysical surveys conducted. They showed something down there that was magnetic, electrically conductive and extra heavy. They drilled two more holes; the drills were blocked by iron too hard to drill, too big to push aside. They had to stop; but they did not give up completely.

285

There is certainly a mass of iron down there—solid metal, at least 100,000 tons, and more likely millions of tons. It is valuable because of its nickel, but so far it has been impossible to mine. Even if a shaft did reach the treasure, the hunks would be difficult to cut up and hoist. The Barringer family now leases the crater as a tourist sight.

More and more people come to see the wonder, because here, plain to the inexperienced eye, is evidence that star-stuff visits us on Earth. What does it mean? To find out, you have to turn to the meteor men. You might call them early spacemen. Long before astronauts and space probes began to stick their noses into stardust, these men studied space with the eyes and ears of telescope and radio. When you piece together what the learned men have written, you begin to understand meteor impact. It makes sense and becomes orderly, like the rest of the Universe.

Professor Fletcher Watson, of Harvard University, tells us that each day at least 1000 million meteors strike the Earth's atmosphere. Most of them, he says, are no bigger than a pin-head and burn up in the air. Their material—about 5 tons a day—is scattered over the planet as dust. Only four or five meteors a day are large enough to pass through the atmosphere and fall on the Earth. There are now over 50 known and acknowledged meteor craters located in Europe, Australia, Arabia, Africa, the Argentine, Siberia and North America.

The real land of craters is eastern Canada. One reason is that the Canadian shield is mostly a granite surface, extremely rigid; even very old craters have not yet been covered over or deformed. Also, the Canadian Air Force has mapped the country; many 'fossil' craters show up only from the air.

Scientist Robert Dietz, formerly an oceanographer at the Navy Electronics Laboratory in San Diego, California, says there must be many more impact sites than we now know. The Moon is covered with meteor craters. The Earth must have taken at least the same bombardment from space. Where are the craters? His answer: do not look only for craters, because on Earth the raised rims weather away, the low places fill with sand and mud, and the rocks bend and heave, rise and sink.

But one effect lasts: a meteor hit sends a shock-wave into the Earth, and this does things to rock that nothing else will do. It cracks rock into 'shatter cones', shaped like ice-cream cones, from a fraction of an inch up to many feet in size. A shatter cone, when struck with a hammer, breaks up into smaller shatter cones. By way of proof, shatter cones have been produced experimentally by shooting into rocks a 'shaped charge'—a front-directed explosive charge in an armour-piercing projectile. Shatter cones are now revealing many old meteor hits.

Shatter cones have solved, according to Dietz, the puzzle of the Vredefort Ring in South Africa. This is not a crater. On the contrary, it is a raised dome of granite, 26 miles in diameter. This, in turn, is surrounded by a further circular pattern of rock folds 130 miles in diameter. Most geologists have doubted that this was a meteor hit, because there was neither a crater nor hunks of iron. But Dietz urged a South African geologist to look for shatter cones. Sure enough, they were there.

Dietz is convinced that a small asteroid, a mile or so in diameter, plunged deep into the Earth here. It opened a crater 10 miles deep and 26 miles wide. The explosion peeled back rock layers like petals of a flower. If the Barringer Thing was a $5\frac{1}{2}$ megaton bomb, this one was $1\frac{1}{4}$ million megatons! The whole world must have wobbled. All this happened a very long time ago. Since then, Dietz thinks, the granite deep down has reacted to the removal of all that weight. It has slowly welled up, filled the crater and bulged up into a dome.

John Reynolds, of the department of physics of the University of California, describes the detective work done on meteorites. Everything about them is studied: chemistry, atomic structure, metallurgy, flight path, etc. Everything is a clue. The nickel-iron shows signs of having cooled and solidified from the molten stage very slowly—this means it must come from within the interior of a fairly large planet. The crystalline structure of the metal shows signs of sudden release of pressure. This means that the planet exploded. The metal contains small amounts of Helium 4. This isotope forms simply by lapse of time, and thus it indicates the time when the meteorite was formed. Scientists have even investigated meteorites—the ones that are rock, not iron—for signs of life. So far they have found no clear-cut yes or no.

John Reynolds says that the age of the meteorite material is about the same as the age of the Earth. The chemical elements of the rest of the Solar System are the same as those of the Earth. It appears that the planets of our Solar System all crystallised at about the same time—4600 million years ago; and that not very long before that, the chemical elements themselves formed 'from primordial matter'.

It is scientifically stated and rather big-scale on the time-and-distance factor, but it still sounds not very different from Genesis.

Next the Planets

Arthur C. Clarke

Soon man will have real knowledge of the planets. Will he find that the Earth is just one of many life-bearing worlds circling the Sun?

Until the advent of radar and space probes, everything we knew about the planets had been painfully gathered, over a period of about a century and a half, by astronomers with inadequate instruments, hastily sketching details of a tiny, trembling disc glimpsed during moments of good sighting. Such moments—when the atmosphere is stable and the image undistorted—may add up to only a few hours in a lifetime of observing.

In these circumstances, it would be amazing if we had acquired any reliable knowledge about planetary conditions; it is safest to assume that we have not. We are still in the same position as the medieval cartographers, with their large areas of '*Terra Incognita*' and their 'Here Be Dragons', except that we may have gone too far in the other direction—'Here Be *No* Dragons'. Our ignorance is so great that we have no right to make either assumption.

As proof of this, let me remind you of some horrid shocks the astronomers have received recently, when things of which they were quite sure turned out to be simply not true. The most embarrassing example is the rotation of Mercury: until a couple of years ago, everyone was perfectly certain that it always kept the same face towards the Sun, so that one side was eternally dark, the other eternally baked. Now, radar observations indicate that it turns on its axis every 59 days; it has sunrise and sunset, like any respectable world. Nature seems to have played a dirty trick on several generations of patient astronomers.

Einstein once said: 'The good Lord is subtle, but He is not malicious.' The case of Mercury casts some doubt on this dictum. What about Venus? You can find, in the various reference books, rotation periods for Venus ranging all the way from 24 hours to the full value of the year, 225 days. But as far as I know, not one astronomer ever suggested that Venus would present the extraordinary case of a planet with a day longer than its year; and, of course, it *would* be the one example which there was no possible way of checking, until the advent of radar. Is this subtlety—or malice?

Look at the Moon. Five years ago, everyone was certain that its surface was either soft dust or hard lava. If the two schools of thought had been on speaking terms, they would at least have agreed that there were no alternatives. Then Luna 9 and Surveyor 1 landed on the Moon—and what did they find? Good, honest dirt.

These are by no means the only examples of recent shocks and surprises. There are the craters of Mars; the unexpectedly high temperature beneath the clouds of Venus; the gigantic radio emissions from Jupiter; the complex organic chemicals in certain meteors; and the clear signs of extensive activity on the surface of the Moon. Now Mars seems to be turning inside-out: the ancient, dried-up sea-beds may be a myth, for it looks as if the dark *Maria* are highlands, not lowlands as we had always thought.

The negative point I am making is that we really know nothing about the planets. The positive one is that a tremendous amount of reconnaissance—the essential prelude to *manned* exploration—can be carried out from Earth orbit. It is probably no exaggeration to say that a good orbiting telescope could give a view of Mars at least as clear as did Mariner 4; and it would be a view infinitely more valuable—a continuous coverage of the whole visible face, not a snapshot of a small percentage of the surface.

Nevertheless, there are many tasks that can best be carried out by unmanned spacecraft. Among these is one that, though of great scientific value, is of even more profound psychological importance. I refer to the production of low-altitude oblique photographs. It is no disparagement of the wonderful Ranger, Luna and Surveyor coverage to remind you that what suddenly made the Moon a real place, and not merely an astronomical body up there in the sky, was the famous photograph of the Crater of Copernicus from Lunar Orbiter 2. When the newspapers called it the picture of the century, they were expressing a universally felt truth. This was the photograph that first proved to our emotions what our minds already knew but had never really believed —that Earth is not the only world. The first high-definition, oblique photographs of Mars, Mercury and the satellites of the giant planets will have a similar impact, bringing our mental images of these places into sharp focus for the first time.

The old astronomical writers had a phrase that has gone out of fashion but that may well be revived: the plurality of worlds. Yet, of course, every world is itself a plurality. To realise this, one has only to ask: how long will it be before we have learnt everything that can be known about the planet Earth? It

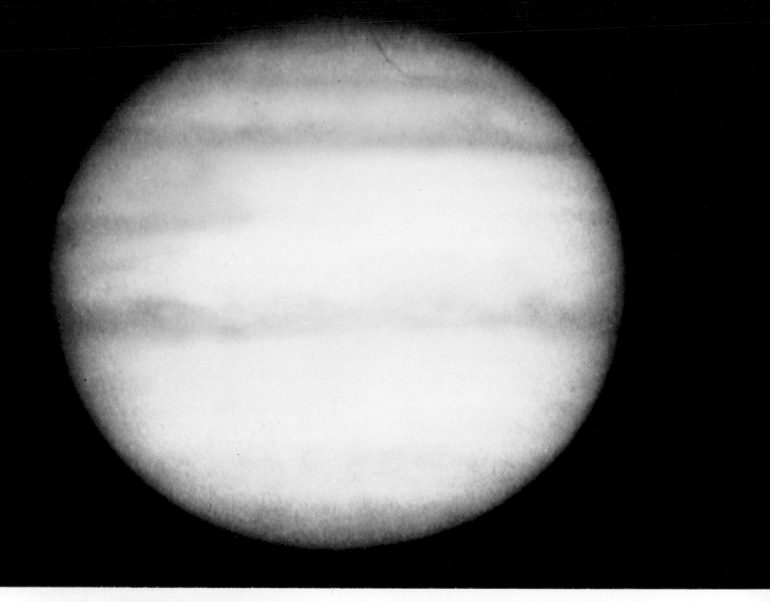

*Jupiter, the giant planet of the Solar System. Its mass
is 300 times greater than the Earth's, and 2½ times
that of all the other planets combined. Its surface
is always veiled in clouds, but in the last few years some
astronomers have begun to think that it may be
teeming with a rich variety of life.*

will be several centuries before terrestrial geology,
oceanography and geophysics are closed, surprise-
free subjects.

Consider the multitude of environments that
exists here on Earth, from the summit of Everest to
the depths of the Marianas Trench—from high noon
in Death Valley to midnight at the South Pole. We
may have equal variety on the other planets, with
all that this implies for the existence of life. It is
amazing how often this elementary fact is overlooked and how often a single observation, or even
a single extrapolation from a preliminary observation based on a provisional theory, has been promptly
applied to a whole world.

It is possible, of course, that Earth has a greater
variety of more complex environments than any
other planet. Like a jet-age tourist 'doing Europe' in
a week, we may be able to wrap up Mars or Venus

with a relatively small number of landings. But I
doubt it, if only for the reason that the whole history
of astronomy teaches us to be cautious of any theory
purporting to show that there is something special
about Earth. In their various ways, the other planets
may have orders of complexity as great as ours. Even
the Moon—which seemed a promising candidate
for geophysical simplicity less than a decade ago—
is already unleashing an avalanche of surprises.

We will encounter the operation of Haldane's Law
—that the Universe is not only stranger than we
imagine, but stranger than we *can* imagine—more
and more frequently as we move away from home.
As we prepare for this move, it is high time that we
faced up to one of the more shattering realities of
the astronomical situation. For all practical purposes, we are still as geocentrically minded as if
Copernicus had never been born: to all of us, Earth
is the centre, if not of the Universe, at least of the
Solar System.

Well, I have news for you. There is really only one
planet that matters; and that planet is not Earth
but Jupiter. My esteemed colleague Isaac Asimov

Even through a small telescope, the rings of Saturn—
which are unique in the Solar System—make the planet
one of the most beautiful in the night sky. The rings,
which are very thin, vary in width from 22,000 to
36,000 miles and are composed of free-travelling particles.
The innermost is 7000 miles from Saturn's equator.

summed it up very well when he remarked: 'The Solar System consists of Jupiter plus debris.' Even spectacular Saturn does not count; it has less than a third of Jupiter's enormous mass—and Earth is a hundred times smaller than Saturn! Our planet is an unconsidered trifle, left over after the main building operations were completed. This is quite a blow to our pride, but there may be much worse to come, and it is wise to prepare for it. Jupiter may also be the *biological*, as well as the *physical*, centre of gravity of the Solar System.

This, of course, represents a complete reversal of views within a couple of decades. Not long ago, it was customary to laugh at the naïve ideas of the early astronomers—Sir John Herschel, for example —who took it for granted that all the planets were teeming with life. This attitude is certainly over-optimistic; but it no longer seems as simple-minded as the opinion, found in the popular writings of the 1930's, that ours might be the only solar system and, hence, the only abode of life in the entire Galaxy.

The pendulum has indeed swung—perhaps for the last time; for in another few decades, we should know the truth. The discovery that Jupiter is quite warm and has precisely the type of atmosphere in which life is believed to have arisen on Earth may be the prelude to the most significant biological findings of this century. Carl Sagan and Jack Leonard put it well in their book *Planets*: 'Recent work on the origin of life and the environment of Jupiter suggests that it may be more favourable to life than any other planet, not excepting the Earth.'

The extraordinary colour changes in the Jovian atmosphere—in particular, the behaviour of that Earth-sized, drifting apparition, the Great Red Spot —hint at the production of organic materials in enormous quantities. Where this happens, life may follow inevitably, given a sufficient lapse of time.

Contrary to popular thinking, gravity on Jupiter would not pose insurmountable difficulties. The Jovian gravity is only $2\frac{1}{2}$ times that of the Earth

289

—a condition to which even terrestrial animals (rats in centrifuges) have adapted. The Jovian equivalent of fish would care little about gravity because it has virtually no effect in a marine environment.

Dr James Edson, late of NASA, once remarked, 'Jupiter is a problem for my grandchildren.' He may have been wildly optimistic. The zoology of a world outweighing 300 Earths could be the full-time occupation of mankind for the next 1000 years.

It also appears that Venus, with its extremely dense, furnace-hot atmosphere, may be an almost equally severe yet equally promising challenge. There now seems little doubt that average temperature is around 700°F; but this does not, as many have prematurely assumed, rule out all possibility of life—even life of the kind that exists on Earth.

There may be little mixing of the atmosphere and, hence, little exchange of heat between the poles and the equator on a planet that revolves as slowly as Venus. At high latitudes or great altitudes—and Venusian mountains have now been detected by radar—it may be cool enough for liquid water to exist. (Even on Earth, remember, the temperature difference between the hottest and the coldest points is almost 300°F.) What makes this more than idle speculation is the exciting discovery, by the Russian space probe Venera 4, of oxygen in the planet's atmosphere. This extremely reactive gas combines with so many materials that it cannot occur in the free state—unless it is continuously renewed by vegetation. Free oxygen in the atmosphere is an almost infallible indicator of life.

On the other hand, it is also possible that we shall discover no trace of extra-terrestrial life, past or present, on any of the planets. This would be a great disappointment; but even such a negative finding would give us a much sounder understanding of the conditions in which living creatures are likely to evolve. This in turn would clarify our views on the distribution of life in the Universe as a whole. However, it seems much more probable that long before we can certify the Solar System as sterile, the communications engineers will have settled this ancient question—in the affirmative.

For that is what the exploration of space is really all about; and this is why many people are afraid of it, though they may give other reasons, even to themselves. It may be just as well that there are no contemporary higher civilisations in our immediate vicinity; the cultural shock of direct contact might be too great for us to survive. But by the time we have cut our teeth on the Solar System, we should be ready for such encounters.

Do not for a moment doubt that we shall one day head out for the stars—if, of course, the stars do not reach us first. I think I have read most of the arguments proving that interstellar travel is impossible. They are latter-day echoes of Professor Newcomb's paper proving that heavier-than-air flight was an impossibility. The logic and the mathematics are impeccable; the premises wholly invalid. The more sophisticated are roughly equivalent to proving that dirigibles cannot break the sound barrier.

In the first years of this century, the pioneers of astronautics were demonstrating that flight to the Moon and nearer planets was possible, though with great difficulty and expense, by using chemical propellants. But even then, they were aware of the promise of nuclear energy and hoped that it would be the ultimate solution. They were right.

Today, it can likewise be shown that various conceivable, though currently quite impracticable, applications of nuclear and medical techniques could bring at least the closer stars within the range of exploration. I would warn any sceptics who may point out the marginal nature of these techniques that, at this very moment, there are appearing simultaneously on the twin horizons of the infinitely large and the infinitely small, unmistakable signs of a breakthrough into a new order of creation. To quote some remarks made recently by a Nobel laureate in physics, Professor C. F. Powell: 'It seems to me that the evidence from astronomy and particle physics that I have described makes it possible that we are on the threshold of great and far-reaching discoveries. I have spoken of processes that, mass for mass, would be at least a thousand times more productive of energy than nuclear energy. . . . It seems that there are prodigious sources of energy in the interior regions of some galaxies, and possibly in the quasars, far greater than those produced by the carbon cycle occurring in the stars . . . and we may one day learn how to employ them.' If Professor Powell's surmise is correct, others may already have learnt, on worlds older than ours. So it would be foolish, indeed, to assert that the stars must be forever beyond our reach.

More than half a century ago, the great Russian pioneer Tsiolkovsky wrote these moving and prophetic words: 'The Earth is the cradle of the mind—but you cannot live in the cradle for ever.' Now, as we enter the second decade of the age of space, we can look still further into the future.

The Earth is, indeed, our cradle, which we are now about to leave. And the Solar System will be the kindergarten of future generations.

The Lunar Colony

Arthur C. Clarke

Before man explores the
Solar System, he will first have to build
permanent bases on the Moon

The cost of maintaining one man on the Moon might be in the region of £20 million a year. In the face of such statistics, it may seem ridiculous to talk of establishing large bases—and even colonies—on the Moon.

But this is looking at the problem through the wrong end of the telescope. It would be more accurate to say that the huge cost makes it mandatory to set up a lunar base, so that it becomes self-supporting in the shortest possible time. The present vast expense of lunar exploration is largely due to the need to carry propellants for the round trip, and the fact that all expendables (food, water, air) must be supplied from Earth. The Pilgrim Fathers would not have done too well if they had had to send the *Mayflower* back to Europe when they became short of breath.

Photographs transmitted back to Earth several hours before the Moon's sunset show the shadow Surveyor 1 cast on the lunar surface. These pictures consist of photographs of small areas, pieced together by NASA scientists to form photo-mosaics of larger areas.

Low, rounded hills, similar in shape to many found in the English Downs, form the horizon north-east of Surveyor 7's landing site. In the foreground, some 18 ft from the camera, is a rock-filled crater about 5 ft wide. Towards the upper right, almost 1200 ft from the camera, is a rock about 20 ft across. Opposite the rock, in the left-hand corner (2100 ft away), is a crater approximately 200 ft in diameter.

Above: an almost vertical view from Apollo 10 of the edge of the Moon's Sea of Tranquillity, where Neil Armstrong and Edwin Aldrin became the first men to set foot on the Moon.

Right: a steep-walled crater on the far side of the Moon, seen from Apollo 10's lunar landing vehicle. Astronauts Stafford and Cernan made four orbits in the landing craft, and took it to within 9 miles of the Moon's surface.

The future of lunar (and, as we shall see later, Solar System) exploration therefore depends on our ability to find supplies of all kinds on the Moon. The most valuable substance of all—as it is on Earth, when in short supply—would be water.

It certainly exists on the Moon; the question is where, and in what form. The free, liquid state can be ruled out—at least near the surface—but ice may occur underground, for in caves where the solar heat never penetrates, the temperature is always far below freezing point. (Radio measurements indicate that only a few feet below the surface the temperature is constant at perhaps $-30°F$.) There are certain lunar formations—low domes—which may indicate the presence of permafrost. At the other extreme, if there are local hot spots, or not-quite-

extinct volcanoes, steam may be available, as well as power and useful chemicals.

These are the optimistic assumptions, which may be wrong. If the worst comes to the worst, it will be necessary to extract water from the minerals in which it occurs; straightforward heating would be sufficient in most cases. During daytime, unlimited quantities of heat can be collected by concave mirrors; however, the physical problem of handling

the amounts of rock involved would be formidable. Since water is 90 per cent oxygen, the two major necessities of life would be provided; but hydrogen would be almost equally important, since this is the best of all rocket fuels. Once it could be liquefied and stored, the economics of Earth–Moon space transportation would be revolutionised.

Beyond water and oxygen lies the much more complex problem of food. Perhaps by the time (around the turn of the century?) we are planning extensive lunar colonisation, the chemists may be able to synthesise any food from such basics as lime, phosphates, carbon dioxide, ammonia and water. This could be done now if expense was no object; it will *have* to be done, *economically*, within the next few decades, to feed Earth's exploding population.

An obvious alternative is soil-less, or hydroponic, farming, already widely used in locations where

The infertile face of the almost full Moon, photographed from Apollo 8, the first space mission to take men out of Earth-orbit. Such expeditions are preparing the way for the eventual colonisation of the Moon, and in 200 years time our satellite may be clothed in the green and blue colours of a fertile world.

land is at a premium; it has also been tried experimentally in the Antarctic and aboard nuclear submarines. Yet another is algae culture; both systems of food production would be ideally suited to the Moon, where there are 14 days of unbroken sunlight—and no bad weather. The plants would not only provide food but would also be an essential part of the life-support system, regenerating oxygen and recycling waste products, just as they do on Earth.

Another idea is more speculative, and I have yet to see it given serious scientific study. If it works, I am prepared to claim it as original; otherwise I shall hastily disown it.

We may be able to develop plants which can grow unprotected on the lunar surface; some desert-adapted forms on Earth give hints as to how this may be done. With a little help from terrestrial geneticists, a lunar flora could be designed; indeed, we may find one already there, which would save us a great deal of trouble. I am sure that I am not the only farmer's boy who felt his fingers itch when he saw the good earth pushed up by Surveyor 1.

Though such speculations may seem premature at the moment, the rate of build-up of the lunar bridgehead may depend upon concepts which today appear no less fantastic. Until we know just what is possible on the Moon and what its natural resources may be, we cannot tell whether its maximum future population will be a few score scientists occupying temporary, inflatable igloos, or millions of men living comfortable and, to them, quite normal lives in huge, totally enclosed cities. The greatest technical achievements of the next few centuries may well be in the field of planetary engineering, the reshaping of other worlds to suit human needs. Upon our own satellite, with Earth close at hand to help, we will learn the skills and techniques which may one day bring life to worlds as far apart as Pluto and Mercury.

The Moon will not only be a training ground for the other planets; it may be an essential stepping stone towards them. If rocket propellants can ever be manufactured there—and this could be done simply by electrolysing lunar water—it could become the key to the Solar System. Spaceships making any interplanetary journey would, on departure or arrival, refuel there. They would probably not land, but would orbit the Moon while specially developed, short-haul tankers brought fuel, and other locally produced supplies, up to replenish them for the remainder of their journey.

Improvements in technology never merely add together; they *multiply*, as the history of commercial aviation has shown. That story will be repeated in space; some of the advances which will make this possible may be: re-usable launch vehicles ('aerospaceplanes'); orbital rendezvous with specialised spacecraft tailored for each stage of the mission; refuelling in orbit; refuelling on the Moon; refuelling from the Moon; nuclear propulsion.

These are all things that can be anticipated, therefore, in accordance with past lessons; we can be sure that the really revolutionary factors are not on this list. (Gravity control? Matter transmission? At this stage, one guess is as good as another.) Nevertheless, the exploitation of the foreseeable techniques to their limit could result in truly commercial space transport being in sight by the end of this century. And perhaps 50 years from now, anyone should be able to afford a visit to the Moon at least once in his lifetime—perhaps to see grandchildren who, having been born under lunar gravity, can never come to Earth and have no particular desire to do so. To them it may seem a noisy, crowded, dangerous and, above all, *dirty* place.

It is strange to think that in a few more years any amateur astronomer with a good telescope will be able to see the lights of the first expeditions, shining where no stars could ever be, within the arms of the crescent Moon. Those lights will spread out over the new world, as they have covered the old; and in a few generations more, they will sometimes be a little hazy. The features near the edge of the lunar disc will no longer appear so crystal sharp in the telescopes of Earth; over the bitter protests of the astronomers and physicists, who now need a new home, the Moon will be acquiring an atmosphere.

Some 200 years from now there will be committees of earnest citizens fighting tooth and nail to save the last unspoilt vestiges of the lunar wilderness.

So You're Going to Mars?

Arthur C. Clarke

A journey to Mars may well be a common adventure in a few years' time: here is the kind of advice the would-be traveller may expect to be given

So you're going to Mars? That's still quite an adventure—though I suppose that in another ten years no one will think twice about it. It's hard to remember that the first ships reached Mars only half a century ago, and that our colony on the planet is less than 30 years old.

I suppose you've read all the tourist literature from the Department of Extraterrestrial Affairs. But there's a lot you won't learn just by reading, so here are some pointers. I won't say my information is right up to date—things change so rapidly, and it's a year since I got back from Mars myself; but on the whole, you'll find it reliable.

The cost of your passage varies considerably according to the relative position of Mars and Earth and, oddly enough, the shortest trips are the most expensive, since they involve the greatest changes of speed as you hop from one orbit to the other. In space, speed, not distance, is what costs money. The cheapest round-trip comes to about £12,500, and most of your fellow passengers will be engineers, scientists or administrators with a job to do on Mars.

I take it you passed the medical examination. The physical strain involved in space flight is negligible, but you'll be spending at least two months on the trip, and it would be a pity if your teeth or appendix started to misbehave.

You're probably wondering how you can possibly manage on your weight allowance. It can be done. Don't take any suits. Inside a spaceship there's no weather. All you'll want is ultra-lightweight tropical kit. When you get to Mars, you'll buy what you need there, and dump it when you leave. Take a camera by all means. There's a chance of some unforgettable shots as you leave Earth in the space liner and when you approach Mars. You can sell a good camera on Mars for five times its price here, and save yourself the cost of sending it home.

The ferry rocket will probably leave from the New Guinea field, two miles above sea level on top of the Orange Range. Why there? It's on the Equator, so a ship gets the full 1000 mph boost of the Earth's spin as it takes off, and there's the whole width of the Pacific for jettisoned fuel tanks to fall into. And if you've ever *heard* a spaceship taking off, you'll understand why the launching sites have to be a few hundred miles from civilisation.

There's really nothing to the blast-off, as long as you're in good health. You just lie down on the acceleration couch, put in your earplugs and relax. About a minute will pass before you'll feel the full strain of the opposition between the Earth's gravitational pull and the rocket's thrust. You *will* notice the noise immediately. It only lasts five minutes; then you'll be up in orbit and the engines will cut out.

There are no viewing ports on the ferry rockets. It takes about 30 minutes to reach the satellite space station, make the necessary steering corrections and match its speed. You'll know when that happens from the rather alarming clang as the air locks make contact. Then you can undo your safety belt and see what it's like being weightless. But hang on to the guide rope while passing through the air lock, and don't try to go flying around like a bird—you may injure yourself.

At Space Station One, which is where the ferries and the liners meet to transfer their cargoes, you'll spend all your time in the observation lounge; everyone does, no matter how many times he has been out in space. I won't attempt to describe that incredible view. In the 120 minutes the station takes to complete its orbit, you'll see the Earth wax from a thin crescent to a gigantic multi-coloured disc, then shrink again to a black shield eclipsing the stars. As you pass over the night side you'll see the lights of cities, like patches of phosphorescence—and the stars! You'll realise that you've never really seen them before.

You'll go aboard the liner when you've had your final medical check, and the steward will show you to the tiny, shelf-size cabin where you'll sleep for the next few months. If you're on one of the larger liners, there'll be about 100 passengers and a crew of 20—a self-contained community floating in a vacuum millions of miles from anywhere, kept alive in a bubble of plastic and metal.

It won't take you long to get used to the ship's gadgets. Handling liquids is the main skill to acquire. Oddly enough, taking a shower is quite simple; you do it in a sort of plastic cocoon, and a circulating air current carries the water out at the bottom. At first the absence of gravity may make sleeping difficult—you'll miss your accustomed weight. But the bunk covers have spring tensioning which is designed to prevent you from drifting out.

The breakaway of the liner from its satellite orbit is gentle. The ship will uncouple from the space station and drift a few miles away. When the atomic drive goes on you'll notice only the faintest of vibrations, and the liner's acceleration will be very gradual. But after a week it will have built up a colossal speed. Then the engines are cut and you carry on under momentum. You'll seem to be motionless—no more aware of your speed than you are now of the Earth's 66,000 mph round the Sun.

During your weeks in space there will be radio and television contact with Earth and Mars, so you'll be able to keep in touch with things—if, in fact, you want to. The ship will have a good library of micro-books. On my first trip, I spent a lot of time learning my way around the stars and looking at clusters and nebulae through a small telescope. Having the stars all round you is an experience you'll never forget.

One of the big moments comes when you realise that Mars has begun to show as a visible disc. The first feature you'll be able to see with the naked eye will be one of the polar caps, glittering like a tiny star on the edge of the planet. A few days later the dark areas—the so-called seas—will begin to appear and, in the week before landing, you'll get to know the planet's geography pretty well.

After the short braking period you'll drop down on Phobos, Mars' inner moon, which acts as a natural space station about 4000 miles above the planet's surface. When the ship has settled down into the landing cradle, the air lock will be coupled up and you'll go through a connecting tube into the port. Then you go inside the centrifuge—a little cabin on a rotating arm—and it will spin you up to half a gravity, or rather more than the weight Mars will give you when you land. This is so that you can practise using your legs again.

There are two ferry rockets in service from Phobos to Mars, each carrying 20 passengers. The descent takes about three hours. The ferries enter the atmosphere at over 5000 mph, and go halfway round Mars before they lose enough speed to land like ordinary aircraft. You'll land at Port Lowell, the largest settlement. The population is more than 20,000 now, I believe. Port Lowell has practically everything you'll find in a city on Earth. From the air, the inflated plastic domes look like a cluster of bubbles, a lovely sight when the sun catches them.

The planet Mars and its glistening polar ice-cap. According to the season, the ice-caps vary in size from about 2000 to 60 miles in diameter. The rest of Mars also shows seasonal changes, and the planet's surface is believed to consist mainly of desert areas and some regions perhaps covered with a lowly form of vegetation.

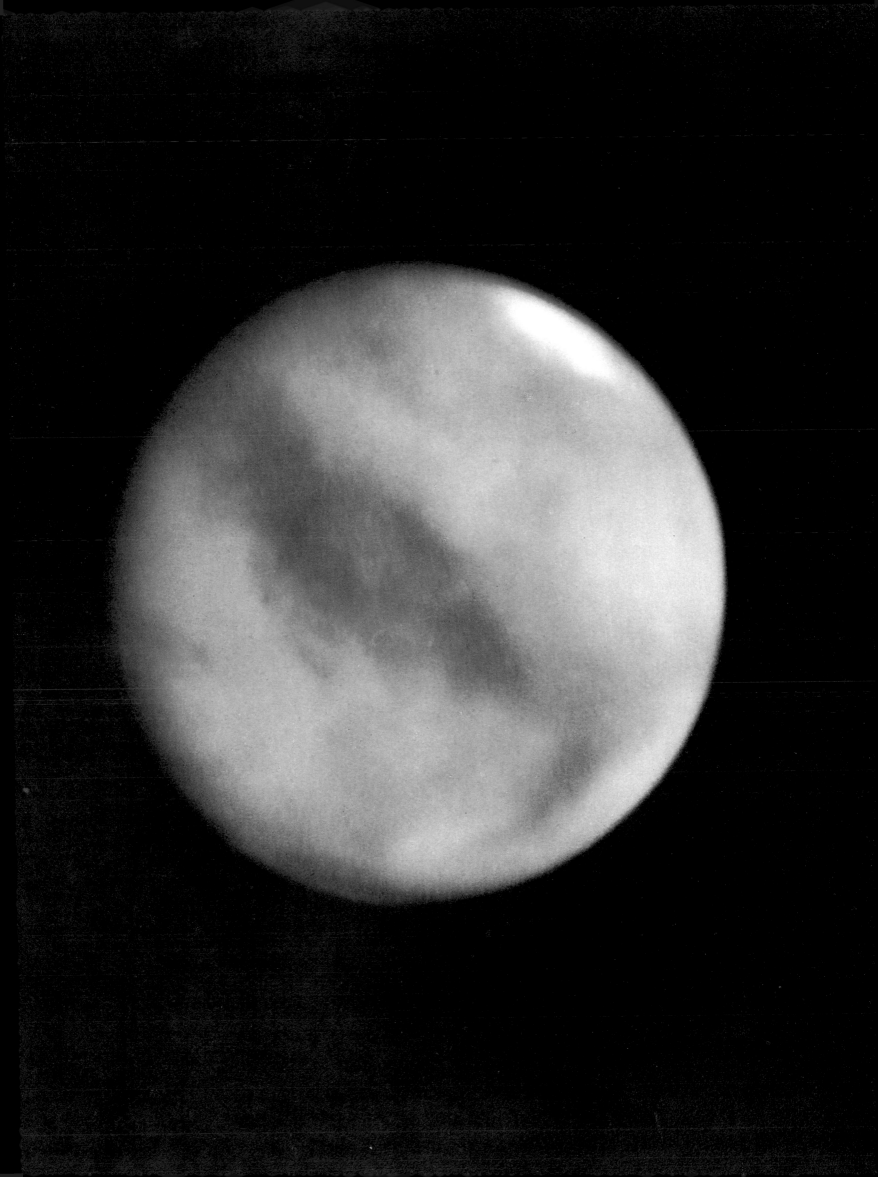

An artist's view of the Martian landscape as
it might look to a man standing on the rim of a
large crater. Prominent details—the low hills, the
intense blue of the sky and the gentle slope of the crater—
are based on data obtained from telescopic
photographs and pictures transmitted by the spacecraft
Mariner 4, which passed within 5700 miles
of the planet. Dust storms like the one shown
blowing up on the left of the painting are believed
to be a common feature of the Martian deserts.

The port, like all the major settlements, lies in
the dark belt of vegetation that roughly follows the
equator and occupies about half the southern hemisphere. The northern hemisphere is almost all desert
—mainly composed of the red oxides that give the
planet its ruddy colour. Some of these desert regions
are really beautiful; they're far older than anything
on the surface of our Earth, because there's been so
little weathering on Mars to wear down the rocks,
at least since the seas dried up more than 500 million
years ago.

Outside the domes, the natural Martian atmosphere is much less dense than that at the top of
Mount Everest, and it contains practically no oxygen.
So when you go out you'll have to wear a helmet,
or travel in one of those pressurised jeeps they call
'sand fleas'. Thanks to the low gravity, enough
oxygen for 12 hours' normal working can be
carried quite easily. Don't attempt to imitate any
of the second-generation colonists you may see
walking about without oxygen gear. They can't
breathe the Martian atmosphere any more than you
can, but like the old-time native pearl-divers, they
can make one lungful of oxygen last them for
several minutes.

The other great obstacle to life on Mars is the low
temperature. The highest ever recorded was in the
80's, but that's exceptional. In the long winters, and

during the night in summer *or* winter, it never rises
above freezing. I believe the lowest recorded is
−190°. For the sort of excursions you'll be doing,
there is a simple, light thermosuit that traps the body
heat quite effectively.

The two methods of transport outside the cities
are sand fleas for short ranges (with a full charge of
power cells, they're good for a couple of thousand
miles) and aircraft for longer distances. Although
Mars seems small compared with Earth, its land
area is almost as great because so much of our planet
is covered with oceans. There are still vast regions
of Mars which have never been properly explored,
particularly around the poles.

Those stubborn people who still persist in believ-
ing that there was once an indigenous Martian
civilisation pin their hopes on these great blanks.
Every so often you may hear rumours that some
wonderful new archaeological discovery has been
made in these wastelands—but nothing ever
comes of it.

Martians or no, you'll be fascinated by the plant
life and by the queer animals that manage to live
without oxygen, migrating each year from hemisphere to hemisphere, across the ancient sea-beds,
in order to avoid the ferocious winter. The fight for
survival on Mars has been fierce, and evolution has
produced some pretty odd results. Don't go investigating any Martian life forms unless you have a
guide, or you may find that you've let yourself in for
some unpleasant surprises.

Well, that's all I've got to say, except to wish you
a pleasant trip. Oh, there is one other thing. My
boy collects stamps, and I rather let him down
when I was on Mars. So, if you could drop me a few
letters while you're there, I'd be much obliged!

298

The Violent Sun

Herbert Friedman

In one second the Sun pours out more
energy than man has used
since the beginning of civilisation

At 2.37 p.m. on November 12, 1960, astronomers in Michigan detected a brilliant explosion on the face of the Sun. Six hours later, a gigantic cloud of solar hydrogen gas, 10 million miles across and still trailing half-way back to the Sun, 93 million miles away, collided with the Earth at a speed of 4000 miles a second.

Though inaudible and invisible, the collision started a violent chain of disturbances on and around the Earth, an electrical and magnetic storm of mammoth proportions. Compass needles wavered erratically. For hours all long-distance radio communications were blacked out. Teletypes printed gibberish. Overhead, sheets of flaming-red northern lights flashed in the night sky, bright enough to be seen through the clouds. Electric lights flickered in farmhouses as if a thunderstorm raged, yet the air and sky were clear and silent.

For more than a week, these chaotic conditions continued. They were clearly the results of the Sun on the rampage. Yet such a storm amounts to no more than a tiny ripple in the usual steady flow of solar energy.

The Sun's power staggers the imagination. In one second, this star of ours (the Sun is, after all, just one of an estimated 100,000 million stars in the Milky Way) radiates more energy than man has used since the beginning of civilisation. The Sun delivers to us in a few days as much heat and light as would be produced by burning the Earth's entire oil and coal reserves and all the wood of its forests. Yet the Earth receives only one half of one thousand millionth of the Sun's radiant energy.

What makes the Sun shine so brilliantly? The answer now accepted as correct is atomic energy. The nuclei, or cores, of hydrogen atoms collide and unite—to form helium nuclei. As the union is accomplished, bursts of energy are given off.

This nuclear fusion actually goes on at a slow pace, atomically speaking. The Sun may be considered as a very slow-burning hydrogen bomb. Only because it is so large is its total production of energy so enormous. Pound for pound, the Sun actually produces less than the human body—two calories per pound daily, while the average human body generates about ten.

Until very recently, man's study of the Sun was seriously hampered by the Earth's murky, shimmering atmosphere, which distorts light beams and blots out the Sun's X-rays and much of its ultra-violet and infra-red radiation. In 1945, rockets became available to carry telescopes and spectrographs above the atmosphere. Now satellites point instruments steadily at the Sun. Huge radar transmitters bounce beams off the swollen outer atmosphere of the Sun and probe its structure and movement. Meanwhile, with the optical spectroscope, we can analyse light arriving from 93 million miles away and tell what the Sun is made of just as accurately as if we had a sample in the laboratory.

Using triangulation with other celestial objects, astronomers have gauged the size of the Sun very accurately. Its diameter of 864,000 miles compares with Earth's 8000. It could hold 1,300,000 Earths.

The spectrum shows that the Sun consists principally of hydrogen. Hydrogen atoms are roughly ten times as abundant there as helium, the next most abundant element, and a thousand times as abundant as carbon, nitrogen or oxygen, which are so common on Earth. Except for the superabundance of hydrogen and helium, the chemical composition of the solar atmosphere is much the same as that of the Earth's crust.

Although the density at the centre of the Sun must be about 11·4 times that of lead, the Sun remains gaseous everywhere. That is, the atoms are free to move about, unlike those in a solid, which are fixed in a regular pattern. Spots on the Sun show us that it rotates from east to west, and in a very peculiar way: different parts spin at various speeds. A spot close to the equator, for example, completes a rotation in 25 days; the polar zone may take 34 days. Most of the changing features observed on the surface of the Sun must be related in some way to this contortion.

When astronomers examine the Sun with a solar telescope, its edge appears sharp, as if it marked a definite surface. This apparent surface is in fact a transparent, though highly luminous, layer of gas about 200 miles thick, called the photosphere. From it comes most of the light we get. Outside the photosphere lie two other layers—a region of flame-like outbursts of gas, called the chromosphere, and an almost endless outer atmosphere, called the corona. All that we know of the Sun's interior is deduced from observation of these three external layers.

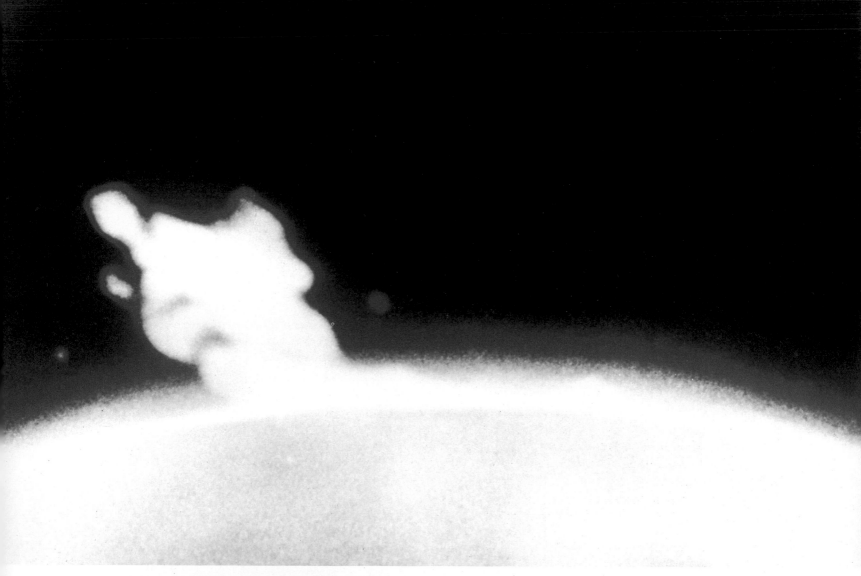

The red, arched flames of a solar flare, or prominence; flares are best observed during a total solar eclipse. When the Moon covers the Sun's disc, the beautiful scarlet atmosphere surrounding the Sun is revealed. From this the flares shoot up, travelling as much as 300,000 miles from the white halo which surrounds the Sun.

We have good reason to believe that at the Sun's centre, close to half a million miles deep, pressure reaches 100,000 million atmospheres. To produce such pressure, we know that gas must be heated to about 16,000,000°C. Sir James Jeans, in *The Universe Around Us*, calculates that a pin-head of material at the temperature of the Sun's core would emit enough heat to kill a man 1000 miles away.

In this nuclear furnace most of the fantastically hot, dense gas is invisible, since nearly all its radiation consists of X-rays produced by nuclear reactions and the collisions of fast-racing nuclei and electrons. The path of an X-ray as it escapes from the core resembles the zigzagging track of the steel ball in a pinball machine. Even though the rays travel at the speed of light—186,300 miles per second —the devious trip to the Sun's surface takes about 20,000 years. During that period the X-rays gradually change. Each time one is deflected, the frequency of its vibration is reduced slightly and its wavelength is increased. In time, the X-rays turn into ultra-violet and visible light.

Most of what we know of the Sun's outer atmosphere comes from studies of solar eclipses. During an eclipse in 1842, astronomers noted the very faint outer atmosphere of the Sun. As the Moon blocked out the brilliant disc, a pearly-white corona with delicate streams and curved arches was revealed. Close to the black edge of the Moon, a reddish ring, the 'chromosphere', encircled the Sun.

The spectrum of the chromosphere and corona reveals a very interesting paradox. The core temperature of 16,000,000°C drops steadily to about 5700°C at the Sun's surface. But in the solar *atmosphere*, the temperature begins to rise again, eventually climbing to several million degrees.

Pictures of the rim show thousands of tongues of gas, called spicules, springing fountain-like above the Sun's surface. They surge up and fall back in five to ten minutes, rising as high as 6000 miles. At any instant as many as 100,000 spicules may be in action. Also, huge streamers of bright gas, called prominences, often loop as high as 300,000 miles into the

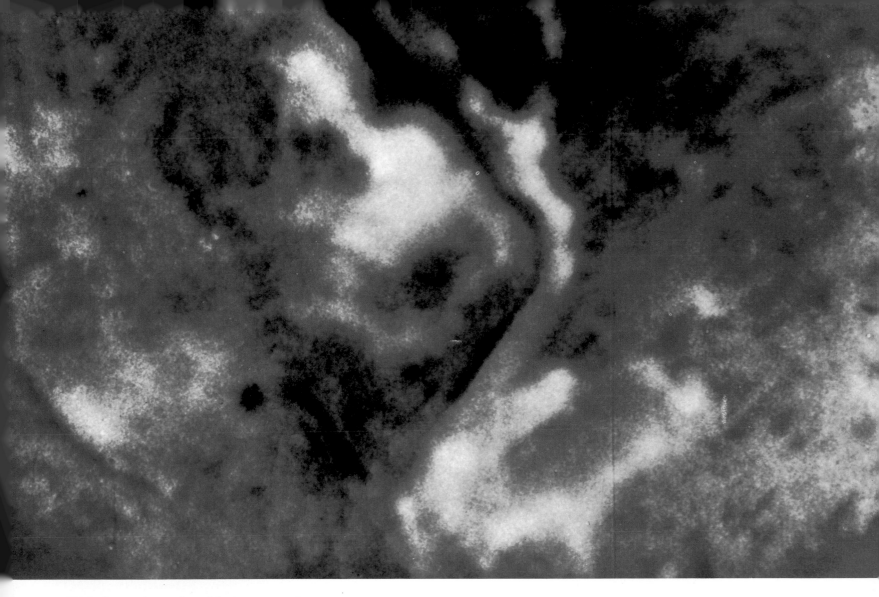

The boiling, violent surface of the Sun, seen under high magnification. Even through a small telescope (which must be fitted with a suitable very dark filter to protect the eyesight), fast-moving sunspots can be seen on the Sun's disc, ranging in size from a few hundred to 60,000 miles in diameter.

corona, then dip back to the photosphere as much as half a million miles away.

Even these dramatic activities of a quiet Sun pale into insignificance beside the explosive phenomenon known as a solar flare. A large flare can erupt in an hour with the force of 1000 million hydrogen bombs. It was such a flare that disrupted earthly communications in November 1960.

Nevertheless, the Sun is a very ordinary star—a yellow dwarf, midway between the largest and the smallest, and between the hottest blue stars and the coolest red stars. To observers on Earth, it is brighter than any other star, though Rigel, for example, is 15,000 times more luminous. And into Antares, a red super-giant, 36 million of our Suns could be fitted.

In time, the Sun's core will deplete its hydrogen: some theoretical calculations indicate that the proportion has decreased from two-thirds to one-third in the past 5000 million years. With the core spent, the thermonuclear reactions will spread to outer portions where unused hydrogen still exists. As the reaction zone moves closer to the surface of the Sun, the tremendous nuclear heat at its core will also move outwards, forcing the Sun to expand. The Sun will then become a giant red star like Antares. It will blow up to a monstrous ball of extremely rarefied, red-hot gas large enough to engulf the four nearest planets—Mercury, Venus, Earth and Mars.

When will the Sun reach this stage? We have no cause for immediate concern—it may take another 5000 million years.

Finally, when all its hydrogen has been converted to helium, the Sun will cool and shrink, ultimately becoming a white dwarf no bigger than the Earth but weighing several tons per cubic inch.

Meanwhile, the Sun is our bridge to the stars. It is the only star whose surface and atmosphere we can study in fine detail. With our magnificent new tools to observe the Sun, the coming years should bring a revolution in our understanding of Earth's bright and awesome companion in the heavens—and of the myriad stars beyond.

301

THE PLANET CALLED EARTH

For the first time in history, man has seen the whole Earth—the scene of all his hopes, fears and ambitions—hanging before him in space. For the first time, he has seen his world for what it is—a solitary, beautiful planet floating in silence. At Christmas 1968, the astronauts of Apollo 8, James A. Lovell, Frank Borman and William A. Anders, became the first men to go out of Earth's orbit and see the world from a distance of some 237,000 miles; below them, less than 100 miles away, lay the desolate surface of the Moon. The heroes of this historic flight described the Earth as 'a blue sphere veiled in clouds'. The record of their journey and the photographs they took on it are some of the most impressive documents of exploration yet offered to mankind. They are graphic evidence of a turning point in human history, and the first signs, perhaps, of a new renaissance.

The Earth rises above the lunar horizon, and bathes part of the spacecraft in the pale glow of Earth-light— light from the Sun reflected on to the Moon from the Earth's seas, continents and clouds.

December 21, 1968, the first stage of a historic journey: the massive Saturn V rocket blasts off from Cape Kennedy in Florida, sending astronauts Borman, Lovell and Anders to the Moon. These men were the first to see the planet Earth from the depths of space.

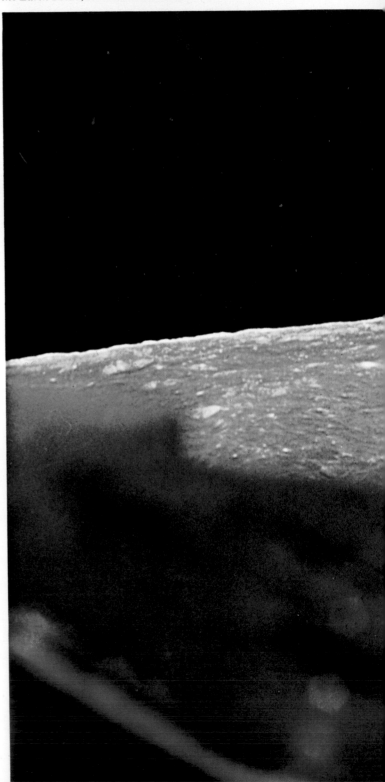

Both sides of the Atlantic Ocean can be seen in this photograph. Clearest is the coast of western Africa, to the right of the globe; to the north are the Algerian desert and the Spanish Sahara.

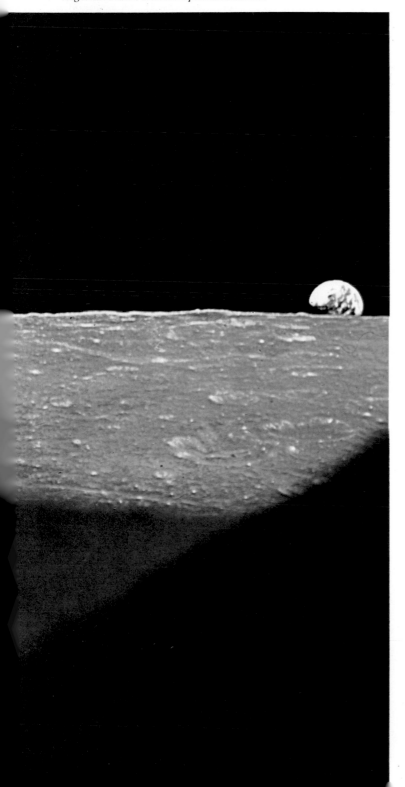

The fertile Earth, fully risen above the barren Moon. In time man may colonise the Earth's satellite and, eventually, turn its desolate, pumice-coloured landscape into a blue, white, green and brown world like our own, the only cradle of life we so far know.

303

Beyond the Solar System

The myriad stars in the Milky Way and in the billions of other galaxies
may be forever beyond our physical reach. But with
optical instruments and radio telescopes we can
study the messages they send us,
and astronomers are now formulating tentative
answers to some of man's age-old questions about the cosmos

Space Flight and the Spirit of Man

Arthur C. Clarke

The exploration of space
may be a vital and necessary stimulus
to the evolution of mankind

In his book *A Study of History*, Professor Arnold Toynbee emphasises 'challenge and response' as the great force shaping the rise and fall of civilisations. It seems to me that the opening of the space age presents a classic example of challenge and response.

My mind is inevitably drawn to the great voyages of discovery of the 15th and 16th centuries. These voyages liberated man's mind from the long trance of the Middle Ages and fed the fires of the Renaissance. Perhaps something similar will happen with space flight. As Sir James Frazer wrote: 'Intellectual progress, which reveals itself in the growth of art and science, receives an immense impetus from conquest and empire.' Interplanetary travel is now the only form of 'conquest and empire' compatible with civilisation. Without it, the human mind, compelled to circle forever in its planetary goldfish bowl, must eventually stagnate.

Though the world is now undeniably space-conscious to an extent that would have seemed unbelievable only a few years ago, it is not yet space-*minded*. And, unfortunately, altogether too many educators, intellectuals and other moulders of public opinion still regard space as a terrifying vacuum instead of a frontier with infinite possibilities.

The possible advantages of space can be best appreciated if we turn our backs upon it and return, in imagination, to the sea. Here is the perfect environment for life—the place where it originally evolved. In the sea, an all-pervading fluid medium carries oxygen and food directly to each organism. The same medium neutralises gravity, ensures against temperature extremes and prevents damage by too-intense solar radiation, which must have been lethal at the Earth's surface before the ozone layer was formed.

It seems incredible that life ever left the sea, for in some ways the dry land is almost as dangerous as space. Because we are accustomed to it, we forget the price we have had to pay in our daily battle against gravity. We seldom stop to think that we are still creatures of the sea, able to leave it only

The launching of Apollo 8 from the Kennedy Space Centre.
The Saturn V rocket thrust astronauts Borman, Lovell
and Anders into the first stage of their 147-hour mission,
during which they orbited the Moon ten times, and became
the first men to enter the Moon's gravity and see its
surface at close quarters—from a height of 70 miles.

On June 3, 1965, Major Edward White climbed out of
a satellite orbiting 100 miles above the Earth and
became the first American to walk in space. A Soviet
cosmonaut, Alexei Leonov, had stepped into space
less than three months earlier. Unlike White, however,
who carried a compressed-air guidance gun,
Leonov was not self-propelled.

because, from birth to death, we wear the water-
filled space-suits of our skins.

Yet until life invaded and conquered the land, it
was trapped in an evolutionary cul-de-sac. The
relative opacity of water and its resistance to movement were perhaps the chief factors limiting the progress of marine creatures. They had little incentive
to develop keen vision or manual dexterity. The
road to further development in the sea is also
blocked by another impassable barrier. The difference between man and animals lies basically in the
possession of fire. A marine culture could never
escape from the Stone Age and discover the use of
metals; indeed, almost all branches of science and
technology would be barred to it.

Perhaps we would have been happier had we
remained in the sea, but no philosopher has ever
suggested that we took the wrong road. The world
beneath the waves is beautiful but hopelessly

limited. No fish can see the stars; we will never be
content until we have reached them.

It cannot be *proved*, of course, that expansion
into space will produce a jump in our development
as great as that which took place when our ancestors
left the sea. We cannot predict the new forces,
powers and discoveries that will be disclosed to us
when we reach the other planets or set up laboratories in space. They are as much beyond our vision
today as fire or electricity would be beyond the
imagination of a fish. Yet no one can doubt that the
increasing flow of knowledge and sense im-
pressions, together with the wholly new types of
experience and emotion, will have a profoundly
stimulating effect upon the human psyche.

Alarm has been expressed at the danger of sensory deprivation in space. Astronauts on long
journeys, it has been suggested, will suffer from the
same symptoms that afflict men who are cut off
from their environment by being shut up in
darkened, soundproof rooms.

I would reverse this argument: our entire culture
will suffer from sensory deprivation if we do *not* go
out into space. There is striking evidence for this. As
soon as we were able to rise above the atmosphere,

a new and surprising universe was opened up, far richer and more complex than had ever been suspected from ground observations.

Even the most enthusiastic proponents of space research never imagined just how valuable satellites would actually turn out to be, and there is a profound symbolism in this.

But the facts of science, priceless though they are, tell only part of the story. Across the seas of space lie the new materials of the imagination; without these raw materials all forms of art must surely eventually sicken and die.

Strangeness, wonder, mystery, adventure, magic —these things, which not long ago seemed lost forever, will soon return to the world. And with them, perhaps, will come again an age of sagas and epics such as Homer never knew.

Though we may welcome this, we may not enjoy it, for it is never easy to live in an age of transition. We must prepare ourselves for painful shocks that will involve our philosophical and religious beliefs. We take it for granted now that our planet is a tiny world in a remote corner of an infinite universe and have forgotten how this discovery shattered the calm certainties of medieval faith. Space will present us with facts that are even more disconcerting.

There can be little reasonable doubt that we shall ultimately come into contact with races more intelligent than our own. That contact may be the most devastating event in the history of mankind. The rash assertion that 'God made man in His own image' is ticking like a time bomb at the foundations of many faiths.

The best examination I have seen of the probable effects of space travel upon our philosophical and religious beliefs was made in a broadcast by Derek Lawden, a New Zealander well known for his work on interplanetary orbits:

'I think man will see himself as one agent by which the whole universe of matter is slowly becoming conscious of itself. He will cease to feel an alien creature in an indifferent world, but will sense within himself the pulse of the cosmos. He'll become familiar with the marvellous and varied forms which can be assumed by matter, and he is certain to develop a feeling of reverence for the awe-inspiring whole of which he is a very small part. I suggest to you that his reaction to these impressive experiences will find its expression in a pantheism which will at last provide a philosophy of life and an attitude to existence which is in harmony with science. I ask anyone who denies this possibility to turn his eyes skyward on a clear night.'

Many will find these thoughts unpalatable; the truth may be yet harder. Perhaps if we knew all that lay ahead of us on the road to space—a hundred or a thousand or a million years in the future—no man alive would have had the courage to take the first step. But that first step has already been taken; to turn back now would be treason to the human spirit.

The eyes of all the ages are upon us now, as we create the myths of the future at Cape Kennedy and Kapustin Yar. No other generation has had such powers and responsibilities. The impartial agents of our destiny stand on their launching pads, awaiting our commands. They can take us to that greater Renaissance or make us one with the dinosaurs.

The choice is ours: it must be made soon, and it is irrevocable. If our wisdom fails to match our science, we will have no second chance. For there will be none to carry our dreams across another dark age, when the dust of all our cities reddens the sunsets of the world.

The Language of the Universe

Ira Wolfert

Strange, newly discovered sounds
from outer space
are baffling astronomers

In February 1968, astronomers in Britain, people who usually remain calm about things like space flights and flying saucers, found something to excite them. It was a long, rapidly varying signal that came out of the sky, and was recorded as a series of precise little jiggles on a tape. It was like a sigh—the drawn-out, tremulous kind of sigh that a troubled man might give.

This in itself was cause for wonderment, but when scientists analysed the signals they were amazed. Although the pulsations were of varying intensity, the period between pulses was always the same—1·33730113 seconds. Nothing known in space emitted a radio signal like that.

Its regularity suggested a technological origin: perhaps it was merely some errant man-made signal bouncing off the Moon, or even a transmission from a deep space probe. But it was observed again and again, coming always from the same place in the sky, showing that its source lay beyond our Solar System.

'Our first, fleeting thought was that this was another intelligence trying to contact us,' said Sir Martin Ryle of Cambridge University; but more sources of similar signals were quickly discovered in other regions of the sky. At this point, it was deemed unlikely that a large number of superior civilisations would be trying to contact us all at once, or that they would squander such colossal power over a broad and continuous range of frequencies—from 40 to 2800 megacycles per second. This was such an inefficient means of signalling that it made no sense.

Something else must be causing the pulses—some natural phenomenon. But what?

When the British scientists announced their discovery in February, 1968, astronomers all over the world jumped for their telescopes. I was in Puerto Rico and made at once for the small city of Arecibo, where astronomers from Cornell University have built a radio telescope that is one of the most powerful celestial sense organs on Earth.

The celestial sighs are caught in a spherical reflector 1000 ft in diameter. The control room, in a building on the west rim, is like the cockpit of a huge spaceship. Lights flutter across banks of electronic counters. Oscilloscopes flicker. An atomic clock gives the time in fractions of a millionth of a second. Computers hum and blink, and from the windows is an unearthly sight—the telescope itself.

A round dish covering 20 acres, it lies over a natural bowl in the mountains that was bulldozed smooth, then replanted to keep it from eroding. The vegetation underneath gets enough sun and rain to keep it lush because the reflector is made of $\frac{1}{2}$ in. open-meshed 'chicken wire', weighing 270 tons.

The receivers and a transmitter are on a movable platform, 435 ft overhead, on railway tracks hung from cables like a suspension bridge. The huge dish reflector catches the signals from space and focuses them at a particular angle, depending on the source from which they come. The angle can then be calculated precisely, and the receiver moved into the correct position to intercept it.

In this way, one can listen in on radio energy emitted from a very large part of the Universe. Fairly recent inventions, and not yet perfected, radio telescopes already can 'see' to a distance of some 12,000 million light-years—three times further than can be seen with optical telescopes.

The strongest signals so far, I was told by Dr Frank Drake of Cornell, then director of Arecibo, were estimated by the British to be originating from about 400 light-years away. Obviously, we were on an exciting voyage of discovery.

An ocean of clues was waiting to be fished. The British had already looked into two hypotheses: was the source of the signals a 'white dwarf'? This is a dying star whose hydrogen fuel is virtually burnt out, a state that our own Sun is expected to reach in about 6000 million years.

Or was it a 'neutron star'? This is a star in an even later stage, collapsing under the weight of its own gravity, shrinking so much that it forms a dense mass which on Earth would weigh 10,000 million tons per cubic inch. Stars vibrating in these death throes would perhaps emit such melancholy exhalations as were reaching Earth.

Measurements showed that the pulses were too slow for a neutron star, too fast for a white dwarf. Where, then, was all the energy coming from? Why were these pulsating stars, nicknamed 'pulsars', never observed before?

Many objects in space radiate electro-magnetic waves as a by-product of their energy. A radio telescope picks up a bedlam of these incoming signals— a ceaseless frying and spattering sound—and what you hear depends, just as with your radio at home, on how the set is tuned. Pulsar signals are relatively weak and are at wavelengths not usually monitored.

The pulsars were discovered by accident in the summer of 1967 by Jocelyn Bell, a graduate student and a member of a group of astronomers led by Dr Antony Hewish. They were working with a new Cambridge University radio telescope specially equipped to record weak, rapidly varying signals, perfect for catching the strange signal that arrived as a weak interference.

Interferences are common and are frequently caused by such earthly things as taxi intercoms; but when the Cambridge astronomers tried to track down this one, they discovered that the signal was extraterrestrial. As they began investigating the nature of their find systematically, mystery began to pile on mystery.

Radio waves, like words, have a grammar and meaning. For example, variation of the energy (or 'loudness') in a sound tells something about the temperature of the electrons which cause the signal. A shift in wavelength gives the speed and direction of the emitter's motion.

A natural amphitheatre in the hills near Arecibo, on the island of Puerto Rico in the West Indies, has been ingeniously converted into a huge radio telescope. This instrument is now receiving radio waves from deep space which are posing new questions, and unsettling old beliefs, about the nature of the Universe.

Such is the language of the Universe, and with it astronomers read radio waves as we read a dictionary, learning from their measurements just what emitted the waves, and what natural process inspired it to do so. But in the case of the pulsars, it was as though the 'words' were written in an unknown tongue, although the Cambridge team did conclude that the signals were coming from a body no larger than Earth. A planet orbiting a distant star? Measurements proved it was not.

Many astronomers joined in the quest. Soon Sir Martin Ryle pinpointed the source. Consulting maps of the sky, he found a faint, bluish glimmer which had hitherto gone unnoticed. Still, it was not exactly where the pulsings seemed to come from. A red star was also found, close enough to be a possibility. But what astronomers really hoped to find was a star that pulsed optically in cadence with the radio waves.

'It's as puzzling as hell,' said Dr Alastair Cameron of Yeshiva University. 'It's spooky,' added Dr Drake. And so I stayed on at Arecibo, staring in wonder at new horizons.

Suppose these pulsars had turned out to be *bona fide* signals from intelligent beings with a technology better than ours. Could we then signal back?

A hopeless enterprise, Dr Drake told me. First, you have to consider the tremendous distance. Though radio waves travel at the speed of light—186,272 miles a second—the closest of these signals was thought to have taken more than 100 years to reach Earth. So, even if we could radio a 'hello', it would be over 200 years before we could hear anybody ask, 'Who's there?'

Arecibo's radio telescope can pick up signals measuring one-thousandth of a millionth of a watt—a noise so faint that it makes a falling snowflake sound like a boulder crashing down a mountainside. If there were a technological civilisation only one or two light-years away—a mere few thousand million miles—we could tune in on its internal communications network, at least on what its television and radio stations were broadcasting a year or so ago. But the distance of 100 light-years or more is at present far too great for the perception of such faint signals as these.

Some day, with improved equipment, we may be able to eavesdrop further out. Then we may be able to learn what such a civilisation has to teach us. Deciphering the language of an unrelated species would be a tremendous problem, but we already have a vital key: the laws of Nature. These laws work the same everywhere in the Universe. Any technological civilisation must know them.

Finally, knowing that the world's astronomers may be struggling with these mournful signals from outer space for years, I left—content to have been for a while a passenger on the voyage of discovery. Content, too, to have had a view of how astronomers react when confronted with any new state of affairs in the Universe.

The plane that took me home flew over the Atlantic in the late afternoon. How strange it felt to be sitting in a golden light looking down at the darkness gathering over the waters below.

In such oceans life began; and primitive creatures, seeing the land, floundered on to it. Now, primitive all over again, life sees the mind-blinding space beyond the sky. Although it can no more comprehend space than a fish comprehends land, it is on the edge of floundering out into it anyway.

Is something calling man without his having heard it yet? Has something been calling life since its beginning? Are there, waiting for us out there, answers to questions we have never even asked? If so, the business of all astronomers, astronauts and men of space may be—in Emily Dickinson's words—'the solemnest business on Earth'.

The Greatest Explosion of all

Earl Ubell

There is growing evidence
that the Universe began with an unimaginably
violent primordial explosion

Within this last year, the astronomers have come closer than ever to deciding which of two theories best answers the awesome question: how did our Universe begin?

New evidence from cosmic light and radio waves arriving on Earth from distant stars has tilted the balance between scientists of two camps: those who believe that we exist in an eternal, infinite, never-changing Universe, and those who believe that the Universe was born in a cataclysmic explosion some 10,000–20,000 million years ago.

An increasing number of astronomers see growing evidence for the big-bang theory. These are the observations that are beginning to convince them:

In the spring of 1965, a metallic horn-shaped antenna, pointed at the sky from a New Jersey hill, detected peculiar radiation that may be a remnant of a white-hot ball of matter and energy—the cosmic egg from which the Universe may have been hatched.

For several years the 200 in. telescope on Mount Palomar, California, has been collecting data on strange objects known as quasars. Brighter than 100 million suns, they stand like beacons on the shore of the Universe, billions upon trillions of miles from us. The quasars appear to be receding so fast that they could signify an exploding Universe.

An English radio antenna has picked up the sounds of worlds we cannot see. The distribution of those radio sources indicates to some astronomers a scattering by a massive explosive force.

The big-bang proponents believe that originally a primal blob of glowing hydrogen shot its fragments far out into space, where they are still travelling at thousands of miles a second. Those speeding wisps of hydrogen, now condensed into star-studded galaxies, make up our expanding Universe. It is as if the galaxies were raisins in a cake mix; as the cake bakes, the raisins move apart in every direction.

That big bang, however, may be just one of an eternal succession of explosions. Some astronomers anticipate that the speeding galaxies will slow down and then start moving back towards one another. Ultimately, they will fall into that primitive ball, only to explode once more and repeat the cycle endlessly. Dr Allan R. Sandage, of Mount Wilson and Mount Palomar Observatories, believes it possible that the Universe renews itself in this way every 80,000 million years.

The new evidence for the big bang has made life difficult for the advocates of the second leading theory, the so-called steady-state theory. These astronomers believe that the Universe has the quality of a field of grass, where individual blades that die are replaced by new shoots. Thus any region of the Universe always retains the same appearance with the same average number of galaxies.

The protagonists of this idea agree that the Universe is expanding. The sight of galaxies flying apart comes from telescopic observation. However, they believe that this results not from an explosion but from some mysterious repulsive force. The steady-state men suggest that new galaxies are continually formed out of hydrogen gas in inter-galactic space, thereby filling the space left by the hurtling galaxies. The hydrogen is created out of nothingness.

Professor Fred Hoyle, of Cambridge University, the leader of the steady-state faction, has modified his theory to fit the recent data. He now says that a limited region of the Universe behaves like the big bang. Beyond lies the unchanging infinity.

Man has always gazed up at the star-spangled night sky and wondered how it came to be. Today

The Mark 1 radio telescope at Jodrell Bank in Cheshire.
The telescope's 250 ft dish is fully movable, to
tune in to radio waves coming from any part of the sky,
and the whole 2500 ton structure rotates on its own
railway track. With the help of such instruments we may
eventually discover how and when the Universe was formed.

astronomers can form theories, and then test them against the observations and measurements of heavenly bodies. Both the big-bang and steady-state theories have observable consequences. But it should be remembered that no astronomer believes that any current cosmology adequately describes the Universe. The theories are only approximations, too simple for the galactic complexities of space.

The big-bang theory was born in 1922, when Dr Alexander Friedman, a Russian mathematician, found an alternative approach to the field equations of Einstein's general relativity theory and went on to predict the possibility of an expanding Universe. By 1928 Dr H. P. Robertson, later of California Institute of Technology, identified the first telescopic

evidence to support that theory. The light from the galaxies, redder than expected, indicated that they were retreating at great speed.

Dr Edwin P. Hubble of the Mount Wilson Observatory also measured the distance to the flying galaxies. The closest galaxy to our own, the Magellanic Clouds, stands some 200,000 light-years from us. That means that a light ray travelling at 186,000 miles a second from that crowd of 100 million stars would take 200,000 years to get to us.

Dr Hubble was amazed to find that the furthest galaxies were travelling the fastest. About the same time a Belgian astronomer-priest, Abbé Georges Lemâitre, suggested the modern form of the big-bang theory, which fitted the Robertson–Hubble observations: as in any explosion, the furthest pieces were flying fastest.

Immediately, questions flooded the astronomical world: how long ago did the bang occur? How were the stars and galaxies formed? How were the many elements—helium, oxygen, iron, uranium and the rest—created?

It has taken 40 years to get a hint of the answers. The hint had to wait for the construction of the giant telescope on Mount Palomar after the Second World War, the development of the atomic-energy theory and the invention of radio telescopes.

The problem of the creation of the elements nearly destroyed the big-bang theory. If the cosmic egg were composed only of hydrogen, how were the heavy elements produced? As the astronomers learnt more about nuclear physics, they realised that the burst of matter occurred too quickly to create any element heavier than helium. There was just no way to account for the other elements.

Then in 1938 scientists discovered that stars burn hydrogen—converting it to helium and extracting energy in the process. That occurs in the heart of the star at 20 million °C. Eventually the hydrogen at the core is exhausted and is replaced by helium. In 1955 a team of scientists at California Institute of Technology showed that the stars could convert that helium into all the elements.

Next the cosmological detectives tried to ascertain the age of the Universe. It had to be older than the Earth, which radio-active rock measurements had revealed to be at least 4600 million years old. Dr Sandage has calculated that the oldest stars in our Galaxy must have been born 12,000 million years ago. He arrived at that figure by determining how long it takes stars to burn up their hydrogen and convert it into helium. Independently, Dr William A. Fowler of Caltech calculated the age of the synthesis of the uranium and thorium found on the Earth. He knew that these elements had been originally manufactured in stars that had exploded long ago and sent their fragments through the Galaxy to become part of the material from which our Solar System was formed. Their age was 12,000 million years. A third measurement made by Dr Sandage indicates an age of 8000 million years for the Universe. The discrepancies disturb the big-bang scientists, but they anticipate that they will be resolved. The great excitement in the last few years has been over discoveries that test the more subtle consequences of the two major theories. In this respect, it is easier to disprove the steady-state theory than the big-bang. If astronomers can prove, for example, that the Universe was expanding faster in the past than it is today, the steady-state theory will fall. To get at past history, astronomers merely look out to greater distances. Since it takes time for light to travel, when they look at galaxies 1000 million light-years away they see the Universe as it existed 1000 million years ago. Therefore they are interested in measuring the speed of recession of the most distant galaxies. If those galaxies are flying faster than the steady-state theory predicts, that will kill the theory.

By 1960 Dr Rudolph Minkowski, then at Mount Wilson and Mount Palomar, had discovered that a galaxy, 3C295, was retreating from us at 70,000 miles a second. It was the most distant galaxy known —perhaps 4000 million light-years away. With that measurement, and a few others, astronomers believed that they had detected a departure from the steady-state prediction. The Universe far away looked different.

But the real break came in February 1963, when Dr Maarten Schmidt of the Mount Palomar Observatory found a quasi-stellar radio source, or quasar, that put out 50 times as much light as an ordinary galaxy. Dr Schmidt was able to detect that quasar because radio astronomers had located areas of the Universe from which radio waves came in torrents. Using the 200 in. telescope to photograph those areas, Dr Schmidt located the quasar.

His significant contribution was the discovery that this and other previously detected quasars were travelling through space as fast as, or faster than, the fastest known galaxies. He has found one quasar, 3C9, moving at 80 per cent of the velocity of light. Dr Schmidt does not know exactly how far away 3C9 is, because astronomers do not know the true nature of the subtle curvature of space.

In an effort to determine the curvature, astronomers have so far taken complex measurements of 22 quasars. However, other quasar-like objects, called blue stellar objects, have been discovered that may help to find the answer faster.

In an approach to the problem of the origin of the Universe, Professor Martin Ryle, working in the 1950's with the radio telescope at Cambridge, mapped the locations of thousands of objects— galaxies and quasars—that are sources of radio waves. Graphs of these radio sources, according to their location and output of radio waves, do not support the steady-state theory.

Not long ago it was announced that a metal horn at the Bell Telephone Laboratories in New Jersey had been receiving a strange radio signal from outer space for a year. The scientists there discovered that the radio waves were coming from all over the sky. Unknown to them, Drs Robert H. Dicke and James Peebles, both of Princeton University, had predicted the existence of those strange radio signals. Since the Universe was once hotter and denser, they reasoned that it should be filled with radiation that eventually cooled as the Universe evolved and expanded. Drs Dicke and Peebles said that ancient radiation, swirling through the Universe, would be detected today as lower-energy radio waves.

Another horn set up by Dr Dicke's research group has also found such radiation. The steady-state theory has thus received still another blow. It has no way to account for such radiation.

Although the big-bang theory seems to be winning, there are still unanswered questions. How far away are the quasars? What caused the explosion? How does the distribution of hydrogen and helium fit into the explosion calculations? According to the present observations, there seems to be more helium than can be accounted for.

Uncommitted to the debate are such critics as Dr Philip Morrison of the Massachusetts Institute of Technology. He declares that astronomers know far too little to make a choice among theories of the Universe and that no theory is adequate at the moment. 'We have been wrong too many times in the past,' he says. 'We do not have enough measurements of distant galaxies to say anything definite. We are in the kindergarten stage of cosmology.'

Perhaps. But astronomers are hopeful that they will soon graduate to the senior school.

Out of this World

Wayne Amos

Amateur astronomers have given their names to comets, and discovered new stars; the adventure of astronomy is open to anyone with a small telescope

I have found a new way to get out of this world. All I have to do is go out in my garden, look into a black tube, and suddenly I am out in space, exploring the rings of Saturn, following the four diamond-like moons around Jupiter or tracing the contours of the mountains and 'seas' of our own Moon.

And I am not alone. The enthusiasm for amateur astronomy is growing all the time, whetted by all the news of space travel. Secretaries of amateur astronomy clubs estimate that there are now at least 100,000 amateurs studying the skies. My telescope only cost about £20. It works on the same principle as the world's largest reflecting telescope on Mount Palomar.

All the amateur astronomers I have talked to say that their new awareness of the vastness of the Universe and the amazing beauty of the heavenly bodies has made them more humble, tolerant, and happier. They confess to a healthy loss of vanity and a more comfortable feeling towards the world. One astronomer told me that he doesn't know of any atheists among professional astronomers—they are all forced to believe in an infinite power.

I know what they mean. These adventures into space are incredibly moving. One evening recently an old friend came over just as I was about to go out in the garden, and he came with me. The Moon was a silver shaving—perfect for observing through a telescope. When it is full, it is too bright. In crescent, when the Sun lights it from the side, the details stand out sharply.

As I focused my telescope, the Moon's craters and mountains came into bold relief. Again I thrilled to see the tremendous ball hanging in space, with no means of support except its centrifugal force outwards, balanced by the pull of gravity from the Earth. It seems to be standing still, but actually it is whirling around the Earth at the rate of 2304 mph.

When my friend looked through the telescope, he gasped, 'I can almost reach out and touch it!'

This was exactly how I felt when I first saw the Moon through a telescope. It changes suddenly from a lovely two-dimensional light to what it really is—a three-dimensional sphere. You feel that you can almost hold it in your hands.

My favourite planet is Jupiter, a glowing pearl with six or seven dark stripes around it. Near it—where you see nothing but dark sky with the naked eye—are usually four of Jupiter's 12 moons, all looking like little diamonds. They go around Jupiter at different speeds, the slowest in 17 days, the fastest in two. When we first looked we could see only three moons, but when we turned back to it an hour later a fourth had appeared from behind the planet.

Stars are glowing suns that give out a light of their own. They are inconceivably far away. If you think of our Sun as the size of a dot over a letter 'i', the next nearest sun is the dot over another letter 'i' ten miles away. The planets are much closer. Like the

The great spiral galaxy in the constellation of Andromeda is some 2 million light-years away. It is one of the nearest and brightest of our galactic neighbours and is easily seen by amateur astronomers. The galaxy is a nearly circular disc, but its inclination gives it an oval appearance when viewed from Earth.

Earth, they move around our Sun; they do not glow like the stars, but reflect the Sun's light.

When you really know the stars, you can become a member of a team of amateurs who are actively helping the professional astronomers. Amateurs send in reports about meteors, the Moon, the northern lights, and about stars that vary in brightness. Thousands of stars grow bright, then dim, then bright again, in periods of time varying from a few hours to several months. Scientists are still unable to explain exactly why this should be so.

There is always the chance, too, that an amateur may make an important discovery. Many comets have been named after amateur observers. Nearly all of the newly discovered stars have been found by amateurs, because they sweep the skies, while professionals concentrate on particular points.

Clyde Tombaugh who at the age of 24 discovered the planet Pluto, began as an amateur; and another amateur astronomer and telescope maker became so proficient that he was asked to give advice during the grinding and polishing of the 200/in. telescope on Mount Palomar.

One of the fascinating things in the sky, and one that frightens me a little, is the faint glow in the constellation of Andromeda. In the glass it leaps out as a luminous glow that seems to come from behind the furthest stars. It is actually the glow from another galaxy—one with millions of stars like our own Milky Way system—and it is about 2 million light-years away from us.

The really staggering thing is that professional astronomers say the Universe probably contains thousands of millions of such galaxies.

To the Stars

Arthur C. Clarke

At last man is breaking free from the Earth;
in time he may also break free
from the Solar System, and explore the stars

Travel to the stars is not difficult, if one is in no particular hurry. Today's vehicles could send substantial payloads to Proxima Centauri, especially if they went by way of Jupiter. Unfortunately, the voyage would take the better part of a million years.

However, no one doubts that there will be enormous increases in spacecraft velocities, especially when we have found efficient ways of harnessing nuclear energy for propulsion. Theoretically, a rocket operating on the *total* annihilation of matter should be able to approach the speed of light— 670 million mph. At the moment, we can reach about 1/20,000th of this figure; clearly, there is plenty of room for improvement.

Let us be very pessimistic and assume that rocket speeds increase tenfold every century. By the year 2000 we will certainly have vehicles capable of reaching the nearer stars in about 100,000 years, carrying really useful payloads of fully automatic surveying equipment.

But there would be no point in building them, for we could be sure that they would be quickly overtaken by the ten-times-faster vehicles we would be building a hundred years later—and so on.

This means that a rocket launched in the year 2000 would take some 100,000 years to reach Proxima Centauri; in the year 2100 about 10,000 years; while one launched in 2400 would take only ten years. Clearly, there is no point in making anything but studies on paper until about the year 2300, when the trip would take 100 years; but after *that*, it is time to start thinking about action. A wealthy, stable, scientifically advanced society would be accustomed to making hundred-year plans, and it might well consider building space probes to survey the nearer stars, as our Mariner space probes have surveyed Mars and Venus. They would report back along tight laser beams to gigantic reflecting telescopes orbiting the Earth; or they might even come back themselves, loaded with quantities of information too enormous to be transmitted across the light-years in a period less than their own transit time.

This proxy exploration of the Universe is certainly one way in which it would be possible to gain knowledge of star systems which lacked garrulous, radio-equipped inhabitants; it might be the only way. For if men, and not merely their machines, are ever to reach the planets of other stars, much more difficult problems will have to be overcome. Yet they do not appear to be insoluble, even in terms of the primitive technology we possess today.

We will first of all assume—and the evidence is overwhelmingly in favour of this—that it is impossible for any material object to attain the velocity of light. This is not something that can be explained; it is the way that the Universe is built. The velocity of light represents a limit which can be more and more closely approached but never reached. Even if all the matter in the cosmos were turned into energy and that energy were all given to a single electron, it would not reach the speed of light, but only 99·9999999999—and so on, for about 160 digits—per cent of it.

We may eventually be able to build rockets driven by the *total* annihilation of matter, not the mere fraction of a per cent which is all we can convert into energy at present. No one has the faintest idea how this may be done, but it does not involve any fundamental impossibilities. Another idea that has been put forward is that, at very high speeds, it may be possible to use the thin hydrogen gas of interstellar space as fuel for a kind of cosmic, fusion-powered ramjet. This is a particularly interesting scheme, as it would give virtually unlimited range, and remove the restrictions imposed by an onboard propellant supply. If we are optimistic, we may guess (and guessing is all that we can do at this stage) that ultimately speeds of one-tenth of that of light may be attained. Remember that to make even a one-way voyage, this would have to be done *twice*—once to build up velocity, the second time to discard it, which is just as difficult and expensive.

On this assumption, we will be able to reach the nearer stars in a few decades, but any worthwhile explorations would still have to last thousands of years. This has led some scientists to make the striking pronouncement that interstellar flight is not an engineering problem, but a medical one.

Suspended animation may be one answer. It requires no great stretch of the imagination to suppose that, with the aid of drugs or low temperatures, men may be able to hibernate for virtually unlimited periods. We can picture an automatic ship with its oblivious crew making the long journey across the interstellar night until, when a new sun was looming up, the signal was sent out to trigger the mechanism that would revive the sleepers. When their survey was completed, they would head back to Earth and slumber again until the time came to awaken once more and greet a world which would regard them as survivors from a distant past.

Another solution was first suggested, to the best of my knowledge, in the 1920's by Professor J. D. Bernal in a long-out-of-print essay, *The World, the Flesh, and the Devil*, which must rank as one of the most outstanding feats of scientific imagination in literature. Even today many of the ideas propounded in this little book have never been fully developed, either in or out of science fiction.

Bernal imagined entire societies launched across space, in gigantic arks which would be closed, ecologically balanced systems. They would, in fact, be miniature planets upon which generations of men would live and die, so that one day their remote descendants would return to Earth with the record of their celestial Odyssey.

One cannot help feeling that the interstellar ark on its 1000-year voyages would be a cumbersome way of solving the problem, even if all the social and psychological difficulties could be overcome. (Would the fiftieth generation still share the aspirations of their Pilgrim Fathers, who set out from Earth so long ago?) There are, however, more sophisticated ways of getting men to the stars than the crude, brute-force methods outlined above.

The ark, with its generations of travellers doomed to spend their entire lives in space, was merely a device to carry germ cells, knowledge and culture from one sun to another. How much more efficient to send only the cells, to fertilise them automatically some twenty years before the voyage was due to end, to carry the embryos through to birth by techniques already foreshadowed in today's biology laboratories—and to bring up the babies under the tutelage of cybernetic nurses who would teach them their inheritance and their destiny when they were capable of understanding it.

These children, knowing no parents, or indeed anyone of a different age from themselves, would grow up in the strange artificial world of their speeding ship, reaching maturity in time to explore the planets ahead of them—perhaps to be the ambassadors of humanity among alien races, or perhaps to find, too late, that there is no home for them there. If they succeeded, it would be their duty (or that of their descendants, if the first generation could not complete the task) to see that the knowledge they had gained was some day carried back to Earth.

At the moment, our whole attitude to the problem of interstellar travel is conditioned by the span of human life. There is no reason whatsoever to suppose that this will always be less than a century, and no one has ever discovered just what it is that makes men die. It is certainly not a question of the body 'wearing out' in the sense that an inanimate piece of machinery does, for in the course of a single year almost the entire fabric of the body is replaced by new material. When we have discovered the details of this process, it may be possible to extend the life span indefinitely if so desired—and this would drastically reduce the size of the Universe from the psychological point of view.

If medical science does not provide the key to the Universe, there still remains a possibility that the answer may lie with the engineers. We have suggested that one-tenth of the speed of light may be the best we can ever hope to attain, even when our spacecraft have reached the limit of their development. A number of studies suggest that this is wildly optimistic, but these are based on the assumption that the vehicles have to carry their own energy sources, like all existing rockets. It is at least conceivable that the interstellar ramjet may work, or that it is possible to supply power from an external device, such as a planet-based laser, or that the Universe contains still unknown sources of energy which spacecraft may be able to tap. In this case, we may be able to approach much more closely to the speed of light, and the whole situation then undergoes a radical change. We become involved in the so-called time-dilation effect predicted by the Theory of Relativity.

Time itself is a variable quantity; the rate at which it flows depends upon the speed of the observer. The difference is infinitesimal at the velocities of everyday life, and even at the velocities of normal astronomical bodies. It is all-important as we approach to within a few per cent of the speed of light. To put it crudely, the faster one travels, the more slowly time will pass. At the speed of light, time would cease to exist; the moment 'now' would last for ever. Let us take an extreme example to show what this implies. If a spaceship left Earth for Proxima Centauri at the speed of light and came back at once at the same velocity, it would have been gone for some eight and a half years according to all the clocks and calendars of Earth. But the people in the ship, and all their clocks or other time-measuring devices, would have detected no interval at all. The voyage would have been instantaneous.

This case is not possible, even in theory, but in 1522 the Western world was suddenly confronted by a paradox which must have seemed equally baffling to many people at the time. Eighteen sailors landed at Seville on a Thursday, whereas by their own careful reckoning it was only Wednesday aboard their ship. Thus they were, in their view, a day younger than the friends they had left behind.

They were the survivors of Magellan's crew—the first men to circumnavigate the world—and they presented the Church with the frightful problem of deciding just when they should have kept the various Saints' days on the latter half of their voyage. Four and a half centuries later, we have learnt to get along with the International Date Line, though it is going to cause us more and more trouble with the advent of global television. Perhaps four and a half centuries from now, time dilation will present no greater intellectual difficulties—though it may cause social ones, when young astronauts return to greet their senile great-grandchildren.

Everything that has been said here is based on one assumption: that the Theory of Relativity is correct. However, we have seen how Newton's theory of gravitation, after being unchallenged for 300 years, was itself modified by Einstein. How can we be sure that this process will not be repeated and that the 'light barrier' may not be shattered, as the once formidable 'sound barrier' was a generation ago?

This analogy is often drawn, but it is quite invalid. There was never any doubt that one could travel faster than sound, given sufficient energy; rifle bullets and artillery shells had been doing it for years. (Man-made objects first broke the sound barrier at least 10,000 years ago, though few people would guess how—a whipcrack is a sonic bang.)

During the last half century, however, the equations of relativity have stood up to every test that can be applied, and millions of dollars' worth of

engineering has been based upon them. The giant accelerators that speed atomic particles up to almost the velocity of light simply would not work unless Einstein's formulas were obeyed to as many decimal places as can be measured.

Nevertheless, there is a faint possibility that even this apparently insuperable barrier may be breached and that we may be able to signal—conceivably, even travel—faster than light. And we might do it *without* violating the Theory of Relativity.

I am indebted to Professor Gerald Feinberg of Columbia University for these ideas, which are taken (I hope accurately) from his stimulating paper 'On the Possibility of Faster Than Light Particles'. Professor Feinberg makes a point which is usually overlooked: the Theory of Relativity does *not* say that nothing can travel faster than light. It says that nothing can travel *at the speed of light*; there is a big difference, and it may be an important one. As Professor Feinberg puts it, the speed of light is a limiting velocity, but a limit has two sides. One can imagine particles or other entities which can travel *only* faster than light; there might even be a whole universe on the other side of the light barrier, though please do not ask me to explain precisely what is meant by this phrase. It may be argued that even if this were true, it could never be proved and would be of no practical importance. Since we cannot travel *at* the speed of light, it seems obvious that we can never travel any faster.

This is taking an old-fashioned, pre-20th-century view of the Universe. Modern physics is full of jumps from one condition of energy or velocity (quantum state) to another *without* passing through the intermediate values. There are electronic devices on the market now which depend on this effect—the tunnel diode, for example, in which electrons 'tunnel' from one side of an electrical barrier to the other without going through it. Perhaps we can do the same sort of thing at the velocity of light. I am well aware that this is metaphysics rather than physics; so are even more *outré* ideas like short cuts through higher dimensions—the 'space-warps' so useful to science-fiction writers. But we have been wrong so many times in the past when attempting to set limits to technology that it would be well to keep an open mind, even about surpassing the speed of light.

J. B. S. Haldane once remarked: 'The Universe is not only queerer than we imagine—it is queerer than we *can* imagine.' Certainly no one could have imagined the time-dilation effect; who can guess what strange roads there may yet be on which we may travel to the stars?

ACKNOWLEDGMENTS

PART ONE: This Planet Earth
AN ISLAND IS BORN, based on *Surtsey* by Sigurdur Thorarinsson, © 1966 Almenna Bokafelagid, published by the Viking Press Inc. WHEN KRAKATOA BLEW UP by Ernst Behrendt, condensed from *Nature Magazine*, © 1946 American Nature Assn. EARTHQUAKES —THE UNDERGROUND MENACE by Ira Wolfert, condensed from *The Denver Post*, © 1958 Post Printing and Publishing Co. BEYOND CONTROL by George Gamow, from *A Planet Called Earth*, published by Macmillan & Co. Ltd., © 1963 George Gamow. THE ATMOSPHERE—OUR INVISIBLE GUARDIAN by George Gamow, from *A Planet Called Earth*, published by Macmillan & Co. Ltd., © 1963 George Gamow. THE WONDER OF WINDS by J.D. Ratcliff, condensed from *U.S. Lady*, © 1965 American Service Publishing Co., Inc. THE HOWL OF THE HURRICANE by Benedict Thielen, condensed from *Holiday*, © 1959 the Curtis Publishing Co. THE MIRACLE OF LIGHTNING by Ira Wolfert, condensed from *Popular Science Monthly*, ©1959 Popular Science Publishing Co., Inc. THE RESTLESS TIDES by K. F. Bowden, from *Oceans*, edited by G. E. R. Deacon, by permission of Geographical Projects, division of Aldus Books Ltd., published by Paul Hamlyn, © 1962 Geographical Projects. HOW RIVERS CHANGE THE EARTH by R. de la Croix, condensed from *Atlas*, November 1966. THE NILE by Lord Kinross, from *Horizon*, Summer 1966, © 1966 American Heritage Publishing Co., Inc. TWENTY TIMES HIGHER THAN NIAGARA by Michael Scully, condensed from *The Kiwanis Magazine*, © 1954 Kiwanis International. THE OLDEST LAKE IN THE WORLD by Pierre Pfeffer, from *Asia: A Natural History*, © 1968 Random House Inc., Hamish Hamilton Ltd. THE WONDER OF SNOW by John Stewart Collis, © 1955 John Stewart Collis, reprinted by permission of Harold Matson Company, Inc. LAND OF FANTASY AND PHANTOM by Thomas R. Henry, condensed from *The White Continent*, © 1950 Thomas R. Henry, published by William Sloane Associates. PORTRAIT OF A DESERT by Edward Abbey, from *Desert Solitaire*, © 1968 Edward Abbey. Used by permission of McGraw-Hill Book Company.

PART TWO: The Miracle of Living Things
THE MARVELS OF CROSS-POLLINATION by Rutherford Platt, condensed from *This Green World*, © 1942 and published by Dodd, Mead & Co., Inc. GOLIATH OF SEEDS by Walter Henricks Hodge, condensed from *Natural History*, © 1949 the American Museum of Natural History. THE AFRICAN BAOBAB by I. M. Wright and O. Kerfoot, condensed from *Natural History*, © 1966 the American Museum of Natural History. PLANTS THAT EAT INSECTS by Jean George, condensed from *Au Grand Air*, © 1962 Jean George, published by Rod & Gun Publishing Co. THE ROCKLAND by N. J. Berrill, condensed from *The Living Tide*, © 1951 N. J. Berrill, published by Dodd, Mead & Co., Inc. THE BARBER'S SHOP OF THE REEF by Irenaus Eibl-Eibesfeldt, from *Land of a Thousand Atolls*, published by MacGibbon & Kee Ltd., © 1964 I. Eibl-Eibesfeldt. English translation © 1965 MacGibbon & Kee. THE SQUID—NATURE'S NIGHTMARE by Ronald N. Rood, condensed from *Down East*, © 1961 Down East Enterprise, Inc. Some of the material in this article is from Frank W. Lane's book *Kingdom of the Octopus* (pub. Jarrolds at 30s.), the major work on the subject, and recommended for further reading. BEWARE THE DEADLY MAN-OF-WAR by Fred Warshofsky, condensed from *National Wildlife*, © 1966 National Wildlife Federation. THE LOBSTER—AN OCEAN ODDITY by David MacDonald, condensed from *The Atlantic Advocate*, published by University Press of New Brunswick, Ltd. KILLER WHALE by William Cromie, condensed from *Rod and Gun*, © 1962 Rod & Gun Publishing Co. NATURE'S MOST ASTONISHING CREATURE—THE BEEHIVE by Jean George, condensed from *Frontiers, A Magazine of Natural History*, © 1966 the Academy of Natural Sciences of Philadelphia. WAR AND PEACE AMONG THE TERMITES by V. B. Dröscher, from *Mysterious Senses*, published by Hodder & Stoughton, © 1962 Gerhard Stalling Verlag, Oldenburg, Hamburg. THE WEIRDEST ORCHESTRA ON EARTH by Jean George, condensed from *National Wildlife*, © 1967 National Wildlife Federation. THAT REMARKABLE CREATURE THE SNAIL by Oscar Schisgall, condensed from *National Wildlife*, © 1967 National Wildlife Federation. WHAT SNAKES ARE REALLY LIKE by Alan Devoe, condensed from *Nature Magazine*, © 1955 American Nature Assn. NOBODY LOVES A CROCODILE by Gordon Gaskill, condensed from *U.S. Lady*, © 1964 American Service Publishing Co., Inc. SURVIVORS OF THE DRAGON AGE by David Fleay, condensed from *Nature Magazine*, reprinted by permission of the American Museum of Natural History. OF SPRING AND AN EGG by Jean George, condensed from *National Wildlife*, © 1966. National Wildlife Federation. THE MIRACLE OF BIRDS by Alan Devoe, condensed from *The American Mercury*, © 1953 The American Mercury, Inc. BIRDS LIVE IN NATURE'S INVISIBLE CAGES by John and Jean George, condensed from *The Christian Science Monitor*, © 1959 The Christian Science Publishing Society. A TOOTH AND A CLAW by Jean George, condensed from *Audubon Magazine*, © 1965 National Audubon Society. ANIMALS CAN BE ALMOST HUMAN by Max Eastman, condensed from *The Saturday Review*, © 1957 Saturday Review Associates, Inc. ARE WILD ANIMALS REALLY WILD? by Andy Russell, condensed from *True, the Man's Magazine*, Canadian edition, © 1960 Fawcett Publications, Inc. HEROES OF THE WILD by Alan Devoe, condensed from *The Minneapolis Sunday Tribune*, © 1954 Minneapolis Star and Tribune Co.

PART THREE: Man and Nature
FIRST OF THE MICROBE HUNTERS by Paul de Kruif, from *The Microbe Hunters*, published by Jonathan Cape Ltd., © Paul de Kruif. FARMING THE SEA-BED by James Dugan, by permission of the *Daily Telegraph*, *Daily Telegraph Magazine*, May 24, 1968, © *Daily Telegraph*. DRUGS FROM THE SEA by Margaret B. Kreig, from *Green Medicine*, by permission of George Harrap & Co., © 1964 under international copyright union by Rand MacNally & Company. BEHOLD THE LOWLY WORM by Arthur Koestler, from *Drinkers of Infinity*, published by Hutchinson & Co. Ltd., reprinted by permission of A. D. Peters Ltd., © Arthur Koestler. LIFE IN A TEST TUBE by Donald Gould, by permission of the *Daily Telegraph*, *Daily Telegraph Magazine*, November 8, 1968, © *Daily Telegraph*. THE WORLD'S MOST EXOTIC NUISANCE by James Poling and John Barr, condensed from *Shreveport Magazine*, © 1964 *Shreveport Magazine*. SPECTACLE OF THE SKIES by Joan Parry Dutton, condensed from *The Denver Post*, © 1959 Post Printing Co. MARTYR FOR A SPECIES by Darwin Lambert, condensed from *Audubon Magazine*, May/June 1968, © National Audubon Society. THE ELEMENTS by Antoine de Saint-Exupéry, from *Wind, Sand and Stars*, © 1939 and published by William Heinemann Ltd. CONFESSIONS OF A TREE SURGEON by W. E. Matthews, by permission of the *Sunday Times*, *Sunday Times Magazine*, April 21, 1968, © *Sunday Times*. AUGUSTO RUSCHI'S JUNGLE PARADISE by Allen Rankin, condensed from *Frontiers, a Magazine of Natural History*, © 1965 the Academy of Natural Sciences of Philadelphia. ASSIGNMENT WITH AN OCTOPUS by Arthur Grimble, from *A Pattern of Islands*, published by John Murray Ltd., © 1952 Sir Arthur Grimble. DOGS AND MEN—THE COVENANT by Konrad Lorenz, from *King Solomon's Ring*, translated by Mrs Marjorie Latzke, published by Methuen & Co. Ltd., © Konrad Lorenz. THE HUSKY —HERO OF THE ARCTIC by Laurie York Erskine, condensed from *National Home Monthly*, © 1949 Home Publishing Co. Ltd. MY WAR WITH THE OSPREYS by John Steinbeck, condensed from *Holiday*, © 1957 the Curtis Publishing Co. Extract (p. 277) from *Audubon Water Bird Guide* by Richard H. Pough, © 1951 Doubleday & Co., Inc. THE COCONUT PALM—NATURE'S MOST BOUNTIFUL TREE by Gordon Gaskill, condensed from *U.S. Lady*, © 1968 American Service Publishing Co., Inc.

PART FOUR: Worlds Without End
THE THING THAT HIT US FROM OUTER SPACE by Wolfgang Langewiesche, based on the following articles in *Scientific American*: 'Meteors' by Fletcher G. Watson; 'The Great Meteor of 1947' by Otto Struve; 'Astroblemes' by Robert S. Dietz; 'The Age of the Elements in the Solar System' by John H. Reynolds; 'The Origin of Meteorites' by Fred Singer; © 1954 Scientific American, Inc.

NEXT THE PLANETS by Arthur C. Clarke, from *Playboy Magazine*, © 1969 by HMH Publishing Co., Inc. THE LUNAR COLONY by Arthur C. Clarke, from *The Promise of Space*, published by Hodder & Stoughton, © 1968 Arthur C. Clarke. SO YOU'RE GOING TO MARS? by Arthur C. Clarke, condensed from *Holiday*, © 1953 the Curtis Publishing Co. THE VIOLENT SUN by Herbert Friedman, condensed from *National Geographic*, © 1965 National Geographic Society. SPACE FLIGHT AND THE SPIRIT OF MAN by Arthur C. Clarke, condensed from *Astronautics*, © 1961 the American Rocket Society, Inc. OUT OF THIS WORLD by Wayne Amos, condensed from *The American Magazine*, © 1953 the Crowell-Collier Publishing Co. TO THE STARS by Arthur C. Clarke, from *The Promise of Space*, published by Hodder & Stoughton, © 1968 Arthur C. Clarke.

ILLUSTRATION CREDITS

'PART PHOTOGRAPHS': 8–9 *Oregon Seascape*, Ray Atkeson; 80–81 *Bee on Flower*, Tony Evans; 210–11 *Forest Clearing*, Swissair Photo AG; 282–3 *Trifid Nebula*, Mount Wilson and Palomar Observatories, © 1959 California Institute of Technology and Carnegie Institution of Washington.

PART ONE: This Planet Earth
11, 12 (left) Sigurdur Thorarinsson; 12 (right) Aevar Jóhannesson; 16–17 (top) U.S. Department of Commerce, Coast and Geodetic Survey; 16–17 (bottom) M. Lockman, Black Star; 22, 23 Crown Copyright Geological Survey photographs, reproduced by permission of H.M. Stationery Office; 24 (left, top right) Camera Hawaii; 24 (bottom right), 25 (top) Josef Muench; 25 (bottom left) Aerofilms; 25 (bottom right), 26 (top left, top right) Picturepoint; 26–27 (bottom) Tor Eigeland, Aramco World Magazine; 27 (top left) B. V. Clarke; 27 (top right) Black Star; 29, 30 NASA; 33 Leo Ainsworth, courtesy of the National Severe Storms Laboratory; 34 (top) Victor Englebert; 34 (bottom left) R. S. Scorer; 34 (bottom right) Camera Press; 35 (top) Bruce F. Moore; 35 (bottom left (2), bottom right) R. S. Scorer; 36 (top) Rapho; 36 (bottom left) Dr T. Ohtake; 36 (bottom right) J. A. Cash; 37 (top) Black Star; 37 (bottom left) Josef Muench; 37 (bottom right) Michael A. de Camp; 39 ESSA; 42 R. C. Jennings, Frank Lane; 43 Picturepoint; 45 Popperfoto; 48 Peter David, Photo Researchers; 51 A. Percival; 52 Mike Andrews; 53 A. Percival; 55 Barnaby's Picture Library; 58, 59 Jack Zehrt; 61 Karl Weidmann; 65 Dr R. E. Longton; 67 Barnaby's Picture Library; 69 Verne Peckham; 70 Michael A. de Camp; 72, 73 Josef Muench; 76–77 Thase Daniel; 78 Monitor Press.

PART TWO: The Miracle of Living Things
85 André Durenceau; 89 (left) Joe Barnell, courtesy of the American Museum of Natural History; 89 (right) F. Jalayer; 90 (top) Eric Read; 90 (bottom) Douglas P. Wilson; 91 (top left) Charlie Ott; 91 (top right) Jane Burton, Photo Researchers; 91 (middle left) U.S. Naval Observatory; 91 (middle right) NASA; 91 (bottom left, bottom right) Douglas P. Wilson; 92 (top) Jan Kepinski; 92 (middle left, middle centre, middle right, bottom right) Douglas P. Wilson; 92 (bottom left) Picturepoint; 93 (top left, top centre, middle right, bottom right) Picturepoint; 93 (top right) Popperfoto; 93 (middle left) Walter Imber; 93 (bottom left) NASA; 93 (bottom centre) Douglas P. Wilson; 94 (top left) Winton Patnode, Photo Researchers; 94 (top right) Picturepoint; 94 (bottom left) Jan Kepinski; 94 (bottom right) Douglas P. Wilson; 95 (top) Jane Burton, Photo Researchers; 95 (middle left) Douglas P. Wilson; 95 (bottom left) Picturepoint; 95 (bottom right) Treat Davidson, Frank Lane; 97 Larry West, National Audubon Society; 98 Robert W. Mitchell; 99 Matthew Vinciguerra; 100 George Holton; 101 Picturepoint; 102 (top) William M. Harlow; 102 (bottom) Hugh Spencer; 105 David Muench; 108 Josef Muench; 111 John Moss; 112 Popperfoto; 113 (left) James Alexander; 113 (right) Larry West, Full Moon Studio; 114 (left) James Alexander; 114 (right) Robert W. Mitchell; 115 (left) James Alexander; 115 (right) Hugh Spencer; 117 Denis Brokaw; 118 William H. Amos; 119 Jack Dermid; 122–3 Jerry Greenberg; 124 James L. Massey; 125 (top) Douglas Faulkner; 125 (bottom) Jan Kepinski; 126, 127 Lee Battaglia; 129, 131, 132, 133, 134, 135 Douglas Faulkner; 137 Peter David, Photo Researchers; 139, 140 Mick Church; 142 Douglas Faulkner; 145 F. Shulke, Rapho; 149 (top left, bottom left) Edward S. Ross; 149 (top right, bottom right) B. B. Jones; 150 Edward S. Ross; 153 James A. Kern; 154 Matthew Vinciguerra; 157 Irvin L. Oakes, Photo Researchers; 159 John Brownlie, Photo Researchers; 162 Stephen Collins; 163 Edward R. Degginger; 164 N. Smythe; 165 (left) Kelly Motherspaugh; 165 (top right) N. Smythe; 165 (bottom right) B. B. Jones; 166 (top) N. Smythe; 166 (bottom) Stephen Collins; 167 (top) Larry West, Full Moon Studio; 167 (bottom) B. B. Jones; 169 Grant Haist; 171 Edward R. Degginger; 172 (top) Jack Dermid; 172 (bottom) Robert W. Mitchell; 175 Fulvio Roiter, *Réalités*; 176–7 (top) James A. Kern; 177 (bottom) Stanley and Kay Breedon; 178 M. K. Morcombe; 179 (top left) A. Y. Pepper; 179 (top right) M. K. Morcombe; 179 (bottom) Stanley and Kay Breedon; 181 Shelly Grossman; 183 Guy Coheleach; 184 Ruth Smiley, National Audubon Society; 186–7 Ray Atkeson; 191 (top) Matthew Vinciguerra; 191 (bottom) Edward S. Ross; 192 T. Eisner; 194 Guy Coheleach; 196 Camera Press; 198 Durward L. Allen; 200–1 Donald Wooldridge; 203 John S. Crawford; 206, 207 (top) N. Smythe; 207 (bottom) Douglas Faulkner; 208, 209 N. Smythe.

PART THREE: Man and Nature
213 (top) R. Clayton, U.S. Coastguard; 213 (bottom) H. M. Sievewright, British Antarctic Survey; 214 Michael A. de Camp; 215 Arthur A. Twomey, Western Ways Features; 216 Prato-Bevilacqua; 217 Guiseppa Mazza; 218 Prato-Bevilacqua; 219, 220, 223 Douglas P. Wilson; 225 Peter Hill; 226 Douglas P. Wilson; 228 *Worm Runner's Digest*; 232 Dr M. F. H. Wilkins, Medical Research Council; 235 Des Bartlett; 236 Jane Burton, Photo Researchers; 239 Rocco Longo; 241, 242 David B. Marshall, Bureau of Sport Fisheries and Wildlife; 245 Josef Muench; 249 Mike Andrews; 251, 252 N. Smythe; 253 Allan Roberts; 254 Leslie Crine; 255 (left) Edward R. Degginger; 255 (right) Leslie Crine; 257, 259 J. H. Wilks; 260 (top left) S. C. Bisserot, Photo Researchers; 260 (bottom left) Jack Dermid, Photo Researchers; 260 (top right) Douglas P. Wilson; 260 (bottom right) Stephen Dalton, the Natural History Photographic Agency; 261 (top left) Jane Burton, Photo Researchers; 261 (top right) G. F. Leedale; 261 (middle) Les Requins Associes; 261 (bottom right) Graham Pizzey, Photo Researchers; 261 (bottom left) Keystone; 263 Constance Warner; 264 Crawford Greenewalt, courtesy of the American Museum of Natural History; 267 Douglas P. Wilson; 269 Osvaldo Langini; 275 Colour Library International; 278–9 Jack Dermid; 280 Popperfoto.

PART FOUR: Worlds Without End
285 Dick Kent; 288, 289 Mount Wilson and Palomar Observatories, © 1965 California Institute of Technology and Carnegie Institution of Washington; 291 NASA; 292, 293 Apollo 8 Express Syndicate; 294 London Express News; 297 Mount Wilson and Palomar Observatories, © 1965 California Institute of Technology and Carnegie Institution of Washington; 298 Chesley Bonestell; 300, 301, 302, 303 NASA; 305 United Press International News Agency; 306 NASA; 309 Cornell University; 311 Aerofilms; 314 Mount Wilson and Palomar Observatories, © 1959 California Institute of Technology and Carnegie Institution of Washington.

ENDPAPERS: Front, *Hydrangea Petals*, Neville Fox-Davis. Back, *Silver Birch Forest*, Adam Woolfit.

FILMSETTING BY PETTY & SONS LTD, LEEDS
PRINTING BY SIR JOSEPH CAUSTON & SONS LTD, EASTLEIGH   BINDING BY HAZELL, WATSON & VINEY LTD, AYLESBURY

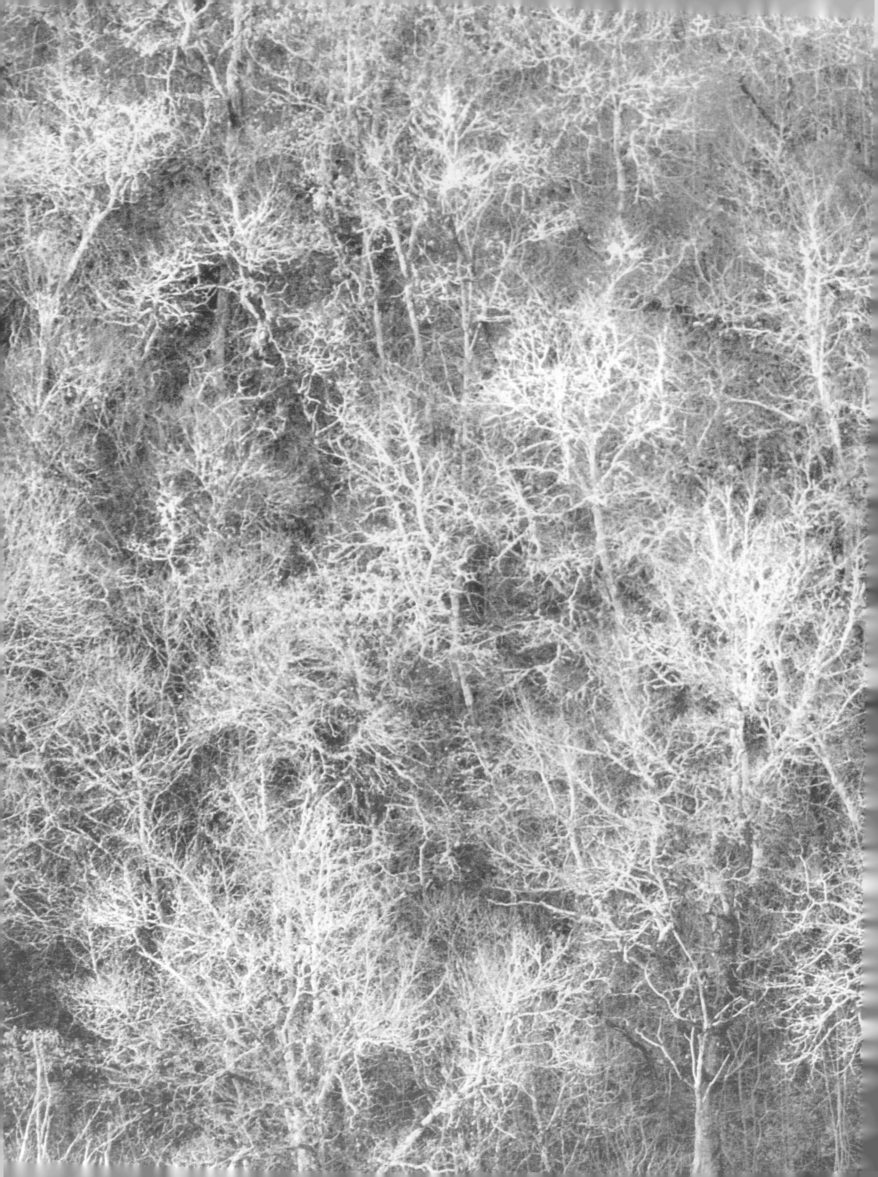